The Principal
as Leader

The Principal as Leader

Larry W. Hughes, Editor

University of Houston

Merrill, an imprint of
Macmillan College Publishing Company
New York

Maxwell Macmillan Canada
Toronto

Maxwell Macmillan International
New York   Oxford   Singapore   Sydney

Editor: Linda A. Sullivan
Production Editor: Laura Messerly
Art Coordinators: Lorraine Woost, Vincent A. Smith
Cover Designer: Thomas Mack
Production Buyer: Pamela D. Bennett
Electronic Text Management: Ben Ko, Marilyn Wilson Phelps, Matthew Williams

This book was set in New Baskerville by Macmillan College Publishing Company and was printed and bound by R. R. Donnelley & Sons Company. The cover was printed by R. R. Donnelley & Sons Company.

Macmillan College Publishing Company
866 Third Avenue
New York, NY 10022

Macmillan College Publishing Company is part of the
Maxwell Communication Group of Companies.

Maxwell Macmillan Canada, Inc.
1200 Eglinton Avenue East, Suite 200
Don Mills, Ontario M3C 3N1

Library of Congress Cataloging-in-Publication Data
The principal as leader / edited by Larry W. Hughes.
     p.   cm.
    Includes bibliographical references and index.
    ISBN 0-02-358441-6
    1. School principals—United States. 2. Educational leadership—
United States. 3. School management and organization—United
States. 4. School personnel management—United States.
I. Hughes, Larry W.
LB2831.62.P75   1993
371.2'012—dc20   93-22764
                                             CIP

Printing: 1 2 3 4 5 6 7 8 9   Year: 4 5 6 7

Foreword

Larry W. Hughes, Editor

How many changes in schooling have been proposed in the past few years? But is anything new? In the words of a veteran (and successful) Houston teacher: "Leave me alone; let me teach." We can't leave this teacher alone. There *are some new things* or at least *some new ways to think about things.* The principal is central to these things.

And, if some of those new things appear at times to be old wine in up-dated casks, that is both unfortunate and untrue. Even if some *is* old wine in new bottles, it is excellent old wine—vintage even (see Tanner, this volume). But, some of it is new wine that promises to be of vintage and some is at peak right now—ready to be consumed.

If there is such a thing as an historical pendulum, then, just as with a clock's pendulum, each swing toward the future never quite returns to the same spot it left. There is change. And, unlike a clock's pendulum, there is progress.

A major issue in school administration these days is leadership, whatever image that might conjure in the minds of practitioners and academicians. The creative and moral leader is sought after, as is the person who can get things done no matter what. Are these mutually exclusively concepts? Not according to the contributors to this book. And the contributors to this book define their terms in ways that will not be misunderstood.

An issue of great importance is the decentralization of much decision-making to school sites. Decentralization is a complex issue, involving questions about what decisions and what latitude and at what level. How to maintain the certain efficiencies of measured centralized control while addressing the inefficiencies of great bureaucratization is among the troubling questions.

And, what of restructuring the curriculum so that it is more responsive to children's needs? What help is there to be found in research and in theory so that these issues might be addressed in something more than a faddish or seat-of-the-pants way? Program reform and program development issues abound.

Human resource development in the school organization is receiving increasing attention—and about time, we would say. Novice teachers and veterans alike require help to be able to adapt better to old challenges and new demands.

Dramatic demographic shifts are occurring in schools and school districts, and this has much implication for school programming as well as school politics. Moreover, much emphasis now must be placed on understanding the cultures of schools and the need to nurture the "creative culture." These considerations have a mighty impact on leadership practices and school effectiveness.

Surrounding all of the aforementioned questions and issues is a legal framework within which all leaders must operate to provide for the lawful and humane school environment.

What is the principal's role in all of this? This book is about the principal as leader—as a person charged with making sense of the issues and directly influencing the way in which the issues are addressed, *for the good of students*. It addresses the issues in a manner very different from the usual text. As a collected work, this book's strength is in the different perspectives the authors bring to their subjects.

The approach has been to focus on instructional and curricular issues and on the principal as a catalyst in the delivery of an excellent program. Certain aspects about the principalship are not addressed. For example, readers will find no specific attention to the public relations role of the principal, nor will readers find a chapter on budget building and financial management, not that these subjects are unimportant. But, we leave the subjects of working effectively with the community and of financial and building management to other writers of other books. Nevertheless, the concepts of leadership we address in part 1 are easily transportable to all of the task areas of the principalship.

Eleven chapters, organized into three parts, comprise the book. In part 1, the focus is the person who is the principal and the environment within which this person interacts with others. The initial chapter examines concepts, theories, and practices of leaders. Remaining chapters in the first part describe the political world of the principal, school cultures, multiculturalism, and ethical frameworks to guide practice.

The focus of part 2 is the several tasks that accrue to the principal, ranging from aspects of the restructuring of the school environment to the improvement of the practice of teaching. Two chapters focus on the improvement of teaching.

One of these is specific to how leaders can help novice teachers have successful experiences. Developing the productive learning environment is the subject of yet another chapter in part 2. The focus of the entire part is on what the principal can and should do to improve children's learning.

Part 3 completes the picture; it includes only one chapter—a major contribution on the subject of the legal framework within which principals must operate.

Each of the authors has taken readily identifiable positions on his or her subject. They were asked to do so. They were also asked to write in the active voice and to take ownership of their ideas. Each has done so. Readers may not always agree with an author's point of view on a particular subject, but they will be challenged to clarify their own points of view.

The authors are not querulous, but they do sometimes quarrel with each other and with the current thinking of others. Good! They express uncertainty about some things. Also good! We are all uncertain about things and often most especially those things others express the most certainty about.

All of chapters are organized similarly. Following an overview, authors develop their conceptual frame and present both theoretical and research perspectives. Implications for action are then presented. Every chapter concludes with a case study or applications exercise in which readers are led to reflect on the material presented as that relates to leadership in the school setting.

The leader as artist, architect, and commissar is the subject of the first chapter. It explores the enigma of leadership *qua* leadership, through the lenses of research, theory, and speculation. The focus is on leadership in the school organization from both a conceptual and a practical perspective. Benedictine precepts, John Wayne, and Machiavelli set the stage for an examination of theoretical and research underpinnings of a more recent vintage. Contingency theories are examined; trait theory is revisited and updated. The relationship to leadership of "venturesomeness," vision, political acumen, and creative insubordination are explored.

In chapter 2, The Political World . . . How Principals Get Things Done, authors Achilles, Keedy, and High continue some of the themes expressed in the first chapter. "As [an] administrator of knowledge workers in a knowledge environment, the principal must understand proven management practices and employ new leadership theories and approaches." Achilles and his colleagues describe some of the most promising techniques and approaches that have issued from their systematic study of excellent schools and those schools striving for excellence. They detail how good leaders get things done to improve their schools. Moreover, they state, "The political world of the principal will, in the future, include considerable ambiguity, diversity, and change." Given this, the authors point out that good principals will evidence a judicious blend of the elements of both leadership and management skills.

Culture is "shared reality," states Norris in chapter 3. Moreover, it is the "creative culture" that offers the promise for the future. She stresses, however, that a creative culture cannot be built by the principal alone. It depends, rather, on the ability of the leaders to inspire the contributions of others in the school—teachers and other professionals, classified staff, students, and patrons. "Whether a school culture is creative or custodial is ultimately a reflection of the personal orientations of the collective membership." Norris's chapter builds on the conceptual frameworks set forth in the first and second chapters. Transformational leadership is the point of departure rather than the transactional leadership characteristic of the static or "custodial" organization.

In chapter 4, Implications of the Multicultural Environment, Baptiste addresses issues having to do with the culturally pluralistic world of the principal. Baptiste provides both historical foundation and prescription for change. He contends that the diversity that characterizes society provides much opportunity for the school leader to greatly enhance the learning of children who will live their lives largely in the twenty-first century—the same century in which those now preparing for school principalships will practice. He examines various levels of multiculturalism and, using his own established typology, discusses the efficacy—or lack thereof—of each. Baptiste argues persuasively that principals and teachers should be operating schools and classrooms at level 3—a level characterized by the principles of equality, recognition, and respect for human diversity, and values that support cultural diversity. This, he avers, will require that principals see cultural diversity as an asset, not a problem. He provides guidance about how to help self and others appreciate the richness of diversity.

What of the ethical behavior of leaders? Craig's chapter, concluding part 1, establishes the need for an ethical framework to guide the leader. He also distinguishes between ethics and morality. He shares the theory and research of Brian Hall regarding values and ethical growth, integrating that theory into observations and implications for the ethical school leader. Craig argues strongly that leadership style is an ethical issue: "Any . . . style that hinders human growth is unethical." Moreover, " . . . the ethical administrator views ethics as a way of life, not merely a technique of moral problem solving."

Part 2 is all about helping teachers teach and students learn. Greer and Short begin the section by examining "restructured" schools and what it is that good principals do that results in maximally effective learning environments. They provide a definitive discourse on what restructuring the schools really is all about. Greer and Short have little patience with sloganeering and establish certain conditions for productive learning environments. Restructuring, they write, "means changing the basic structure of the schools." This is not tautology. The authors are making a point: " . . . many have applied the word [restructuring] to mean any change in programs, instructional techniques, or teaching arrangement," but Greer and Short mean something different by the term. They write about fundamental changes in the way curriculum and instruction are delivered to students—a school organized consistent with the way young people grow and learn is contrasted to a "factory assembly-line production mode." And they write about how their kind of restructuring has been accomplished in certain schools. The chapter is replete with illustrations of exemplary current practices.

In chapter 7, Program Development, Cordiero pursues a different tack. She uses the metaphor "play director" to describe the role of the principal in program development. Not content with simply adjusting the status quo any more than are Greer and Short, she establishes the "roles of the players" and uses the results of field research to guide principals in what might be done to bring about change. She develops a description of the stages of change that a principal must realize will occur and suggests ways of shortening the time spent in each stage before reform will be realized. She also deals with those organizational conditions that get in the way of change and suggests ways of overcoming them.

Tanner's position in chapter 8 is that much is known about how principals can help teachers improve instructional practice. She presents the combined lessons of research and practice in a persuasive way. One section of her chapter is given over to a description of three major examples of practices principals can apply in working with teachers to improve instruction. She writes too about a newly developing colleagueship of principals and teachers. She sees promise in the movement to place more emphasis on decision-making at the school site: "The practical affairs of improving teaching include working with teachers on school-based issues or problems." Tanner provides a strong historical anchor as well, "For what has been a new mode of instructional leadership—the democratic-participatory approach—was developed by educators in the first half of the twentieth century and is based on Dewey's concept of problem solving for instructional improvement."

Weise and Holland continue the discussion about improving teaching practices in chapter 9. They focus on a special problem: what to do about nurturing those new to teaching. They conclude that certain practices are expected of an effective principal, relating to the development of all faculty, but that the needs of novice teachers are special. Of critical importance is that principals communicate and model the culture of the school and make the mission clear. To do this principals must make clear the connections between the visible strategies that the novice can see and the values, beliefs, and attitudes that undergird those strategies. Novice teachers are entering a totally new culture, and principals must not overlook the lack of experience the novice has with that culture. Common ways of thinking, belief patterns, reward structures, and work-group standards must be learned. It is the principal's responsibility to truncate the time required for this learning.

In chapter 10, the focus shifts to students and their academic performance. Achilles and Smith contend that principals can ensure a no-fail school experience even for at-risk students, and they provide strategies to do this. Principals have a direct responsibility for stimulating the academic progress of students—*all students*, they aver. Beginning with the research-established premise that pupil attendance is the single most important factor in academic achievement, they examine why pupils do and do not attend school regularly and what the leader must do about it. Strategies for providing a school that is safe, orderly, and inviting, and that projects a culture of success are presented. Promoting and monitoring the academic success of all pupils is the theme of this chapter. Readers will enjoy the not-so-subtle distinction Achilles and Smith make between "pupils" and "students" and the implications that distinction has for action by the principal.

Part 3 is composed of a single chapter: Building Leadership and Legal Strategies. Strahan develops a description of the legal framework within which principals must operate to provide for the lawful and the humane school environment. He writes " . . . knowledge and sensitivity to areas of potential litigation is vital to successful leadership." And, "It cannot be emphasized enough that appropriate, well-conceived rules and regulations, consistently and equitably enforced, often precludes effective litigation." Strahan argues persuasively that principals must be prepared to lead program development while at the same time administering a plethora of policies, regulations, state statutes, and federal law, all of which control or have an impact on various facets of the behavior of staff and students. He uncovers the land mines, presents the potential legal entanglements, and provides directions for good practice.

Our hope is that readers will find the individual chapters stimulating and the book of significant help in the improved practice of the principalship. And we wish for you a good intellectual journey.

Acknowledgments

We wish to thank the reviewers of this text: Gary M. Crow, Louisiana State University; John C. Daresh, University of Northern Colorado; Thomas G. Evans, director of middle schools, Kansas City, Missouri, and University of Missouri-Kansas City (adjunct); India J. Podsen, Georgia State University; Linda Sue Warner, University of Kansas; Frederick C. Wendel, University of Nebraska-Lincoln.

Brief Contents

Contents

Chapter 8 *The Practical Affairs of Improving Teaching*   *185*

LAUREL N. TANNER

Chapter 9 *The Principal and Novice Teachers*   *215*

KAY R. WEISE AND PATRICIA E. HOLLAND

PART

1

The Person and the Setting

PART 1 contains five chapters, all having to do with aspects of organizational leadership. Hughes sets the stage, in chapter 1, with a review of extant theories of leadership and the relationship of these to practice as a school principal. He concludes that to be an effective leader requires the interacting elements of artist, architect, and commissar.

In chapter 2, Achilles, Keedy, and High compare good management practices with good leadership practices, concluding that both are essential to the effective school. They focus on ways principals get things done within an organizational context and present strategies for encouraging leadership from the faculty.

In the third chapter, Norris focuses on the organization itself. She describes both custodial and creative organizational cultures, contending that it is a creative culture that undergirds the effective school. She returns to the notion of the principal as artist, architect, and commissar and provides a framework for practice.

In chapter 4, Baptiste explores the implications a culturally pluralistic society has for school leadership. He argues for a "Level Three" educational environment, one in which the true meanings of multiculturalism are realized. And he holds the principal responsible for achieving this level. Guidelines and processes by which this may be attained in all schools are presented.

Chapter 5 concludes part 1 with an examination of the nature of ethics and morality in administrative behavior. Craig discusses several theoretical frames and then suggests the implications of these to the educational leader who wants to make ethical and moral decisions. He examines stages of ethical and moral growth and submits that as individuals go through the different stages they will make decisions differently.

1

The Leader: Artist? Architect? Commissar?

Larry W. Hughes
The University of Houston

"American organizations have been overmanaged and underled."
  Warren Bennis

"The best of all leaders is the one who helps people so that, eventually, they don't need him."
  Lao Tzu

"And so then the question is: How can leaders be prepared? . . . I wish I knew."
  Stephen F. Bailey

Overview

"You know where I first learned about leadership?" asked a soon–to–retire and successful principal of 27 years. "I learned about it the same place you did—at the movies. I went to school at the John Wayne College of Leadership. You remember. There was John, at the front of the cavalry unit, and just over the hill were the Apaches. And John raised his saber and said 'Charge!' and, as one, a hundred mounted soldiers moved forward, some to certain death. Big John abided no nonsense. Took me a long time to realize it really doesn't work that way." He went on: "I'm just glad I didn't take that post–graduate course in the Clint Eastwood Department of Human Relations. Would have been just too much to unlearn."

The image of an exhorting John Wayne charging with his troops over this or that battlefield is not an unappealing view of what it is that a leader does, but as my correspondent pointed out, it doesn't often "work that way." How does it work? There is an almost timeless quality to inquiries and discourses about leadership; people have mulled the subject and considered the puzzle for centuries.

In A.D. 529, St. Benedict promulgated the Benedictine Rule to guide the abbots in leading the monastery:

> As often as any important business has to be done in the monastery, let the abbot call together the whole community and himself set forth the matter. And, having heard the counsel of the brethren, let him take counsel with himself and then do what he shall judge to be most expedient. Now the reason why we have said that all should be called to council is that God often reveals what is better to the younger. Let the brethren give their advice with all deferences and humility, nor venture to defend their opinions obstinately, but let the decision depend rather on the abbot's judgment, so that when he has decided what is the better course, all may obey. . . . But if the business to be done in the interests of the monastery be of lesser importance, let him use the advice of seniors only. (1952, p. 25)

St. Benedict's early text about what the nature of leadership should be in a formal organization is instructive. Even in that most hierarchical of hierarchical organizations, the pre–Vatican II Roman Catholic Church, specific directions were given to involve staff in the issues and problems confronting the organization—and at the operational site, no less!

A thousand years after St. Benedict's guidelines were offered, Niccolo Machiavelli (1964; orig. 1517) provided further guidance to the aspiring leader. For those words I refer the reader to the original source, *The Prince*. Unfortunately, Machiavelli's name has become synonymous with intrigue and sinister behavior. Those may be unfair appellations: Machiavelli's purpose was to analyze what practices had brought about political success in the past and to deduce, from those, principles that would lead to success in the future. *The Prince* may have been an attempt at scientific inquiry, but many of the practices Machiavelli discovered that worked were not the sort that rested on very firm moral ground. "Be as moral as you must" was the admonishment.

The subject of leadership has been of interest to people for centuries, but truly systematic study about leadership is of relatively recent vintage, St. Benedict notwithstanding. Moreover, prescriptions about what leaders should do must not be confused with descriptions about what leaders actually do.

Leadership, as a subject, is elusive. Benedictine rules, *The Prince*, John Wayne—these, no matter how intuitive, insightful, or pragmatic, do not offer an adequate buttress to a study of what it takes to guide successfully an organization to persisting pinnacles of excellence.

This chapter is in five parts. The first part establishes a theoretical and research frame. Contingency theories are discussed and trait theory is revisited. The next part examines leadership in the complex organization, introducing the notions of creative insubordination and "venturesomeness." In the third part, the focus is on the vision and political acumen of the leader. The fourth part contains a discussion of the leader as artist, architect, and commissar; the chapter concludes with a case study for reflection.

Conceptual Frame

No great effort will be made here to detail the rich body of research and theoretical constructs that have characterized the study of leadership and management during the first half of the twentieth century. Many standard works provide excellent grounding in the historical foundations of what is now known about leadership in complex organizations. (Hunt, 1991; Bass, 1990; Vroom & Jago, 1988; Boyan, 1988; and Wexley & Yukl, 1984, offer a good start.)

Schweiger and Leana (1986), Yukl (1981), and Locke and Schweiger (1979) all have conducted extensive reviews of extant research on leadership and leader behavior. Only one conclusion is certain: there is vast variability in the results, when studies are compared. This caused Schweiger and Leana to conclude that "essentially, no single approach, whether autocratic, consultative, or totally participatory, can be effectively employed with all subordinates for all types of activities" (p. 159).

Accordingly, one must be skeptical of simplistic models of leadership. The nostrums of Blake and Mouton, McGregor's Theory Y, Likert's System 4, Ouchi's Theory Z, as examples, are of limited use. Such models are not adequate—no more than Taylor's scientific management or the works of Mayo and Lewin are adequate—to explain what truly happens in a work force of interacting humans. For this reason, the focus of this chapter is on leadership theories that recognize the diversity that is characteristic in work organizations—diversity in individual perceptions about the work, in understandings and commitments to organizational or leader goals, among attitudes and orientations to life generally. This chapter explores leadership theories that take into consideration the varied nature of power and influence among workers and managers, and the attitudes and perceptions of those to be led about how designated leaders are supposed to behave. It may be as important to study "followership" as it is to study leadership. That will not be done here, however, except by implication.

In my opinion, contingency or situational theories offer the most useful perspectives in any inquiry about the complexities of leadership. But, before this chapter concludes, I will also make a not reluctant return to trait theory, as well. First, though, let us examine leadership from a contextual, or situational, perspective.

Fiedler's Contingency Model

That leadership may be a product of at least three components—the leader, the led, and the situation in which they all function—is increasingly apparent. For this premise, we consider the work of Fiedler and others. Fiedler (1967) was one of the earliest researchers to advance a complex explanation of how the leader influences the attainment of organizational goals. Fiedler's contingency model of leadership effectiveness is, as he has written,

> a theory which states that the group's performance will be contingent upon the appropriate matching of leadership style and the degree of favorableness of the group situation for the leader, that is, the degree to which the situation provides the leader with influence over his group members. The model suggests that group performance can be improved either by modifying the leader's style or by modifying the group–task situation. (p. 262)

Fiedler reasoned that he could get insights about important characteristics of leaders by having them describe people with whom they most disliked working. He used a bipolar adjectival scale to measure this, and the result was the least–preferred coworker scale (LPC). Those who described their LPC in unfavorable terms were labeled "task–oriented." Those who described their LPC in favorable terms were labeled "relationship–oriented." In early writings, Fiedler described task–oriented leaders as "autocratic" and relationship–oriented leaders as "participative." But later studies indicated the distinction between the two was not that simple.

Fiedler's premises and model are curious and interesting. They are discussed in the abstract more often than in the particular. As more studies were conducted and LPC scores were compared to objective criteria of work–group performance, researchers discovered that the range of effective behaviors was very wide. In some instances, high LPC leaders were highest in performance; in others, they were lowest. Many kinds of work groups were studied: basketball teams, army tank crews, school faculties, production line workers, and others (Crehan, 1984; Singh, 1983; Martin, Isherwood, & Lavery, 1976; McNamara, 1966).

The inconsistency was a puzzle. Ultimately, Fiedler decided it could best be explained by classifying the situations within which decisions affecting the work group occurred. According to Fiedler, three critical elements determined the "favorableness" or "unfavorableness" of a situation: leader–member relations, task structure, and leader position power.

Leader–member relations.   Leader–member relations are favorable when followers are trusting, like the leader, and are compliant when directed to do something. There is a willingness on the part of group members to follow their leader. According to the contingency model, the better leader–member relations, the more favorable the situation is for the leader.

Task structure.   Task structure is favorable when leaders and, presumably, followers know exactly what to do and how to do it. The tasks may be complex or simple, as long as the procedures to accomplish the work objective are well known and the leader and group members have the ability to perform them. The more highly structured the task, the more favorable the situation is to the leader, according to the model.

Leader position power.   Leader position power relates to the power in the formal position the leader has in the organization. The freedoms to hire, fire, reward, or punish followers (subordinates) are aspects of this element. The model posits that the stronger the leader's position power, the more favorable the situation is to the leader.

Implications.   Clearly, the most favorable of all situations would be when leader–member relations were good, the task to be accomplished was structured, and the leader had much position power. Alas, often such is not the case. But, Fiedler argued, leader effectiveness, and thus group performance, depends on the nature of the interaction of leadership style and situation favorableness. Different situations require demonstrations of certain styles. McPherson, Crowson, and Pitner (1986) state:

> . . . a low–LPC leader will be more effective when the situation is either highly favorable or highly unfavorable. A high–LPC leader is more effective in moderately favorable or unfavorable situations. Fiedler contends that when a mismatch between leadership orientation and the situation exists, it is easier to change the situation— through changes in responsibilities and power—than it is to change the leader's personality . . . (p. 236)

Hughes and Ubben (1989), using Fiedler's elements, extrapolated the kind of "productive leadership styles" required according to the situational differences that might exist in any problem to be solved (pp. 11–12). Figures 1–1 and 1–2 depict the differences in style that could be expected to have the greatest likelihood to be efficacious.

But the evidence about contingency theory is contradictory. In a meta–analysis, Peters, Hartke, and Pohlman (1985) noted that even though the theory is reasonably well supported, most of the supportive data have been obtained in laboratory settings. Field–based studies, they write, have been less supportive of the theory.

A debate continues about contingency theory's central concept—the LPC. The true meanings of this simple scale—that is, its construct validity—have not been established (Vecchio, 1983; Rice, 1978). It is not really clear why a low–LPC leader is more effective in some situations and a high–LPC leader in others. Nor is it certain how the two kinds of leaders differ in behavior, nor what it is these leaders *do* that increases the performance of work groups.

Leader-Member Relations	Power Position	Productive Leadership Style
Good	Strong	Task-oriented
Good	Weak	Relationship-oriented
Moderately Poor	Strong	Relationship-oriented
Moderately Poor	Weak	Task-oriented

Figure 1–1
Effective leader behavior in the *unstructured* work environment (an explication of Fiedler's contingency theory).
Source note: From *Elementary School Principal's Handbook: Guide to Effective Actions*, 3rd ed. (p. 11) by Larry W. Hughes and Gerald C. Ubben, 1989, Boston: Allyn & Bacon. Copyright c 1989 by Allyn & Bacon. Reprinted by permission.

Leader-Member Relations	Power Position	Productive Leadership Style
Good	Strong	Task-oriented
Good	Weak	Relationship-oriented
Moderately Poor	Strong	Relationship-oriented
Moderately Poor	Weak	Relationship-oriented

Figure 1–2
Effective leader behavior in the *structured* work environment (an explication of Fiedler's contingency theory).
Source note: From *Elementary School Principal's Handbook: Guide to Effective Actions*, 3rd ed. (p. 12) by Larry W. Hughes and Gerald C. Ubben, 1989, Boston: Allyn & Bacon. Copyright c 1989 by Allyn & Bacon. Reprinted by permission.

Hersey and Blanchard

Hersey and Blanchard (1982) offer a conceptual framework that seems to be of more immediate practical use than Fiedler to the leader. The situational variable in the Hersey–Blanchard model is the maturity of the work group. *Maturity* is defined as the "readiness to tackle the task facing the group." *Readiness* could be defined as the degree to which group members have the requisite skills, the amount of trust among and between group members (as well as their trust of the leader), and the nature of commitment to organizational goals, among other characteristics.

Hersey and Blanchard name four leadership styles: telling, selling, participating, delegating. These styles are effective, according to Hersey and Blanchard, depending on the maturity of the work group and, more importantly, depending on the maturity of the individual subordinate. Leaders would be expected to vary their modes from subordinate to subordinate if individual subordinate's stages of development varied.

Given the nature of the task and the subordinate's maturity, the leader might be in a telling mode, or any of the other three modes, in any given situation. A low level of maturity, Hersey and Blanchard submit, would require "telling": the leader would spell out the task to be accomplished, arrange the conditions under which the task is to be accomplished, and provide close supervision. As group or individual maturity increased, the leader would move more toward participating and ultimately to delegating.

Vroom and Jago (1988) offer a perspective on this model:

> Hersey and Blanchard refer to the model as a life–cycle theory and draw an analogy between leader–follower and parent–child relations. Just as parents should relinquish control as a function of the increasing maturity of their children, so too should lead-ers share more decision–making power as their subordinates acquire greater experi-ence with and commitment to their tasks. (p. 52)

Thus, the model may be useful in helping someone analyze situations and determine the leadership approach likely to be most effective. But, Ubben and Hughes (1992) note, "[Hersey–Blanchard] suffers from an inadequate research base. Neither the model itself nor any of its components has been validated" (p. 6). A more extensively research–based theory, and one that is behaviorally anchored, is path–goal theory.

Path-Goal Theory

Path–goal theory is situational, but it focuses on the end product—goal attain-ment—rather than on elements such as task specificity, environment, group maturity, and relationships with the leader. It emphasizes how leaders can influ-ence workers' perceptions about their work, their own personal goals, and the various ways (paths) available to the attainment of these goals.

The theory is essentially an effort to explain how leader behavior affects the motivation and satisfaction of subordinates. Building on earlier work by Evans (1970), Robert House (1971) formulated a theory that included situational variables:

> . . . the motivational function of the leader consists of increasing personal payoffs to subordinates for work–goal attainment, and making the path to these payoffs easier to travel by clarifying it, reducing roadblocks and pitfalls, and increasing the oppor-tunities for personal satisfaction en route. (p. 324)

Path-goal theory has two major postulates. First, subordinates will accept the leader's behavior when they perceive that behavior either as an immediate source of satisfaction or as instrumental in obtaining future satisfaction. Second, the leader's behavior will increase the effort expended by subordinates when the latter perceive effective performance as a means to satisfying important needs and when they perceive the leader as assisting in their attainment of that level of performance (House & Mitchell, 1974).

Path-goal theory characterizes leader behavior in four classifications: directive, supportive, participative, and achievement-oriented. Each of these kinds of behaviors is seen as appropriate under certain circumstances, which links the theory directly to contingency theory. Indeed, it makes path–goal theory a contingency theory.

Directive leadership provides subordinates with specific guidelines for action, with the leader setting and maintaining performance standards. A directive leader style increases subordinate motivation in situations where there is ambiguity. Subordinates who are uncertain about what is expected of them or what needs to be done will look to the directive leader for certitude.

Supportive leadership focuses on the well–being of subordinates. There is an obvious concern for subordinate satisfaction. This style is especially appropriate in stressful environments. Stress may occur because of any number of factors. For example, the required tasks may be boring, or subordinates may not be sure of their ability to carry out the required tasks successfully.

Achievement–oriented leadership sets goals that are challenging yet attainable, and encourages goal attainment by expressing confidence in subordinates' abilities to reach these goals—individually or collectively.

Participative leadership solicits subordinates' ideas and suggestions in problem identification and problem resolution. It is a consultive mode. Such a situation would be, for example, one in which subordinates have a stake in any action that is taken, are competent to analyze the problem, and can "make or break" the implementation of any decision. Participative leadership is appropriate, as well, when the task to be accomplished or the problem to be solved is "unstructured," that is, a leap into the unknown in which little previous experience or policy guidance is available.

According to path–goal theory, the effect of leader acts on motivation, satisfaction, and goal attainment depends on the situation. Characteristics of subordinates (e.g., ability, personality, perceptions) and characteristics of the environment (e.g., nature of the task, work norms, reward structures, climate, and culture) determine both the potential for increased worker motivation and the way the leader must act.

Siegel and Lane (1987) describe the implications of path-goal theory as follows. Effective leaders, they write,

1. Ascertain their subordinates' needs and structure the outcomes in order to satisfy those needs.
2. Remove obstacles hindering subordinates from attaining their goals.
3. Coach and counsel subordinates individually.
4. Reward subordinates for attaining their goals. (p. 499)

Although it seems intuitively sound and useful, path–goal theory suffers currently from a lack of persuasive research. Nine years after Schriesheim and Kerr's inconclusive review of research about path–goal theory (1977), Indvik (1986) was also unable to find sufficient evidence to confirm the theory. However, earlier than Indvik, Yukl (1981) concluded that the lack of conclusive results of much of the validation research could be due to methodological flaws. Clearly, more research needs to be conducted.

Vroom–Yetton/Vroom–Jago

In 1973, Vroom and Yetton proposed a model of leadership that focused on decision–processing practices of leaders. The model is based on an analysis of how leader behavior affected the degree to which decisions made would be implemented by subordinates. More recently, Vroom and Jago (1988) have refined and extended the model.

Sometimes labeled a "normative theory," the model attempts both to describe and to prescribe appropriate leader behavior, given certain situational elements. The research and writings of Maier (Maier & Verser, 1982), Tannenbaum and Schmidt (1958), and Simon (1947) are fundamental to the Vroom–Yetton and Vroom–Jago models of leadership. Earlier, Maier (1963) wrote of the need for the leader to consider both the technical quality requirements of the decision and the need for work group acceptance of the decision. Tannenbaum and Schmidt (1958/1973) asserted that a leader's choice of decision-making processes reflected forces in the leader, forces in subordinates, and conditions in the environment. Tannenbaum and Schmidt presented a continuum of leader behavior extending from the "boss tells" to the "group decides."

Much earlier, Simon wrote of the "zone of acceptance." His reasoning was based on responses to two questions. First, is the issue relevant to others in the organization? Second, do others in the organization have the expertise to solve the issue? If the answer to both questions is no, then whatever decision is made is likely to fall within the subordinate's zone of acceptance and require little or no involvement in the decision making. If the answer to either question is yes, then, according to Simon, there is a need to engage subordinates in some way to examine alternatives.

Both Vroom–Yetton and Vroom–Jago build on their predecessors' work. That decision situations vary and group maturity differs among work group units is implicit. Also implicit is that some problem situations cry out for great use of the wisdom existing in the work group, while other situations require nothing more than someone who is willing to say yes or no.

As models of leadership, the Vroom–Yetton and Vroom–Jago models are narrow in focus. These models focus on one aspect of leadership—decision making—and more specifically the nature and degree of subordinate participation in decision making. The conceptual frame provides a classification of the problem-solving processes available to a leader to arrive at a decision that is at once good (technically sound) and maximally feasible (acceptable by subordinates and therefore implemented). For problems confronting a work group, these models use a taxonomy of five decision options: autocratic (two alternatives), consultive (two alternatives), and consensus (one choice).

The model is designed to cause the leader to make a rational choice among the alternatives, to reach a decision that is both good and feasible. The leader needs to make correct judgments about what is "so" in the situation, in order to arrive at a decision process that offers the best possibility to arrive at the maximum feasible decision.

The leader's most important responsibility is to correctly diagnose the nature of the problem facing the organization and to choose an appropriate decision process to resolve the problem. The guiding questions are whether the leader has sufficient information to make the decision (and if not whether it is known where or from whom that information is available); whether group acceptance is critical to implementation; and whether group members could be counted on to make a decision in the best interests of the organization. Considering these questions results in selection of the decision option most likely to result in a satisfactory resolution.

Factors such as the press of time and whether the problem provides an opportunity for the leader to help the work group develop problem-solving capabilities ("maturity") are also important aspects of the model (Vroom & Jago, 1988; Ubben & Hughes, 1992; McPherson, Crowson, & Pitner, 1986).

Even with the constrictions of the Vroom-Jago process, however, any principal would be better off to use it, if only as an intelligent thought process, when confronted with a problem of great complexity and importance. Doing so at least reduces the odds of making a bad decision. Moreover, it encourages the involvement of those in the organization who will have to implement the decision, an involvement that seems to make sense to me. Tanner, Achilles, and Greer and Short (all this volume), among others, agree, as well, and write to the same issue in their chapters.

Trait Theory Re–visited

A recent reevaluation of research about traits of leaders suggests there is much that is positive to be considered about trait theory. Even with some evidence to the contrary, some traits have been consistently linked to leaders: intelligence, dominance, self–confidence, and high energy/activity level are noted again and again. People other than leaders may possess some or all of these traits, and some leaders in some situations don't possess all; yet that does not deny the importance of the characteristics nor refute the correlations that have been discovered.

In their review of trait research, House and Baetz arrived at three conclusions:

1. Leadership exists only with respect to others—thus, interpersonal skills are important if others are to be influenced.
2. Leadership requires the personal motivation to be influential—thus, dominance and drive will be related to leadership.

3. Task accomplishment to achieve organizational goals is a part of the drive—thus, a need for achievement and a desire to excel are related to leadership. (Shaw, 1979, p. 352)

Bennis (1982) has also written about the traits leaders exhibit and contends that five characteristics comprise the leader:

1. Leaders had a strong *vision* of where the organization needed to go and strong orientation to established outcomes.
2. Leaders were able to *communicate* this vision to others, often using metaphors as the communication device.
3. Leaders were *persistent*. Failure was viewed as an opportunity to learn and they were able to stay the course in the instance of of–the–moment setbacks.
4. Leaders *knew their organization* and found ways and means to overcome obstacles.
5. Leaders *empowered others* and developed an environment within which workers strove for excellence. Workers were given the clear sense that they were essential to progress and goal accomplishment. (p. 85)

In this regard, Maccoby's work (1981) also provides insights: "[Leaders] do not lead by fear, domination, or seduction. They are not especially charismatic, and their faults are apparent" (pp. 219–220). Maccoby's study of six leaders in private-sector and public-sector organizations and at various hierarchical levels found similarities, although no single model could be represented.

The six leaders in the Maccoby study shared personality traits such as intelligence, ambition, will, and optimism.[1] All were "persuasive communicators." There was no common pattern to their childhood experiences, but all had been "competitors," five on athletic teams. "And, all shared a critical attitude to traditional authority" (p. 220).

Maccoby's six leaders combined traditional traits with "new qualities in ways that might appear to be contradictory" (p. 220). Such traits as institutional loyalty were combined with risk taking and willingness to experiment with social reform in the name of humane goals.

Maccoby concluded:

What is most significant to developing leadership is three qualities all six share which correspond to the most positive attributes of the new social character: a caring, respectful, and responsible attitude; flexibility about people and organizational structure; and a participative approach to management, the willingness to share power. Furthermore, they are self–aware, conscious of their weaknesses as well as strengths, concerned with self–development for themselves and others. (p. 221)

---

1.   Maccoby studied a production line foreman, a union leader, a Scottish plant manager, a Swedish chief executive officer, an assistant secretary of a federal bureau, and a congressman.

And So We Know . . .

Contingency theory, path–goal theory, Vroom and Jago's conceptual and contextual frameworks, and trait theory make clear the complexities of studying leadership and the uncertainties of the research results. Leadership cannot be studied without context. The nature of the work organization impinges mightily on the effectiveness of the leader. Achilles, Keedy, and High write to this point in chapter 2.

For now, let us turn to the work organization and the nature of leadership therein.

Leadership in the Complex Organization

The culture of an organization has an effect on attempts to lead, as do the perceptions a leader has of his or her organizational role. It may be much harder to be a leader in some school systems than in others. Some types of formal organizational structures seem designed to thwart change and creative adaptation. Highly centralized (tall) organizations or Likert (1961) Systems 1 and 2 organizations would appear to diminish significantly the efficacy of leadership behaviors at the school-building level. Bureaucratic and highly centralized organizations seemed designed to create work groups of low maturity, to use Hersey and Blanchard terminology.

Yet some principals in highly bureaucratic and centralist school districts are able to "work the system" in such a way that they have a great impact on school programming and school effectiveness at the school level. To that subject we will return in the section on political acumen and vision later in this chapter. First, let's examine leadership in a total organizational setting.

More important than the particular organizational structure of the system as a whole may be the perception principals have of the roles they are to play in the system and the perceptions their teachers have of the adequacy with which they are fulfilling that role. The works of Blase and Kirby (1992), Scotti (1987), High and Achilles (1986), and Burns (1978), among others, help in the consideration of this aspect and are generally representative.

Burns distinguishes between transformational leaders and transactional leaders. He submits that transactional leaders are the most common in organizations. The transactions involve relationships with both the supra organization and the employees. Leaders get things done by making tasks clear and providing such rewards as are at their disposal—favors, pats on the back, awards—to staff members who perform appropriately; that is, who behave congruently with organizational expectations.

Burns' notion of the transformational leader is different. Transformational leaders have a different mental set. They use their knowledge and skills to work both internal and external to the organization to map new directions, to secure and mobilize old and new resources, and to respond both to present challenges and what they perceive to be future challenges. Such leaders, he writes, assume change is inevitable. Indeed, they see it as necessary and strive to cause it.

The transactional leader is a maintainer and is competent in intensely stable organizations where there is little or no perceived need for change. A solid, even effective, status quo is maintained as long as resources are adequate to supply the needed services.

In organizations fraught with challenges from both inside and outside result-ing from impelling societal expectations, demographic shifts, new knowledge, and social and technological revolutions, a different kind of leadership is required. Such a leadership requires vision, political acumen, and an environ-ment within which leaders and followers work together for the good of the whole rather than for the usual rewards for performing congruent to larger organiza-tional expectations. Synergy rather than the effective use of individual energy is the goal.

It is stimulating to think of social systems theory, and especially the popular Getzels–Guba model (1957), in this regard. The administrator's role in a social system model is most often described as that of the "transactor" trying to make matches (fits) between "organizational expectations" and "individual needs–dispositions" to provide for the maximally productive organization. Burn's concept of the transformational leader is in interesting juxtaposition to this.

Creative Insubordination/Mapping the Organization

Organizations vary from the highly bureaucratic to the loosely coupled. Most school organizations have tended to the bureaucratic. Making one's way through various bureaucratic levels while at the same time being "site–based" requires deft maneuvering in centralist organizations. There are the rules, you see: good rules and bad, old rules and new, complied with rules and avoided rules, necessary rules and foolish rules. These are the bases of formal organizational structures. Yet leaders have been able to be transformational in even the most centralist of systems.

The administrator–bureaucrat is bound to support the rules, though perhaps wearily so. But, I suggest, leaders know it is best sometimes to not ask permission (considering it better "to beg forgiveness" after the fact). Leaders rarely seem bothered by rules that make no sense or that in a given situation do not lead to the best solution to a problem. They "map" the organization.

The culture of rules and rules observance.   Consider Newton Minow's obser-vations about certain nations and what I will call the culture of rules and rules observance. Minow, a former chairman of the Federal Communications Commission, is reported to have made the following observation about different organizational arrangements (and the culture of governments): "In Italy . . . under the law everything is permitted, especially that which is prohibited" as contrasted with France where "everything is permitted except that which is prohibited" and Germany where "everything is prohibited except that which is permitted" and the [former] Soviet Union where "everything is prohibited, especially that which is permitted."

Mapping the organization.   These observations apply as well to the culture of other complex organizations. School systems may be like any of these; principals need to figure out what the organizational culture is, and plan accordingly. Some people succeed in what would appear to be most unlikely environments. Leaders map the environment and work the system, ignoring the rules when necessary, enforcing them when necessary and "misunderstanding" them when necessary.

Is this a new idea? Since A.D. 1744, maybe. In 1744, Giambattista Vico (1948) wrote, "Men of limited ideas take for law what the words expressly say. Intelligent men take for law whatever impartial utility dictates in each case." Gender specificity by Signore Vico notwithstanding, the point is well made. And I label such behavior "creative insubordination" and submit this as a characteristic of leaders.

"Venturesomeness."   In a seeming extension of both Burn's transformational leader concept and of the notion of creative insubordination, Vanderstoep, Anderman, and Midgley (1991) studied the relationships of principal venturesomeness to school culture, to teacher commitment, and to student commitment. *Venturesomeness* was defined as the extent to which a teacher saw the principal as displaying risk–taking behavior, courageous decision making, or other activities indicative of an achievement–oriented leader.

Principals who often take risks and are goal–oriented, Vanderstoep and colleagues argued, would be more likely to stress accomplishment, mastery, and high achievement than principals who take risks only infrequently, are creative also only infrequently, and work to maintain the status quo.

While no significant relationship was found between teacher commitment and student commitment, principal venturesomeness was a strong predictor of an "accomplishment culture" (stress on excellence, peer pressure to do a good job, encouragement to make suggestions about how the school could be improved), and that, in turn, was a strong predictor of teacher commitment (identifying with the school, taking pride in being a part of the school, and having a strong sense of ownership in the school). And so now we have "venturesomeness" to add to the rich genre leadership.

Vision and Political Acumen

Ubben and Hughes (1992) argue that political acumen is characteristic of effective principals. And they describe this, in part, as ". . . knowing when to break the rules, when to short circuit the system. . . . Good leaders seem to know when it is more important to risk having to beg forgiveness as against asking permission" (p. 8). They were not the first to advance this argument (see, for example, Cuban, 1986, pp. 107–119). But, other than in pieces published largely for professors, the idea is seldom discussed in the literature, and then it is often described only cryptically. The phenomenon is grist for a lot of story telling at conferences for school administrators, however.

Studies by Bridgeland and Duane (1986), Blank (1987), Chusmire and Koberg (1987), Scotti (1987), and others address this. The Duane, Bridgeland, and Stern (1986) study of principals' ability to cope with "turbulence" lends perspective. They found that effective principals function well within a bureaucratic structure and become adept at "adaptation and improvisation," using such techniques as denial/avoidance and passive adaptation. They concluded that principals are more involved in political behavior today than in the past and use "intense" persuasion mixed with gaming, while recognizing and accepting diversity. Effective principals are challenged by complex and ambiguous events, finding in such events the opportunity to implement their own selected courses of action.

Leaders in the school bureaucracy seem able to balance the inherent conflict between attention to teacher and individual school needs and central office mandates. A key leadership function is establishing goals which others agree with and commit to, and then helping everyone—staff, students, community—realize the school belongs to them—it's their school, and what happens is their responsibility. Leaders, it appears, encourage the empowerment of others who also have a stake in the success of the enterprise.

Successful principals get goal consensus by working with the staff to establish a collective vision of what the school might become—more importantly, a vision of what each student might become. Keedy (1991) discovered that the four principals in his study did not enter their schools with any sort of pre–conceived vision. Their school improvement visions seemed driven within an organizational context. These principals built their and other's visions by "scanning" the environment for any attractive opportunity to improve their school. They were, in a word, opportunists. They didn't like what they saw in the present environment. Students, in their opinions, were not learning as well or as much as possible, so the principals sought ways to correct this. Moreover, they usually found that the instructional staff was not only receptive but eager to cooperate.

And So Then . . .

The Leader: Artist, Architect, **and** *Commissar*

Based on the complexities of the theoretical and research bases of leadership, what can be said about the leader? Style seems to vary; physical size seems to vary; neither an autocratic nor a human relations approach nor both in balance seems unerring; situation and work group "maturity" are inadequately documented in field settings. Are we back to Steven Bailey's lament about leaders: "I wish I knew?" I don't think so. The pieces seem to be lying around, and if we don't know how, or even whether, all of them fit together, we can still surmise some of the placements.

The qualities imbued in the effective leader seem to relate to creativity, a finely–tuned sense of what it will take to achieve a desired goal (planning) *and* a driving singleness of purpose. Degrees of imagination, planning skills, and singleness of purpose are not absent in any person, but for many there is a decided loading in one quality or another. The qualities are understood more easily in the extreme.

If leaders are agents of change—or better, agents of growth—then what is to be learned from the research base about what good leaders do? How can it be summed up? How do good leaders really function and what circumstances and situations offer the best possibilities for success? A leader essentially would seem to be some blend of artist, architect, and commissar.

Artist

I think of the artist as a creative virtuoso—contemplative and unfettered by constraints of the mundane world, giving birth to ideas and concepts and the notion of *what might be*. Could an organization be led effectively only by the artist? Probably not well for very long. The very notions of contemplation, of reflection, of unconcern with the "real" world suggest a personality and disposition that is antithetical to working for long in any sort of organization, save that of a research and development department. Artists are a curious sort and apparently not given to the constraining forces characterizing most formal organizations and certainly not inclined to the sort of linear planning upon which organizational change seemingly takes place.

Too, a cursory review of the work of Mintzberg (1973) about the nature of managerial work or of research conducted by Kmetz and Willower (1982), Martin and Willower (1981), and others, who in a manner replicated Mintzberg's studies, applying both his methods and his terminology to elementary and secondary school principals, would seem to shatter a notion of any person acting *only* as an artist being an effective principal for long. Fragmented days characterized by innumerable interruptions, chance encounters, unanticipated problems from out of the blue, often heuristic in nature, would seem counter to reflection and contemplative behavior. Yet, just paragraphs before I have called the leader a visionary. This is more than suggestive of contemplation and of reflection and not a little suggestive of speculative artistry.

Architect

Let's think then about an architect—not an artist perhaps, but certainly not a person of bureaucratic disposition nor of great constraint, yet possessing a decided sense of direction and goal orientation. Is a leader best described by this metaphor? Certainly, aspects of the job require a kind of design work. Could the architect be an effective leader? Maybe, once the "educational specs" were conceived. Do architects implement? To a degree, I suppose, but few edifices would be realized without a "clerk of the works"—a day-to-day driver, evaluator, procurer, overseer, who follows the plan and sees that others follow the plan. Architects don't do such things very often, and some probably would not be happy if they did, nor even be very good at it. For this, send in a commissar!

Commissar

> I believed . . . that a leader could operate successfully as a kind of advisor to his organization. I thought I would avoid being a "boss." . . . I thought that maybe I could operate so that everyone would like me—that "good human relations" would eliminate all discord and disagreement. I couldn't have been more wrong. It took a couple of years, but I finally began to realize that a leader cannot avoid the exercise of authority any more than he can avoid the responsibility for what happens in his organization. (McGregor, cited in McPherson, Crowson, & Pitner, 1986, p. 220)

These words were attributed to Douglas McGregor as he left the presidency of Antioch College. They lend a perspective to the tasks of the leader and lead us to the third aspect of leadership—getting the right things done.

The commissar is a person of action. Put commissars in charge of a sloppy operation, and it gets sorted out quickly. The commissar has the charts, and no matter if the sea is choppy, the foreign port is the goal and the ship is seaworthy. Sextant at the ready, firm grasp on the wheel, it's full speed ahead.

Good commissars are essential when much work needs to get done. Commissars need neither prodding nor pushing; indeed, it is they who do the prodding and pushing.[2]

Commissars understand and appreciate the ways of other commissars; architects understand and appreciate the ways of other architects; artists understand and appreciate the ways of other artists. And, leaders understand and appreciate all three, and they exhibit the attributes of all three. So, it is not artist, architect, *or* commissar; it is artist, architect *and* commissar. I leave the reader then with three premises:

- Leaders have a vision—a sense of what might be and what ought to be, a decided and advertised point of view, a point of view that others know about.
- Leaders have a plan—a design—about how to get there, as well. They know what needs to be done.
- Leaders are *determined* to get there, no matter what, through all available means and even means that may not be immediately available. Leaders seem to be internally driven to achieve the goal. They understand the organization, the nature, needs and limitations of the work group, and what it is going to take to achieve the goal.

These three qualities are present always—they are even interactive—but each predominates at various times. Leaders also seem to have a finely tuned sense of

---

2. I must give credit to Arthur Koestler for this notion. He wrote about the creative leader as both "yogi *and* commissar" in *The Act of Creation*, London: Hutchinson & Co., Ltd., 1964.

their own dispensability but do not appear to be troubled by this. Or, at least, it does not get in the way of their doing what they believe needs to be done.

Does this suggest that organizations might best be led by triumvirates? One an artist; one an architect; one a commissar? Ancient Rome tried triumvirates. A few school systems have tried to have co–principals. Neither arrangement was to any positive result. It just doesn't work well in those ways. Rather, it is the dynamic interaction of the three qualities in one person that makes the difference.

Leaders get the right things done in the *right* ways. They have the vision and the plan *and the will to get it all accomplished* on time and within budget.

SUMMARY

In this chapter, I have explored the several dimensions of leadership from a historical and a current research perspective. Neither of these perspectives may be very stimulating to the casual reader, nor, I suppose, even to the graduate students for whom the book really is written. But there is much to be known about qualities of leadership and how it is that leaders lead. Those who would try to lead may be served best by having at hand lessons from the past and the research base of the present.

The first two parts of the chapter presented the theoretical and research frame and discussed the nature of leadership in complex organizations. The second part concluded with a discussion of creative insubordination and venturesomeness as aspects of leadership. Leader vision and political acumen were the subjects of the third part. Good leaders know how to work the system and when to beg forgiveness rather than ask permission. The body of the chapter concludes with the premise that the leaders manifest the qualities of artist, architect, and commissar.

What follows is an opportunity for the reader to reflect on the research and premises that have been advanced and to assume an active role in the analysis and solution of an administrative problem of some complexity.

THEORY INTO PRACTICE: A CASE STUDY FOR REFLECTION

You have accepted an assignment as principal of one of the largest schools in the district. The school is widely recognized as being a trouble spot. Antagonism between teachers and administrators abounds. There have been threatened work stoppages and even the department heads, some of whom are members of the union as well, show antagonism toward the administration. They identify with the teachers. And no one, including yourself, is especially pleased with a new state mandate with regard to "career ladders" and "pay for performance." (You know it's going to be difficult to implement these under any circumstance.)

This is your first principalship and you are anxious to do well. However, during your first month on the job, you have not had much success in gaining the acceptance of the eight department heads. They seem friendly in interactions with each other but noticeably cool and suspicious toward you.

The superintendent visited you today. One of the curriculum projects on which a task force in your school is working is six months overdue and unless completed soon, outside funding—"seed money" which is desperately needed— will be in jeopardy. You were previously unaware that this problem was so severe, and your boss indicates that immediate action is required.

You know that some of the department heads are skeptical of the value of the project in question. It will require a complex organizational change. Ultimately, it may result in the collapsing of two departments into one budgetary unit, the reassignment of one department head, and a reduction of six teachers and one para–professional.

You reflect on the issues and do what?

GUIDING QUESTIONS

1. What are the problems and sub–problems?

2. What theoretical constructs might help you analyze the situation and suggest courses of action? For example, how might Fiedler's contingency theory describe the situation with regard to leader–member relations, task structure, and leader–position power. Does Hersey and Blanchard's conceptual frame- work offer any assistance? Is there any help from Vroom–Yetton? Or, Maier? Or, House?

3. Make and state any assumptions with regard to any of the above, and suggest a course of action consistent with your assumptions and analysis.

4. What outcomes do you desire?

5. What do you think are your personal strengths and weaknesses in the solution to this problem?

6. Generate a set of alternative actions, and select a plan of action.

7. What will you accept as indicators of the success of your plan?

REFERENCES

Bass, B. M. (1990). *Bass and Stodgill's handbook of leadership* (3rd ed.). New York: Free Press.

Bennis, W., (1982, May 31). Leadership transforms vision into action. *Industry week*, 55.

Blank, R. K. (1987). The role of the principal as leader: An analysis of variation in leadership of urban high schools. *Journal of Educational Research*, *81*, 69–79.

Blase, J., & Kirby, P. C. (1992). *Bringing out the best in teachers: What effective principals do.* Newbury Park, CA: Corwin Press.

Bridgeland, W. M., & Duane, E. A. (1986). The leadership of principals: Coping with turbulence. *Education*, *107*, 212–219.

Boyan, N. J. (ed.), (1988). *Handbook of research on educational administration*, New York: Longman.

Burns, J. M. (1978) *Leadership*. New York: Harper Torchbooks.

Chusmire, L. H., & Koberg, C. S. (1987). Organizational culture relationships with creativity and other job–related variables, *Journal of Business Research*, *15*, 397–409.

Crehan, P. (1984). *A meta–analysis of Fiedler's contingency model of leadership effectiveness.* Vancouver: The University of British Columbia.

Cuban, L. (1986). Principaling: Images and roles, *Peabody Journal of Education*, *63* (1), 107–119.

Duane, E. A., Bridgeland, W. M. and Stern, M. E. (1986). The leadership of principals: Coping with turbulence. *Education*, *107* (2), 212–219.

Evans, M. G. (1970). The effects of supervisory behavior on the path–goal relationship. *Organizational Behavior and Human Performance*, *5*, 277–298.

Fiedler, F. E. (1967). *A theory of leadership effectiveness*. New York: McGraw–Hill.

Getzels, J., & Guba, E. (1957). Social behavior and the administrative process. *School Review*, *65*, 423–441.

Hersey, P., & Blanchard, K. (1982). *Management of organizational behavior: Utilizing human resources* (4th ed.). Englewood Cliffs, NJ: Prentice–Hall.

High, R., & Achilles, C. M. (1986). An analysis of influence–gaining behaviors of principals in schools of varying levels of instructional effectiveness. *Educational Administration Quarterly*, *22* (1), 111–119.

House, R. J. (1971). A path–goal theory of leader effectiveness. *Administrative Science Quarterly*, *16*, 321–339.

House, R. J., & Baetz, M. L. (1979). Leadership: Some empirical generalizations and new research directions. In B. J. Shaw (ed.) *Research in organizational behavior*, Greenwich, CT: JAI Press.

House, R. J., & Mitchell, T. (1974). Path–goal theory of leadership. *Journal of Contemporary Business*, *3*, 81–97.

Hughes, L. W., & Ubben, G. C. (1989). *The elementary principal's handbook guide to effective action*. Boston: Allyn and Bacon. (chapter 1, especially.)

Hunt, J. G. (1991). *Leadership: A new synthesis*. Newbury Park, CA: Sage.

Indvik, J., (1986). Path–goal theory of leadership: A meta–analysis. *Proceedings of the 46th annual meeting of the academy of management*, 189–192.

Jago, A. G. (1982). Leadership: Perspectives in theory and research. *Management Science*, *23* (3), 316–318.

Keedy, J. L. (1991). *School improvement practices of successful high school principals*. West Carrollton, GA: The West Georgia Regional Center for Teacher Education.

King, B., & Kerchner, C. T. (1991, April 5). Defining principal leadership in an era of teacher empowerment. Paper presented at the Annual Meeting of the American Educational Research Association, Chicago, Illinois.

Kmetz, J. T., & Willower, D. J. (1982). Elementary school principal's work behavior. *Educational Administration Quarterly, 18* (4), 62–78.

Likert, R. (1961). *New patterns of management.* New York: McGraw–Hill.

Locke, E. A., & Schweiger, D. M. (1979). Participation in decision making: One more look. In B. Shaw (ed.), *Research in organizational behavior* (vol. 1). Greenwich, CT: JAI Press.

Maccoby, M. (1981). *The leader.* New York: Simon and Schuster.

Machiavelli, N. (1964). *The prince* (M. Musa, trans). New York: St. Martin's Press. (Original work published in 1517)

Maier, N. R. F. (1963). *Problem solving discussions and conferences.* New York: McGraw–Hill.

Maier, N. R. F., & Verser, G. C. (1982). *Psychology in industrial organizations.* Boston: Houghton–Mifflin.

Martin, W. J., & Willower, D. J. (1981). The managerial behavior of high school principals. *Educational Administration Quarterly, 17* (1) 69–90.

Martin, Y. M., Isherwood, G. B., and Lavery, R. G. (1976). Leadership effectiveness in teacher probation committees. *Education Administration Quarterly, 12,* 87–99.

McNamara, V. (1966). Directive leadership and staff acceptance of the principal. *Canadian Administrator, 6,* 5–8.

McPherson, R. B., Crowson, R. L., & Pitner, N. J. (1986). *Managing uncertainty: Administrative theory and practice in education.* New York: Merrill/Macmillan.

Mintzberg, H. (1973). *The nature of managerial work.* New York: Harper and Row.

Norris, C. (1990). Developing visionary leaders for tomorrow's schools. *NASSP BULLETIN, 74* (526), 6–10.

Peters, L. H., Hartke, D. D., & Pohlman, J. T. (1985). Fiedler's contingency theory of leadership: An application of the metaanalytic procedures of Schmidt and Hunter. *Psychological Bulletin, 97,* 274–285.

Rice, R. W. (1978). Construct validity of the least preferred co–worker LPC score. *Psychological Bulletin, 85,* 1199–1237.

St. Benedict, (1952). *The rule of St. Benedict* (Abbot J. McCann, trans.). Westminster, MD: Newman Press, p. 25.

Schriesheim, C. A., & Kerr, S. (1977). Theories and measures of leadership: A critical appraisal of current and future directions. In J. G. Hunt and L. L. Larsen (eds.), *Leadership: The cutting edge.* Carbondale, IL: Southern Illinois Press.

Schweiger, D. M., & Leana, C. R. (1986). Participation in decision making. In E. Locke (ed.) *Generalizing from the laboratory to field settings: Findings from research in industrial/ organizational psychology, organizational behavior, and human resource management.* Lexington, MA: Lexington Books.

Scotti, W. H. (1987). Analysis of organizational incongruity using teacher perception of the principal's leadership behavior, *Education, 108* (1), 26–33.

Shaw, B. J. (1979). *Research in organizational behavior,* Greenwich, CT: JAI Press.

Siegel, L., & Lane, I. M. (1987). *Personnel and organizational psychology* (2nd ed.). Homewood, IL: Irwin.

Simon, H. A. (1976). *Administrative behavior*, (3rd ed.). New York: The Free Press.

Singh, R. (1983). Leadership style and reward allocation: Does the least preferred co–worker scale measure task relation orientation? *Organizational Behavior and Human Performance*, *32*, 178–197.

Stogdill, R. M. (1974). *Handbook of leadership: A survey of theory and research.* New York: The Free Press, 35–91.

Tannenbaum, R., & Schmidt, W. H. (1973). How to choose a leadership pattern. *Harvard Business Review*, 36, 95–101. (Original work published 1958)

Ubben, G. C., & Hughes, L. W. (1992). *The principal: Creative leadership for effective schools* (2nd ed.). Boston: Allyn and Bacon.

Vanderstoep, S. W., Anderman, E. M., & Midgley, C. (1991). The relationship among principal 'venturesomeness,' and stress on excellence, and the personal engagement of teachers and students. Paper presented at the Annual Meeting of the American Educational Research Association, Chicago, Illinois.

Vecchio, R. P. (1983). Assessing the validity of Fiedler's contingency model of leadership effectiveness: A closer look at Strube and Garcia. *Psychological Bulletin*, *93*, 404–408.

Vico, Giambattista (1948). *The new science.* (T. G. Bergin and Max Harold Fisch, trans.). Ithaca, NY: Cornell University Press.

Vroom, V. H., & Jago, A. G. (1988). *The new leadership: Managing participation in organizations.* Englewood Cliffs, NJ: Prentice–Hall.

Vroom, V. H., & Yetton, P. W. (1973). *Leadership and decision making.* Pittsburgh: University of Pittsburgh Press.

Wexley, K. N., & Yukl, G. A. (1984). *Organizational behavior and personnel psychology*, Homewood, IL: Richard D. Irwin. (especially chapters 7, 9, and 10).

Yukl, G. A. (1981). *Leadership in organizations.* Englewood Cliffs, NJ: Prentice–Hall.

SELECTED READINGS

Bass, B. M. (1990). *Bass and Stogdell's handbook of leadership* (3rd ed.). New York: The Free Press.

Boyan, N. J. (1988). *Handbook of research on educational administration.* New York: Longman. (Part 2, especially.)

Duane, E. A., Bridgeland, W. M., & Stern, M. E. (1986). The leadership of principals: Coping with turbulence. *Education*, *107* (2), 212–219.

Getzels, J. W. (1979). Problem–finding and the inventiveness of solutions. *Journal of Creative Behavior*, *9* (1), 12–18.

Hughes, L. W., & Ubben, G. C. (1994). *The elementary principal's handbook: A guide to effective action* (4th ed.). Boston: Allyn and Bacon.

Hunt, J. G. (1991). *Leadership, a new synthesis.* Newbury Park, CA: Sage.

Jago, A. J. (1982). Leadership: Perspectives in theory and research. *Management Science, 23* (3), 316–318.

Leithwood, K. A., & Montgomery, D. J. (1986). *The principal profile*. Research in Education Series 113. Toronto: OISE Press.

Maccoby, M. (1981). *The leader*. New York: Simon and Schuster.

Norris, C. J. (1990). Developing visionary leaders for tomorrow's schools. *NASSP Bulletin, 74*, (526), 6–10.

Norris, C. J., & Achilles, C. M. (1988). Intuitive leadership: A new dimension for education leadership. *Planning and Changing, 19* (2), 108–117.

Short, P. M., & Spencer, W. A. (1990). Principal instructional leadership. *Journal of Research and Development in Education, 23* (2), 117–121.

Ubben, G. C., & Hughes, L. W. (1992). *The principal: Creative leadership for effective schools* (2nd ed.). Boston: Allyn and Bacon.

2

The Political World of the Principal: How Principals Get Things Done

C. M. Achilles
University of North Carolina–Greensboro

J. L. Keedy
North Carolina State University

R. M. High
University of Tennessee

Overview

This chapter features several guiding theories or maps of the territory that help to explain key aspects of administration and how those theories relate to an administrator's actual performance. We discuss some activities of principals who work to improve schools in the maze of *restructuring* and then draw

Thanks to various people who read and commented on early drafts of this material and to anonymous reviewers for helpful comments, including Susan Hoover and Steve Price. Dale Brubaker, University of North Carolina at Greensboro, was particularly helpful. Any inadequacies in the text, however, are the authors' own.

A special thanks to the students, teachers, and administrators who participated in some of the research upon which parts of this chapter are based, and to personnel of the Clovis, CA, schools and the (then) superintendent, Dr. Floyd Buchanan, 1990 California Superintendent of the Year, for some ideas and examples used in this chapter and also in chapter 10 of this volume.

explicit connections between these activities in practice and several theoretic and research–based considerations.[1]

In this chapter, administration is described as consisting both of management and of leadership efforts, with the administrator engaging in moral and ethical behavior to bring about school improvement (see Craig, chapter 5, this volume). The unique management/leadership blend in the school or immediate work setting (situation) and within a larger environment (context) defines an individual's administrative style. Successful strategies for school improvement such as norm setting, teacher collegial groups, expertness or expert power, and problem identification are related to research and theory. We draw attention to issues surrounding accountability to stakeholders and explore the professional rights and responsibilities of educators in improving education. After discussing some current changes and speculating a little about the future, we conclude with some activities built upon ideas in the text. Selected readings supplement text references.

Conceptual Frame[2]

As soon as humans formed groups, there was a leader. The concept and practice of leadership has drawn considerable attention. Historians have chronicled leadership; behavioral scientists have studied it; authors have written about leaders. As discussed in chapter 1, leaders are often the stuff of myths, stories, sagas, and epics. When humans made their organizations more complex, leadership tasks multiplied as did terms for goal–directed activities of groups. Sometimes people use the terms *leadership*, *management*, and *administration* interchangeably; other times, they define the terms differently, often attributing value (e.g., good or bad) to them. Meanings change over time. By the 1990s, the "in" thing was to be an "instructional leader." But how?

People tend to set up dichotomies to help them analyze things—good/bad, hot/cold, art/science. To simplify analysis and discussion, they may separate concepts that, in real life, work together—note Getzels and Guba's (1957) idea of "conceptually independent and phenomenally interactive." Ideas in this

---

1.   *Restructuring* as used here is the evolution or the transition of schools from mass-production entities into professional or caseload work environments. It may include organizational or structural changes or changes in governance or processes, or both. Greer and Short (chapter 6) discuss in detail restructuring as primarily an organizational or structural change.

2.   Permission to draw extensively from Achilles, C.M. (1992, January), "The leadership enigma is more than semantics," *Journal of School Leadership*, 2(1), 59–65, is gratefully acknowledged. This section of the chapter is taken with only slight change from that source.

chapter build on the conceptually independent/phenomenally interactive nature of administration as the composite of leadership and management. It is exciting to think of the principal only as Leader. However, as sure as a shingle—no matter how thin—has two sides, there are complementary views of the principal's job. Part of the confusion in thinking clearly about a principal's full range of tasks is based in semantics and basks in the aura of the concept, "Leader." Who doesn't want to be called Leader, even if he or she is efficient and effective in manager–type tasks?

Unfortunately, by connotation, leadership has come to be considered good, while management has paled in comparison. Is the person in charge a leader or a manager? Language clarity influences how we think about and actually treat the subject (or object) of that word; words and symbols are the building blocks for thoughts about and concepts of whatever words represent. Language clarity can help in debates about whether someone is a leader or a manager.

This relatively long–lived, dichotomous battle has not advanced the theory and practice of leadership and management very far. Murphy, Hallinger, and Mitman (1983) count among the problems of research on leadership some misconceptions about both management and leadership. They note that management and leadership are often considered extremes on a single continuum: "New effectiveness activities are leadership, while unpopular practices are sorted into the management bin" (p. 299). Figure 2–1 portrays this value–laden view in which leadership is good and management is bad, a concept that does little to help one understand the actual operations of a complex organization.

Rather than viewing leadership and management on a good–bad continuum, consider each as a factor that can be described by appropriate adjectives, such as good or bad. As shown in figure 2–2, one can think of good leadership and bad; of good management and bad.

Conceptually separating management and leadership helps to show that these terms really are interrelated. While *leadership* may describe dynamic efforts, such as translating into action a vision for the organization, creating change, and developing new policies, *management* emphasizes a supportive status quo to provide people stability and balance in the workplace so that they can work in relative comfort. Organizations need clear, consistent, and expeditious ways to deal

Figure 2–1
Leadership and Management
on a "Good–Bad" Continuum

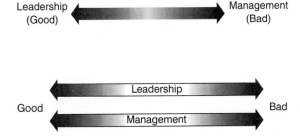

Figure 2–2
Leadership and Management
as Separate Factors, Rather
Than on a Continuum

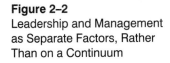

with routines (such as payrolls, reimbursements, and vacations). In this sense, the status quo keeps the organization on an even keel so that members understand what is required and how they need to behave to help achieve organizational goals. Some aspects of an organization must remain stable so others can change without chaos. Good management is positive and necessary.

Cuban (1990) explained the difference between leaders and managers by framing the distinction as a duality: managers accept goals of others, but leaders define, examine, and refine goals; managers try to avoid conflict, but leaders seek conflict as opportunity for growth. Managers solve routine problems, but leaders seek and define problems (Achilles & Norris, 1987–88). Managers do things right, but leaders do the right things (Bennis & Nanus, 1985).

Management is not by itself bad or less important than leadership. Paradoxically, leadership is not likely to occur easily unless management provides consistency and a nurturing status quo in which there are few surprises. "All organizations tend to make the roles and standard operating procedures the dominant force in organization life" (Starratt, 1991, p. 190). This is management (albeit not particularly enlightened). Starratt, citing Eisenstadt (1968) continues: "On the other hand, organizations, paradoxically, are the only places in the modern world where freedom and creativity can be exercised in any significant way" (p. 190).

Management is important in administering education. Tanner, Schnittjer, and Atkins (1991) note: "Performing management functions is a continuing activity for a high school principal, who faces many responsibilities and is hampered by the amount of time available to carry them out," and "in a recent survey by The National Association of Secondary School Principals (NASSP) 70% of the principals specified time spent on administrative details and lack of time to do their jobs as obstacles" (p. 211). Tanner, Schnittjer, and Atkins list such things as meetings, reports, compliance with rules and policies, telephone interruptions, and staff evaluation, as examples of management tasks that have to be done (p. 215). One might add bus schedules and safety procedures to the list of management tasks that usually have to be done *before* there is time for "leadership" activity.

Hughes and Ubben (1989) discuss the two dimensions of the principalship as managerial behaviors and as leadership behaviors that principals apply to five functions:

- curriculum development
- instructional improvement
- pupil services
- community relations
- financial and facility management (pp. 3–9)

Successful administrators lead and manage. The operational trick is for principals to get the ship sailing smoothly so they and others can do their jobs creatively.

Leadership and Management: The Organizational Context

The task of running a complex operation is *administration*, a task with two dimensions. One dimension, embracing activities related to change and dynamism, is *leadership*. The other dimension, encompassing productive efforts to manage a status quo in which people can work comfortably, is *management*. This conceptualization frames administration within current theory and practice. For example, depending upon a particular situation (context), the administrator evokes leadership or invokes management by following the ABC rule. By alternately using the *A*ccelerator, the *B*rake, and *C*ruise Control the administrator guides the dynamic organization.

The good administrator reads the context correctly and knows how much pressure to apply, when to apply it, and why. In the real world of running complex organizations, the person in charge must attend *both* to leadership tasks and to management tasks. A successful organization doesn't have leaders running one way and managers another. The successful principal administers a complex organization that is part of a larger social and political context. Figure 2–3 depicts administration as a moral/ethical act occurring in an organizational context *within* a larger environmental context. The administrator—exercising leadership skills—helps establish the goals, mission, and shared vision for the organization itself, and for the organization within a larger context. When the vision is shared, processes and structures to guide goal attainment can be built and used.

Administrators fulfill two roles and must operate in a moral–ethical framework. As *managers*, they maintain a productive status quo; they conserve useful and facilitative policies and procedures. As *leaders*, they work to change goals, policies, and procedures in response to or in anticipation of internal (organizational) and/or external (environmental) concerns, issues, or problems. The site where the administrator works is an organization with goals and people and processes embedded in an external environment—a *context*. In a school, major foci are

Figure 2–3
The Leadership/Management/
Administration Relationship,
Showing Interrelatedness
of the Terms in Context

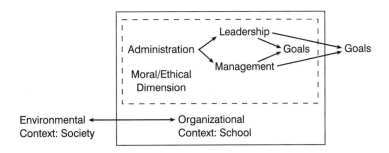

The Ethical/Moral School Administrator		
Major Focus	Manager Actions	Leader Actions

Curriculum
    Goals
    Materials
    Sequence
    Structure
    Budget		

Instruction
    Goals
    Interaction
    Process
    Budget		

Other Elements
    e.g.: School and
    Community,
    Culture/Climate,
    Situation/Setting, Staff
    Development, etc.		

Figure 2–4
Sample of School Administration Concerns Within the Manager/Leader Framework and Related to Major Foci of Schooling. What Actions Might the Ethical/Moral Administrator Take?

curriculum, instruction, and selected other activities as dictated by the situation and the context. Figure 2–4 shows a sample of these relationships.

The successful principal applies the "craft" of administration (Blumberg, 1989) by the judicious balancing of the art of leadership and the science of management to improve the curriculum, instruction, and other pertinent elements of school. By thoughtfully adding to figure 2–4 elements of a specific school setting, a principal could categorize and assess important site–specific school–improvement actions.

Applying these ideas to the challenge of future paradigm shifts (not just changes in the rules of the game, but the formulation of a new game), Barker (1992) notes that the administrator manages within a paradigm but leads between paradigms (p. 164). This notion adds powerful future–orientation and change–orientation roles to the principal–as–leader tasks of the site administrator.

Management as Unilateral Use of Power: Leadership as Instilling Shared Vision

Principals who get things done understand the management and leadership dimensions of administration. Studies show that principals beginning their tenures in out–of–control schools use a particular blend of these two dimensions: The use of managerial skills may *precede* use of leadership skills. Four successful high school principals used their positional authority and management techniques to get control of their schools by making unilateral decisions (Keedy, 1991a). Influenced by their biographies and professional experiences, their senses of mission were related both to personal survival and to restoring order. Although the principals were hired to lead these schools, vignettes from this research on four principals (Burke, Brown, Jackson, & Lee) and their schools show how these principals used the management function to pave the way for later leadership initiatives (Keedy, 1991a). It may be necessary to use power unilaterally as a means to establish structures and processes that will then accommodate shared governance.

The Management Phase: A Sense of Control and Stability[3]

Burke wanted to make Nottingham High School (NHS) safe enough for his own children. (Both children eventually did attend and graduate from NHS). He also wanted to provide an appropriate curriculum for all students. These were his missions. First, he had to deal with personnel problems that kept faculty members from concentrating on teaching. He soon discovered that he had a divided faculty and that "certain faculty members tended to get into trouble" (Keedy, 1991a, p. 92). His predecessor had not clarified the distinction between administrative and teacher roles, and some teachers, acting as informal leaders, were making administrative decisions. Burke hired a data clerk, reorganized the master schedule to equalize class and teaching loads, and differentiated administrative and teacher roles.

Before teachers got to know him, he unilaterally appointed some new department heads to break up power cliques among the NHS teachers. He closed the two lounges (one used by whites and the other by blacks) and opened one new workroom and one lounge. Burke also had to get students under control. This led to physical confrontation, including four fights. On different occasions, two students tried to run over him with their cars. One joke around school during the first years was that the principal spent more time in court hearings for in–school drug and alcohol consumption than he spent at NHS!

---

3.   Names and places are fictitious; data are real.

Burke and the other principals in the study gained control over their schools by assessing situations quickly, by "laying down the law" and by enforcing it. This may be viewed as riot control. Brown commented on his situation, "One would have to be an idiot to have any questions about what had to be done" (Keedy, 1991a, p. 28). Many interactions centered on power politics. Because his school was fairly small (28 full–time teachers), Brown determined that students needed only three minutes, instead of five, to pass between classes. One board member actually timed corridor passings because he had heard complaints about the shortened time. Brown prevailed.

The Leadership Phase: Sensing and Developing the Vision

With the schools under control (a process that took between six months and two years), these four principals *then* articulated strong visions that were neither rigid blueprints for action nor predetermined at the beginning of the principals' tenures. (Bennis & Nanus, 1985, defined *vision* as an uncommon ability to visualize a better future for an organization.) The visions were interactive and iterative; principals compared rough drafts of their visions with perceptions of teachers and community leaders (e.g., influential parents), and they were influenced by institutional contexts. As these principals built their visions, they began practicing leadership skills: they could now lead their staffs because they had management and control, and they knew where they were going!

The principals generally shifted strategies from direct action to a propitious use of influence, a constant ingredient in the leadership dimension. They established conditions in which teachers had choices relating to professional opportunities and growth, and, in Brown's case, opportunities to influence the future of Monroe County High School (MCHS) directly. Brown knew that teachers had to share both the responsibility and the initiative for school–wide decisions if MCHS were really going to improve. With the help of a professor from a nearby university, Brown and the teachers established a shared–governance structure.

Burke already had developed an ability to influence people, and he asserted this ability after NHS was under control. When decisions had to be planned or made, he quickly gathered a few teachers and counselors with important knowledge and expertise and used them as sounding boards. He also influenced certain entrepreneurial teachers to lead in developing programs directed at meeting the curricular needs (e.g., science, math, and at–risk students).

Jackson was influenced by the changing demographics at Carmichael High School (CHS) which was about 70 percent African-American by the time of this study. He spent much time with students for whom high school might be their best (and last) chance to set a pattern of success in life. In the corridors and school office, Jackson constantly asked seniors about their vocational plans for the next year. Jackson recognized that he had been quite autocratic. He enlarged his management team, which eventually operated as a participatory decision–making unit. As school demographics changed, Jackson realized the need for full commitment of his staff to deal with changing student expectations of school.

During his third year at Wells High School (WHS), Lee felt a need to employ more teacher input. He established a teacher liaison group. Although WHS had the ingredients for a good school—a hard-working and well-trained faculty, successful parents with high expectations for the schooling and success of their children, and many students ambitious to attend top colleges and universities—the parents had nevertheless been sending their children to independent and parochial schools. They had become disenchanted with WHS, a school they perceived as chaotic and as a drug haven. Lee and the faculty had to market WHS to an upper–middle-class community. Under Lee's leadership, WHS gained community acceptance as an alternative to independent and parochial schools. Enrollment increased.

Theoretical Discussion

In these four out–of–control schools, management and leadership were sequential stages. The principals used management and personal strength to gain control of the schools (exerting power and authority). In envisioning their school improvement platforms, they began to use influence and to collaborate with selected teachers on school improvement projects. This finding of an initial use of power followed by careful use of influence supports work of High and Achilles (1985) who found that high–achieving principals used power and expertness to gain control and then used influence to encourage trusted teachers to accept leadership roles.

These principals were not middle managers carrying orders from their superiors in a hierarchical chain. They did not wait until downtown administrators called them before making decisions. To the contrary, they implemented their visions partly because they were able to establish autonomy from their central offices, and sometimes from their school boards. Indeed, central office personnel may be as much a hindrance as a source of support and backing in efforts to improve schools (Keedy, 1991b; Conley, Dunlap, & Goldman, 1991). Successful principals are driven by vision and judgment, and not by rules and bureaucratic procedures (Louis & Miles, 1990). As Hughes (chapter 1) concluded, successful principals have mastered the crafts of "creative insubordination" and of venturesomeness.

In shifting from use of power to use of influence, these principals employed a modification of Halpin's (1966) initiating structure and consideration dimensions. Whereas Halpin concluded that both initiating structure and consideration were necessary for good leadership, emphasis on structure in out–of–control schools may precede extensive use of consideration. Because they had to get their schools under control merely to survive, these principals initiated structure unilaterally ("Here's what I expect of you. Here's what you can expect from me").

After the schools were under control, they emphasized consideration, mutual respect, and trust. For new principals in out–of–control schools, the ability to change gears may be a pivotal skill in getting things done.

Recent research on power (Dunlap & Goldman, 1991) shows that gaining power to share power, or *facilitative power*, rather than the use of power as domination seems appropriate for collegial operation of schools as professional environments for learning. Facilitative power fits the leadership concepts recognized as important in school improvement.

Two Strategies for Encouraging Teacher Leadership

Good principals know the importance of management. If faculty meetings are chaotic because of lack of agendas, or discipline is poor because duties are not assigned, then crucial time and energy are spent putting out brush fires. The game can become survival or just getting through the day. Strong management provides consistency and stability ("I know what to expect from my principal in parent conferences"). How pleasant it could be if this were all that we needed—consistency, constancy, and calmness like "Tradition" in the little village of Anatevka in *Fiddler on the Roof*. Alas, there is more. Change will occur, but to work with change one must know the local norms; as the song in *The Music Man* warns, "You gotta know the territory."

Leadership has been viewed as largely principal–centered in an industrial–age school, mimicking the economy's moribund, assembly–line industries. Major change [e.g., school–based management, shared decision–making by principals and teachers, school choice, and student–centered learning (Murphy, 1990)] may lead to the professional settings needed to improve teaching and learning for an information age. Leadership in this new age will include teachers *and* principals. Two strategies principals can use to gain influence with their staffs and to prepare teachers for tomorrow's leadership demands are *norm setting* and *teacher collegial groups* (TCGs).

Getting Things Done by Establishing Rules of the Game: Norm Setting

Norms are behavioral expectations that personnel find valuable to conform to and comply with (Homans, 1958). These expectations are based on values and beliefs. Norms are not policy and regulations—sometimes downplayed by better principals—passed down by the central office or the State Education Agency (SEA). Norms, instead, are the way we do things around here (Lortie, 1969). In schools, norms should have a moral aspect; they are products of principal–teacher interactions—often spontaneous and informal (Peterson, 1977–78).

Principals are gatekeepers in schools; they have the positional influence to help shape new roles. Observations in six effective elementary schools indicated *how* principals set norms (Keedy, 1982). Of the 14 norm–setting behaviors identified, the 4 most important were human relations, resource provider, authority of position, and modeling:

- *Human relations*. The principal relates in ways that make teachers want to comply: They like their principal and how he or she treats them. Principals set expectations by believing in and assuming the best of teachers. (This is akin to power of personality, French and Raven's (1959) *referent* power, or perhaps to charisma.)
- *Resource provider*. When teachers need things, the principal delivers. Resources are anything the principal can use to satisfy teacher needs: materials, student discipline, insulating teachers from parents, organizational maintenance. (This is similar to French and Raven's *expert* power.)
- *Authority of position*. Principal pulls rank (acts like a boss). Teachers conform when the principal uses pressure and unilateral decision making because he or she is responsible for performance in the schools.
- *Modeling*. There are two types. First is a conscious effort: "Look, I'm doing it; certainly you can do it." The second type is an unaware effort communicated through interactions with teachers, who then do the same thing.

Of these four categories, resource provider may have the most potential for developing teacher leadership. This technique is related to the *exchange system*: principals—meeting teachers' professional needs as resource provider—fulfill teachers' psychic and work needs, so that teachers can produce the daily effort required for good teaching (Lortie, 1975). The more a principal can do for teachers—as enabler—the more the principal can expect from teachers in return (Blumberg & Greenfield, 1980). Two participating principals explained the system as they saw it:

- "If you provide something for teachers, they'll do something for you."
- "I identify teacher needs and meet them. Then I can expect teachers to comply with what I believe defines good teaching behavior."

Principals in the Keedy (1982) study addressed specific needs of teachers. In one school, teachers had complained that parents were intruding on their classrooms, and the principal responded by changing the system so that parents waited for their children in the school office. Another principal was excellent at getting extra money for materials and equipment for teachers. A third principal who was a reading specialist set up individualized programs for students whom teachers referred because of learning problems. Principal expert knowledge paved the road to school improvement.

In meeting teacher needs, the six principals in the Keedy (1982) study used exchange–system activity to structure norm–setting behaviors. Some behaviors (e.g., the ones that the four high school principals in the out–of–control schools study used early in their tenures) related to teacher needs for organization maintenance and stability (management). The principals were meticulous about distributing supplies, keeping the duplication machine in order, and so on. The schools ran smoothly. When interviewed, no teacher complained that the school was poorly run. Principals used strong management skills to collect the goodwill credits necessary to exchange later with teachers for important changes. A well-managed school established a contract that let the principal get important things done at the central office.

Principals can use norm–setting behaviors to establish the collegial tone necessary for Glasser's (1990) "professional learning school" of the future. Through careful management and by exchanging resources with teachers and central office, savvy principals build credits to get commitments for designing improved school environments. Similarly, Keedy (1991a) identified teachers with leadership potential as "entrepreneurial program managers."

Getting Things Done in Collegial Cultures: Power Through Teacher Collegial Groups (TCGs)

A vibrant role alternating between good management and quality leadership will help the principal establish a community of learners in the school. School restructuring to develop a professional environment includes changing isolated classrooms into collaborative workplaces. Teachers will change their roles from dispenser of information to large groups, to facilitator and coach of student–centered learning in a caseload format. Students, teachers, and parents/guardians will become partners in expanding the learning agendas and environments.

Can we expect teachers to be creative and collaborative with students if principals do not set the tone? Can principals exert leader roles if central office expects only good managers who never rock the boat? Reform requires new degrees of professional freedom at all levels for, as Sarason (1972) says: "You cannot create the conditions which enable others to change unless those conditions exist for you" (p. xiv). Principals must learn to mirror new classroom relationships in their own interactions with teachers. Key leadership strategies will include organization development, staff development, strategic planning, and school improvement.

How do principals create collegial norms in schools? Principals can manage the schedule to provide opportunities for collegiality: mentoring, within–department and grade–level cooperation, team or grade–level curriculum planning, cooperative teaching, peer observation, coaching, and so on. By playing a networking role, principals can develop opportunities for teachers to help one another improve their classroom teaching. Teacher Collegial Groups (TCGs) are one strategy that leaders can use to professionalize the teacher workplace.

A crucial premise undergirds TCGs: Teachers themselves are excellent resources for professional change and growth (Carnegie Forum, 1986). TCGs provide teachers most committed to improving their teaching with new and diverse opportunities to learn about teaching. TCGs can take several formats, but typically each teacher formulates a year–long focus for a series of meetings— usually 8–10 per year. A primary–grade teacher might want to decrease time for reading groups and increase whole–group instruction. A history teacher might want to use cooperative learning groups for student analysis of historical issues.

Teachers in TCGs deliberate on alternatives to established practice. As action researchers, they develop and try out "gameplans" that are incremental steps, listing strategies to be followed for two–four weeks as they seek to achieve their year–long focus. Using group analysis, critique, and encouragement at each monthly TCG meeting, teachers discuss progress made on gameplans established at the previous session. This sharing leads to the formulation of another game-plan to be tested during the weeks until the next TCG meeting. As this cycle continues, teachers reflect on their successes; they become analysts, problem-solvers, and professional critics of their own teacher styles.

Keedy and Rogers (1991) reported how TCGs helped teachers in one school improve. The norms of collegiality and of professionalism (e.g., exchanging motivation and discipline strategies with other teachers) replaced the tradi-tional norms of isolation and of cordiality. For instance, the status of Charlene (a special education teacher) increased among her peers as her reputation for differentiated instruction spread through the TCG networks. Charlene con-cluded: "We are the ones who know best what needs to be done for our stu-dents and for our school. Sometimes teachers who are having troubles try to solve their problems alone and end up spinning their wheels and getting nowhere. This [TCG] prevents that" (interviewed by White, 1990). The TCG is a practical strategy for increasing collegiality and for preparing teachers for major school–based leadership roles.

Using an adaptation of the TCG, Achilles and Gaines (1991) established the School Improvement Group Network (SIGN) that featured group effort to iden-tify goals, set gameplans and improve schools. The SIGN included the principal as a key player with a group of three to five teachers. The school–site SIGNs met together monthly for a full day to plan and share. A professor linked the SIGNs to research and theory to support the change effort. SIGNs were successful in several ways: Change occurred, principals learned and practiced group skills, and the idea expanded from five to all schools in the system. The TCG was indi-vidual teachers coming together to develop group support for individual game-plans; the SIGN was teacher–principal groups from schools coming together for school–wide and even district–level change. The TCGs and SIGNs are examples of teacher empowerment strategies.

In both TCGs and SIGNs, the participants initially defined and stated clearly the problems they would address. They applied their professional skills to find and define the problems that they would then use their knowledge and skills to solve. This professional involvement in determining the problems they would work on (ownership) helped the participants avoid lethargy and burnout as a function of being removed from key decisions, for as Grumet (1989) noted,

"Burnout is less about being overworked than feeling responsible for the experience of children and forbidden to shape that experience" (p. 22).

Getting Things Done: Collegial Cultures

Many administrator preparation or in-service programs include work on problem solving; few have structured instruction in problem finding or problem posing. Among others, Getzels (1985, 1979) has addressed the issue of "problem" and noted that there are two "problems": the problem of the problem and the problem of the solution. Getzels (1979) quoted Einstein on the crucial importance of formulating the problem correctly: "The formulation of a problem is often more essential than its solution" (p. 5). If two pilots of equal skill are flying identical airplanes that develop the same malfunction, the pilot who correctly identifies the problem and applies the appropriate correction for that problem is more likely to land the plane safely than the pilot who does not identify the problem correctly (and who might even take action that would worsen the situation and result in a crash). A person who identifies and poses a problem correctly can work at solving the correct problem (Jackson & Achilles, 1990). The professional's and leader's task is primarily to *find* and *define* the problem correctly. Given the problem and clear instructions, a skillful manager or technician should be able to *solve* the problem.

Getzels (1979) summarizes his work on types of problems by listing three generic problem situations: "(1) presented problem situations, (2) discovered problem situations, and (3) created problem situations" (p. 7). Hughes' (chapter 1) concept of the principal as artist, architect, and commissar; Getzels' (1979) formulations; and some current research and current trends may help us understand better the principal's role in the arena of "problem."

Using Getzels' framework (1979, pp. 7–8), in a *presented problem situation*, a "problem" with a known formulation, known method of solution, and known answer is proposed by others and given to a problem solver. The problem–solver needs only to know *how* to solve it and does not need to apply the professional skills of diagnosing. (If the side of a square is three inches, what is its area?) In a *discovered problem situation*, the problem exists, but the problem finder/problem solver defines it. The problem may or may not have a known formulation, known method of solution, or known solution. The problem finder looks around, asks "What is going on here?" and engages the problem. (Why do children initially seem eager to go to school, but by grade three or four start to dislike school?) In a *created problem situation*, no problem is evident until someone creates or invents it. An artist creates a painting; a poet creates an ode. Here someone asks "Why?" or "Why not?" Consider the following situations in terms of problem types:

- A principal tells teachers to improve discipline by using detentions.
- A legislature requires that schools decentralize in a particular way.
- A principal asks teachers to find ways to help pupils learn better.
- Fifty–five pupils appear for cheerleading tryouts.

An organizational restructuring that may really only be administrative delega-tion is a presented problem. A substantive restructuring that places in the hands of those providing the service the responsibility for *defining* problems and prescribing for their solutions may be a discovered problem situation. For the presented problem situations of the principalship, we need Hughes' commis-sars—they ask few questions and know how to get the job done. For discovered and created problem situations, we need the architects and artists. Table 2–1 provides a summary of similarities implied in Hughes' commissar–architect–artist image, the three problem situations suggested by Getzels, the focus of the question, and the general type of knowledge employed to solve or work on the question.

In the TCG and SIGN models, some evidence indicates that teachers and administrators are energized to employ their professional abilities in discovered problem situations. As the SIGN project evolved (1989–92), changes occurred in the source of the problem identification. In the first year, each school team iden-tified its problem(s) and set its own goals. Goals and processes, although shared among school teams, were different based on each school's service area and faculty concerns.

By 1992, at administrative urging, all schools were encouraged to align their goals with accreditation–agency plans for site–based school improvement; all were challenged to use the SIGN process to develop five–year plans. The func-tion of the teams then involved a presented problem and basically the delegation of a task. This may have been needed, but in the presented problem situation the principal became a commissar—and the task was merely to get an externally defined and pre–determined job done. However, the task of determining how to do the presented job was still left to those who would be responsible for doing the job. This is a half–way step between the administrator's need to be in control and the teacher's interest in involvement and problem definition. Wimpelberg

Table 2–1
Some interesting similarities among ideas and concepts presented in this chapter.

Principals' Role[1]	Nature of Problem Situation[2]	Focus or Type of Question[3]	Type of Knowledge Employed[3]
Commissars (managers)	Presented	How	Practice or craft (use of ideas or theory)
Architects (leaders)	Discovered	What	Science (analyzing or theory testing)
Artists (leaders)	Created	Why	Art (conceptualizing or theory building)

[1]Hughes (this volume).   [2]Getzels (1979).   [3]Achilles (1988, p. 51).

and Boyd (1991, p. 249) credit Waterman (1987) with coining the term *directed autonomy* to explain this half–way step—between releasing professional energy (discovered problem) and simply directing energy toward a task (to "do this," the presented problem). This step is a presented problem, but the method of solution, and perhaps the solution, are not known. "Accountability, under directed autonomy, becomes translated into delegated responsibility" (Wimpelberg & Boyd, 1991, p. 249). This compromise may retain some of the fun and professional challenge of being the architect of a better condition, but the potential vision and creativity of the artist have been subsumed into painting within pre–determined, numbered spaces.

Delegation is not necessarily involvement or the creative use of professional skills; important considerations are ownership and what is delegated. Getting things done in collegial cultures requires careful attention to problem finding, not just to problem solving.

Applying What We Know to a Future Vision: How *Will* Principals Get Things Done?

Involvement/Expert Power

Influence, as defined by High (1984), is "a combination of applied power and authority—social control of subordinates—subordinate consent—mediated by the persuasion of subordinates" (p. 4). Leadership and influence are nearly synonymous. How do principals exert leadership (influence)? Where does the potential for or source of influence originate? Relying on French and Raven's (1959) five bases of social power, with the addition of two other research–based power bases, High and Achilles (1985) reported on seven sources of influence available to principals. Those sources are:

- Principal as Expert: Valued expertise
- Principal as Legitimate Authority: Positional perquisite
- Principal as Norm Setter: Modeling desiderata
- Principal as Enabler: Selective rewards
- Principal as Coercer: Negative emphasis
- Principal as Involver: Teacher empowerment
- Principal as Referent: Personality plus

From the study of 4 effective (improving) schools and 15 "other" schools, High and Achilles (1985) found that teachers in improving schools believed that their principals actually relied most frequently on expert, norm–setting, and legitimate authority as sources of influence. The teachers believed that these same three sources of influence contained the most potential for getting them (the teachers) to make changes. Teachers from the "other" schools believed that their principals relied most frequently on legitimate authority, involvement, and refer-ent power as sources of influence. They agreed with teachers in the effective schools, however, in selecting expert, norm–setting, and legitimate authority as the three most *potentially* influential of the seven original sources of power.

A subtle but important difference in the effective schools is the alignment of what sources of influence/power teachers perceived principals as actually using and the sources of power teachers said had potential for influencing them in their jobs. Aspects of providing areas of expertise and of setting norms (model-ing) seem closer to ideas of facilitative power (Dunlap & Goldman, 1991) than to traditional concepts of power. Principals who provided important expert knowl-edge (e.g., community relations or resource acquisition) and who "walked their talk" by modeling desired behaviors had schools perceived as effective (based on pupil outcomes, professional observation, and questionnaire responses from vari-ous groups). There was congruence between how these principals got and used their influence and what teachers said had potential for influencing their behav-iors as teachers.

Principals in the 15 "other" schools were seen by their teachers as high on involvement, but involvement itself was not high on the list of potential sources of influence. This finding raises the question of "involvement in what?" Too much involvement, or involvement in mundane or management tasks may be seen as taking time from teaching or as busy work. Finding the proper balance of involvement may reflect differences between the technician's task of problem solving vs. the professional's metier for problem finding.[4]

Principals who bring valued knowledge and skills to the workplace and model desired behaviors (e.g., setting norms) are using their influence not to hold power, but to share power among the professionals in the school. They will handle routine tasks unobtrusively and expeditiously; they will challenge their colleagues to find and solve problems through the beneficial application of state–of–the–art knowledge and skills.

Prospect: The Reality of Routine and the Vibrancy of Vision

This section provides some futuristic ideas about how the principal will get things done in the emerging school that will be a social–service hub in the com-munity (Kirst & McLaughlin, 1990) and be filled with "knowledge workers" (Glasser, 1990).

Signs of change abound around us. Drucker (1989) claimed that we entered the twenty–first century in 1973 but most people didn't realize it. Toffler (1990) described the movement from muscle to money to mind, roughly equal to the agrarian, industrial, and information ages. Schools and school leadership change also. The administrator will be both a *conserver* of what is useful and a *catalyst*

---

4.   For additional information about involvement, see Achilles & Smith, chapter 10.

for what needs to be changed. While orchestrating a safe and orderly environment that reflects continuity, conservation, and reasonable expectations, the principal will challenge professionals to use their skills to improve what they do. The risk–taking principal will find and pose problems of professional interest. The principal will coordinate the involvement of key groups in helping set the goals that activate the vision/mission developed through open group processes representing the growing diversity and ambiguity in society. The paradox is this: as people become better educated, they develop healthy skepticism and ask difficult questions. In successfully educating their clientele, educators increase diversity and ambiguity, thus complicating their jobs if they continue to approach those jobs in traditional ways.

Getting Others Going

The principal is not only the cheerleader of the group working for school improvement but also the school's rockets and rudder providing thrust and direction. The principal is the teacher of teachers and of other adults. In a well–run school, the principal shares with faculty/staff and school patrons elements of leadership and management so that the faculty/staff assume both leadership and followership roles. The leader/follower roles are complementary; an understanding of administration elements should help a person in both roles. Although principals must know principles of pedagogy to help teachers plan instruction for young people, principals can energize teachers by employing principles of adult learning (andragogy) and of *synergogy* (Mouton & Blake, 1984), which combines the best elements of pedagogy, of andragogy, and of human relations/group processes.

Likert (1961) proposed a highly developed organizational theory (System 4) to improve organizations and their products, to help reduce conflict in organizations, and to build an organization and a society for the future. System 4 requires leaders who have exceptional human relations skills; its key ideas include "a high degree of group loyalty . . . favorable attitudes and trust among (all members) . . . high levels of skill in personal interaction, group problem solving. . . . *These skills permit effective participation in decisions on common problems* [italics added]" (p. 99). For the complexity of System 4, the leadership must be "technically competent" and hold "high performance goals" (p. 99). Specifically, Likert's System 4 requires that those in charge develop "a highly effective social system of interaction, problem solving, mutual influence, and organizational achievement" (p. 99). These ideas sound much like elements of Total Quality Management (TQM) as described by W. Edwards Deming (1986) and as being advocated to help improve education (e.g., see Holt, 1993). They also sound like the "idealized" restructured school operating with high levels of teacher empowerment and professionalism. Likert's later work (1976) emphasizes the importance of a System 4–type structure to deal with conflict in organizations—and school administrators assuredly deal with conflict.

Araki (1990–91) reported that school administrators spent as much as 40 percent of their time in conflict management (p. 23). Araki also noted that institutions, such as schools, based on "traditional organization theory . . . lack the capacity to deal successfully with the conflicts created by the new demands which recently legitimated values are placing on them" (p. 19), and that management and organization theorist Rensis Likert "believed that to facilitate applying a more effective system of organization . . . several major aspects of his (Likert's) System 4 organizational theory needed to be operationalized" (p. 19). Among the key ideas are linking pins and the linked multiple overlapping groups, and integrative goals and consensus in problem solving, or win–win strategies (p. 19).

In this model, personnel form overlapping groups with a few people serving as "linking pins," joining the groups to coordinate efforts and to improve communications. Groups develop clear goals and resolve conflicts through consensus techniques to achieve win–win solutions that help people work harmoniously in goal achievement. Following this model, principals help establish the groups, serve the linking–pin function in several groups, and use consensus–building skills to help groups achieve useful solutions.

The effective principal is to be a communication center for the education hub of the future. The principal will receive, process, and send out vast amounts of information and use an adaptation of a social–interaction model to guide carefully–planned change (Havelock, 1969; Achilles & Norman, 1974). Using techniques of synergogy (Mouton & Blake, 1984) and of group processes, the principal will lead groups through a rational change model to achieve group consensus on goals and processes. In this model, the principal–as–leader helps people move from Level I activity (awareness of or knowledge about a need to change) through trial (skill building) to the everyday use of the new knowledge/skill (transfer) and into continuous self–renewal through contemplation and reflection. Table 2–2 shows an abbreviated plan for the change model, indicating the purposes of the stages in the model and their relationships to change (Achilles, 1988). This communication–based model of change seems appropriate for guiding the development of learning efforts for knowledge workers.

Teaching has been, and is, mostly a female endeavor, but education administration has been a primarily male enterprise. Site–based management as applied to education has the potential to increase teacher decisions over the content, methods, and resources related to teaching *and* to increase the involvement of women as leaders in the profession (Glazer, 1991, p. 328). In the political world of the future, the principal must attend to new school and schooling concepts that build on feminist issues and that rely on an increasing emphasis of female leadership.

The Principals' Power Prerequisites

Older, industrial–age concepts of power as domination will give way to power through knowledge and understanding of how people learn and achieve in a

Table 2–2
Model for directing positive change using a social interaction
and communication–based process.

Level of Activity	Purpose(s)	Relation to Change	Proposed Method(s)
I	Understanding. Conceptual control.	Awareness/interest. Knowledge of new ways. Get things started. *Initiation.*	Lecture. One-way didactic with some question & answer (Q&A). Dissemination.
II	Build skills. Expand the knowledge base.	Trial/evaluation. *Implementation,* even on a pilot basis. Confirmation.	Two-way communication. Q&A, discussion, and critique. Case studies. Observation/demonstration.
III	Synthesis. Transfer skills and knowledge.	Use/adoption or adaptation. *Incorporation.*	Practice and feedback. Simulation and role play. Involvement/coaching. Action plans.
IV	Application of skills/knowledge. Self-assessment.	Institutionalization and renewal.	Counseling. Consulting. Synthesis. Analysis of practice. Reflection.

Terms and ideas in the model are from several sources, including Rogers (1962), Havelock (1969), Rogers and Shoemaker (1971), Achilles and Norman (1974), and Berman and McLaughlin (1977, 1975). Adapted from Achilles (1988, pp. 48–49), where a more complete model is presented. In the field of public opinion, Yankelovich (1991) identifies the three stages of "consciousness raising," "working through," and "resolution" as needed in changing from mass opinion to public judgment (pp. 63–65).

modern world. Leaders will learn "facilitative power" (Dunlap & Goldman, 1991). The leader of the future will seek power to share it and to help others get things done (Joseph, 1991). The principal will be the leader of the school, among many leaders of knowledge and learning; he or she will work not only with the knowledge professionals in education but also with diverse family and community members who will be stakeholders in the knowledge business.

Not every idea from business administration is directly applicable to education (due to many factors, such as different goals, different methods, and different outcomes and outcome measures); however, some business ideas may help the principal improve schooling efforts. In adapting business ideas, the leader must keep firmly in mind the differing goals or ends of business and education. Those differences are clear in this statement: business deals in dollars; education deals

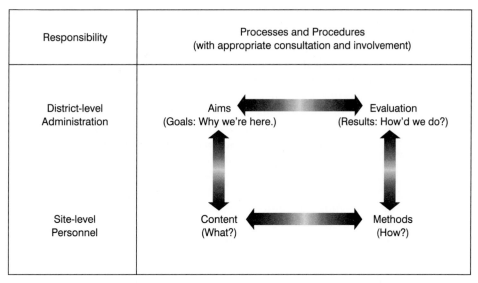

Responsibility	Processes and Procedures (with appropriate consultation and involvement)
District-level Administration	Aims ⟷ Evaluation (Goals: Why we're here.) (Results: How'd we do?)
Site-level Personnel	Content ⟷ Methods (What?) (How?)

Figure 2–5
Synopsis of the ACME Model, Showing Levels of Responsibility and the Flow of
Involvement in Empowering Those at the Site to Get the Job Done

in sense. Some business–related concepts that seem to make sense as applied
to education include the Total Quality Management emphasis on quality
and some business theorists' ideas relating to worker involvement and training,
attention to clients, and the need to work closely with suppliers—in the case
of schools, to work closely with parents. A focus on quality, careful work with
parents/family, and the use of power to empower others will be part of each principal's survival kit.

Barker (1992) believes that Deming's (and others') ideas about Total Quality
will dominate work in the future, including knowledge work. A key element of
TQM is constantly "asking people to do it better tomorrow than they did it today.
It's called 'continuous improvement'. . . . This starts with a belief that everyone
can be inventive and innovative" (p. 133). Some of the practices and tenets of
site–based management will help here. New ideas directly applicable to education will be needed. How can the principal activate some of these ideas?

The Clovis Unified School District in California pioneered many "information–age" ideas for education, including a move by 1972 to site–based management, careful use of productive competition to develop school faculties as teams,
and a structured, results–oriented accountability model that opened the way
for professionalizing teaching (Strother, 1991). The Clovis "accountability
model" has four components with clear definitions of responsibility at two levels
(see Strother, 1991, pp. 6–10 and pp. 38–41 for more detail). The two levels
of responsibility shown in figure 2–5 are the district–level administrative and

governance personnel (essentially a service orientation) and the site–level personnel (essentially the knowledge workers). With consultation and input, administration sets district goals and establishes the evaluation process. Pupils must attain desired exit skills, but in heterogeneously–grouped classes teachers are responsible for the curriculum, texts, methods, and processes of achieving the goals (few goals: many methods).

The four components of the Clovis model (which for convenience we call the ACME model, for its acronym) include those shown in table 2–3. Responsibility for Aims and Evaluation rests primarily with district administrators and governance personnel; responsibility for Content (the *what*) and Method (the *how*) rests squarely with building–level administration and teachers. Within the realm of effective teaching, those at the school site are responsible for achieving the districts' Aims; in return, *they have direct control of ways to achieve the Aims.* In this model, those who have the responsibility for events are held accountable for achieving them through a predetermined evaluation process based on clear and mutually understood goals.

This version of the model suggests but does not detail its complex underlying assumptions, including the revitalized role for central office, pupil assignments, processes, and so on. The central office must remove the hurdles so that site personnel can achieve the Aims. Accountability is at the classroom level and is

Table 2–3
Components of the ACME model.

Component	Description
Aims	The system's mission, goals, directions, philosophy. This is a clear statement of expectations or anticipated outcomes. Outcomes are specified in five areas, such as academics, community involvement, co–curricular participation, etc. One goal simply stated is that at least "90 percent of students are working on grade level" (Strother, 1991, p. 5). (This is *Why* the system exists.)
Content	The curriculum, activities and opportunities provided so students can achieve the aims. (This is the *What* element.)
Method	The processes for implementing the content; instruction and ways to achieve the aims. (This is the *How* element.)
Evaluation	The accountability effort. This includes ways to evaluate and report effectiveness and progress toward achieving the established aims (p. 38, adapted).

measured by achievement of Aims at each school site. This encourages uniform goal attainment across the district and reduces inter–school differences.

Principals of the future will be leaders of schools that move from a boss–centered, top–down power model to a client–centered, service–unit model. The essentials of this change appear in a comparison of figures 2–6 and 2–7. The traditional model (figure 2–6) depends upon the familiar but increasingly archaic assumptions upon which it was based such as downward flow of power, clear hierarchial levels, clear chain of command, status by position, and restricted communication channels. The client–centered model in figure 2–7 will require new assumptions: facilitative power, consensus building, service orientation, status by competence, open communications and decisions made close to the customer

Figure 2–6
Typical School Hierarchy Based on Boss–Centered and Authoritarian Administration and Use of Power

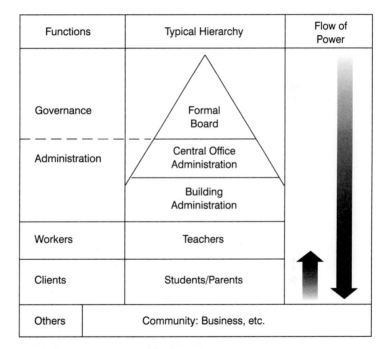

This figure appears in a slightly different form in "A Tesseract in Progress: Back to 2002" by C. M. Achilles (1992, Fall/Winter), *The Record in Educational Administration and Supervision*, *13*(1), 15. Reprinted by permission. Permission to reproduce figure 2–7 has been granted by R. Calabrese, editor for an issue of *The Bulletin* of the National Association of Secondary School Principals (NASSP), and is gratefully acknowledged. This figure may appear in somewhat different form in C. M. Achilles, "Democracy and Site–based Administration: Education's Successes Increase Its Woes" (*NASSP Bulletin*, under review, 1/93).

Figure 2–7
School Hierarchy of the Future,
Encouraging Responsiveness
to Clients and Facilitative Use
of Power

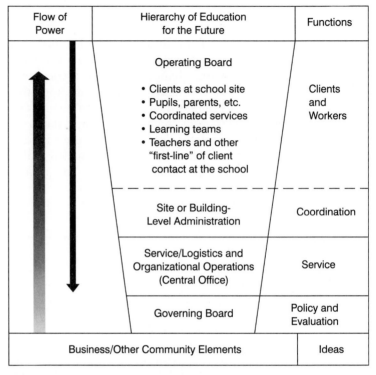

Flow of Power	Hierarchy of Education for the Future	Functions
	Operating Board • Clients at school site • Pupils, parents, etc. • Coordinated services • Learning teams • Teachers and other "first-line" of client contact at the school	Clients and Workers
	Site or Building-Level Administration	Coordination
	Service/Logistics and Organizational Operations (Central Office)	Service
	Governing Board	Policy and Evaluation
	Business/Other Community Elements	Ideas

This figure appears in a slightly different form in "A Tesseract in Progress: Back to 2002" by C. M. Achilles (1992, Fall/Winter), *The Record in Educational Administration and Supervision*, *13*(1), 15. Reprinted by permission. Permission to reproduce figure 2–7 has been granted by R. Calabrese, editor for an issue of *The Bulletin* of the National Association of Secondary School Principals (NASSP), and is gratefully acknowledged. This figure may appear in a somewhat different form in C. M. Achilles, "Democracy and Site–based Administration: Education's Successes Increase Its Woes" (*NASSP Bulletin*, under review, 1/93).

where, in effect, the clients become an *operating board* influencing the organization's daily operations.[5] New concepts of power, professionalism and leadership will require new concepts of organization. The outline in figure 2–7 may guide considerations of "organization" for the future.

---

5.   For additional information, see Achilles & Smith, chapter 10.

SUMMARY

The 1990s are a time of transition for society and for education. As the administrator working with knowledge workers in a knowledge environment, the principal must understand proven management practices and employ new leadership theories and approaches. In this chapter, we have established a research- and logic–driven language and framework for analyzing and categorizing a principal's administrative behavior as a judicious blend of management and of leadership elements. By relying on field studies and research on practice, we have provided examples of how principals get things done to improve schools. A typical pattern was that the principals first took command of the management details and then, through human relations, norm setting, TCGs, use of expert power to help teachers, and distribution of resources the principals moved into the leadership arena. The norms of reciprocity and of exchange and applications of procedures to achieve total quality aided leadership efforts.

The chapter describes one operating model in which a clear distinction of responsibility exists between administration and professional teaching. That model, refined in the Clovis, California, schools during the 1980s offers one strategy for moving toward the knowledge community of the future (Strother, 1991). The chapter also touched on issues of involvement, redefinition of power as facilitation rather than domination, the use of expertness to improve the teaching condition, the potential of restructuring to bring more women into decision making in schools, the extension of schools into communities, and a professional model of accountability.

We speculated in this chapter about social changes and education demands that will challenge principals as leaders. In the future, the political world of the principal will include even more ambiguity, diversity, and change than it has in the past. Times will be exciting. Consider the following topics explored in this chapter:

- The principal as teacher of teachers and other adults; for example, the TCG (Keedy & Rogers, 1991) and SIGN (Achilles & Gaines, 1991)
- The principal as a link pin (Likert, 1961; 1976)
- The principal as expert (High & Achilles, 1985; Hughes, this volume)
- The principal as communication hub, "switchboard," and change facilitator
- The principal as facilitating positive use of power by others (Dunlap & Goldman, 1991; Joseph, 1991), and as increasing the power/influence of women through encouraging teachers to make important decisions (Glazer, 1991)
- New concepts of community and of school governance, in which the traditional hierarchy disappears and the separation of governing board from operating board gains in utility

- Educators' continuing successes in raising education levels in society add to the principal's challenges as better educated clients ask increasingly more from education
- Education providing information–age answers to unlock the inevitable, perplexing changes and paradigm shifts of the future

As society moves into the information age, educators will become increasingly responsible for defining the problems they must address. Older ideas of educators simply doing what society asked—of applying solutions externally developed to problems externally promulgated—will fade as an enlightened society comes to understand the moral and ethical implications of working with children who are the future. Major changes in how educators do the business of education will challenge the principal–as–leader.

THEORY INTO PRACTICE: ACTIVITIES FOR REFLECTION

1. Read Glasser's article about the quality school (see References). Reflect on the ideas and then informally interview some colleagues. How do you assess the extent to which teaching in your school is student–centered? Who is doing most of the work—the teachers or the students? How can Teacher Collegial Groups (TCGs) support teachers who want to turn more responsibility for choice of assignments to students?

2. Which teachers in your building would benefit most from participation in a TCG? What characteristics do they share? What tactics could you use to implement a TCG into your school? (Little's work on school norms of collegiality and experimentation is interesting background reading—see References).

3. Meet informally with two or three of your colleagues. Explain what norms are, how they can help professionalize schools, and some ways principals can set norms. Mention that the exchange system is a major key in setting norms. Record your colleague's reactions: what practical advantages did they see in norm setting? (One–two pages). Share this with others.

4. In clear, concise, and cogent language, develop a case study using ideas/issues from your setting (one–two pages). Include enough information that others in the group can get involved in the case. Emphasize a *problem* that needs to be solved. Discuss the case and some proposed courses of action.

5. Refer to figure 2–4. Fill in cells in that matrix using the lead/manage concepts for administration. Consider important actions needed to encourage education excellence in your own setting.

A TASK FOR THE ADMINISTRATOR

There continues to be great concern about making major changes in education—
Restructuring, Rediscovering, Reinventing. In contemplating those three Rs,
we surely need some vision of the school of the future and of the people who
will lead such a school. This gives rise to at least three question areas:[6]

1. The Vision: conceptualizing schools for the future.
2. What are the qualities that education leaders will need to meet and
   carry out the dream in the schools of the future?
3. What do we need to do to cultivate and develop leaders who can
   implement this dream? (By *we*, we mean anyone interested in education improvement.)

To translate these three questions into practice, consider a favorite saying of
Dr. Floyd Buchanan, long–time superintendent of the Clovis Unified School
District: "A fair break for every kid." Use this expression as the basis for building
a *vision* of a school or of a program that you—as administrator—would encourage. What 5–10 elements would your new school (program) emphasize? Why are
these components important given the future of schooling as you perceive it and
"a fair break for every kid"?

ONE TYPE OF ORGANIZATIONAL ANALYSIS

Peter Senge (1990) identified seven "Learning Disabilities" (pp. 18–25) of
organizations. In summary form, those seven learning disabilities are as follows:

1. Belief that I am my job
2. Feeling that the enemy is out there
3. Illusion of taking charge
4. Fixation on events (True proactiveness comes from seeing how *we*
   contributed to our problems (p. 21). Threats come not from events
   but from slow gradual processes.)
5. The boiled frog syndrome. (If put into hot water, a frog will jump
   immediately out; a frog in cool water will stay in the water as it is
   heated to boiling and kills the frog.)
6. Delusion of learning from experience.
7. Myth of the "management team" (Most management teams break down
   under pressure—Argyris, p. 25.)

---

6.   These three questions were adapted from materials used in Cycle III of the Danforth
Foundation's Professors Program. The Danforth Foundation credited The National Center for
Educational Leadership, Harvard University, for generating the question ideas from the
"Reinventing School Leadership" conference, September 26–27, 1990.

Consider your own school or administrative unit. Evaluate your own setting relative to these seven learning disabilities. You may need to consult *The Fifth Discipline*, pages 18–25, for some guidance. Refer to Cordiero (chapter 7, this volume) for additional details about the ideas included in *The Fifth Discipline*.

How would ideas in this chapter help you to avoid some of these organizational learning disabilities? Consider such ideas as TCGs, ACME, the Three Problem Situations, the conceptual framework of administration as a combination of management and leadership.

REFERENCES

Achilles, C. M. (1988). Unlocking some mysteries of administration and administrator preparation: A reflective prospect. In D. Griffiths, et al. (Eds.), *Leaders for America's schools* (pp. 41–67). Berkeley, CA: McCutchan.

Achilles, C. M. (1992). The leadership enigma is more than semantics. *Journal of School Leadership*, 2(1), 59–65.

Achilles, C. M., & Gaines, P. (1991, May). Collegial groups in school improvement: Project SIGN. Paper presented at the annual meeting of the American Educational Research Association, Chicago. (ERIC–ED 332300)

Achilles, C. M., & Norman, C. D. (1974, Fall). Communication and change in education. *Planning and Changing*, 4, 138–142.

Achilles, C. M. & Norris, C. (1987–88). Vignette: Alas! A report of a new commission on excellence in leadership. *National Forum of Educational Administration and Supervision Journal*, 5(1), 103–106.

Araki, E. T. (1990–91). Managing conflict in the schools with System 4. *National Forum of Educational Administration and Supervision Journal*, 7(2), 18–30.

Barker, J. A. (1992). *Future edge*. New York: William Morrow and Company, Inc.

Bennis, W., & Nanus, B. (1985). *Leaders: The strategies for taking charge*. New York: Harper and Row.

Berman, P., & McLaughlin, M. (1975; 1977, April). *Federal programs supporting educational change: Factors affecting implementation and continuation* (Vols. IV & VII). Santa Monica, CA: Rand.

Blumberg, A. (1989). *Administration as craft*. Boston: Allyn and Bacon.

Blumberg, A., & Greenfield, W. (1980). *The effective principal: Perspectives in school leadership*. Boston, MA: Allyn and Bacon.

Carnegie Forum. (1986). *A nation prepared: Teachers for the 21st century*. New York: The Carnegie Forum on Education and the Economy.

Conley, D. T., Dunlap, D. M., & Goldman, P. (1991). *The vision thing and school restructuring*. Paper presented at the annual convention of the University Council for Educational Administration, Baltimore.

Cuban, L. (1990, February 28). Leading, managing defined. *Leadership News*, p. 7. American Association of School Administrators (AASA).

Deming, W. E. (1986). Out of the crisis. Cambridge, MA: Massachusetts Institute of Technology: Center for Advanced Engineering Study.

Drucker, P. (1989). *The new realities*. New York: Harper and Row.

Dunlap, D., & Goldman, P. (1991, February). Rethinking power in schools. *Educational Administration Quarterly, 27*(1), 5–29.

Eisenstadt, S. N. (1968). *Max Weber: On charisma and institution building*. Chicago: University of Chicago Press.

French, J. R., & Raven, B. (1959). The bases of social power. In D. Cartwright (Ed.), *Studies in social power*. Ann Arbor, MI: Research Center for Group Dynamics, Institute for Social Research, University of Michigan.

Getzels, J. W. (1985). Problem finding and the enhancement of creativity. *NASSP Bulletin, 69*(482), 55–61. (ERIC: EJ 325260)

Getzels, J. W. (1979). Problem finding and research in educational administration. In G. L. Immegart and W. L. Boyd (Eds.), *Problem finding in educational administration* (pp. 5–22). Lexington, MA: Lexington Books.

Getzels, J. W., & Guba, E. G. (1957, Winter). Social behavior and the administrative process. *The School Review, 65*(4), 423–441.

Glasser, W. (1990). The quality school. *Phi Delta Kappan, 71*, 424–435.

Glazer, J. S. (1991, August). Feminism and professionalism in teaching and educational administration. *Educational Administration Quarterly, 27*(3), 321–342.

Grumet, M. (1989, January) Dinner at Abigail's: Nurturing collaboration. *NEA Today, 7*(6), 20–25.

Halpin, A. W. (1966). How leaders behave. *Theory and research in administration*. New York: Macmillan.

Havelock, R. G. (1969). *Planning for innovation through dissemination and utilization of knowledge*. Ann Arbor, MI: Center for Research on Utilization of Scientific Knowledge.

High, R. M. & Achilles, C. M. (1985). An analysis of influence–gaining behaviors of principals in schools of varying levels of instructional effectiveness. *Educational Administration Quarterly, 22*, 111–119.

High, R. M., Achilles, C. M., & High, K. (1989, April). Involvement in what? Teacher actual and preferred involvement in selected school activities. Paper at the annual meeting of the American Educational Research Association, San Francisco. (ERIC ED 336856)

Holt, M. (1993, January). The educational consequences of W. Edwards Deming. *Phi Delta Kappan, 74*(5), 382–388.

Homans, G. (1958). Social behavior as exchange. *American Journal of Sociology, 63*, 597–606.

Hughes, L. W., & Ubben, C. G. (1989). *The elementary principal's handbook: A guide to effective action*, 3rd ed. Boston: Allyn and Bacon.

Jackson, C. J., & Achilles, C. M. (1990, Spring). Education reform depends on problem clarity. *Planning and Changing, 21*(1), 26–33.

Jackson, J. (1966). A conceptual and measurement model for norms and roles. *Pacific Sociological Review, 24*, 35–47.

Joseph, J. A. (1991, Winter). Leadership for America's third century. *National Forum of Phi Kappa Phi, LXXI*(1), 5–7.

Keedy, J. L. (1982). A factor in principal effectiveness: Norm setting. *The Catalyst for Change, 11*(3), 26–29.

Keedy, J. L. (1991a). *School improvement practices of successful high school principals.* Unpublished manuscript.

Keedy, J. L. (1991b). *Using school–site, contextual research: Contributions to a new EA paradigm.* Paper presented at the annual conference of the University Council for Educational Administration, Baltimore.

Keedy, J. L., & Rogers, K. (1991). Teacher collegial groups: Promoting professional dialogue for organization change. *The Journal of School Leadership, 1*(1), 65–73.

Kirst, M., & McLaughlin, M. (1990). Rethinking policy for children: Implications for educational administration. In B. Mitchell & L. Cunningham (Eds.), *Educational leadership and changing contexts of families, communities and schools.* Eighty–ninth Yearbook of the National Society for the Study of Education, Part 2. Chicago: University of Chicago Press.

Little, J. W. (1982). Norms of collegiality and experimentation: Workplace conditions of school success. *American Education Research Journal, 19*(1), 325–340.

Likert, R. (1961). *New patterns of management.* New York: McGraw Hill.

Likert, R., & Likert, J. (1976). *New ways of managing conflict.* New York: McGraw Hill.

Lortie, D. (1969). The balance of control and autonomy in elementary school teaching. In A. Etzioni (Ed.), *The semi–professionals and their organizations.* New York: The New York Free Press.

Lortie, D. (1975). *Schoolteacher: A sociological study.* Chicago: University of Chicago Press.

Louis, K. D., & Miles, M. B. (1990). *Improving the urban high school.* New York: Teachers College Press.

Mouton, J. S., & Blake, R. R. (1984). *Synergogy.* San Francisco: Jossey–Bass.

Murphy, J. (1990, October). *Restructuring schools: Looking at the teaching–learning process.* Paper presented at the annual convention of the University Council for Educational Administration, Pittsburgh, PA.

Murphy, J., Hallinger, P., & Mitman, A. (1983, Fall). Problems with research on education leadership: Issues to be addressed. *Educational Evaluation and Policy Analysis, 5*(3), 297–305.

Peterson, K. (1977–78). The principal's tasks. *Administrator's Notebook, 26*(8).

Rogers, E. M. (1962). *Diffusion of innovations.* New York: The Free Press.

Rogers, E. M., & Shoemaker, F. (1971). *Communication of innovations: A cross–cultural approach.* New York: The Free Press.

Sarason, S. (1972). *The creation of settings.* San Francisco: Jossey–Bass.

Senge, P. (1990). *The fifth discipline.* New York: Doubleday.

Starratt, R. S. (1991, May). Building an ethical school: A theory for practice in educational leadership. *Educational Administration Quarterly, 27*(2), 185–202.

Strother, D. B. (1991). *Clovis California schools: A measure of excellence*. Bloomington, IN: Phi Delta Kappa Center for Evaluation, Development, Research.

Tanner, C. K., Schnittjer, C. J., & Atkins, T. T. (1991, May). Effects of the use of management strategies on stress levels of high school principals in the United States. *Educational Administration Quarterly, 27*(2), 202–224.

Toffler, A. (1990). *Powershift*. New York: Bantam Books.

US Department of Education. (1991, April). *America 2000*. Washington, DC: Author.

US Department of Labor. (1991, June). *What work requires of schools*. A SCANS Report for *America 2000*. Washington, DC: Author.

Waterman, R., Jr. (1987). *The renewal factor*. New York: Bantam Books.

White, B. (1990, March 24). Teachers version of study hall. *The Atlanta Journal Constitution*, p. 7E.

Wimpelberg, R. K., & Boyd, W. L. (1991, Winter). Restructured leadership: Directed autonomy in an age of educational reform. *Planning and Changing, 21*(4), 239–253.

Yankelovich, D. (1991). *Coming to public judgment*. Syracuse, NY: Syracuse University Press.

SELECTED READINGS

These readings supplement ideas in the text, clarify and extend some of the narrative, and open doors to new concepts or ways of considering leadership and strengthening management performance.

Barker, J. A. (1992). *Future edge*. New York: William Morrow and Company, Inc.

Pfeiffer, J. W., Goodstein, L. D., & Nolan, T. M. (1989). *Shaping strategic planning*. Glenview, IL: Scott, Foresman & Co.

Rost, J. C. (1991). *Leadership in the 21st century*. New York: Praeger.

Senge, P. M. (1990). *The fifth discipline*. New York: Doubleday.

Toffler, A. (1990). *Powershift*. New York: Bantam Books.

Yankelovich, D. (1991). *Coming to public judgment: Making democracy work in a complex world*. Syracuse, NY: Syracuse University Press.

3

Cultivating Creative Cultures

Cynthia J. Norris
University of Houston

Overview

In this chapter, I will explore school culture through the lens of creative thought. Leaders will be encouraged to be creative and responsive to the many variables that impact their schools. Emphasis will be placed on the value of individual members' contributions to the emerging needs within school settings, and school principals will be challenged to provide the leadership necessary for cultivating those creative contributions. All organizational members must feel free to question and to endeavor to understand the organization in light of the various needs of its members; there must be a climate of openness that will embrace a new way of doing business when current practices prove outdated. Emphasized in this chapter will be the importance of leadership as the pivotal force in shaping the

Many of the examples quoted in this chapter are the result of field work and reaction papers developed by students in classes in the principalship. I would particularly like to acknowledge these students for their contributions: Martha Dykes, David Ford, Edwin Hebron, Raymond Lowery, Ann Plummer, and Edward Vargas.

creative attitude of the organization—not only through the personal creativeness displayed by the school principal, but also through the inspiration given to others for creative contributions. Leadership will be viewed as a proactive rather than a reactive process.

How today's leaders respond to their environments in support of their ethical values is, of course, important. Even more crucial, however, is whether they serve as transformers of a better society. A need exists for leaders who will search diligently for the discrepancies between "what is" and "what should be." An equal need exists for leaders who will act on this knowledge in ways that will benefit the organization and its members. Leaders must view the environment as an extension of the school; they must foster means of embracing and cultivating that environment to promote the welfare of all human life. No longer can they afford to perpetuate an existing order; they must become, instead, active, dedicated shapers of a future reality—one committed to the advancement of human potential.

The link between personal thought process and the leader's potential for becoming a visionary leader who will inspire the visions of others is the emphasis of this chapter. Creativity is explored in various stages as it relates to rational and intuitive thought, and the concept of visioning is developed against that backdrop. Case studies demonstrating differing leadership perspectives in action are presented for reflection with suggested activities for further study.

Conceptual Frame

Behind every great achievement there is a dreamer of great dreams. (Greenleaf, 1977, p. 15)

In the midst of educational turmoil and unyielding cries for accountability, bright hope emerges that challenges one to dream for better days. It is a glimmer—a possibility—for improvement. It is the emergence of a leader—a school principal capable of envisioning and cohesively blending the values, hopes, and dreams of organizational members into concert.

What is necessary to promote the visionary leadership needed for a new educational age? That in essence is the central question explored in this chapter. Leadership is possible for those individuals capable of dreaming, those who have something worthwhile to dream about, and those who can shape dreams into reality.

Change is inevitable. How educators learn to function within a changing world will determine the survival of our educational system. Today's principals need to view their schools as part of a larger whole and "facilitate patterns of change and development that will allow their identity to evolve along with the wider system" (Morgan, 1986, p. 245). One cannot fully appreciate the qualities necessary for such creative leadership without some understanding of the context in which that leadership must occur.

Understanding Schools as Organizations

Convention is a great discourager of originality. (Osborn, 1957)

Before schools can be appreciated as separate cultures, they must be understood collectively as organizations. Schools operate as unique identities different from business and industrial settings. They deal with variable resources, large spans of control, inconsistent standards for determining efficiency and effectiveness, and a technology that is unclear at best. Schools consistently lack four qualities necessary to be considered "tightly coupled"—i.e., organizations able to operate as "rational models." Weick (1982) classifies those needed qualities:

1. consistent goals and standards
2. predictable problems and solutions
3. continuous inspection and corrective feedback
4. coordinated information dissemination

All four of these qualities must be present if schools are to function as "business models."

Tightly coupled organizations can operate rationally (i.e., in a mechanistic fashion) because their environments are stable and their methodology is clear. By contrast, schools must survive in the midst of much uncertainty and environmental turbulence, a loosely coupled situation.

This loosely coupled nature offers schools an opportunity to remain flexible and adaptable to their everchanging environments. If this flexibility is allowed to prevail, schools can continually renew themselves and evolve with their environments. However, when structures are superimposed in efforts to make schools carbon copies of industrial settings, the organization's potential for growth and regeneration is usually lost. People's creativity is squelched and they become disillusioned, often leaving the organization for positions where their abilities can be realized. If they remain, they either try to change the system or they "adapt" by becoming complacent and conditioned to the imposed structures (Dyer & Dyer, 1965).

What conditions presently exist in schools? State department regulations, minimum competency testing programs, and various other mandated reform efforts have inundated today's schools with structures designed to streamline, predict, and measure their effectiveness. At the very time when educators should be questioning the relevance of current practices, they have reacted to the challenges for accountability by tightening existing procedures. Such rigidity has focused on a perpetuation of the tried-and-true rather than a creative exploration of new methods and approaches.

Loose coupledness yields little advantage unless perceptive organizational members and leaders provide purpose to an otherwise drifting team. If no individuals think beyond "the way things have always been done around here" to a better way—if no leaders serve as transformers of the organization—the organization is not likely to move in any purposeful direction.

Central to this issue is the notion that collective decision making at the grass-roots level will bring about creative decisions that will promote positive responses to the problems facing today's educators. Riding on the crest of such thinking is the notion of site-based management. All this sounds positive and should prompt the beginning of a real transformation in public schools.

However, research on the initial impact of site-based management suggests that even when opportunities are afforded teachers to be change agents in the decision-making process, little real change occurs (Malen, Ogawa, & Kranz, 1989). This research shows that although teachers may be given the opportunity to make significant decisions, they are often governed by what they think is expected of them by their administrator; or, when they do make decisions, those decisions are often simply a rehash of the way things have always been done. If creativity is widely dispersed among the teacher population, as is commonly believed, why do conditions remain the same?

Real transformation will occur only as subordinates are inspired through a creative coach who facilitates an open climate that encourages others to question existing practices and to envision more appropriate ways of doing business. Such a leadership orientation may require that leaders themselves examine and modify the very nature of their own thought, as they seek to inspire others in similar transformation.

Exploring School Culture

Organizations are in essence socially constructed realities that rest as much in the heads and minds of their members as they do in concrete sets of rules and relations. (Morgan, 1986, p. 131)

A school's culture is a representation of what its members collectively believe themselves to be: it is their self-concept. It reflects what they value and what they express to others as being important. Just as an individual's self-concept shapes his or her personality, so does an organization's perception of itself shape what it ultimately becomes, or what it represents to others.

Culture is a shared reality (Morgan, 1986; Sergiovanni, 1990). Because it is constructed over time, culture includes both past and present perceptions. Its perceived reality is reflected in its symbols, rituals, and purpose. Cultures may be cohesive or fragmented, strong or weak, and functional or dysfunctional depending on the degree to which its members share the same reality.

A shared reality, whether functional (effective) or dysfunctional (ineffective), relates to the cohesiveness with which organizational members bond together in a united purpose (Sergiovanni, 1990). It is certainly true that before a culture can function effectively, it must be cohesive, yet a functional culture in its truest form involves far more than cohesiveness. It involves the moral and ethical direction of that purpose and the degree to which the purpose is true to the reality it represents. To bond together under misguided principles, or according to an outdated reality, is counterproductive to school improvement. This is true even if those misguided principles do reflect current thought legislated and blessed by a society directed toward accountability. A culture that does not recognize the needs of human beings within its circle, that does not examine those needs in light of current structures and practices, and that does not proactively embrace a set of common beliefs aimed at eliminating the wrongs of that society and paving a way for its renewal, is a dysfunctional culture. It is dysfunctional even though it may succeed in the accomplishment of its goals and even though it may work concertedly with one purpose. We are accountable as educators—yes; but we are accountable first and foremost to the advancement of the human spirit!

Culture has been defined as a shared reality constantly moving and dynamic. Morgan (1986) likens this characteristic to a river—calm on the surface but wrought with turbulence underneath. The ebb and flow of human existence is constantly shaping and reshaping the culture to fit with organizations' preconceived notions of themselves. This characteristic, known as *autopoieses*, signifies a need to self-produce. Often the conceptualization of who we are becomes so cohesive and rigid that we react to our external environment by manipulating the variables to preserve and conform to our notion of self. As Weick (1985) notes, "A coherent statement of who we are makes it harder for us to become something else" (p. 385). Strong cultures are often rigid and custodial in orientation. Their tenaciousness renders them less perceptive to changing needs and more prone to adapt than to innovate. Wessley High School exemplifies this characteristic.

Wessley High School.   Wessley is a 60–year–old inner city high school located in a large metropolitan city. It is a predominantly minority high school in a deteriorating economic area. A blighted field and low-cost, poorly maintained housing are directly across the street. The surrounding neighborhood is characterized by deteriorating housing with garbage and litter filling the streets and ditches.

The school has a rich heritage; many prominent leaders, both state and national, graduated from Wessley during its days of glory. In recent years, the school has declined, partially due to the "skimming off" of "brighter" students for the city's magnet school program. There is much talk of "what could be" or "ought to be," but an unfocused atmosphere exists in terms of *how* to accomplish this need.

Parents express great dissatisfaction with the administration of the school and seem to agree that the school "could use a good academic program and better discipline. . . . It needs music, vocational courses for more careers . . . more practical work."

Although teachers verbalize that "all students can learn," some question exists about whether they truly believe that the present student body at Wessley is really capable of achieving. There is too much focus on the Wessley of yesterday and the idea that the cream of the crop has been skimmed away through magnet programs. Not a single student at Wessley is classified as gifted, and little attention is directed toward excellence among the existing student body. Expectations at Wessley seem directed toward minimum competency—meeting the basic requirements. Expectations appear to center on student *effort*, compensating for what students can't do instead of developing/capitalizing on what they *can* do. Teaching activities lack inspiration, and many teachers seem to have little motivation to provide positive role models.

Lesson plans are often sketchy and there seems to be little, or no, long-range planning by teachers. Coordination of subject areas is facilitated by block scheduling; however, there is no evidence of a system to facilitate planning across subject boundaries. This failure to plan jointly prohibits the possibility of an integrated teaching/learning process. A lack of relatedness and isolation of subject areas makes it difficult for students to be provided with a curriculum that is experientially based and related to their lives. Meaning is thus hampered.

This example demonstrates how one school, preoccupied with its past reputation and self-concept, is failing to recognize the need to embrace its new environment and develop a culture beneficial to its members. In failing to examine its preconceived notion of self in relation to its larger environment, the organization neglects the very students it serves.

One reason cultures become obsolete is that they often remain locked into a custodial rather than creative orientation. Let us explore these different cultural types.

Cultural Types

> Paradoxical as it seems, the rational mind prefers the rules it invents to the process of invention. (Samples, 1980, p. 106)

Organizational cultures reflect a collective mind-set of custodial or creative orientation. As outlined in Table 3-1, one approach is reactive; the other proactive. One views its environment as acting *upon* it; the other embraces its environment as an extension of itself and moves in a proactive way to shape an organization which is vibrant and dynamic.

Custodial Organization.   In a *custodial organization*, the emphasis is on streamlining, repetition, and predictability. Leadership is directed toward problem-solution related to emerging issues. The approach is that of single-loop learning (Argyris, 1982), in which efforts are expended toward compliance with preexisting norms.

Single-loop learning follows three steps:

1. establishing a norm
2. monitoring for compliance of that pre–established norm
3. taking corrective action aimed at bringing the organization back into compliance (Argyris, 1982; Morgan, 1986)

Single-loop learning is characteristic of the custodial organization, which "is concerned with achievement of known, predictable measurable items or goals in accordance with familiar, unchanging doctrines, procedures and methods" (Dyer & Dyer, 1965, p. 33).

Table 3–1
Comparisons between custodial attitudes and creative attitudes.

Custodial vs. Creative Leadership	
Custodial Leaders	Creative Leaders
Maintain routines. When questioned about them, automatically defend them	Ignore routines. When made aware of such procedures, automatically try to innovate

Show ingenuity only in improving efficiency of present methods, which are characterized by:
    Simplification
    Streamlining
    Mechanization
    Repetivity
    Predictability
	Develop completely new missions and products; operations are noted for:
	    Basic design changes
	    New breakthroughs
	    Variations
	    Unpredictability

Replace creative persons by custodial ones	Replace custodial persons with creative ones
Seek perfection of the status quo: drill and inspect	Seek new horizons— Speculate and imagine
Fear any change; resent new ideas; cannot understand why anyone wants to change what is already working well enough	Resent frustration; cannot understand reluctance to try new ideas
Find that leadership can be summed up in formulas like: "Be firm, fair, and friendly"; "know your job"; "know your men"; "work through people"; and "be a man"	Equate good leadership with those willing to listen to new ideas, and to be enthusiastic in stimulating change

Adapted from Dyer & Dyer, 1965, p. 39.

Organizations are able to maintain their stable identities through a process of negative feedback that allows them to monitor and adjust any deviations from the preexisting norms they have set. No effort is made to question the appropriateness of those norms if they prove to be dysfunctional. The organization rushes on totally oblivious to the changing needs of the larger environment.

Such a culture would be considered strong in the sense that it is able to maintain itself, but rigid cultures can "program the minds of people in such a way that issues of reality come into question" (Sergiovanni, 1991, p. 223). Organizational maturity itself causes this entrenchment. "Culture preserves the glories of the past and hence becomes valued as a source of self–esteem and as a means of defense rather than for what it represents and the extent to which it serves purposes," according to Schein (cited in Sergiovanni, 1991, p. 224). This attitude is exemplified by Southview High School.

Southview High School. Southview High School is an inner–city school located in the heart of Mountain Crest, the nicest neighborhood in a large metropolitan city. The facade of the 1930s limestone building faces the boulevard. At the other end is the Mountain Crest Country Club. Unlike the country club, Mountain Crest opens its doors to a mixed population.

Mountain Crest High School boasts a strong heritage and a rich tradition, based on the thousands of graduates who have graced its halls over the past 54 years. It was the first high school in the western part of the city and was considered "the place to be" for future professionals.

The school has grown from 750 students to 2,000 students over the past 50 years. As enrollment increased in the 1960s and 1970s, the school became overcrowded. Forty wooden, temporary buildings were used as additional classrooms until two additions to the original building were completed in the 1980s.

Entering 1 of the 10 doors to the foyer of Mountain Crest, one is struck by the cultural diversity of the students who fill the wide, slightly dirty halls. The students are loud, and they congregate in single-race groups in front of lockers and display cases filled with trophies, anti–drug literature, school photographs, and student projects. The air is filled with energy as students move happily but leisurely to classes.

The school is racially mixed (30 percent white, 30 percent black, 30 percent Hispanic, and 10 percent other, mostly Asian). The whites come from the surrounding affluent neighborhood, the Hispanics from nearby areas, and the blacks are bused in. The PTA is recognized statewide, but, unfortunately, few black, Hispanic, and Asian parents belong to the organization.

Mountain Crest's academic position is enhanced by its strong, although mostly white, faculty. Although the school has had four principals in the past five years, all department heads and major program coordinators have held their positions for at least five years. Teacher turnover is low.

Today, Mountain Crest High School with 2,000 students is at peak enrollment and again is overcrowded. The school PTA has taken the lead in the community to decrease school population by 800 students. Their proposal, which has been taken to the school board, calls for a reduction in transfer students who live outside the school zone. To date, no minority organizations have mobilized to block this effort of white parents within the school zone. Mountain Crest, which was one of the top five high schools in the United States in the 1950s, still prides itself as the best in the city, but it is fighting to maintain its identity and position within the district.

Mountain Crest High, like Wessley High (described in an earlier example), is preoccupied with the glories of the past and has failed to recognize the diverse needs of its total student body. No real integration of cultures exists in either of the schools, and eventually both will lose their battles to preserve themselves unless they consider more carefully the norms from which they operate.

Creative Organization.   The custodial organization is in sharp contrast to the creative organization, which operates from a double-loop approach (Argyris, 1982). In the *creative organization*, norms are questioned in light of new situations that emerge. A proactive orientation questions the appropriateness of existing practices and endeavors to develop new missions and products suited to the changing needs of the organization. *Double-loop learning* is a four-stage process that raises the question "Why?" As in single-loop learning, norms are established and monitoring occurs; however, if discrepancies exist, the norms, as well as the results, may be questioned. Double-loop learning is a dynamic process focusing on problem finding, as well as problem solving (Getzels, 1979). It paves the way for organizational renewal. The custodial, single-loop, approach is an example of "doing things right"; the creative, double-loop approach, seeks to do "the right thing" (Bennis & Nanus, 1985).

Just as organizations reflect these separate orientations, so do the leaders who represent them. A special kind of leadership is needed that results from the innate way in which one thinks. Such leadership not only thinks creatively, but inspires this quality in others by promoting an emotionally safe climate, which fosters the questioning of existing practices.

Transformational Leadership

> The art of the creative leader is the art of institution building, the reworking of human and technological materials to fashion an organism that embodies new and enduring values. (Selznick, 1957, p. 28)

Leadership inspires a relationship between leaders and followers. The quality of that relationship and the resulting individual and organizational benefits are determined by leadership type.

Burns (1979) defines two leadership types: transactional and transformational. *Transactional leadership* is a "bargain basement" approach offering to the followers specified external rewards and privileges in exchange for the completion of duties and responsibilities outlined by the organization. It rests on a foundation of external rewards and is an exchange characterized by duty. Transactional leadership centers in the *mind* of the follower (Sergiovanni, 1990), for it is a rational agreement to work toward organizational goals and values in exchange for rewards offered by the leader. Transactional leadership operates at the "receive, respond" level of affective development where followers give "lip service" to those goals and values with little or no personal commitment to them. Such *espoused theory* (what is professed to be of value, rather than what is demonstrated by one's behavior) does little to enhance the development of the individual or the organization.

Transformational leadership builds on a transactional approach by elevating the organization and its members to higher levels of moral response. Tranformational leadership serves as the igniting force, uniting members in a mutually beneficial and transforming shared purpose.

Transformational leadership/followership operates from the *heart* as well as the mind (Sergiovanni, 1990) and cuts to the core of personal values and character. It is a moral response reflected in the individual's behavior ("theory in use") resulting from those values.

Transformational leadership in its highest sense moves an organization from its custodial orientation to a climate of creative awareness and response. Transforming leaders reflect upon the reality of current conditions and dare to question existing practices. They consider future trends and conceptualize new pathways. A sensitivity to the human condition is evidenced by their efforts to create new avenues of understanding for all groups. In chapter 1, Hughes emphasizes that transformational leadership impacts not only the internal organization, but its larger environment as well. It is a powerful leadership force based on personal influence rather than authoritative directives and succeeds in transporting followers from a "zone of indifference" (Barnard, 1968b) to one of committed acceptance.

Barnard (1968b) speaks eloquently of the moral dimensions of leadership, calling attention to "moral creativeness" as "the highest expression of responsibility" (p. 261). The leader *alone* does not create anything of lasting value. That creation comes about through *cooperation*, and it is the work of the organization as a whole. The leader accomplishes this through the "creation of faith" by serving as a catalyst for human effort. "Cooperation, not leadership, is the creative process; but leadership is the indispensable fulminator of its forces" (Barnard: 1968b, p. 259). Such leadership is defined as:

> . . . the power of individuals to inspire cooperative personal decision by creating faith: faith in common understanding, faith in the probability of success, faith in the ultimate satisfaction of personal motives, faith in the integrity of objective authority, faith in the superiority of common purpose as a personal aim of those who partake in it. (p. 259)

Today's leaders *must* become risk takers—not in a reckless sense, but from a *committed* perspective. Leaders must be willing to venture into uncharted waters when organizational reality beckons. Principals have a responsibility to facilitate growth: organizational growth, personal growth, and the growth of others. For some principals, meeting this responsibility may require the development of previously unclaimed potential.

Gardner (1963) says that most of us have really not developed our potentialities because the circumstances of our lives never called them forth. He defines potentialities as "the full range of his [man's] capacities for sensing, wondering, learning, understanding, loving and aspiring" (pp. 11–12). Visionaries, he says, are those who "look forward to an endless and unpredictable dialogue between [their] potentialities and the claims of life—not only the claims [they] encounter but the claims they invent" (p. 11). Such individuals are the creative leaders.[1]

The Creative Leader

> He who cannot change the very fabric of his thought will never change reality. (Admar Sedat)

Personality variables exist that operate in direct contrast between leaders (creators) and managers (custodians) (Zaleznik, 1977). These differences are manifested in a person's respective orientation toward goals, human relationships, work, and self. *Custodians* have passive, impersonal attitudes toward goals, which they view as necessary ingredients for the fulfillment of organizational purposes. *Creators* view goals from an inward desire to improve the organization. The attitude of the custodian is in contrast to the creator who exercises a personal and active interest in goals and who, through personal commitment and influence, is able to alter positively the thinking of others.

The nature of work is, likewise, viewed differently by custodians and creators. Custodians are basically interested in keeping an organization on an even keel; they endeavor to coordinate people and ideas into a smooth organizational operation directed toward maintaining the organization in its present state. Creators, by contrast, operate from a high-risk position; they initiate new approaches to problems and explore issues that require more effective resolution.

In the realm of human relations, yet another contrast exists between the creator and the custodian. A custodian tends to seek out others for work and collaboration, avoiding solitude if possible. Although custodians desire the company of others, they lack the empathy and intuitiveness necessary for relating to others' thoughts and feelings. Creators, on the other hand, possess the capacity to empathize with others and to be perceptive of others' reactions to events and situations.

Custodians are characterized by bureaucratic school cultures noted for their conservative, unmoving nature. It becomes almost the duty of the custodian to maintain the status quo, to make only minor changes, and to achieve perfection

---

1.   In chapter 2, Achilles, Keedy, and High discuss the important functions of the administrator (one who *properly* balances managerial duties with the excitement of leadership). I believe that both are essential skills for today's principal. The importance of balancing structure (management) with randomness (leadership) is discussed in detail later in this chapter. There is, however, an unfortunate connotation attached to the word *management* that has little to do with the important *job* of management and more to do with how one manages. It is to this connotation of the word *management* that the following section is addressed, rather than to the job of management itself.

of the routine. As noted by Dyer and Dyer (1965), "the custodial manager recognizes any change as a threat to the predictability of his management and therefore to the efficiency he has achieved" (p. 35).

The creative nature of leaders has been celebrated throughout the literature. Rogers (1976) emphasizes that its characteristics spring from a "creative ego" marked by "individuality, uniqueness and identity" (p. 297). Creative leaders possess courage and a confidence in their pursuit of ideas; they are more concerned with finding a better way than with accepting a solution that may already appear adequate.

Leaders possess self–actualized creativeness in contrast to the special talent creativity so often equated with the word *creative* (Maslow, 1976). They "do not cling to the familiar, nor is their quest for the truth a catastrophic need for certainty, safety, definiteness and order" (p. 89). For these leaders, self-actualized creativeness is "emitted" or radiated and "hits all of life regardless of problems" (p. 91).

What implications does this contrast between creative and custodial style have for school principals? A custodial approach to management is less demanding and less risky than creative leadership; however, leadership is essential for organizational growth and survival. It is particularly important during times of adversity. Principals have been charged with the monumental task of educational renewal. This can only be accomplished if they cease to operate from a custodial perspective.

Unity of Thought

> To the extent that creativeness is constructive, synthesizing, unifying, and interpretive, to that extent does it depend upon the internal integration of the individual. (Maslow, 1976)

The alteration of one's leadership pattern depends to a great extent upon an internal unity. Creative people are not polarized in their thinking process but incorporate, instead, both conceptual and analytical processes in a complementary manner (see table 3-2). DeBono (1971) terms these processes *lateral* (first stage) and *vertical* (second stage) thinking. In the creative process, the mind shifts continuously between a lateral mode and a vertical mode as ideas are created, developed, and refined.

Organization management entails both analytical (vertical) and intuitive (lateral) skills. Mintzberg's (1976) study supported this concept and confirmed Barnard's (1968a) belief that the real keys to management are contained in the realm of intuitive thought.

Contrary to popular belief, fostered by preparation programs that emphasize quantitative analysis, managers favor an intuitive, verbal mode of communication and are not inclined to depend on hard data as the basis for finalizing decisions. They have difficulty delegating because organizational knowledge is stored in their subconscious (Mintzberg, 1976).

Table 3-2.
Comparisons between lateral
thinking and vertical thinking.

Lateral vs. Vertical Thinking	
Vertical Thinking	**Lateral Thinking**
Is selective; judges	Is generative
Shows concern for stability	Shows concern for change
Proves and establishes points or relationships	Moves from one concept to another
Looks for what is right	Looks for what is different
Looks for answers	Looks for questions
Is analytical	Is provocative
Is concerned with where an idea originates	Shows concern for where an idea leads
Functions step by step, sequentially	Is holistic; jumps in thinking
Chooses what is to be considered	Welcomes intrusions — sets off new ideas
Goes along with the obvious	Explores beyond the obvious
Promises at least a minimal result	Increases the chances of a maximal result, but makes no promises
Develops an idea	Originates an idea

Adapted from DeBono, 1971, p. 5.

Educational researchers have replicated Mintzberg's study, adapting it to superintendents and to principals at the elementary and secondary level (Duigan, 1980; Willis, 1980; and Martin & Willower, 1981). Few differences were found among the natures of these administrative positions. These studies suggest that the need for intuitive, or lateral, thinking is most pronounced among school leaders. As Duigan (1980) explained:

> Over 47% of the decisions made by the superintendent were classified as non–programmed decision, or decisions for which there existed no clear method for handling them. In these instances the (leader) found himself in a "de novo" situation and had to fall back on his expertise and creative ability. (p. 18)

Leaders must understand that the rational thought process, although important, is not always a superior method for making effective decisions. The nonlogi-
cal process is equated with "common sense, experience, originality and a sense of
adventure" (Barnard, 1968a, p. 306). Both logic and intuition have their place in
effective leadership. Barnard gives the following guidelines for determining the
appropriate thought process:

1. If the purpose is to *ascertain truth*, emphasis should be placed on the
   rational process. Under such conditions, the past or the present is in view,
   and conclusions can be subject to test and review.
2. If the purpose is to *determine a course of action*, one looks to the future,
   and the thinking process demanded is speculative with less emphasis
   on rationality.
3. In attempting to *persuade*, one should lean strongly on the sensing,
   intuitive nature and not let logic get in the way.

Creative Leadership

The scarce people are the ones who have the know–how, energy, daring and staying
power to implement ideas. . . . [C]reativity without action oriented follow–through is
a barren form of behavior. In a sense, it is irresponsible. (Levitt, 1963, p. 96)

Creative leadership, as defined in this chapter, is the ability to bring about
constructive change. Such leadership is innovative and demands a capacity to
conceptualize the creation of new avenues for change (i.e., ability to determine a
course of action), as well as an intuitive awareness in working with and through
people to move the organization forward (i.e., power of persuasion). A leader is
an expert at utilizing the abilities and skills of all organization members in a
creative manner beneficial both to the organization and to the personal development of its members.

Levitt (1963), in relating the field of management to the creative thought
process, separates the process into two factors: creativity and innovation. He
explains that *creativity* is thinking up new things; whereas, *innovation* is doing
new things. Hughes (chapter 1) suggests that the creative quality of leadership is
personified in the artist. The artist/leader is the "creative virtuoso" who "gives
birth to ideas and concepts and the notion of *what might be*." Certainly then, the
leader and followers, through coordinated efforts, must provide structure and
shape to the ideas that are generated. This is the work of the architect/leader
who, according to Hughes (chapter 1), brings a "decided sense of direction and
goal orientation" to the process of leadership. Finally, the creative cycle is complete when the commissar/leader inspires organizational members to bond
together in completing the task. As Achilles, Keedy, and High (chapter 2) suggest, the true administrator is one who combines these elements in a most effective manner and works with others to accomplish the goals of the organization.

The embodiment of purpose through the leadership process requires that
a leader possess the ability to sense organizational needs from a holistic

approach, and that he or she have an insightfulness, or intuitive feel, for what the organization can become. The leader must possess a vision. Katz (1974) defines this ability to see the whole as conceptual skill and notes that it enables leaders to act so that their decisions advance the overall welfare of the organization. Barnard (1968a) also stresses that conceptualization is a process of sensing the wholeness of the organization and that it "transcends the capacity of merely rational thought." It is, he believes, pertinent to "feeling, judgment, sense, proportion, balance, and appropriateness." It is a matter of art rather than science and is aesthetic rather than logical (p. 306). Conceptual ability is crucial in steering an organization toward a direction of accomplishment and growth; it is the mark of leadership (Greenleaf, 1977).

Artist, Architect, and Commissar Revisited

> Our thinking mind is mainly two-fold: a judicial mind which analyzes, compares, and chooses; a creative mind which visualizes, foresees, and generates ideas. Judgment can help keep imagination on the track, and imagination can help enlighten judgment. (Osborn, 1957, p. 52)

In the realm of creativity, the interrelatedness of rational and intuitive thought is crucial. Although many point to the intuitive nature as the realm of creativity, it is only as the rational mode selects, refines, and structures that a creative product results.

Creativity is a continuous process that moves through four stages: preparation, incubation, illumination, and verification (Wallas, 1926). During the stages of preparation and verification, a vertical thinking process is employed, which focuses on one's ability to think rationally—i.e., to determine the truth. The emphasis is on sequencing the known into patterns that facilitate the assimilation of information and the formation of judgments based on factual data. This emphasis shifts during the incubation and illumination stages, and the thinking mode becomes one of intuitively searching for new ideas and holistically viewing situations from a feeling or insightful perspective. Principals can learn to use these stages to maximum advantage as they seek to work with their organizations in the cultivation of a school climate characterized by a creative visionary perspective.

Cultivating Creative Climates

Stage 1: Preparation (What?)

Creative climates are based on a strong foundation of preparation that includes both cognitive and affective dimensions. During *preparation*, the individual's focus is primarily one of rational inquiry. The purpose is to find answers—to solve problems by exploring the many alternatives that have been tested, proven, and found workable. The preparation phase is also the time for exploration beyond the already known, for examining past assumptions, and for clarifying espoused theories. Although preparation is primarily a time of rational, vertical thinking, the individual must remain open to many viewpoints and incorporate intuitive skills in reading situations, subtle signs, and feelings.

Today's principals must develop a broad knowledge base that can serve as a springboard for later reflection. The preparation stage is characterized by hard work and study. During the preparation stage, principals are encouraged to do the following:

- Search for breadth.
- Expand their horizons.
- Read widely.
- Let their curiosity take them wherever it will.
- Be open to experience and stimuli of all sorts—
  both from within themselves and the world around them.
- Understand problems and define them accurately.

Preparation is the first stage of problem analysis, and it necessitates the accumulation of much data. The richness of this data will come from the variety of sources that contribute to it: books, articles, reports, visits to other schools/districts, conversations with others in similar situations, and action-based research. Preparation is also a time to enhance environmental awareness. As previously emphasized,

> awareness should extend to a developing understanding of the human beings that make up the educational system. Who are these individuals? What unique problems face them as they seek to find meaning in their lives? As the leader confronts such questions, problems are identified. *What is* is then measured against *what should be*; needs are identified. The leader comes to terms with the important question: What do I really believe that schools should be? (Norris, 1991, p. 118)

Additionally, one must ask—how does this compare with what currently exists in this school? Having asked and answered these questions, the principal has tentatively identified the problem. As the principal/leader continues to explore and learn more about the situation, the real issues emerge and the problem may be redefined. Greater clarity brings us closer to the true reality of the situation.

Preparation is the knowledge stage that supports all other stages of the principal's developing vision for the school. If the preparation is based on inaccurate knowledge or assumptions, there is little likelihood that the resulting vision will be effective or reflect the reality of the organization's needs.

Principals can facilitate the preparation stage for others by sharing knowledge and encouraging others to study issues and increase their own understandings. Allowing opportunities for sharing knowledge and learning through others is of major benefit. Travelling to other districts, visiting others' classrooms, and encouraging staff to share ideas from journals and engage in their own action-based research are important things the principal can do to enhance the group's knowledge base.

Stage 2: Incubation (How? Why?)

Incubation marks the second stage in creating a workable vision for any organization. It is an intuitive, lateral thinking stage in which the subconscious blends past knowledge as the mind becomes detached, or moves away, from logic. During this period, the individual does not analyze or form judgments, but instead breaks old patterns and connections by allowing the mind to explore possibilities based on information previously acquired. During the incubation stage, principals are encouraged to do the following:

- Detach their minds from, or "sleep on," the problem.
- Postpone judgment to allow association to occur.
- Allow their senses to come into full play on other aspects of the environment as the problem "ferments" in the back of their mind.
- Step out of the rut of habit, and try to make different connections.
- Think metaphorically (i.e., look at one thing and see another).

"New pathways, approaches, or possibilities will not evolve if the leader continues to hold fast to past courses of action. There must be an attitude of openness—a receptivity to change" (Norris, 1991, p. 118). Incubation is often the most difficult stage for leaders who are conditioned to past approaches and methods of solving problems. As previously discussed, a custodial orientation on the part of many leaders causes them to hold on to the safety net of experience even when that old way of operating was not effective. Only as leaders sharpen and develop the thoughtful side of their nature—only as they allow their minds to wander into the regions of the *metaphoric mind*—can they see beyond the present state of affairs to the realm of possibility. As Gardner (1963) expressed it, "Vision is possible to those who allow themselves to step back from life and question its relevance—to consider its possibilities" (p. 19).

Incubation will not occur unless time is provided for it. That time is based on what Arieti (1976) calls "aloneness." It is during inner silence, or inactivity, that we remove ourselves from the mundane and discover our own creativeness. Arieti stresses that aloneness is not a passive state but is, instead, a time when we allow those hidden parts of ourselves to add to the richness of life.

Not only must today's principals find time for and allow themselves personal freedom for their own reflection, but they must also encourage the same in others, fostering an open, accepting climate where mutual trust is paramount. Leaders should likewise provide stimulation for creative thought by encouraging and rewarding new ideas on the part of others.

Stage 3: Illumination (If?)

This stage is the essence of creativity, for it is with *illumination* that the idea is born.

> It is in the illumination stage that leaders embrace tomorrow! They recognize that all answers are not indelibly engraved in the past. Possibilities become vivid: leaders

discover what their course of action should be. What they (suddenly or) intuitively discover is really based on a strong foundation of rational thought. Ethical, moral choices are made based on subconscious feelings of rightness. (Norris, 1991, p. 119–120)

During the illumination stage, principals are encouraged to do the following:

- Allow images to take form.
- Translate those images into words.
- Trust in themselves and the ideas they generate.
- Communicate those images to others in ways that help them understand the images, too.

As a developer of others, the principal should facilitate the illumination stage for others by encouraging the sharing of new ideas. Several techniques of group processing (i.e., brainstorming, etc.) can provide vehicles for sharing ideas; however, unless the principal has established a climate of trust and appreciation for the ideas of others, few ideas will be generated.

Stage 4: Verification (How?)

Having an idea is one thing; providing a structure to that idea so that it can be used is something else. According to Norris (1991), "All intuitive thinking must be translated into the linear order of rational thought if it is to be articulated and eventually put to use" (p. 120). The process of creativity, or *visioning*, is incomplete until the judicial mind examines the creative idea, selects what is relevant, and begins to form a structure for its implementation. This is the stage of *verification*, and it provides principals and staff with opportunities to do the following:

- Examine the ideas in relation to personal and organizational values.
- Correct discrepancies by modifying the ideas or the previously established norm.
- Deduce immediate and long-range consequences.
- Shape and arrange the results of inspiration.
- Demonstrate so as to validate to others.

This stage can be facilitated by working through a series of questions that might be used by the leader alone or jointly by the leader and other members of the organization:

1. Is my (our) vision consistent with the greater vision, or mission, of education?
2. Does it promote, or hinder, actualization of that mission?
3. Is my (our) vision consistent with my (our) own value system and the educational platform that I (we) espouse?
4. Is it morally and ethically sound?

5. Should I (we) modify the vision—or the platform, philosophy that I (we) originally espoused?

Finally, the ideas must be given form and structure if they are to make any difference in the goals of the organization. Structure and direction must be facilitated through a systematic plan of action. Included in that plan must be an analysis of the guiding factors and values that support the vision, along with the goals and objectives that provide the pathway for attainment. Convincing others to join in the plans for implementation and to contribute their ideas helps ensure that the vision will be realized.

This final stage does not happen overnight. It requires for its fulfillment the bonding of purpose addressed earlier in this chapter. Its transformational nature requires that the leader possess those qualities characterized by transformational leadership.

SUMMARY

Schooling has reached a turning point. The survival of mass public education and continued renewal depends on the creative spirit and courage of leaders at the school site. They are in a unique position to evaluate current needs and visualize more appropriate futures based on that reality.

This chapter has explored creative culture-building. The principal has emerged as the energizer and facilitator of this process. It has stressed, however, that cultures—shared realities—are cooperative arrangements that can not be fully actualized by the leader alone. Purposeful direction depends on the leader's ability to inspire the creative contributions of others.

Whether a school culture is creative or custodial is ultimately a reflection of the personal orientations of the collective membership. Leaders are challenged to develop personal qualities conducive to creative thought, such as openness, tolerance for ambiguity, and risk taking. They are also encouraged to establish a climate of support and emotional safety that will inspire similar thought patterns in others.

Creative leaders recognize that excellence is facilitated through a bonding of purposes and values rather than through imposed structures designed to streamline, predict, and quantify objectives. Creative cultures, in turn, are characterized by participants who examine current practices in relation to emerging organizational needs. Through a process of double-loop learning, those participants dare to question existing practices and to search for emerging problems, as well as, solutions. Their proactive response allows them to remain flexible rather than rigid as they deal with emerging needs. Leaders and followers unite in creating an organization that is beneficial to all.

THEORY INTO PRACTICE:
A CASE STUDY FOR REFLECTION

Driving north on Main Street, over the old city bridge, just on the other side of downtown, one is greeted graciously by a sign reading, "Bienvenidos— Welcome to Near Northside." A few feet beyond this welcoming sign is a tunnel, about a third of a mile long, the top serving as a crossover for railroad cars. Driving through the tunnel, one expects the usual aura of apprehension at the opposite end. On the other side, one sees an array of abandoned warehouses, preceded by a smorgasbord of retail shops. The concentration of businesses mimics a small city. In the midst of this "city" stands the community school.

Approaching the institution, one comes to a fenced–in parking lot with two sets of gates; one is never opened. Teachers gain entrance to the building from the parking lot by way of a smaller gate. There are chains on all gates facing the street. The school's building is a three-story, red brick structure whose glass facade reaches from the first to the third floors. Damage is obvious to the second-floor glass. At the very top, just below the eaves, appears the school's name. To the right, there are no windows—only a twelve-foot, red brick wall that provides partial view of the second and third floors. On the red brick wall appear fragments of carved letters taken of the previous site and cemented on this wall, making a nostalgic reference to the past. Behind this wall is hidden an old building that was also part of the past. It stands alone.

As visitors enter the building, they are greeted by the institution's mission statement: "Every child can learn." To the left of the school's entrance is the office, set apart from the main hall. There are two doors—one for entering, the other for exiting. Between these two doors is a glass display case, empty, showing no sign of pride, past or present, nor anticipation of future success. It is a sign of unconditional surrender. Graffiti and smoke-damaged lockers are exposed. So are the broken lockers. Corridor walls are severely damaged, and once-concealed pipes are now exposed. Many of the classrooms have no windows, and rooms with them have a casement window or two. Too many layers of dark and rusty paint, like the coloring of politics, hide the truth of education. One notices that the doors at the east end of the building are unlocked, opened, and in need of repair. A chain dangles from the door bar.

Students are not current with the latest fads but are triumphantly tough and streetwise. During the changing of classes, some students carry no supplies but positively make their way to class. Others stop to shoot the breeze with their comrades.

No student organizations exist in the school, with the exception of a student council. Around contest time, an overnight rush takes place to gather students for the math contest, which usually has good results. This year there were no sponsors for the school newspaper or yearbook. Recently, a faculty member volunteered to sponsor the school's cheerleading team. There is no apparent unity among the faculty.

Teachers place emphasis on textbook and drill book learning. The district's curriculum guide is used as a tool to determine objectives and/or teaching strategies. The school has an after-school tutoring program, and approximately 60 percent of the students enrolled in the program attend.

The school operates like a machine. Teachers are to sign in no later than 7:45. At almost that time, a flux of teachers rushes in one door; they sign in, check their boxes, and rush out. The principal, the engine that drives the organization, on occasion stands at the end of the counter, uttering, "Good morning." To an observer, it is the New York subway, with its many ticket-stamping devices and turnstiles. If there were a real cadence to this, one could imagine the sound of the subway: turnstiles turning, doors opening and closing, and people rushing to their destinations.

Because of the very nature of its business, this organization depends on a rigid bell schedule. This bell allows for the structured, routinization of the organization. The ringing of the bell, like pressing the On button of a machine, starts the mechanization/activities of the organization (machine).

Students feed into the classrooms like paper into a machine. They are imprinted, and as if on an assembly line, are passed on, or moved on, for another imprint. The clerical staff, arriving before their working time, sit at their desks, unable to strike the next key on the typewriter: "It's not time yet. I don't get paid to work extra." Like the remote control of a jukebox, the human entity of the organization cannot function until the button has been pressed or the quarter inserted. Administration says to teachers, "You must teach and the students must learn for the 45 minutes that they are in your class." Teachers respond, "All a teacher has to do to get a good evaluation is put on a good show." The bell rings; the curtain goes up. Teachers, like puppets on a string electronically controlled, begin their movements, stopping only at the sound of the bell.

In this school certain activities must be performed without question:

- showing up for work at a certain hour
- giving instructions
- reporting to parents every three weeks
- evaluating students
- following policy

The language used and the conversations explored are understood among the people of this culture:

- "Students, today the objective is . . . "
- "By the end of the lesson you will . . . "
- "Teachers, you must modify your lesson . . . "
- "Teachers, the curriculum guide . . . "
- "The first appraisal period is . . . "

Teachers assemble in the lounge and the conversations begin:

- "Jack just cannot learn."
- "Oh! Sally is just driving me crazy."
- "I tell you, our discipline problems are getting out of hand."

Evident to most observers is the penetration of yet another culture within the school:

- "Why are so many of our boys wearing black t–shirts?"
- "It seems like we are having a lot of gang fights this year."
- "What is going on?"

There is considerable fear among the staff that gangs are infiltrating the school environment. These gangs/groups, like the fragmented faculty, have divided loyalties.

The female principal, an astute professional whose aggressive self–confidence begs to be tested, makes strong attempts to run the organization with an iron hand: "I am not _____ (the former leader). I am now your principal, with new rules and regulations that we all will follow." Although the teacher group has no formal or recognized leader, it makes itself known by constantly refusing to volunteer or accept extra duties: "She's crazy if she thinks I'm going to do it. Let her write me up."

The culture of each of these groups cannot tolerate the absolute control by one individual or small group. Yet, at least on the surface, the mechanization keeps the organization afloat and in rhythm. The doors open and close, buttons are pressed, bells ring and the work begins.

GUIDING QUESTIONS

1. Compare Northside's culture with a similar school culture you may have experienced. What elements of each culture are tightly coupled? In what ways do these elements suggest a custodial orientation? What effect does the tightly coupled framework have on organizational members?

2. What behaviors are displayed by each school principal? How do their respective styles affect the tone of the organization? Is the thinking style displayed by these principals lateral or vertical? How does this style limit their effectiveness as leaders?

Driving to Taylor Elementary, a school located within the inner loop of a large metropolitan city, one passes boarded up homes and block after block of dilapidated apartments. People stroll languidly and purposelessly through the residential areas. That this is one of the more depressed areas of the city, both economically and, seemingly, spiritually is evident with every abandoned business and with every adult male and female whom one sees passing his or her day sitting idly on a front porch stoop or a littered curb or street corner. Then, as if transported by some means depicted in science fiction, one arrives at the more immediate residential area of the school. In this area, one sees a dramatic change in not only the quality of homes, but also in the home maintenance and apparent pride of ownership. The homes are well kept; paint is immaculate. The lawns are well–clipped, hedged, and edged. The people who live in the houses seem to have direction and purpose in their lives, in contrast with the people in the dwellings outside the school's immediate area.

The school itself is a model in maintenance, reflective of pride in the surroundings. Physically the school is lovely. The building sparkles with freshness and is cheerful and clean throughout. Atria are carefully planted with a variety of vegetation. All are well cared for, blooming and fresh. They have been carefully nurtured and the whole school is involved in maintaining their health and well being. No graffiti besmirches even the remotest corners of this school's bathrooms. No trash or litter is evident in any corner. Inside the classrooms, one finds the space neat and embellished with the work and lessons that students complete in the course of their day. Rooms have an inviting and warm feeling that sends out the signal that whoever lives and works there is happy and productive.

The whole school is involved in the growth and nurturing of its students. The care and satisfaction in this is apparent from the calm peace of the corridors and the smiles and warmth of the children themselves. There is pride here, and strength, and a promise of better things to come. One surmises that whoever is in charge at this school has infused this sense of worth and pride in all who are a part of the organization.

The principal in charge, Mrs. Franklin, is a woman of great strength and fortitude. Her eyes embody confidence and vitality, and project a frankness and candor that make one feel welcome. She shakes hands like a person who is fully aware and satisfied with who she is and where she is going. That she exudes confidence and direction confirms itself not only in her nonverbal message but also in her voice and in her message, "Invest in the Future," which is an integral part of the school's mission.

Living up to her own maxim, Mrs. Franklin does not stand in the way of the children at Taylor. Instead, she has expanded their world view and enriched many dimensions of their personality and intellect. Mrs. Franklin is a risk–taker in attempting to succeed at a mission. Quite aware of the lack of earlier board policy to support many of her endeavors; she nevertheless plunged deeply into undesignated waters in an effort to match the school's reality to its mission, goals, and objectives. One plunge that Mrs. Franklin took was to initiate the development of the school's curriculum. Using local private schools that cater to the elite as her models, she took on the school's curriculum goal: the teaching of "basic skills of life." The objectives became the attainment of "good discipline, good vocabulary skills, great literature, good books, good paragraph meaning, math skills, and developmental science." The school bootlegged a science lab, and two foreign languages were taught in sophisticated language labs. French was chosen for its "global appeal."

Taylor Elementary became a magnet school for physical development during the years of desegregation. Mrs. Franklin accepted the principalship of the physical development magnet but felt that students would not select a magnet program for simple exercise routine. A more extensive program was designed that was divided into five parts:

1. traditional, interpretative, and native dance
2. parallel bars
3. floor exercises
4. lifetime sports
5. fencing

In addition, students currently participate in ballet, square dance, and creative dramatics.

"Two things everyone understands—a smile and music," says the principal. Hence, Taylor's smiling musicians can boast of their accomplishments. The sixty-member school choir has received national recognition. Some students also participate in a Suzuki Violin Program, and many are winners of local music awards.

Mrs. Franklin is proactive, but there is no "big boss." She selects her teachers with care, demanding and expecting a level of commitment similar to her own. She tells them from the start, "If you do not want to serve, do not come here." She is nurturing to all the school's population: students, staff, parents, and community members. Her collaborative approach to decision making provides opportunities for all to have input in school decisions.

Not standing in the way of children has caused Mrs. Franklin to extend her efforts into the community. She believes in keeping her finger on the pulse of the extended environment of the school. Her public relations efforts come in many forms and are directed at personalizing the Taylor experience. Greeting students at the bus stop, walking through the community, greeting parents by name, and fussing over faculty achievement are common activities during the course of her day. Her standards are high and are reflected in her manner. She is responsible for knowing each child she serves so that she can provide the best possible services and offer them a chance to have a better day than their parents have had. "It's not what you do that counts," she states, "It's what you do for children."

The location of Taylor Elementary is important to Mrs. Franklin and her staff. It *is* a ghetto school, in an area of town known for the easy availability of drugs, high crime rate, and low incomes. Because of its environment, some would assume that the school would match the stereotype of an inner-city school: undisciplined, tattered, unkept, and forlorn. Yet instead of the stereotypical inner-city school, Taylor Elementary is a shining monument to the potential of all children.

GUIDING QUESTIONS

1. How has this principal "embraced" the larger environment in developing a vision based on the school's reality? Compare the approach to double-loop learning.

2. Relate the four stages of creative visioning to the development of a vision for Taylor Elementary. Is the vision a shared one or does it exist only in the mind of the leader? Support your position.

3. What characteristics of the lateral thinker and the creative leader are displayed by the principal? How do her behaviors appear to affect the rest of her staff? Would you consider this leader to be transactional or transformational? Why?

REFERENCES

Arieti, S. (1976). *Creativity: The magic synthesis.* New York: Basic Books.

Argyris, C. (1982). *Reasoning, learning and action.* San Francisco: Jossey–Bass.

Barnard, C. (1968). Mind in everyday affairs (a Cyrus Fogg Bracket Lecture presented at the Engineering Faculty and Students of Princeton University, March 10, 1936). In C. Barnard, *Functions of the executive* (2nd ed., pp. 302–322). Cambridge, MA: Harvard University Press.

Barnard, C. (1968). *Functions of the executive* (2nd ed.). Cambridge, MA: Harvard University Press.

Bennis, W. & Nanus, B. (1985). *Leaders: The strategies for taking charge.* New York: Harper & Row.

Burns, J. (1978). *Leadership.* New York: Harper & Row.

DeBono, E. (1971). *Lateral thinking for management.* London: American Management Association.

Duigan, P. (1980). Administrative behavior of school superintendents: A descriptive study. *Journal of Educational Administration, 28*(1), 5–25.

Dyer, F., & Dyer, J. M. (1965). *Bureaucracy vs. creativity.* Coral Gables, FL: University of Miami Press.

Gardner, J. W. (1963). *Self renewal.* New York: Harper & Row.

Getzels, J. (1979). Problem-finding and research in educational administration. In Immegart, G. & Boyd, W. (Eds.), *Problem finding in educational administration* (pp. 5–22). Lexington, MA: D.C. Heath.

Greenleaf, R. (1977). *Servant leadership.* New York: Paulist Press.

Katz, R. L. (1974). Skills of an effective administrator. *Harvard Business Review, 52*(5), 90–102.

Levitt, T. (1963). Creativity is not enough. *Harvard Business Review.*

Malen, B., Ogawa, R., & Kranz, J. (1989). *An analysis of site based management as an education reform strategy*. Salt Lake City, UT: The University of Utah.

Martin, W., & Willower, D. (1981). The managerial behavior of high school principals. *Educational Administrative Quarterly*, *17*(1), 69–90.

Maslow, A. (1976). Toward a psychology of being. In A. Rothenburg & C. Housman (Eds.), *The creativity question* (pp. 296–305). Durham, NC: Duke University Press.

Mintzberg, H. (1976). Planning on the left side and managing on the right. *Harvard Business Review*, *54*(4), 49–58.

Morgan, G. (1986). *Images of organizations*. Cambridge, MA: Sage Publications.

Norris, C. (1992). Developing a vision of the humane school. In B. Barnett, F. McQuarrie, & C. Norris (Eds.), *The moral imperatives of leadership* (pp. 106–128). Memphis, TN: National Network for Innovative Principal Preparation.

Osborn, A. (1957). *Applied imagination*. New York: Charles Scribner's Sons.

Rogers, C. (1976). Toward a theory of creativity. In A. Rothenburg & C. Housman (Eds.), *The creativity question* (pp. 296–305). Durham, NC: Duke University Press.

Selznick, P. (1957). *Leadership and administration: A sociological interpretation*. New York: Harper & Row.

Sergiovanni, T. (1990). *Value-added leadership: How to get extraordinary performance in schools*. New York: Harcourt Brace Jovanovich.

Sergiovanni, T. (1991). *The principalship*. Boston: Allyn and Bacon.

Samples, R. (1980). *The metaphoric mind*. Reading, MA: Addison Wesley Publishing.

Wallas, G. (1926). *The art of thought*. New York: Harcourt, Brace.

Weick, K. (1982). Administering education in loosely coupled schools. *Phi Delta Kappan*, *63*(10), 673–676.

Weick, K. (1985). The significance of culture. In P. Frost, L. Moore, M. Louis, C. Lundberg, & J. Martin (Eds.), *Organizational culture*. Beverly Hills, CA: Sage.

Willis, Q. (1980). The work activity of school principals: An observational study. *The Journal of Educational Administration*, *218*(1), 26–53.

Zalenik, A. (1977). Managers and leaders: Are they different? *Harvard Business Review*, *55*(3), 67–78.

SELECTED READINGS

Barth, R. (1990). *Improving schools from within*. San Francisco: Jossey-Bass.

Bass, B. (1985). *Leadership and performance beyond expectations*. New York: Free Press.

Bennis, W. & Nanus, B. (1985). *Leaders: The strategies for taking charge*. New York: Harper & Row.

Burns, J. (1978). *Leadership*. New York: Harper & Row.

Colton, D. (1985). Vision. *National Forum of Phi Delta Kappa*, *65*(2), 33–35.

DeBono, E. (1971). *Lateral thinking for management*. London: American Management Association.

Hughes, L. & Ubben, G. (1989). *The Elementary Principal's Handbook: Guide to Effective Action* (3rd ed.). Boston: Allyn & Bacon.

Morgan, G. (1986). *Images of organizations*. Beverly Hills: Sage Publications.

Norris, C. Developing visionary leaders for tomorrow's schools. *NASSP Bulletin, 74*(526), 6–10.

Norris, C. J. & Achilles, C. (1987). Intuitive leadership: a new dimension for educational leadership. *Planning and changing, 19*(2), 108–117.

Schein, E. (1985). *Organizational culture and leadership*. San Francisco: Jossey–Bass.

Sergiovanni, T. (1992). *Moral leadership*. San Francisco: Jossey-Bass.

Ubben, G., & Hughes, L. (1992). *The principal: Creative leadership for effective schools*. Boston: Allyn and Bacon.

4

The Multicultural Environment of Schools: Implications to Leaders

H. Prentice Baptiste, Jr.
University of Houston

Overview

This chapter describes the multicultural environment and the rationale for multicultural education in U.S. schools. It also explains the historical development of multicultural education, discusses current trends in the field, and provides a typology for internalizing multiculturalism in educational settings. The chapter ends with a section about the future of multicultural education and educational leadership. Throughout the chapter specific implications are included for educational leaders.

Conceptual Frame

The United States is and has always been a culturally diverse society. From the very beginning, with the exception of the Native Americans, groups from

I wish to express my appreciation to Ms. Deborah Saldaña for her library research and other contributions to the writing of this chapter.

different countries with their own separate and unique cultures came here, willingly or otherwise. Over the years, each of these immigrant groups has contributed to make this nation what it is today. Being a culturally diverse society does not guarantee that a society is also culturally pluralistic. In a culturally pluralistic society, members of diverse ethnic, racial, religious, or social groups maintain autonomous participation in and development of their traditional culture or special interest within the confines of a common civilization (Bennett, 1986; Suzuki, 1979). America is not yet a culturally pluralistic society.

The government of the United States is based on the notion that it is the responsibility of the citizens to participate in the democratic society for the good of all people. A prevailing idea has been that in order to have a successful democratic society, an educated citizenry was essential. To that end, part of the responsibility of the public educational system has been to prepare youth to participate in society. Therefore, developing a culturally pluralistic society must begin with multicultural education programs in schools.

The Multiethnic Society

According to Appleton (1983), the United States shows signs of accepting cultural pluralism as a social ideal. Recent legislation, as well as additional funding at the federal and state levels for projects targeting ethnic minority concerns, is beginning to address issues relevant to these groups. Our educational institutions are beginning to include curricula that recognize the cultural diversity that exists in their student populations. Further evidence is displayed in the efforts of scholars and researchers to identify and investigate issues surrounding cultural diversity and the needs of those students whose cultures differ from the dominant group.

Because the United States is a multiethnic society that has not yet evolved into a culturally pluralistic society, certain problems exist. One such disturbing problem is discrimination. Discrimination limits certain groups that have racial, ethnic, religious, or other cultural differences from full participation in society. This is not a new phenomenon. During the later 1800s and early 1900s, Americans were concerned about the ever increasing numbers of immigrants to the United States. Africans and Asians were arriving, and changes in the border with Mexico caused an increase in the Mexican population. Also at that time more than 20 million Eastern and Southern European immigrants arrived in the United States. Not only were these immigrants poor, but they were also perceived as racially inferior to those already resident in the United States (Perkinson, 1991; Suzuki, 1979). This discrimination toward newly arrived immigrants led to the Americanization concept.

The Americanization Concept

Cubberly (1909), a distinguished and well-respected educational leader of the early twentieth century, wrote the following in his book *Changing Conceptions of Education*, which typifies the Americanization concept:

The southern and eastern Europeans are a very different type from the north Europeans, who preceded them. Illiterate, docile, lacking in self-reliance and initiative and possessing none of the Anglo-Teutonic conceptions of law, order and government, their coming has served to dilute tremendously our national stock, and corrupt our civic life . . .

Our task is to break up their groups or settlements, to assimilate and to amalgamate these people as part of our American race, and to implant in their children, so far as can be done, the Anglo-Saxon conceptions of righteousness, law and order and popular government, and to awaken in them reverence for our democratic institutions and for those things in our national life which we as people hold to be of abiding worth. (p. 768)

Because of his stature in the educational community, Cubberly's suggestions went unchallenged and his recommendations were instituted in the schools. His philosophical views, thus institutionalized, stripped the children of newly-arrived immigrants of their cultural heritage.

Adults were also included in the Americanization process. Theodore Roosevelt denounced the idea of hyphenated Americans (Krug, 1976, p. 8). He perceived names like *Irish-American* or *Italian-American* as disloyal to the United States. He felt that a person could not hold allegiance to both the United States and some other nation. Many immigrants were coerced into abandoning their cultural heritage to gain a "new and better" American life. In reality, the Americanization process was an assimilation to Anglo-Saxon culture (Banks, 1991; Baptiste, 1986; Perkinson, 1991).

The Melting Pot

In the early 1900s, the United States was desperate to achieve a society in which there were few if any cultural differences among its people. Another sociological ideal presented was the melting pot theory, which was based on the concept that a new hybrid would result if all of the diverse sociocultural groups contributed to society. These contributing groups would then form a superior American society. The melting pot theory was never a reality because the mixing of the many diverse groups did not occur. What did occur was the making of the melting pot myth. In 1908, Zangwill's play *The Melting Pot* (1922/1908) portrayed to the American public the inaccurate notion that the hybrid had been achieved through this process, when in reality there was never a melting pot.

Cultural Pluralism

The last emerging social ideal of the early twentieth century was proposed by Horace Kallen in *Cultural Pluralism and The American Idea* (1956; originally published in the early 1920s). His theory was that of cultural pluralism, but the concept was not fully understood by American society at the time. Kallen met with fierce opposition, and as a result, his proposed culturally pluralistic model was not adopted. However, during the 1960s, it reemerged as a viable sociological model for American society.

According to Appleton (1983), "the first and most obvious characteristic of a model society characterized by cultural pluralism is that of cultural diversity" (p. 21). In this society, groups from different value-systems, races, religions, ethnicities, and other types of diversities coexist. Each of these groups is allowed to maintain its unique cultural lifestyle. However, the groups work together in our democratic society to promote the common values and goals of democracy. The educational process through which cultural pluralism is achieved is called *multicultural education* (Baptiste & Archer, 1993); the individual or educational environment learns and internalizes the goals of a culturally pluralistic society.

The Culturally Diverse Society

Current data reveal that unlike in previous eras, recent immigrants are arriving from non-European countries. The vast majority of immigrants are coming from Asia and Latin America. Since 1981, only 11 percent of legal immigrants have come from Europe, the remainder are primarily from the Philippines, Korea, China, Mexico, and Cuba (Banks, 1991; Bennett, 1986).

By the beginning of the year 2000, one third of the population of the United States will consist of people of color (Banks, 1991; Grant & Secada, 1990). In 1984, 36 percent of the babies born in the United States belonged to non-white mothers. By the year 2000, projections for this group of children under the age of 18 will be at least 38 percent (Committee for Economic Development, 1987). Additionally, many of these children will be poor. The percentage of poor children and people of color in the United States has been steadily rising in recent years. As a group, children are the poorest segment of the U.S. population. Nearly 20 percent of all children under 18 currently live in families whose income falls below the poverty line. Both African-Americans and Hispanics are much more likely to be poor than European-Americans. This trend will continue in the future. Part of the ideology of a culturally pluralistic society is to help bring into the mainstream all segments of the society and to work for the betterment of those groups that have become disadvantaged due to prior exclusionary practices.

Role of Educational Institutions

Because public school is the most common shared experience for most Americans, the United States has depended upon schools to Americanize its citizens. Unfortunately, the focus on schooling in the United States has been primarily on the enhancement of one group's culture and the corresponding neglect of the culture of other groups. Because they have excluded information on the cultures of non-whites in their curricula, schools in the United States have long promoted the view that Nordic Anglo-Saxon superiority exists in all aspects of life while simultaneously promoting the inherent inferiority of non-Nordic origins of life (Baptiste, 1989).

American schools have become monocultural environments that present only a narrow view of the essence of human experience through the Western Civilization curriculum. By doing so, schools have denied children of color the opportunity to view themselves and their cultures as having value and worth, and as having made many and varied contributions to the dominant culture (Banks, 1991).

Disadvantage in the Educational System

Multicultural education is a process by which individuals and groups can learn to internalize the facts of cultural pluralism, to bring about a society that recognizes cultural diversity. Equitable coexistence among the cultural groups that constitute this society is an essential goal.

Steps need to be taken toward achieving educational equity for all groups of students. Historically in this country, children of color and the disadvantaged have not been given equal opportunities in the public educational system. The system has failed to meet their special needs and now should begin to address some of the problems that it has inadvertently, unintentionally, or systematically created or helped to perpetuate.

Funding Practices.   Jonathan Kozol (1991) cites the lack of adequate funding for inner-city schools as a source of inequities in the public schooling system. According to Kozol, the basic formula for education financing at the state level is the "foundation program." This program allows a local tax to be levied on the homes and businesses within a district to support public education. The same tax rate is issued for both the richest district and the poorest district in the state. Based only on this, inequities occur in the amount of funds available to the respective districts because the value of the homes and businesses in wealthier districts are higher than those in poorer districts. The state, recognizing that the poorer districts may not generate enough money, then provides "sufficient funds to lift the poorer districts to a level (the foundation) roughly equal to that of the richest district" (p. 208). As proposed, this should allow for equalization of all school districts. However, this is not the case.

The states, in order to entice wealthier districts to accept the foundation level, also provide additional funding to the wealthier districts. If this were not enough, normally the wealthier districts determine the foundation. The foundation is not set at the level of the richest district but rather at a much lower foundation:

> The low foundation is a level of subsistence that will raise a district to a point at which its schools are able to provide a "minimum" or "basic" education, but not an education on the level found in rich districts. (Kozol, 1991, p. 208)

In adhering to the foundation program, many states perpetuate the unequal education system that favors the rich. Use of this school funding process is under increasing fire, and recent state court actions are providing a basis for some change (Kozol, 1991), albeit slow and inadequate.

Monocultural Curriculum.   The curriculum poses additional problems for the non-white students in the schools. Currently the curriculum in U.S. schools does not present the cultural views and contributions of people from groups other than the dominant culture (Anglo-American/Eurocentric). It is essential that the curriculum reflect the culturally diverse nation in which we live, so that all members can gain a better appreciation of the diversity that exists.

In the past, white students have appeared to benefit from the Euro-American world view because their culture was more attuned to this view. These students have rarely been required to be "bicultural, bilingual, bicognitive" (Pine & Hilliard, 1990, p. 596). However, this is the norm for children of color. They have been required to adapt to the dominant culture.

Racism—Institutional and Otherwise

Another dilemma for non-white students is racism. Racism persists at the individual level—there are still those who believe that people of a particular group are inferior based solely on physical traits. Racists think that racial groups other than their own are intellectually, psychologically, and morally inferior to their own.

Racism has also been institutionalized through U.S. laws, judicial decisions, customs, and practices. Often, laws and judicial decisions support inequalities among the different ethnic groups. An example is the U.S. Supreme Court decision in *Plessy v. Ferguson* in 1896, which allowed segregation in public schools based on the separate but equal doctrine. The separate but equal doctrine was decided to be inherently unequal in the U.S. Supreme Court decision of *Brown v. Board of Education of Topeka* in 1954.

The process of multiculturalism through education will assist all students in their understanding of the cultural diversity that composes our society. Such understanding will help eliminate the racism and discrimination that are alive and well in U.S. society today.

Through the public school system, the United States has the responsibility and obligation of continuing to pass on the values and beliefs of a democratic society. Because this country was founded on the tenet that all are created equal, all should have equal opportunities and equal access to a better life. If schools embrace the concepts of cultural pluralism, members of all groups will benefit.

Current Trends in Multicultural Education

Much of the current literature on multicultural education recognizes the importance of the preparation of educational leaders and teachers for culturally diverse schools and classrooms. Multicultural education cannot and will not be successful without principals and teachers who are able to provide both the environment and the instruction conducive to the goals of multiculturalism. The literature suggests that administrators and future teachers need to be prepared to address both the educational and the cultural needs of their students (Reed, 1992; Ford, 1992; and Kraig, 1992). Three major areas are stressed as critical for future and current principals and teachers:

1. preparation for the teaching of language minority students
2. recognition of the learning styles of culturally different students
3. high expectations for culturally different students

These concepts are not new to educational leadership and teacher education programs, but they have not generally been associated with helping to accomplish the goals of multicultural education.

Teaching Language Minority Students

The recruitment and preparation of teachers for language minority students has become increasingly more important given the recent estimates on the number of language minority children. Garcia (1990) reports that the estimates range from 1.3 to 3.6 million. According to him, the divergence in the estimates is caused by the procedures used to obtain the count of language minority children. Of the total number of language minority students in the United States, the majority have Spanish language backgrounds. Projections for the year 2000 suggest that the proportion of children in the United States with Spanish language background will be about 77 percent of the total number of language minority children in U.S. schools (Garcia, 1990).

All of these students will require some type of bilingual education programs. Garcia notes that several possible programs exist for the language minority students: Transitional Bilingual Education, Maintenance Bilingual Education, English as a Second Language, Immersion, Sheltered English, and Submersion. The types of programs selected must meet the needs of the language minority population in a particular school district. The most critical component of the bilingual education program is the training of the classroom teacher. These educators must be taught to be supportive of the languages and cultures of their students.

Recognizing Diverse Learning Styles

University educational leadership and teacher-training programs as well as inservice programs for those currently working in schools must provide information about the various teaching and learning styles. Style differences reasonably occur among administrators, teachers, and students and also between the students and the curriculum. Anderson (1988) discussed the two basic cognitive styles, field-dependent and field-independent, as they related to the learning styles of various ethnic groups. In his paper, he cites several studies on the differences in ethnic groups.

Field-dependent learners tend to prefer to learn in groups and to interact with the teacher. They may require more extrinsic reinforcement and more structure from the teacher in terms of organization of learning experiences. *Field-independent students* appear to be able to respond better to independent and individualized instruction. Unlike field-dependent students, they are more likely to respond to intrinsic motivation (Witkin, Moore, & McDonald, 1974).

Also of importance is the orientation of the teacher. *Field-independent teachers* prefer a relaxed teaching situation with the instructional emphasis on cognitive or theoretical issues while *field-dependent teachers* are more comfortable with class discussions and interaction with students. Witkin et al. (1974) provide additional information about the learning and teaching styles of field-dependent and field-independent individuals.

The key issue with learning and teaching styles is that teachers must be able to identify the methods of instruction that best suit the learning styles of their students. Differences in learning styles should not be misunderstood and lead to discriminatory practices but rather should be utilized to help students reach their full potential (Bowen & Bowen, 1992).

Maintaining High Expectations

Principals should recognize that the attitude of the teacher is paramount not only in accomplishing the goals of multicultural education but also for the educational success of students. Studies have consistently shown that students of teachers who are not motivated to teach and who have low expectations for their students do not perform as well academically as students whose teachers have high expectations (Good, 1981).

Tracking is a form of teacher-expectation for students. According to Good and Brophy (1990), teacher-expectations have a direct relationship to the tracking system, which is used in many schools. Teachers in the Good and Brophy study who taught low-track classes showed less initiative and creativity in their teaching. Good and Brophy also present studies that suggest that most teachers prefer to teach high-track classes and that those teachers tend to emphasize more higher order thinking skills.

Principals and teachers must begin with positive attitudes toward their minority students and respect them as individuals. Too often, principals and teachers use varying student backgrounds as an explanation or excuse for poor achievement instead of raising the level of expectation for students. They must demand maximum effort from all students, regardless of race, gender, religion, social economic status, or physical abilities, and accept no less.

If teachers are to be successful in the education of culturally different students, they must communicate their expectations to students, show an interest in the students' culture, and make objectives not only descriptive of learning outcomes but also clear and understandable. Teachers and principals should use positive reinforcement often and continually let the students know how well they are doing in class. Principals can do this both directly and by example.

Internalizing Multiculturalism:
A Typology for the Learning Environment

The educational system is composed of various educational environments. Each educational environment has key personnel who are responsible for the climate of that environment. The various educational environments include classrooms/ teachers; schools/principals; districts/central office administrators; principal and teacher education programs/professors; and governmental agencies/politicians. Multiculturalism, in order to be successful, requires internalization at the individual, group, and institutional levels.

I first proposed a typology of multicultural education in 1983 (Baptiste, 1983). Since then, I have further developed and refined my typology of multiculturalism (Baptiste & Archer, 1993). It is my hypothesis that the internalization of multiculturalism in an educational environment or agent can occur on one of at least three conceptual levels. A distinct set of characteristics identify the conceptual level of multiculturalism the educational environment has reached.

The levels in this typology are distinct, each level having parameters that define its specific characteristics. The typology takes into consideration qualitative as well as quantitative differences with respect to the levels of multiculturalism. The qualitative differentiation has the three levels—product, process, and philosophical orientation—which show the type and content of integration of multiculturalism. Each level similarly shows a quantitative differentiation.

All formal educational processes will display the same basic components when functioning at Level One of the typology. Keep in mind that there are two parts—i.e., environments (classrooms) as well as personnel (teachers). Thus a classroom will function at a certain level because the teacher is operating at that level of the typology.

Internalization of multiculturalism is an evolutionary process. There are two aspects to the evolution in an educational environment—quantitative and qualitative. Quantitative measures of the educational environment considered in the typology show that environments differ in the following categories:

- number of cultural/ethnic groups
- number of workshops, courses, or activities devoted to multiculturalism
- ethnic/cultural make-up of faculty and students
- amount of funds allocated for the multicultural program

The qualitative dimensions of multiculturalism in the typology are these:

- product
- process
- philosophical orientation

Without internalization of the qualitative dimension, the prescriptive goals of multiculturalism cannot be achieved.

Level One

This level is characterized as additive and tangible. Multicultural education is manifested as single-focused events, such as cultural celebrations, ethnic-specific courses, and unrelated cultural topics added at various times to the regular curriculum (see Figure 4–1). Sleeter and Grant (1987) identified approaches to multicultural education in which teaching the culturally different, human relations, and the single-group studies all qualify as Level One of the typology.

Culturally Different Groups.   Teaching about culturally different groups by educators is the method most widely used by those people who realize that they are not meeting the needs of their students of color (Sleeter & Grant, 1987). According to Baptiste (1992), these educational entities are functioning at Level One of internalizing the concepts of multiculturalism. That is to say, they recognize the need to help students of color (African Americans, Asian Americans, Native Americans, and Hispanic Americans) become competent in the culture of the majority group while simultaneously learning about, maintaining, and feeling pride in their own cultures. Educators at this level stress individual achievement and social mobility, but they fail to focus on the underlying problems resulting from the fact that the majority race has dominated capitalism in this society. They do not address the issues of surrounding the unequal access to goods and services. They are mainly concerned with race and ethnicity only.

Programs are instituted at this level are shallow, dealing only with special occasions or events. No attempt is made to effect any sweeping curricular changes. The emphasis is on adding activities to the lessons. At this level, the programs are limited to students of color. Unfortunately, in schools and districts where little or no racial diversity exists, even this limited approach is often deemed unnecessary.

Programs involved at this level may show a strong commitment to the educational needs and the overall welfare of children of color. However, because they are an additive approach, they may try to address issues in a broad manner instead of being more specific. An example is the use of the term *Hispanic* to identify all children of Spanish heritage or surname, while in reality students whose first language is Spanish come from many different countries and cultures (Mexico, Cuba, Puerto Rico, Argentina, and many others). The same applies to the term *Asian*, which with similar lack of precision, treats Japanese, Chinese, Korean, Vietnamese, Laotian, Cambodian, East Indians, and others as one group. Students must be identified as to their specific origin because teaching strategies and learning styles differ among the culture groups.

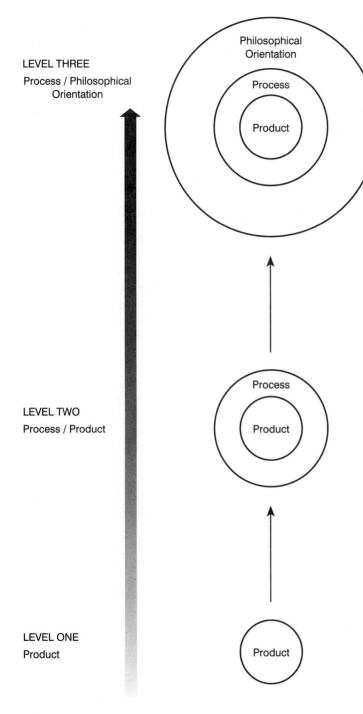

LEVEL THREE

Process / Philosophical
Orientation

LEVEL TWO

Process / Product

LEVEL ONE

Product

Figure 4–1
Typology of Multiculturalization
Modified from Baptiste, 1989.

Characteristics
• A philosophy permeated by the
principles of equality; recognition
of and respect for human diversity;
values that support cultural diversity
• All children valued
• All pedagogy restructured or
reconstituted to exemplify the basic
tenets of multiculturalism
• Cultural diversity regarded as an
asset not a problem
• A moral commitment to social
action for equity
Programs
• There are no specific identifiable
programs operating at this level

Characteristics
• Confluent relationship between
product and process
• Theoretical referent link with
practical applications
• Curriculum restructured to include
various cultural and ethnic
perspectives
• Steps taken to institutionalize
various facets of multiculturalism
• Broad conceptual framework
formed to guide amalgamation of
multiculturalism with education
programs
Programs
• Cultural diversity approach:
Understanding of culture and its
parameters; moves toward
institutionalizing cultural diversity
as both product and process

Characteristics
• Single focus, additive, tangible
• Cultural celebrations limited to
students of color
Programs
• Cultural differences limited to
students of color or minority
students
• Human relations: Promote
positive self image; usually in
elementary schools, schools
undergoing desegregation
• Single group studies: Emphasis
on one ethnic, racial, or cultural
group; geared toward ethnic
studies, intent is "quick fix"

A weakness of programs that operate on Level One of the typology lies in the fact that educators using this approach tend to rely on these programs exclusively. They ignore or are not aware of other models of multicultural education. Because these programs are multicultural education for children of color, those who use these methods do not feel it necessary to broaden their scope to include a multicultural process that emphasizes the necessity of exposing all children to the cultural diversities that exist in the United States.

Groups at Level One have a commitment to students of color who have been denied access to full participation in the educational system because of language or cultural difference. They promote a method that implies that these children of color should learn to adapt to a different culture, and, unfortunately, the method does not require that those in the dominant culture make any changes or learn anything about other cultures. The burden is, as it has always been, on those in the minority to change in some way to accommodate the majority. The only difference between the programs on this level and the *cultural assimilation approach* (the process by which an individual or group acquires the culture traits of a different ethnic group) is that people of color are allowed to maintain their own cultural heritage while learning about the new culture.

Human Relations.   The goal of Level One programs for recognizing the cultural diversity that exists is to assist students of different cultural backgrounds to communicate and get along with each other. Another aim is to promote a positive self-image so that students feel good about themselves.

These programs are usually introduced in elementary schools. They support the use of nonstereotypical materials and activities that promote interaction among the different groups. Schools addressing problems of desegregation generally try to implement this approach because it emphasizes ideas and suggestions about how to help students understand cultural differences between and among their classmates.

One of the reasons this approach is placed in Level One of the typology is that after communication and understanding between the groups has been achieved, this approach has no other agenda—it identifies no other problems to be addressed. No effort is made to deal with other problems, which militates against the achievement of a culturally pluralistic society. Unless other problems are addressed, a culturally pluralistic society will not be achieved.

Single-Group Studies.   The single-group method of multicultural programming places its emphasis on one racial, ethnic, or cultural group. This approach is geared toward ethnic studies. This Level One approach may identify one or more specific ethnic groups to be included as units of study (an additive approach).

Perhaps the most salient characteristics of all Level One programs are their reactive posture and lack of institutionalization. In these programs, tangibles are used to suggest something other than the real intent of the program. Often, the cultural/ethnic emphases are for specific populations and are limited geographically. Usually the catalyst for initiating these programs is external pressure brought about by interest groups, social pressure, or community ethnic groups. The intent is a quick fix to the problem without real change to existing programs or policies.

Level Two

Qualitative differences exist between Levels One and Two. At Level Two in the typology, a confluent relationship exists between product and process. In Level Two entities, the tangible products are embedded in a matrix of process. An entity at this level possesses a theoretical referent link with practical applications, allowing multiculturalism to take on a broader base as it is incorporated into the infrastructure of the entity.

At Level Two, multicultural concepts are integrated into all educational components. For example, the curriculum is restructured to include various cultural and ethnic perspective on topics, events, and concepts. Generic components of multicultural education and strategies for incorporating them are identified for implementation. Additionally, steps are taken to institutionalize various facets of multiculturalism. Specific courses and related experiences are formalized within the program. A broad conceptual framework is formed at this level, one that guides the amalgamation of the principles and goals of multiculturalism with the other components of the educational programs.

Cultural Diversity Approach.   The cultural diversity approach to multicultural education is included in Level Two of the typology. Those who incorporate this approach begin by gaining an understanding of culture and its parameters. Next, they acquire knowledge about the contributions of ethnic, racial, and cultural groups to U.S. society.

Discussions of gender and social class are included in the activities of programs using the cultural diversity approach. At Level Two, care is taken not to replace one type of human diversity with another (i.e., sexism or classism does not become a substitute for racism). One of the concerns with this approach revolves around the controversy regarding other diversities. Many programs do not include gender, class, or handicap in their approach to multiculturalism. This is limiting because these groups may be interrelated to race and ethnicity and therefore deserving of inclusion in this approach.

The cultural diversity approach has other limitations. It does emphasize culture, but, as with the programs of Level One, it fails to deal with social stratification. By excluding these issues, educators send the message that the important aspect of multicultural education is only to allow culturally different groups to maintain and value their cultural differences. This cultural diversity approach does go beyond those of Level One by moving toward institutionalizing multiculturalism as both a product and a process.

Level Three

Achievement of Level Three in the typology is accomplished only after successful completion of Level Two. Level Three represents a highly sophisticated internalization of the process of multiculturalism and the added dimension of a philosophical orientation that permeates the educational environment. This pervasive quality causes the educational entity to respond to its mission and goals in a manner consistent with the conceptualized principles and goals of genuine multiculturalism.

In order to achieve Level Three status, an educational entity must emerge from the product stage of Level One and the combination product/process stage of Level Two to a sophisticated and regenerative conceptualized knowledge base for multiculturalism.

The goals of Level Three programs are extended to help students "gain a better understanding of the causes of oppression and inequality and ways in which these social problems might be eliminated" (Suzuki, 1984, p. 308). Activities at this level point to the unequal inclusiveness of various groups in U.S. society, exploring and examining the underlying reasons. At Level Three, cultural diversity is regarded as an asset rather than a problem, and the appreciation of diversity is used to progress toward a culturally pluralistic society.

> A philosophy based on the principles of equality, recognition and respect of human diversity, and a sense of moral commitment serves as the blueprint for the emergence of a multicultural process which leads to cultural pluralism. Although the legitimacy of multiculturalism is no longer a question, debatable issues do exist. These issues serve to further the refinement and expansion of knowledge from new perspectives. Finally, this level has a matureness in conceptualization, rationalization, and direction (Baptiste & Baptiste, 1980, p. 44).

Administrators and other educators operating at this level have internalized a philosophy of the basic tenets of multiculturalism that provides them with support and a commitment to action. They are social activists.

Multicultural Education and Educational Leadership: The Future

A comprehensive definition of multicultural education written by Suzuki (1979) describes succinctly the goals of multicultural education:

> Multicultural education is an educational program which provides multiple learning environments that properly match the academic and social needs of students. Through this process the program should help students to respect and appreciate cultural diversity, overcome ethnocentric and prejudicial attitudes, and understand the social-historical, economic and psychological factors that have produced the

contemporary conditions of ethnic polarization inequality and alienation . . . Finally, it should help them conceptualize and aspire toward a vision of a better society and acquire the necessary knowledge, understandings and skills to enable them to move the society toward greater equality and freedom. . . . (p. 48)

After reading this definition, most people understand clearly that schools in the United States are currently addressing few if any of the goals for achieving a cultural pluralistic society through multicultural education.

Schools as they exist today are failing to meet the academic and social needs of a large group of students, specifically the racial and ethnic minorities. Racism, sexism, and other inequities abound and are being fueled by an educational system that perpetuates these forms of discrimination through the Eurocentric/ Anglocentric curriculum.

At-Risk Students

A growing number of school children in the United States are considered to be at risk for failing in school. Literature suggests that children may be at risk due to factors relating to their socioeconomic status (poverty), family background (single-parent homes), or community (drugs or youth gangs). In reality, these children are at risk because they are unable to take full advantage of the education opportunities available to them. A look at the current population of students in U.S. schools shows that about one of five school-age children lives in poverty (Natriello, McDill, & Pallas, 1990). Suzuki (1979) writes, "schools have not met the education need—either academic or social—of many racial and ethnic minorities particularly those who are poor, because they are victimized by the sociocultural milieu of the schools, which is biased against them" (p. 47). He further believes that *all* children are victimized because the sociocultural structure of schools has reinforced and perpetuated prejudicial attitudes and values, and therefore not given children an opportunity to develop their capacity for understanding and critically analyzing problems that exist in society. This condition is elucidated by the following:

> The schools today are ill-equipped and ill-designed to accommodate the students of today. Although almost every aspect of American society has entered into the technological age, the American school system remains in the industrial age. The programs, curriculum, and even buildings are essentially the same as they were fifty years ago. Probably the only thing which has changed is the learner. Because of the conditions which exist for disadvantaged youths, they bring to the schools a completely different set of problems and concerns which the schools need to address. (Baptiste, 1992, p. 13)

Without opportunities to develop and foster the moral commitment, children will not have the skills necessary to bring to fruition a culturally pluralistic society in the future.

Schools of the Future

By the year 2020, students of color will make up about 46 percent of the nation's student population (Natriello, McDill, & Pallas, 1990). Recently, the United States has experienced a large influx of immigrant students; more than 600,000 people legally immigrated in 1986 and 1987 (Banks, 1991). Moreover, these figures do not reflect the large but undetermined number of illegal and undocumented immigrants, so the total number of immigrants is considerably larger than acknowledged.

> The influence of an increasingly ethnically diverse population on the nation's schools is and will continue to be enormous. In 25 of the nation's largest cities and metropolitan areas, half or more of the public school students are students of color. (Banks, 1991, p. 15)

In Texas, the state education agency reported that the population of students of color in the public schools exceeded the percentage of white students for the first time during the 1991–92 school year. While the number of students of color has been increasing, the number of minority teachers has been declining steadily in the United States, as has the number of minority college students entering teacher education programs (Grant & Secada, 1990; Pine & Hilliard, 1990).

Because of these trends, most teachers currently in the classroom and those in teacher education programs will find themselves teaching a racially, socially, and culturally diverse student body (Natriello, McDill, & Pallas, 1990). According to Pine and Hilliard (1990), diversity within the public school faculty is absolutely essential. Children will learn to respect differences among cultural groups if they have the opportunity to interact with members of other groups and to observe the cultures of diverse faculties. Furthermore, minority teachers as role models are important and beneficial to children of all racial and ethnic groups, thus making them important to all cultures.

SUMMARY

In the coming years and into the twenty-first century, educational leaders will have to become multiculturalists. The cultural diversity of society has been and will continue to be an asset to the United States. A culturally pluralistic society in which there is unity within the diversity will only become a reality if educational leaders emerge as multiculturalists. It is assumed that educational leaders will function personally at Level Three of the typology—they have internalized the processes involved in evolving as multicultural agents through a philosophical orientation. Having arrived at this point, the educational leaders must then make a commitment to ensure their schools function as multicultural entities.

All children in the United States deserve what public education has promised them—a quality education that will enable them to function fully and successfully in the complex society of today. In order for multiculturalistic educational leaders to provide this, we must recognize that a culturally diverse student population requires a culturally diverse faculty. It is going to become increasingly more difficult to obtain a culturally diverse faculty in the future, but every effort should be made to achieve this goal.

An important component of Level Three multicultural programs is the school and classroom climate. Educational leaders on these campuses set the tone by instituting school-wide philosophies that demonstrate that *all* students are respected, and that racism and discrimination of any type will not be tolerated. A further underlying philosophy acknowledges that cultural diversity is positive and to be valued because it leads to a broadening of the educative experiences for all students.

The multiculturalist leader is a transformational leader, as opposed to a transactional leader (Hughes, chapter 1), and is therefore aware of the hidden curriculum that includes teacher attitudes and expectations, grouping and tracking of students and instructional strategies, school disciplinary policies and practices, and school and community relations. By working to eliminate negative attitudes and procedures, the multiculturalist is committed to transforming the total school environment so that the schools are not "culturally depriving" any students (Benninga, 1991).

Issues surrounding equity in education become particularly significant to the multiculturalist. Bennett (1986) writes that "educational excellence in our schools cannot be achieved without educational equity. Equity in education means equal opportunities for all students to develop to their fullest potential" (p. 13). Equity according to her is not to be taken to mean equality or sameness. Because cultures are different and students come to the educational system with varying experiences, equal treatment or equal programs may not be of value. What is necessary is to provide those experiences that will enable all students to develop to their fullest potential.

One of the most important components that goes into developing the educational leader as a multiculturalist is understanding the relationship between multiculturalism and character development. A major purpose of the public educational system is to provide training in citizenship and pass on to youth the moral values and beliefs of the democratic way of life. These values include fair play, concern for excellence, respect for law, willingness to work hard, the ability to delay gratification, a sense of service, commitment, self-discipline, self-reliance, trust, honor, and loyalty, and most are common to all cultures.

The educational leader must display these values as a role model for the students, teachers, and staff. Additionally, the multiculturalist must demand that these values be modeled by teachers and staff. Values are instilled in the students through the curriculum and also through the school programs and overall environment of the school. If students are respected by educational leaders and teachers, they learn to respect themselves and others.

I am not suggesting that all the problems that exist in society can be solved through the multiculturalization of the educational system. However, I do believe that schools in the United States need major reforms to address the needs of a group of students who have been underserved by the system to date. A step toward the reformation process is creating schools that are able to service culturally diverse student populations. These multicultural schools can then begin to help develop the intellectual, social, and overall growth of all students.

THEORY INTO PRACTICE: A CASE STUDY FOR REFLECTION

School district Alpha-Beta has a reputation as an outstanding school district. A high percentage of its past students has attended colleges and universities. The district has also had more than its share of regional science fair winners and National Merit Scholars. The faculty and administrators, for the most part, have remained stable in the district. However, during the past two years, the demographics of the student body have begun to change ethnically, socially, and economically.

GUIDING QUESTIONS

As an observer of this school district reflect on the following:

1. If the district's leadership tends to ignore these changes and continue to "conduct business as usual," what may happen to this school district's reputation?

2. If you were a principal (elementary, middle, or high school) where the aforementioned changes were evident, what steps or process(es) would you implement to enable your school to continue to make a positive contribution to the outstanding reputation of the Alpha-Beta district?

3. What actions would you take and why?

4. What would be your short-term goals and objectives?

5. What would be your long-term goals and objectives?

REFERENCES

Anderson, J. A. (1988). Cognitive styles and multicultural populations. *Journal of Teacher Education, 5,* 2–9.

Appleton, N. (1983). *Cultural pluralism in education: Theoretical foundations.* New York: Longman.

Banks, J. A. (1991). *Teaching strategies for ethnic studies*. Boston: Allyn and Bacon.

Baptiste, H. P., Jr. (1983). Internalizing the concept of multiculturalism. In R. J. Samuels & S. L. Woods (Eds.) *Perspectives in immigrant and minority education* (pp. 294–308). Washington, DC: University Press of America.

Baptiste, H. P., Jr. (1986). An Inquiry on the Status of Multicultural Education in Teacher Education in Texas. Occasional paper number 2. Texas Association of Teacher Educators.

Baptiste, H. P., Jr. (1989). Multicultural education and urban schools from a sociohistorical perspective: Internalizing multiculturalism. In Joe L. Burbin (Ed.), *School leadership: A contemporary reader* (pp. 187–204). Newberry Park, CA: UCEA and Sage Publications.

Baptiste, H. P., Jr. (1991). *Developing the multicultural process in classroom instruction: Competencies for teachers* (Draft of 2nd ed.). Houston, TX: University of Houston.

Baptiste, H. P., Jr. (1992). Conceptual and theoretical issues. In H. C. Waxman, J. Walker de Felix, J. Anderson, & H. P. Baptiste, Jr. (Eds.), *Students at risk in at risk schools* (pp. 11–16). Newberry Park, CA: Corwin Press.

Baptiste, H. P., Jr., & Archer, C. M. (1993). A comprehensive multicultural teacher education preparation program: An ideal whose time has come. In Mary Atwater (Ed.), *Multicultural education: An invitation to all*. Athens, Georgia: Educational Materials Center, University of Georgia.

Baptiste, H. P., Jr., and Baptiste, M. L. (Eds.). (1980). *Multicultural teacher education: Preparing educators to provide educational equity* (Vol. 1). Washington, DC: American Association of Colleges for Teacher Education.

Bennett, C. (1986). *Comprehensive multicultural education: Theory and practice*. Boston: Allyn and Bacon.

Benninga, J. S. (1991). Moral and character education in the elementary school: An introduction. In J. S. Benninga (Ed.), *Moral character and civic education in the elementary school*. New York: Teachers College Press.

Bowen, D. N., & Bowen, E. A. (1992). Multicultural education: The learning style aspect. In C. A. Grant (Ed.), *Toward education that is Multicultural: Proceedings of the First Annual Meeting of the National Association for Multicultural Education* (pp. 266–276). Morristown, NJ: Silver Burdett Ginn, Inc.

Brown v. Board of Education of Topeka, 347 U.S. 43 (1954).

Cubberly, E. (1909). *Changing conceptions of education*. New York: Riverside Educational Mimeographs.

Ford, B. (1992). Developing teachers with a multicultural perspective: A challenge and a mission. In C. A. Grant (Ed.), *Toward Education that is Multicultural: Proceedings of the First Annual Meeting of the National Association for Multicultural Education* (pp. 132–138). Morristown, NJ: Silver Burdett Ginn, Inc.

Garcia, E. E. (1990). Educating teachers for language minority students. In W. Robert Houston (Ed.), *Handbook of research on teacher education* (pp. 717–729). New York: Macmillan.

Good, T. L. (1981). Teacher expectations and student perceptions: A decade of research. *Educational Leadership, 38*(5), 415–422.

Good, T. L. & Brophy, J. (1990). *Educational Psychology: A Realistic Approach* (4th ed.). New York: Longman.

Grant, C. A. (1992). Multicultural education: Examining the why, what, how. In C. A. Grant (Ed.), *Toward Education that is Multicultural: Proceedings of the First Annual Meeting of the National Association for Multicultural Education* (pp. 5–9). Morristown, NJ: Silver Burdett Ginn, Inc.

Grant, C., & Secada, W. G. (1990). Preparing teachers for diversity. In W. Robert Houston (Ed.), *Handbook of research on teacher education* (pp. 403–422). New York: Macmillan.

Kallen, H. (1956). *Cultural pluralism and the American ideal*. Philadelphia: University of Philadelphia Press.

Kozol, J. (1991). *Savage inequalities: Children in America's schools*. New York: Crown Publisher, Inc.

Kraig, G. M. (1992). Implementation of a multicultural education in teacher training program. In C. A. Grant (Ed.), *Toward Education that is Multicultural: Proceedings of the First Annual Meeting of the National Association for Multicultural Education* (pp. 139–47). Morristown, NJ: Silver Burdett Ginn, Inc.

Krug, Mark. (1976). *The melting of the ethnics: Education of the immigrants, 1880–1914*. Bloomington, IN: Phi Delta Kappa Educational Foundation.

Natriello, G., McDill, E., & Pallas, A. M. (1990). *Schooling the disadvantaged*. New York: Teachers College Press.

Perkinson, H. J. (1991). *The imperfect panacea: American faith in education, 1865–1990*. New York: McGraw-Hill, Inc.

Pine, G. J., & Hilliard, A. G. (1990, April). Rx for racism: Imperatives for America's schools. *Phi Delta Kappan 71*(8), 593–600.

Plessy v. Ferguson, 163 U.S. 537 (1985).

Reed, D. F. (1992). Preparing teachers for multicultural classrooms. In C. A. Grant (Ed.), *Toward Education that is Multicultural: Proceedings of the First Annual Meeting of the National Association for Multicultural Education*. Morristown, NJ: Silver Burdett Ginn, Inc.

Select Committee for Economic Development. (1987). *Children in need: Investment strategies for the educationally disadvantaged*. New York: Research & Policy Committee.

Sleeter, C. E., & Grant, C. A. (1987, November). An analysis of multicultural education in the United States. *Harvard Educational Review*, *57*(4), 421–439.

Suzuki, B. H. (1979). Multicultural education: What's it all about? *Integrated Education*, *17*(1–2), 47–48.

Suzuki, B. H. (1984). Curriculum transformation for multicultural education. *Education and Urban Society*, *16*, 294–322.

Witkin, H. A., Moore, C. A., & McDonald, F. J. (1974). *Cognitive style and the teaching/learning processes*. (Cassette Series 3F). American Educational Research Association.

Zangwill, I. (1922). *The Melting Pot: Drama in Four Acts*. New York: Macmillan. (Originally produced in 1908)

SELECTED READINGS

Banks, J. (1991). *Teaching strategies for ethnic studies*. Boston: Allyn and Bacon.

Baptiste, H. P., Jr. (1989). Multicultural education and urban schools from a sociohistorical perspective: Internalizing multiculturalism. In *School leadership: A contemporary reader*. Newberry Park, CA: Sage Publications. (Reprinted from *Journal of Education Equity and Leadership, 6*(4), 295–312.)

Fuchs, Lawrence H. (1990). *The American kaleidoscope race, ethnicity, and the civic culture*. Hanover, NH, and London: Wesleyan New England.

Garcia, E. E. (1990). Educating teachers for language minority students. In W. R. Houston (Ed.), *Handbook of research on teacher education* (pp. 717–729). New York: Macmillan.

Hughes, L. W., Gordon, W. M., & Hillman, L. W. (1980). *Desegregating America's schools*. New York: Longman. (See chapters 10 and 11, especially.)

Kozol, J. (1991). *Savage inequalities: Children in America's schools*. New York: Crown Publishers.

Nieto, S. (1992). *Affirming diversity: The sociopolitical context of multicultural education*. New York: Longman.

Pine, G. J., & Hilliard, A. G. (1990, April). Rx for racism: Imperatives for America's schools. *Phi Delta Kappan 71*(8), 593–600.

Suzuki, B. (1979). Multicultural education: What's it all about? *Integrated Education, 18*(1–2).

Waxman, H. C., Walker de Felix, J., Anderson, J. E., & Baptiste, H. P., Jr. (1992). *Students at risk in at-risk schools: Improving environments for learning*. Newbury Park, CA: Corwin Press.

5

Ethical Frameworks to Guide Action

Robert P. Craig
University of Houston

Overview

How does ethics apply to educational leadership? Why does it matter whether ethical considerations are a part of administrative decision making? This chapter addresses these kinds of questions by developing an ethical framework to aid educational leaders.

Ethics is integral to administrative practice. I will sharply distinguish morality from ethics (*morality* being an historically conditioned, systematically developed theory of human obligation and responsibility; *ethics* being a personal commitment to and critique of moral theory as it applies to human growth and problematic situations). In this chapter, the most common approach to moral decision making within any institutional context—"The five steps involved in moral decision making" (Fox & DeMarco, 1990)—is critiqued and supplanted by an approach that considers the humane and ethical development of the educational leader.

I will share three approaches to the nature of moral obligation:

• deontology, which emphasizes duty and adhering to prescribed moral principles

111

- teleology, which stresses the greatest amount of good derived from a solution to a moral problem and focuses on the consequences of one's actions
- virtue ethics, which emphasizes the human characteristics, dispositions, and attitudes an ethical person needs to make moral decisions, concerning itself with the sort of person one ought to strive to become

Two illustrations, demonstrating the applicability of ethics to administrative practice, will help the reader "walk through" the three approaches.

The chapter concludes with a discussion of the theory and research of Brian Hall regarding values and ethical growth. This conceptual framework is integrated into my remarks about "visionary" educational leadership.

Conceptual Frame

Most philosophers distinguish between morality and ethics, although the issue itself is a philosophical question. Like the meaning and nature of philosophy itself, which is a philosophical question open to reasoned argumentation and interpretation, so is the issue of the difference(s) between morality and ethics. In this chapter, the two terms are used in the following way:

- *Morality* refers to socially accepted rules which center on one's self-interest. "Always cross the street at the light" is an example.
- *Ethics* refers to rules that are (at least somewhat) other-oriented. "Do not take things that do not belong to you" is an example.

Another way to view the distinction is to note that ethical theory is the philosophy of the nature and justification of ethical principles, dilemmas, and decision making. Morality, on the other hand, refers to various traditions concerning right and wrong (Beauchamp, 1982). Because moral traditions develop historically, it follows that morality is a product of social interaction that is learned as one matures. Ethics, though, encompasses theories, rules, and criteria for selecting among alternate principles. These may or may not be related to a moral theory or tradition. Ethics also encompasses processes of moral problem solving—that is, choosing which tradition, if any, is applicable to the moral situation. Ethics, then, is a way of life. Morality consists in historically-developed, internally-consistent theoretical systems regarding "what" one ought to do. Morality is one type of fuel or food necessary to consider when making an ethical decision.

Although the distinction between the two terms is valid, the terms are used synonymously at the level of administrative practice (Craig, 1990a). At the very least, ethics and morality are not readily distinguishable in administrative decision making and policy formation. In this chapter, the distinction is used as consistently as possible when the issue warrants it—that is, when moral reflection on an issue is aided by ethical inquiry.

The purpose of the initial part of this chapter is to develop both the theoretical and research foundations for ethical decision making within a public school setting. The first task is to discuss three theories of moral obligation (*moral*, because the issue of obligation generally occurs within a social system or tradition). The three theories of moral obligation are deontology, teleology, and virtue ethics.

Deontological Theories

An example may be helpful. Why is it wrong for the administrator of a public school to intentionally deceive the teachers? Some might argue that informing teachers of the probable closing of the school would merely lead to anxiety and diminished productivity and commitment. In other words, sharing this information may cause more harm than good. Others argue that the teachers have a commitment to the school and deserve to be told.

A deontological moral theory would strongly suggest that the teachers should be told. The reason has nothing to do with evaluative judgments of the consequences of the information, nor with the virtue formation of the principal. Rather, the decision that informing the teachers is the only possible moral decision is derived from the nature of human duty. Although there will be disagreement about the exact features of the nature of duty, *deontologists agree that doing one's duty is the main criterion of a moral act*. The reasons are various, but all are based on the application of a moral principle(s): the teachers have a right to know, which is violated when this information is withheld; teachers need to be respected as persons, which also is violated when this information is withheld. How are teachers to make proper choices regarding their future (which is one criterion of respecting them as persons) if they do not have access to this information? The preceding discussion is merely a sketch of deontology. More discussion about it will ensue later in this chapter.

Teleology

Although teleology has many forms, the most prevalent teleological system is utilitarianism (Mill, 1859/1959). *Utilitarianism* is both a social theory and a theory of moral inquiry. This theory of moral responsibility emphasizes the effect or consequences of a moral decision or action.

Under the theory of teleology, intentionally deceiving teachers is morally wrong due to the short-term and long-term consequences. In the short term, they are not permitted to get their affairs in order, to revise their resumes, and to begin searching for other teaching positions. In the long term, they are not being permitted the opportunity to go through the grieving process that accompanies the loss of one's job, and they may be hampered in securing other positions.

The teleologist, then, is concerned with the end, goal, or consequences of one's actions. In situations in which it is impossible to predict consequences, the teleologist suggests that the individual choose the alternative most likely to produce the most good and the least harm. When should the administrator inform the teachers about the school's closing? To do so too soon may hamper morale, and may even cause some teachers to be overly concerned with future employment or to be so angry that they neglect the students. To inform them too late may issue in the consequences previously noted in the case of not informing them at all. The administrator, then, if he or she is a teleologist, would weigh the circumstances, consider the individual teachers' personalities, note the type of job market, and so on, before informing the teachers. A basic question to ask, for the teleologist, is this: Which action will produce the most good and the least harm?

Virtue Ethics

Virtue ethics is a bit more difficult to describe. The emphasis is neither on principles nor consequences; rather the focus is on developing individuals of character. The basic issue is: What sort of person, in the sense of virtue, character, or what philosophers sometimes refer to as excellences, do we want public school administrators to be?

Aristotle (1947), for instance, argues that friendship is integral to human and social development. The ability to develop friendships, and the interpersonal skills this demands, forms a core virtue for Aristotle. The administrator who possesses this set of characteristics is better able to identify with and to have empathy for teachers and staff. The cardinal virtues of courage, justice, temperance, and piety have traditionally been associated with the good person. Likewise, religions such as Christianity and Buddhism emphasize the virtues of compassion and love. The point is that the virtuous person is the good person, or at least the virtuous person is more likely to act in a good way in specific situations: to inform the teachers concerning the closing of the school, for instance.

The reason the virtuous person acts this way is because he or she has practiced truth telling to such an extent that it has become almost second nature. Merely to perform a virtuous act every now and then does not constitute a virtuous person. The person of virtue acts certain ways habitually; virtue becomes a way of life.

It is possible to combine the three approaches to moral responsibility—not in the sense of eclecticism, but in the sense of using the various approaches in light of one's ethical development. It is my opinion, following the work of Murdoch (1969), that taking ethical responsibility indicates a type of human growth. Thus, merely to state an ethical dilemma, or what is referred to as "quandary ethics" (Pincoffs, 1971), and resolve it through some type of pre-established model, misses the essence of ethics: As Pincoffs (1971) writes:

> A well-founded ethics would encourage the development of moral sensitivity, but discourage the entertainment of moral quandaries which arise out of moral ineptness . . . That the moral philosopher can be thought of as prescribing a regimen for a healthy moral life rather than a cure for particular moral illness would surely not be news for Aristotle. (p. 555)

Let me, then, examine more deeply, and in relationship to the general theories of moral responsibility, what the ethical life, as opposed to mere moral decision making (quandary ethics), is like. This necessitates a discussion of the nature and characteristics of the ethical life.

The Ethical Life

In any leadership position, there are institutional rules and policies that must be followed. This is the moral realm previously mentioned. Humans have discovered that following certain rules and procedures facilitates efficiency and accomplishes specific tasks more deliberately. Hall passes, for instance, are useful in controlling students and in identifying individuals who should not be in the school. It may seem odd to term such behavior *moral*. However, in an important sense, the moral life is the "conserving" life; that is, the moral is that which, if done properly, meets individual needs (students being able to go to various places in the school with a hall pass) and institutional needs (the necessity for order).

Teleological theories of moral responsibility, such as utilitarianism, undergird this type of moral decision making. Although utilitarianism has various forms—act and rule utilitarianism, for instance—the basic premise of utilitarianism is the consideration of the greatest good (the greatest good for students and for the school, in the example).

Similarly, institutional (and classroom) rules concerning fairness are moral rules in that their intent is to benefit the individual student and school. Rules of fairness are usually deontologically based; that is, a rule of fairness, such as "give every student equal consideration as far as possible" presupposes a moral principle: the principle of justice (Rawls, 1971). To treat students fairly is also to treat them justly, in this view. Although philosophers will argue the merits of particular cases, "quandary ethics," general consensus exists about the different types of theories of moral responsibility.

A difficulty arises in that an administrator can follow a theory of moral responsibility and can treat teachers justly but do so for the wrong reasons. Even Aristotle (1947) noted that reasons are essential to the ethical life. Put bluntly, an administrator can consider the interests of teachers in making a particular decision but do so merely to avoid conflict: the action is moral but not ethical. This is one reason the distinction between the moral and the ethical is important. Moreover, I am arguing that the moral is tied to a theory of the good that is historically developed and that considers the interests of oneself and others (the good of the school, for instance). This is the conserving function of morality. And who would deny that rules and procedures are necessary? Without them life within the school becomes chaotic. But, also, I, for one, would not want to identify the moral (the following of rules, principles, and so on) with the ethical.

Failure to clarify the difference(s) between morality and ethics has led to dangerous consequences. Since Kant (1938/1964), who believed in the ability of humans to use reason so as to treat each other as ends rather than as means to institutional success, and Hegel (1929/1967), who believed that history was purposeful, many contemporary philosophers, perhaps unwittingly, have destroyed traditional characteristics of the self. For Sartre (1947/1965), for instance, the basic human virtue seems to be freedom (or perhaps a form of sincerity). For many analytical philosophers, reasonableness seems to be the basic virtue.

Many contemporary philosophers seem to have eliminated the question "What ought I to do?" in favor of "What does ought mean?" (Craig, in press). One needs to have a clear idea of the meaning of *ought* before one makes a moral decision, but it is illogical to suggest that questions of meaning or of the use of language comprise philosophy in general and moral philosophy in particular.

Likewise, ethical theory can benefit from psychology; that is, the insights of contemporary psychology should inform the study of and the practice of ethics. The work of Freud (1962) is a case in point. If human nature were as positive, and if human and social growth were as optimistic as thinkers such as Sartre (1947/1965) suggest, perhaps freedom and sincerity would be two hallmark virtues. But as Murdoch (1969) notes:

> Freud takes a thoroughly pessimistic view of human nature. He sees the psyche as an egocentric system of quasi-mechanical energy, largely determined by its own individual history, whose natural attachments are sexual, ambiguous, and hard for the subject to understand or control. Introspection reveals only the deep tissue of ambivalent motive, and fantasy is a stronger force than reason. Objectivity and unselfishness are not natural to human beings. (p. 104)

Without arguing for the truth of Freud's insights, moral philosophers, as well as public school administrators, should at least appreciate the darker side of human nature, what Jung (1932/1971) refers to as the "shadow." We will return to the issue of human development when discussing the "Phases of Consciousness" of Brian Hall (Hall, 1986; Hall & Thompson, 1980).

Although much of the preceding discussion is quite theoretical (almost pedantic), the intent is not to display theory for theory's sake. Rather, it is to note the importance of the distinction between morality and ethics; and to approach the doing of ethics with some intelligence. A philosopher ought not apologize for theorizing, after all that's the name of the philosopher's game. Yet theory needs to relate to practice.

It would be a serious error to imagine that the imposition of rules and procedures totally defines either morality or ethics. We all know of rules and procedures that exist for administrative convenience only and do not relate to the benefit of students. But the ability to critique rules and procedures is not synonymous with being an ethical administrator. Ethics is related to behavior; while morality may or may not be, depending on the development of virtue of the administrator, among other things.

Let me be a bit more precise. The ethical person possesses certain types of characteristics. One is the ability to "pay attention to" others. This "paying attention to the other" is natural, as humans are communal beings. We exist with others, and unless we suffer some pathology, we "pay attention to others" for our own good, if for no other reason initially. Yet to consistently "pay attention to others," in the sense of being there for them and considering a particular issue from their point of view, requires effort and training (Hall, 1986).

One trait of the ethical person is his or her ability and willingness to be concerned about the other. For example, when a teacher comes to an administrator with a personal problem that is affecting his or her work, the ethical point of view would be to pay attention to another human being in distress. This requires empathy and disinterestedness—not solely considering the good of the school but "paying attention to" the suffering of this particular teacher. Ethics requires energy.

A second criterion of the ethical person is that he or she possesses the knowledge that values are somehow unitary. Aristotle (1947) noted that humans naturally seek unity—that unity is one criterion of intellectual development and understanding. This idea is not as odd as it may seem at first. Even the natural sciences seek unity—as shown by the various attempts at unified field theory currently in vogue, in which physicists are attempting to *unify* the various sources of energy.

The way value terms are used betrays a natural bent toward unifying the virtues. When asked about the nature of *courage*, for instance, people define it in relationship to other virtues, such as "acting unselfishly," "being calm in the face of danger," and so on. Although this may not be the exact type of unity sought, the argument illustrates the human need for value/virtue unity. Different traditions defend different hierarchies of value/virtue. Christianity, for instance, considers love the primary value/virtue from which others flow.

Finally, the good itself is transcendent; that is, the good (and the values and virtues encompassed by it) is not arrived at through scientific or empirical arguments. Philosophers traditionally have noted that the object of the human will, the good, transcends the will. The good is not a product of the will, but is discovered through the will. It is this sense in which the good is transcendent; it is beyond the purview of contemporary science, as well as beyond assimilation by human will.

In fact, it is by losing one's ego in the ethical act of helping another—performing the act because the other is suffering or is in need—that transcendence occurs. One has, as it were, transcended ego needs, drives, and concerns for the benefit of another. Yet the human will never fully grasp nor encompass the good. Plato argued that we can experience the transcendence of beauty (Taylor, 1956). Beauty is experienced in objects that are beautiful. But not so with the good. There will always be an ineffable aspect to the good. As G. E. Moore (1948) noted, the good is indefinable, while beauty is not.

The ethical person, then, is oriented toward the good; and he or she has developed the ability to "pay attention to" the other. He or she does this based on the idea of a hierarchy of values (unity). The value of the individual in a particular circumstance, coming to the administrator to share a personal dilemma, is higher than the value of completing whatever paperwork was underway. Doing the ethical usually gives pleasure, but one does not perform the ethical act to acquire pleasure. In the ethical act, one holds personal interests or ego needs in abeyance, as it were, thus transcending the self.

From the moral point of view, one could say "I did what I should have—what the principle or rule required of me." The ethical point of view might note that doing the moral is not enough, as the individual has chosen values, indeed chosen commitments and a way of life, that go beyond mere rule following—yet recognizing the importance and necessity of rules. This point will be made clearer in the discussion later in this chapter of a particular scenario within a public school.

The Research of Brian Hall

Is there any empirical basis for the distinction between morality and ethics? And what is the practical import for public school administrators?

Brian Hall, a professor of pastoral psychology at Santa Clara University, has been researching humans values development for more than 20 years. His early work (Hall, 1976) considered Phases of Values growth in relationship to processes such as values clarification. In 1980, Hall and Helen Thompson wrote *Values and Leadership*, in which they further refine and develop the Phases of Consciousness. Finally, Hall and Ben Tonna, a Catholic priest whom Hall met when involved in educational and pastoral work in Latin America, developed the Hall-Tonna Inventory of Values (1986), a forced choice Inventory. The Hall-Tonna Inventory of Values supplies data regarding one's Goal Values, or the values that form the basis of one's commitments, and Means Values, those values by which the individual actualizes the Goal Values (Hall & Thompson, 1980). The Hall-Tonna Inventory of Values also supplies data about one's leadership style, ethical profile, time management, spiritual development, and skill growth.

For these past several years, I have used the Hall-Tonna Inventory of Values with health care and public school administrators (Craig, 1989, 1990a). From my research, as well as Hall's continuing study of values development, several points need to be made:

1. One's ethical posture depends largely on one's values commitments.
2. Ethics is not merely a process of decision making but interrelates with the individual's world view and values growth.
3. The primary, although not exclusive, reason for regression relates to the fact that humans have needs (psychological, social, sexual, and so on) that if not met lead to behavior the individual usually would not cherish— selfish and egotistical behavior for self-preservation, for instance.

4. It is possible to consciously develop ethically; in fact, to do so is one sign of human maturity.

5. Values and ethical growth are dependent, in large part, on skill development.

6. One's value commitments are mainly derived from one's Phase of Consciousness and the contingencies of life.

7. It is possible, perhaps more probable than many people will admit, that one regresses to a lower Phase of Consciousness, especially when stressed, anxious, or pressured.

The following section describes the Phases of Consciousness.

Phases of Consciousness

The basis of Hall's theory and research is somewhat complicated. His commitment to developmental psychology is evident in the idea of Phase development. Likewise, humanistic psychologists, such as Maslow, are frequently quoted as reliable sources who undergird Hall's views. Finally, he is fond of quoting theologians and artists, especially novelists. This is both a blessing and a curse. Determining the main influence on Hall's theory and research is not possible; there have been many. This makes Hall's language difficult, at best. Unfortunately, much of his language relates to religious and/or humanistic psychological sources. This makes the language somewhat clumsy, perhaps even romantic; and his ideas are immediately discredited by people who have no interest in either religion or humanistic psychology.

With these disclaimers in mind, what does Hall mean by a Phase of Consciousness? Hall and Thompson (1980) write:

> The behavior characteristic of a Phase of Consciousness is determined by three factors: 1) how the world is perceived by the individual; 2) how the individual perceives the self functioning within that world; and 3) what human needs the self seeks to satisfy. (p. 33)

Consciousness simply means the developing awareness by an individual that there are many possible meanings to life and that different values can take on increasing importance. Hall's theory is descriptive, not prescriptive.

Phase One.   At Phase One, "the individual is struggling to survive, and has a limited view of anything beyond physical satisfaction and needs" (Hall, 1986, p. 85). Put another way, the self finds itself in a situation it does not understand and for which it has not developed the skills to cope. One's reality seems mysterious and threatening; one's physical and psychic existence seem to be at stake. In such a situation, values such as self-preservation and security become motivating factors in one's behavior. These are the Goal Values, which "are ends in themselves and which constitute the core of meaning" (Hall & Thompson, 1980, p. 51) for the individual. His/her moral decisions, then, are made in light of these value commitments. And the primary Means Values, or way the individual usually seeks to actualize the Goal Values, are safety and security.

The administrator whose world has suddenly taken an oppressive and capricious turn, presenting an administrative situation he or she does not understand and feels incapable of interacting with, may become so overwhelmed that decisions are made by fiat so as to preserve the self. Teachers' (and other staffs') best interests are of little concern in that case. The only good is the survival of the individual administrator.

Phase Two.   Phase Two consciousness "is quite distinct in that the self now realizes that survival requires social interaction, and requires that interest and attention be given to the perspective of others . . ." (Hall, 1986, p. 85). The individual at Phase Two has developed a wider perspective, including the interest of others. The human need shifts from self-preservation to belonging.

> The self seeks to belong in a significant human environment and to be approved by significant persons. (Hall & Thompson, 1980, p. 51)

This educational leader, then, is motivated by such Goal Values as family/belonging, self-worth, and self-competence/confidence. Usually, instrumentality and education are thought to be Means to accomplish this. The educational leader derives a sense of self and worth through institutional affiliation. Often he or she may be the company person, viewing the moral point of view as synonymous with institutional (or district) rules, policies, procedures, and regulations. Thus, someone who does not follow this agenda is often perceived as disloyal. Institutional loyalty is important for the growth of all and for the smooth functioning of the school—or, at least, consistent disloyalty by a large number of staff will hinder success. An administrator can be warm and caring, yet maintain institutional rules as the modus operandi for his or her moral decisions. Yet the administrator is unlikely to choose immoral means to accomplish institutional ends: the end does not justify the means. Because belonging is an important value, others are not treated unjustly or immorally. This behavior would alienate the educational leader from others and not meet the Goal Value orientation.

As previously noted, the individual, when stressed or uncertain tends to revert to a lower Phase of Consciousness. As one's awareness can be expanded, it can also be restricted. If the educational leader begins to sense a lack of belonging, for instance, he or she will feel personally threatened and probably become autocratic and rigid, not realizing, of course, that this behavior causes further alienation.

Phase Three.   Hall (1986) describes Phase Three in the following way:

> Phase III is revolutionary in that the self now begins to act on the environment in creative ways, not simply to react to it. Phase III is a stage of essential integration as the self feels conscience and recognizes that it exists not in reaction to the external only, but also to the internal world of psychic energy. (p. 85)

The educational leader who is at Phase Three is driven by such Goal Values as life/self actualization, service/vocation and human dignity. The Means Values include empathy and independence. The point is that the administrator begins to become aware of a reality or world larger than the school, and/or becomes aware of ethical issues within the school—as opposed to survival or institutional demands. Treating teachers fairly is done not merely because it increases institutional commitment but because it is the way teachers ought to be treated. This indicates the development of conscience, as institutional reality is perceived as a project in which the educational leader must participate: the must being normative.

Phase Four.   At Phase Four consciousness, the individual views himself or herself as integral to the global environment. Consciousness goes beyond either self or institution. The educational leader begins to view the school as one system (although consisting of subsystems) within an even larger system (all the districts in the state, perhaps), and so on.

Goal Values that energize the individual at Phase Four are intimacy/solitude and transcendence, among others. Interdependence is an example of a Means Value. The ethical posture of an educational leader at this Phase is to harmonize the seemingly disparate concerns and interests within the school. This is not a utilitarian position but a deontological one based on the belief in the interdependence and interrelationship of all things. This is a metaphysical view. Thus, teachers' interests are considered not because the educational leader fears personal survival, nor because he or she values belonging, nor even because this is the good thing to do, it is good in itself in the ethical sense. Rather, teachers' interests and concerns are valued because teachers interrelate in an essential way with other communities that interrelate and are interdependent, such as students, parents, the community, and the society.

It is difficult to tell which Phase of Consciousness the educational leader is at by simply observing behavior. The administrator could be warm and caring and be at Phase Two, Phase Three or Phase Four. To clarify which Phase of Consciousness the educational leader is at, one must ascertain the reason the educational leader makes a particular decision. Are teachers' interests and concerns valued and acted upon because the administrator wants a smooth-functioning school where everyone is happy and works together as a family (Phase Two)? or because it is ethically right to consider teachers' interests (Phase Three)? or because teacher interests interrelate to other interests which further interdependent realities (Phase Four)?

Skills and Moral, Ethical, and Values Development

Lawrence Kohlberg (1981) has noted that *empathy*, being able to put oneself in another's place, is a skill necessary for moral development. In Hall's scheme, empathy is a skill certainly necessary for growth to Phase Three. But, as Hall

(Hall, 1986; Hall & Thompson, 1980) argues, the relationship between values growth and skill development is contextual. Hall and Thompson (1980) write:

> The Phase Two values associated with belonging—being liked, peer support, duty-obligation, responsibility—become internalized as the individual becomes skilled in interpersonal behaviors. Similarly, the values related to success—competence, achievement, education, productivity—are achieved as the instrumental skills that enable the individual to do a task are developed. Values as skills are more easily understood when they are considered in a specific context. (p. 52)

According to Hall (1986), skill development is a necessary but not a sufficient condition for values/ethical growth. Perhaps this is what Aristotle (1947) had in mind when he noted that the development of virtue demands practice. One may perform a virtuous act, but that differs from being virtuous. Although Kohlberg (1981) criticized this approach by referring to it as "the bag of virtues approach" to moral development, his arguments are not convincing. Certainly, as Kohlberg (1981) contends, one can perform acts of virtue mindlessly, or the acts can be mere repetition without proper intent, but it does not follow that practice has no place in ethical growth. The point is that skill development is necessary to ethical growth.

In order to function as an educational leader, instrumental skills are required. These are the skills associated with any profession or craft. As Hall (1986) writes:

> Instrumental skills are then a combination of the tool with the intellect. Any profession takes a combination of these. . . . A plumber must know about the design of houses and the sizes and material composition of piping, and he or she must have the physical skills to accomplish the given tasks. (p. 141)

Today an educational leader needs to be computer literate. Likewise, such activities as budgeting and scheduling require instrumental skills, the tools of the administrative trade, as it were. With the development of adequate instrumental skills comes administrative and personal competence, that is, instrumental skills are related to the development of an adequate self-concept. And this is a necessary condition for values/ethical growth.

A second set of skills are interpersonal. These include the ability to be empathetic, to listen attentively, to pay attention to another, and so on. As previously noted, the ethical life depends on such skills. Hall (1986) argues that:

> Critical to the mature development of interpersonal skills is self-awareness and knowledge of one's emotional and imaginal life, in the past and the present. Such an awareness plus the skills that come with it is not something that is learned intuitively; it has to be learned formally. . . . (p. 141)

"Paying attention to the other" and putting one's ego in abeyance, as it were, are not natural activities. They must be learned through practice. Yet the development of interpersonal skills occurs, or is simultaneous with, growth to the Phase Three of Consciousness.

A third skill mix is imaginal skills. These are

. . . the peculiar blend of internal fantasy and feeling that enables a person to externalize one's ideas and images in an effective manner. Basically it is the ability of the person to transform internal images into external structures that are workable in the world. (Hall, 1986, p. 139)

The development and use of imaginal skills are important in two senses:

- They allow the individual to synthesize the seemingly disparate data of experience, to perceive hidden meaning in the data, and to transform complex data into simple ideas. Such skill development is essential for an educational leader to take the complexity of institutional experience and to derive meaning from it.
- They form the basis of skill integration. They have "the peculiar quality of synthesizing all the other skills" (Hall, 1986, p. 14).

The other set of skills necessary for ethical growth is systems skills. These skills enable the individual "to see all parts of a system or an institution as they relate to the whole" (Hall, 1986, p. 147). Often, educational leaders, especially assistant administrators who usually are responsible for the myriad issues relating to student discipline, view their activity as "putting out fires." As a result, they miss the opportunity to envision their responsibility within a larger social and ethical context. The development and use of systems skills enables the educational leader to view "putting out fires" within the mission and holistic enterprise called a school.

System skills demand the ability to use the other three skill clusters to move beyond the integration of disparate experience within the school (imaginal skills) to viewing administrative activity within a holistic pattern of learning and student growth. One manner of developing systems skills is through group dynamics training, which allows the individual the opportunity "to move beyond assessing data (imaginal skills) to seeing new possibilities (Hall, 1986, p. 148).

Hall-Tonna Inventory of Values

Although there are other instruments on the market (The Personal Values Inventory, for instance), the Hall-Tonna Inventory of Values is especially relevant to this discussion. The Hall-Tonna Inventory has undergone extensive reliability and validity studies (Hall, Harari, Ledig, & Tondow, 1986). The Hall-Tonna Inventory supplies information concerning several areas of human growth—the individual's Ethical Profile, Leadership Style, Faith Growth, and Skill Development—as no other instrument by itself does. Part of the feedback sessions that result from using this Inventory includes a process of clarifying and understanding one's values and ethical posture—and suggested ways to develop this understanding, especially as this information impacts ethical decision making.

The process is not entirely rational; the use of the imagination is required. I have written elsewhere that ethical decision making, viewed merely through the lenses of logic and rationality, is one-sided (Craig, 1974). Put differently, logic and rationality (instrumental skills) are at the disposal of the imagination, and not vice versa, as researchers such as Lawrence Kohlberg (1981) have argued.

The process of values/ethics clarification and articulation consists of three parts:

1. Feedback regarding the educational leader's value clusters
2. Development of Values Convergence Statements
3. Development of Values/Ethics Action Plan

As Hall and Ledig (1986) note, one's value cluster can be unhealthy. Thus, after discussing the values profile of the educational leader(s), as the process achieves the best results in a group setting, the Values Convergence Statement is developed. Part of the feedback process is to discuss one's Phase of Consciousness, Skill, and Ethical Profiles, and so on. A meaningful Values Convergence Statement cannot be developed without this information.

When doing feedback sessions, individuals are often shocked with some of the information they uncover. The first time I completed the Hall-Tonna I was so amazed at the Ethical Profile, which indicated I was beginning to develop a point in which ethical choices were not merely black and white, I shouted out, "This can't be right. I have a Ph.D. specializing in ethics." The other group members, who knew me quite well, calmed me and then informed me that they perceived my ethical universe to be consistent with the Profile. When someone is shocked by a particular type of information, and verbalizes their feelings as I did, it often indicates the information is correct.

Cycles of Growth

An individual's value clusters represent a personal and unique way of perceiving the world. Along with Phases of Consciousness, of which there are substages of each of the four phases, Hall (1986) has discerned seven cycles of growth. Hall and Ledig (1986) write:

> Let us imagine that life is a journey and that somehow through our life circumstances and the choices we make about these circumstances we travel through seven cycles of growth. Each of these cycles represents a unique world view, new experiences and the challenge of learning a whole new set of skills. (p. 10)

The seven cycles of growth indicate, in reality, a more precise way of describing one's journey through the Phases of Consciousness. Although this sounds complicated, it really is not.

In the *Primal Cycle* (first) of growth, which encompasses the first Phase of Consciousness, the individual experiences reality as mysterious, even alien. Reality is perceived, at least at the feeling level, as being controlled by a distant authority. Security and material ownership are important, as the individual is concerned with physical survival.

Educational leaders in this cycle would base ethical choices merely on self-interest, which they view as the paradigm for everyone else's ethical choice. The main requirement for development to the next cycle depends on the development and use of the imagination—to imagine other possibilities, to imagine oneself in control so as to limit the threat of impersonal control of one's life, and so on.

The *Familial Cycle* (second) bridges Phases One and Two. Educational leaders in the Familial Cycle of growth use the image of the home as the paradigm for understanding experience and reality. The school is viewed as a family, and the intimacy and closeness of family living is the yardstick for interaction of the educational leaders. When the school no longer seems to have a family atmosphere, the educational leader experiences a sense of alienation. Thus, friends and associates become important in shielding the individual from an unfriendly universe, and the values of hospitality and respect for authority take on increasing importance.

In the Familial Cycle, the rightness or appropriateness of one's moral choices are measured in relationship to rule-following articulated by legitimate authority. This is the deontological moral framework, in which the moral principles of fairness and mutual respect form the basis of moral action—that is, specific modes of rule-following. Similarly, fairness and mutual respect support the family-like environment. To avoid a rigid and narrow approach to others and/or to institutional life, objective study, through education, perhaps, takes on increasing importance.

At the *Institutional Cycle* (third), which encompasses Phase Two consciousness, the struggle is to be successful, in an institutional sense, and to please those (usually superiors) who are viewed as controlling one's future. One aspect of growth occurs when the individual is able to balance those things with the development of strategies to please his or her family. Divided loyalties exist—between the institution and the family—and further growth necessitates meaningfully meeting the demands of both.

Moral choice is based on following legitimate authority: the law, government, the church, or other respected institutions. But if the individual is unable to follow this moral choice he or she may become rigid and be perceived as being authoritarian. Thus, the development of interpersonal skills allows the person to relate to others in such a way as to avoid rigidity (appearing as if he or she is always right); and the refinement of administrative skills allows the educational leader to function more efficiently. Finally, the development of the critical ability to evaluate and critique values of the family and rules of the school (among other respected institutions) leads to further growth.

The *Intrapersonal Cycle* (fourth) of growth bridges Phases Two and Three. The development to this cycle begins a radical departure in perspective and ethical (as opposed to moral) framework. The educational leader begins to perceive uncertainty in reality; institutional rules and norms are no longer as binding as they once seemed. Policies and procedures that once seemed certain and appropriate might begin to be seriously questioned. In fact, the individual is beginning to think that ethical values are relative. Thus the need occurs to find a center of values in one's life and to discover one's own place in the meaning and scheme of things.

At the Intrapersonal Cycle, because the resolution of ethical issues no longer relates solely to moral principles and to institutional rule-following, the individual no longer perceives these issues to be black and white. Although it is becoming more difficult to make ethical (as opposed to moral) decisions and commitments without hesitation and reservation, such struggle and uncertainty is a sign of positive ethical and human growth. It is essential, then, for the educational leader who is at this Cycle to be able to assess effectiveness and decision making in light of both this new growth and the reality of the institutional situation. Without this balance, the educational leader will be perceived as disloyal or incompetent. And because the individual is struggling to discover values and an ethical framework within an uncertain world, the study of equality, justice, and life-development issues takes on increasing importance.

The *Communal/Collaborative Cycle* (fifth) embraces Phase Three consciousness. Individuals in this cycle are increasingly discovering that they have talents and gifts not previously known. It is beginning to be realized that these gifts, such as delegation or interpersonal gifts, are integral to growth and to being a productive educational leader. Along with this comes the realization that institutions, such as schools, are more successful to the extent that they are humane. Accordingly, the educational leader increasingly attempts to humanize the workplace.

This cycle of growth has defined a clear set of personal values and an ethical framework, and ethical choice is predicated upon living life according to these newly chosen humanistic values. One acts, that is, through conscience. Institutional rules, guidelines, and policies are thought to be important, but they will be adapted and/or modified if they neglect the equitable, fair, and humanistic development of all concerned.

Again a balance is demanded for further growth—this time a balance between time devoted to work and professional growth and having the support and affirmation of peers so as to avoid disillusionment and misunderstanding.

The *Mystical Cycle* (sixth) bridges Phases Three and Four. At this cycle of growth, reality itself, in its various forms, is perceived to be a gift, which demands the individual's involvement. A balance is again indicated: a balance between work and professional growth and involvement with others and time for personal intimacy and solitude.

The educational leader's ethical choices are now informed by the awareness of the rights and dignity of all people. Unjust institutions will not be tolerated. In fact, the educational leader will probably assess his or her particular school in light of just such ethical criteria. Further growth is accomplished by the development of systems and imaginal skills, especially growth to the awareness and recognition of a global view of the world.

The *Prophetic Cycle* (seventh) of growth encompasses Phase Four consciousness. In this cycle, the educational leader recognizes that his or her particular institutional success is ultimately expressed at a global level and necessitates the collaboration of all social institutions. Such awareness is not merely theoretical, for the individual usually feels called to participate in community activity in light of this new growth. One develops such ethical commitments as improving the balance of material goods, among other goods, for humans, beginning with the institution one directs (or, more accurately, with which one shares responsibility). To continue at this cycle, one needs to continually recognize areas of growth, as well as note how he or she acted when at other cycles. Having peers who represent and can articulate the various moral and ethical concerns at each cycle of growth is one way to accomplish this.

Perhaps an example will help clarify the Phases of Consciousness. Merely by observing administrative practice it is difficult, if not impossible, to pinpoint an individual's particular Phase of Consciousness. The reasons the educational leader gives for the specific behavior usually indicate the Phase of Consciousness. For instance, educational leaders could use site-based management because they viewed the school as an interdependent aspect of a larger whole consisting of the district, the community, and so on—a Phase Four orientation. Or they could use it because they knew and felt it to be their moral responsibility—a Phase Three orientation. In a Phase Two orientation, educational leaders might use site-based management to feel accepted, affirmed, and approved—because it is the thing to do; everyone else is trying it. Or they could use it because they don't know what else to do—a Phase One orientation.

The Ethical Educational Leader

What are the implications of the preceding discussion for educational leadership and moral/ethical decision making? In the first place, it means that ethics is the name of nothing clear. Ethics does not have a unitary definition. As individuals go through different stages of moral/ethical growth, they will make moral/ethical decisions differently from other administrators who are at a different stage or phase. The stages or phases of moral/ethical development are tied to a particular cycle of growth.

Returning to the issue of the impending closing of a school, an administrator who is at the Second Cycle will use criteria related to a legitimate authority. Is there a school or district policy concerning communication with teachers, in the event of an impending school closing? If not, what advice can the educational leader get from business or industrial management regarding downsizing or the closing of a facility? The educational leader will tend to follow the direction of such perceived legitimate authority.

This approach is deontological in that a moral principle is inherent in whatever decision is made—perhaps the principle of truthtelling or doing no active harm to another. The legitimate authority provides the justification for the reliability and accuracy of the principle. In other words, the moral principle is not the product of conscience.

There is a teleological aspect to the moral decision, but the projected consequences are ascertained from the legitimate authority. They are not reached through reasoned analysis. The educational leader has developed to the point of performing virtuous behavior in light of legitimate authority. Put another way, the educational leader has developed the virtue of prudence and rule-following in response to legitimate authority. Thus the moral decision is not made collaboratively nor is it a product of conscience.

A different administrator, at Cycle Four, the Intrapersonal Cycle, is beginning to perceive that the rules of legitimate authority are relative, at least in the sense that different legitimate authorities will differ on what action to take. The educational leader recognizes that the issue is not black and white, that whatever decision is made will have benefits and drawbacks.

If the administrator views the decision in light of the interests and functioning of the school—as if the decision impacts human beings—he or she will make the decision by embracing such humanistic values as the good of the teachers, students, school, and so on. Again there are deontological aspects to the ethical decision, namely the principles of fairness and human best interest. The teleological aspect will be viewed in light of the humanizing effect of a particular decision. And the administrator has developed the virtues of fairness and respect for others. Although the decision to inform the teachers is the product of conscience, it is not a collaborative decision. An educational leader at Cycle Five, though, would use a participatory or collaborative style of ethical decision making.

In summary, although ethics is the name of nothing clear, it is related to several factors:

1. the cycle of growth of the educational leader, with the accompanying value clusters, virtue characteristics, and mode of decision making
2. the skill development of the individual
3. the way the educational leader perceives himself or herself in relationship to the reality of the school (Phase of Consciousness)

The two examples that complete this section suggest how this works in actual practice. One is a conflict-of-interest situation, and the other is a question of administrative management style.

Conflict of Interest

The administrator is being pressured by a particular family to pay attention to the number of minorities who are in the Gifted and Talented Program. The family contends that, with the large number of minorities in the program, their daughter (who is white) will suffer when it comes to being accepted into a particular private high school. The family has political power within the community; the mother is an important lawyer, and the father is a surgeon. Thus they can mobilize others within the community to put various kinds of pressure on the administrator. Is there a "correct" ethical way to respond to this issue?

Deontological Approach.   A strictly deontological approach, which is highly rational, would consider moral principles that relate to the issue. Usually in a deontological system, a hierarchy of moral principles exists, and the charge is to sort them rationally and apply them. One's duty will then be clear, and one ought to, indeed has the moral responsibility to, act on one's duty.

According to the deontologist, the concept of duty is independent of the concept of good, and actions are not judged moral because of their consequences. Factors other than good actions, good consequences, and good results determine the rightness of actions. Such principles as are inherent in keeping promises, fair and equitable distribution of goods and services, and/or abiding by a contractual relationship constitute the rightness of actions (or constitute moral actions). The reason is that it is one's duty to abide by the above three situations. It is not because breaking promises shatters human trust (consequences) that keeping one's promises is a moral act; rather, it is because humans have a "duty" to keep promises.

Deontology, then, is a deductive and rational moral system. The logic is unassailable:

1. It is one's duty to keep promises.
2. X is a situation in which I promised to do Y.
3. Therefore, I ought to do Y.

Thus, for the deontologist, there are many nonconsequential relations, such as promise-keeping, parent-child relations, teacher-student relations, physician-patient relations, and friendship, that are intrinsic to the moral life.

Likewise one's motivation is important for the deontologist. One keeps a promise not out of fear, nor because he or she will benefit from keeping promises, but because it is the right thing to do even if the greatest good is not obtained. This is really another way of saying that one has intrinsic duties based on moral principles—everyone should keep promises because promise-keeping is derived from the prima facie duty of fidelity (Ross, 1930).

Another version of deontology, a Kantian sort (Kant, 1938/1964), stresses the universal moral principle inherent in doing one's duty. As Kant argues, one should act not only "in accordance with duty, but for the sake of duty" (p. 73). And, for Kant, an action is moral if it is performed by an agent who possesses "a good will"—one has a good will if moral duty is based on a universalizable (everyone ought to do X) rule or principle. In this version of deontology, one ought to keep promises because keeping promises is a universalizable moral rule.

We need not argue the complexities of a deontological position. We merely want to understand it so as to apply a deontological perspective to the moral dilemma under discussion. It will become clear that the major difficulty with a strict deontological approach is that humans often have conflicting duties.

Does the administrator have a moral duty to make sure the Gifted and Talented Program is equally distributed, open to all students who have the qualifications? On any approach, the answer is yes. Otherwise, the program would be meaningless because the criteria for admission are not adhered to, or a hidden agenda is inherent in admission to the program, such as emphasizing minorities, which, on the surface, would be discriminatory.

From the way the moral dilemma is stated, there is no way of discerning whether the parents' motive is purely selfish, based on the desire for their daughter to attend one of the best private schools. A dialogue with the parents, indeed with all concerned, would be needed. It might be discovered that the parents have a point.

Teleological Approach.   In a teleological moral system, the educational leader would ask questions about the consequences of acting. In utilitarian moral theory, the desire is to secure the greatest possible balance of good consequences over the least possible balance of bad consequences (Bayles, 1966). The purpose of morality, for the utilitarian (the most prominent form of teleology), is to promote human welfare by minimizing harms and maximizing benefits.

Utilitarianism is not devoid of moral principles. In fact, maximizing benefits and minimizing harms itself is a moral principle. Inherent in any teleological system are moral principles. For instance, utilitarianism understands morality to include shared rules of fairness, justice, and other principles of the moral life (Mill, 1959; orig. 1859). Thus teleology, especially the utilitarian sort, is a social philosophy. The point is that the consequences of a particular action form a kind of calculus to define moral activity—maximizing benefit. The moral principles are not followed because of one's duty, as in deontology, but because following them maximizes benefits for human beings: it makes the school run more smoothly and decreases the possibility of discrimination.

Taking a utilitarian position, the administrator would investigate the parents' charge because doing so will potentially cause the Gifted and Talented Program to run more efficiently, serving the benefit of the greatest number of acceptable students. But efficiency is not the only value valuable in utilitarianism. In fact, efficiency is an instrumental value, or a means to an end. Efficiency, then, is the means for maximizing the good. But what is the good? Utilitarians argue that the good is that which is intrinsically good, that which is not merely a means. Equality, fairness, and human happiness are thought to be three intrinsic goods. They are conditions that are good in themselves, without reference to further consequences. In fact, all human values are thought to be measured by the standards of intrinsic goods or values. An *intrinsic value* is one that is possessed for its own sake.

In the dilemma under discussion, the educational leader, if using a utilitarian approach, would ask questions about human preferences. This is not to suggest that any preference is commendable. Preferring to treat children in a discriminatory fashion is not good because it does not maximize the good for those children treated this way. To maximize the good, then, is to maximize the agreed-upon preferences. The preference for those involved in the school, administrators, parents, community, and so on, is to have a Gifted and Talented Program that truly identifies gifted and talented children, based on agreed-upon criteria. If the program is not performing this function, it is not maximizing the good for which it has been established. If it is performing toward its pre-established purpose, and the parents of the girl still pressure minimizing the number of minority children in the program, the administrator knows the issue is something else. Thus, using either a deontological or teleological moral system, the educational leader can assess the moral appropriateness of both the program and the parents' demand.

Quandary Approach.   Is this all there is to ethics? The above is an example of the "quandary approach" to moral decision making. Both deontological and/or teleological systems are workable and are important rational factors in moral problem solving. The method has at least four factors:

1. Using the concepts of deontology and/or teleology, one articulates the moral dilemma as fully as possible.
2. One assesses how much the dilemma is being driven by the special interests of parents.
3. One articulates the appropriate type of motivation, based on the stated purpose of the program and on appropriate moral principles.
4. One states the conclusion in light of the moral theories.

In some cases, this process is not as easy to use—times when there are conflicts of moral principles or when consequences are not so black and white. This alone indicates that the moral dilemma approach to moral decision making does not constitute the whole of ethics.

Without the development of certain virtuous characteristics, the educational leader may simply give in to the demands of the parents. In the actual case on which this discussion has been based, the educational leader "paid serious attention to" those involved in the scenario. The parents, the student, teachers, and other concerned individuals were consulted so the educational leader could view the situation from their points of view. This is not only sound administrative practice but is integral to virtue ethics. It would have been easier, and taken far less time, if the educational leader had merely presupposed that the parents' demand was mere self-interest and not paid attention to it. Alternatively, he or she could have noted the political power of the parents and their importance and interrelationship with the community and simply given in to their demands. It took courage, insight, care, and respect for others to initiate the process of ethical inquiry. The virtuous administrator, then, recognizes the situation as an ethical question in the first place and takes the proper steps (which demand such virtues as courage and truth-seeking) to ensure that a just solution (another hallmark virtue) is found.

Now let's consider a second issue: the educational leader's management style.

Management Style

The issue of administrative management style is an ethical issue. Any management style that hinders human growth is unethical. This follows from both a deontological and a teleological moral system.

If one accepts the moral principle that one should not actively harm another, and if it is admitted that hindering emotional and psychological growth is an example of active harm, then it follows deontologically that any management style that hinders such growth is immoral. Likewise, if one of the purposes of public schools is the emotional and psychological growth of all concerned (at least to the extent that they do not leave schooling emotionally and psychologically worse), then it follows teleologically that any management style that hinders such growth is unethical.

Different levels of leadership style exist (Hall, 1986). Consider two: the paternalistic/maternalistic leader and the participatory leader. The paternalistic/maternalistic leader tends to dominate and does not encourage (or even allow) people to grow. Subordinates are dependent upon him or her. The subordinates—assistant administrators, department chairs, teachers, and so on—are viewed in the parent-child model, and it is the responsibility of the leader to develop those under his or her charge, as it is the purpose of parents and teachers to develop the child. A paternalistic/maternalistic educational leader does not respect the self-esteem and autonomy of subordinates. This behavior does not allow their growth as either professionals or as human beings. It logically follows, then, that a paternalistic/maternalistic leadership style leads to immoral behavior—manipulating others for a preestablished goal. (Although I will not argue this, there may be times where these styles might be appropriate on a temporary and limited basis.)

On the other hand, participatory leadership styles do encourage emotional and psychological growth. Discussing participatory leadership, Hall and Thompson (1980) write:

> Participatory leadership can be achieved by persons whose skills enable them to function comfortably within Phase Three consciousness and whose vision includes a Phase Four view of the world as mystery-to-be-cared-for. With the emergence of Phase Three consciousness, the individual experiences personal authority as unique; he values, in a new way, his personal creativity and imagination. This is . . . the leader so desperately needed in our times. (p. 81)

Without necessarily agreeing with Hall and Thompson's assessment of the leadership situation, it is easy to note that a participatory mode of management is more likely than a paternalistic/maternalistic one to develop others' emotional and psychological growth. What is really being asserted is that the ethical, as opposed to the merely moral, participatory educational leader possesses characteristics and virtues other styles of leadership do not possess.

SUMMARY

What has been suggested in this chapter is that the ethical educational leader is more than a person capable of moral decision making. A major concern of the ethical administrator is the development of ethical sensitivity in himself or herself and within the school. Why should ethical sensitivity be developed? The stated assumption is that people and institutions should develop as harmoniously and integratedly as possible. It cannot be proven that personal and institutional holism and integration are the sine qua non of the ethical life—nor that they epitomize the ethical person. This is being assumed. The integrated person looks at experience from both a cognitive and an affective dimension, from both a left- and a right-hemisphere orientation, from both a moral and ethical perspective, and so on.

Brian Hall's research was used as a framework for discussion of such growth. It is assumed by many philosophers, from Plato to Kant, that human and institutional integration represents the "highest" achievement of human beings. Kant (1938/1964) refers to this as the creation of a "kingdom of ends"—an institutional and social situation in which humans treat each other as ends, possessing worth and dignity. Likewise a number of historical religions, including Christianity and Buddhism, suggest that human holism epitomizes the human spiritual quest: the individual who is able to integrate his or her physical, psychological, emotional, and spiritual selves.

How is this ethical person developed? As with ethics itself, there is a mysterious aspect to human nature. No single, simple path results in the ethical (and thus integrated) person. But the development of ethical sensitivity is one condition (Craig, 1990b). The ethical administrator has developed an ethical awareness—an awareness of the worth and dignity of others—and a sensitivity to conditions that violate human worth and dignity. Ethical sensitivity or awareness is like other types of awareness, the awareness that one is tired or hungry, perhaps.

The individual's awareness of proper ethical behavior becomes second nature. This sensitivity is developed through practice, through treating others as beings of both worth and dignity, and, thus, through the development of virtue. But there is an additional element that can be defined as vision. It is the Phase Four vision of the interrelatedness of all people and things. This, and the values inherent in Phase Four, is the stimulus or motivation for being ethical.

Consider this illustration: The principal of a high school with almost 4,000 students in the Houston area, upon accepting the position, met with the faculty and staff during the summer. He shared with them his vision for the school, which was to decentralize and to create a form of participatory democracy. He would help in the facilitation of decisions, but he would not make them unilaterally. He primarily viewed himself as being there for the students, so he developed an open-door student policy. He also stated that he would help anyone who felt that he or she could not or would not like to work in such an environment find another position, preferably a better position than their present one. One administrator and a number of teachers requested transfers.

Without discussing his management strategy with any precision, a few comments are in order. When asked why he chose such a participatory management style, he answered that in his experience and based on his assumptions (which had been learned) about how humans grow and work best, participatory democracy is the most suitable management style for an institutional environment. When asked why an educational leader should be concerned about the emotional and psychological growth of teachers and staff, and not solely be concerned about student growth, he stared in amazement and responded, "How could anyone question this?"

I wrote he "learned" that this vision is the most suitable to human growth. In other words, the administrator develops through distinct lifestyles or phases of understanding his experience and reality. Yet not every administrator or teacher is capable of functioning well within such a vision. Because this vision demands growth, as well as more responsibility for individuals over their own work-destiny, not everyone should be required to operate in this fashion. In fact, it would be immoral (doing harm to the individual) to require it. Some individuals are not ready, for they are at different phases of ethical growth.

It certainly is the case that public school administrators should be trained in moral problem solving, should be able to take a moral dilemma and go through a deontological and teleological assessment of it. But I am arguing for more. I am arguing that the technical administrator views ethics as a way of life, not merely as a technique of moral problem solving. The ethical administrator has a vision that includes the interrelatedness of all those involved in the school and community. As I have noted elsewhere (Craig, 1989), this is one necessary condition for the development of ethical sensitivity, viewing others as beings with respect and dignity. The other piece is the development of virtue through arduous practice: treating others justly and respectfully over a long period of time may result in a virtuous person—a person who respects others because they are like oneself and ought to be treated that way.

The rest is mystery not susceptible to quantification, nor even description. I am talking about human nature and the possibilities of human growth. This is metaphysics in the traditional sense. As George Bernard Shaw remarked about Christianity, the major problem with such an approach to ethics is that so few have ever tried it.

Enough is known about human development to note under which conditions humans grow best. Enough is also known about human development to know under which conditions humans are unlikely to grow. That the moral educational leader is possible is a matter of fact. Many educational leaders have developed the ability to use various methods of moral problem solving. That the ethical educational leader is possible is also a matter of fact. That such an educational leader ought to be developed is a matter of belief, hope, and vision.

THEORY INTO PRACTICE: A CASE STUDY FOR REFLECTION

You are the principal of a large, inner-city middle school. The district has mandated that every middle school have a Character Education Program. You need to select one department chairperson and one teacher to attend district in-service programs to prepare teachers for the program. The in-service programs are a "train the trainer" process, so the two individuals chosen will be involved in initial training and programmatic development.

GUIDING QUESTIONS

1. What characteristics would you look for in recommending these two individuals and why? What would you tell them to convince them of the importance of this endeavor?
2. One of the teachers asks you if you don't see an inconsistency in a "mandated" Character Education Program. Do you? How would you respond?
3. After training, the two individuals begin presenting in-service programs in your school regarding the "nuts and bolts" of the program. This is the approach taken at the district level. Is there other information you think the teachers ought to have? What? And for what reason?
4. It is almost immediately noticed, and verbalized by a number of students and a few concerned teachers, that the program is for and evaluates the progress of students only. These articulate individuals feel that, if the program is going to be meaningful, teachers and the administration would need to be involved—the teacher and administrators need to go through the same (or a similar) process and evaluation the students are going through. Otherwise, it is argued, the assumption is that all teachers and school administrators are already virtuous and need no improvement. Also, without this involvement the program is merely another authoritarian, white, middle-class imposition of values on inner-city students, or so this vocal constituency strongly suggests. What would you say and do about their proposal, and why?
5. No matter what your decision, how would you like to evaluate progress in the area of Character Education? What are some assumptions and moral issues inherent in the program and in any method of evaluation you choose? Be specific.

REFERENCES

Aristotle. (1947). *Nichomachean ethics*. New York: Random House.

Bayles, E. (1966). *Pragmatism in education*. New York: Harper.

Beauchamp, T. (1982). *Philosophical ethics*. New York: McGraw-Hill.

Craig, R. (1974). Lawrence Kohlberg and moral development: Some reflections. *Educational Theory, 24*, 4–16.

Craig, R. (1980a). Accountability and responsibility: Some fundamental differences. *Proceedings of the Midwest Philosophy of Education Society*. Carbondale, IL: Southern Illinois University Press.

Craig, R. (1980b). Kohlberg's justification of stage theory: A critique. *Focus on Learning, 21*, 21–24.

Craig, R. (1989). Institutional democracy in health care: A plan. *Thresholds in Education, 10*, 36–41.

Craig, R. (1990a). Ethics and educational leadership. *Texas Study of Secondary Education Research Journal, 46*, 20–24.

Craig, R. (1990b). Reflections on values: Research and commentary. *Educational Horizons, 68*, 168–171.

Craig, R. (1990c). To live is to be a searcher of wisdom. *Curriculum Review (29)*, 7–9.

Fox, R., & DeMarco, J. (1990). *Moral reasoning: A philosophic approach to applied ethics*. Fort Worth: Holt, Rinehart and Winston.

Freud, S. (1962). *Civilization and its discontents*. New York: W. W. Norton.

Hall, B. (1976). *The development of consciousness: A confluent theory of values*. New York: Paulist Press.

Hall, B. (1986). *The Genesis effect: Personal and organizational transformations*. New York: Paulist Press.

Hall, B., Harari, O., Ledig, B., & Tondow, M. (1986). *Manual for the Hall-Tonna inventory of values*. New York: Paulist Press.

Hall, B., & Ledig, B. (1986). *Lifestyle workbook: A guide for understanding the Hall-Tonna inventory of values*. New York: Paulist Press.

Hall, B., & Thompson, H. (1980). *Leadership through values*. New York: Paulist Press.

Hall, B., & Tonna, B. (1986). *Hall-Tonna inventory of values*. New York: Paulist Press.

Hegel, G. W. F. (1967). *The phenomenology of mind*. New York: Harper & Row. (Original work published 1929)

Jung, C. (1971). Aion: Phenomenology of the self. In J. Campbell (Ed.), *The portable Jung* (pp. 139–162). New York: The Viking Press. (Original work published 1932)

Kant, I. (1964). *Groundwork of the metaphysics of morals*. New York: Harper & Row. (Original work published 1938)

Kohlberg, L. (1981). *The philosophy of moral development* (Vol. 1). San Francisco: Harper & Row.

Mill, J. S. (1959). *On liberty*. London: J. W. Parker. (Original work published 1859)

Moore, G. E. (1948). *Principia ethica*. Cambridge: Cambridge University Press.

Murdoch, I. (1969). On "God" and "Good." In M. Grene (Ed.), *The anatomy of knowledge* (pp. 68–91). New York: Routledge and Kegan Paul.

Pincoffs, E. (1971). Quandary ethics. *Mind, 80,* 552–571.

Rawls, J. (1971). *A theory of justice*. Cambridge: Harvard University Press.

Ross, W. D. (1930). *The right and the good*. Oxford: Oxford University Press.

Sartre, J. P. (1965). *The philosophy of existentialism*. New York: Philosophical Library. (Original work published 1947)

Taylor, A. E. (1956). *Plato: The man and his work*. Cleveland: World Publishing Company.

SELECTED READINGS

Beauchamp, T., & Bowie, N. (1983). *Ethical theory and business* (2nd ed.). Englewood Cliffs, NJ: Prentice-Hall, Inc.

Brinton, C. (1990). *A history of western morals*. New York: Paragon House.

Facione, P., Scherer, D., & Attig, T. (1991). *Ethics and society*. Englewood Cliffs, NJ: Prentice-Hall, Inc.

Hall, B. (1986). *The Genesis effect: Personal and organizational transformations*. New York: Paulist Press.

Jacobs, J. (1989). *Virtue and self-knowledge*. Englewood Cliffs, NJ: Prentice-Hall, Inc.

Peters, T. (1987). *Thriving on chaos: Handbook for a management revolution*. New York: Alfred A. Knopf.

Sergiovanni, T. (1990). *Value-added leadership: How to get extraordinary performance in schools*. New York: Harcourt, Brace, Jovanovich.

P A R T

2

Improving Instruction and Learning

PART TWO is about the role of the principal as an instructional leader—as a person who gives guidance to and facilitates the accomplishment of persisting pinnacles of curricular and instructional excellence.

Greer and Short lead off in chapter 6 with an examination of what it means to restructure the learning environment. They lead readers through an exploration of schools that are in various stages of restructuring and detail the activities of the principals in those schools. What their research indicates works and does not work are investigated. They discuss what the principal needs to know and do in order for successful restructuring—restructuring that results in a positive learning environment—to occur.

Cordiero's focus in chapter 7 builds on the concepts presented previously. She writes of the "learning organization" and the principles on which such organizations are developed. Using the metaphor of the principal as play director, she describes the dynamics of program reform.

In chapter 8, Tanner provides both an historical anchor and a futuristic enactment as she sets forth the "practical affairs" confronting the principal who wants to improve instructional performance. She writes of collaborative ventures in the improvement of teaching and learning. She also writes about the processes involved in promoting higher order thinking.

Few problems are as severe as those perceived by the first-year teacher. Thrust at once into the real-world environment of helping others learn, some learners who are more reluctant than eager, the first-year teacher's days are fraught with frustration. "Going home for good by Thanksgiving" is more than an aphorism; it's a stark reality for many new teachers. How the principal can nurture new teaching talent is the subject that Weise and Holland address in chapter 9. They describe the needs of novice teachers and provide guidance to the principal about how to work effectively with new staff so that the new staff succeed. Recent research is reported that describes how solid support bases can be established so that novices can develop their instructional skills.

And what of the students themselves? In chapter 10, Achilles and Smith focus on such fundamental issues as attendance, school climate, teacher and parent involvement, health, clear mission, and a caring environment as essential aspects in stimulating high academic performance of "pupils."

6

Restructuring Schools

John T. Greer
Georgia State University
Paula M. Short
Pennsylvania State University

Overview

It is hard to visit any school in the United States without encountering a restructuring project. Reading programs are being "restructured." Teacher responsibilities are being "restructured." Site-based management is "restructuring" the school system. In short, restructuring appears to be every educator's preoccupation.

This chapter focuses on the principal's role in restructuring efforts. We begin with a perspective of restructuring that we have used in work with two Danforth Foundation Projects over the past four years (Greer & Short, 1993; Allen, Greer, & Slawson, 1990). The first of the projects was an investigation of the teacher empowerment process used in nine schools across the nation. The second is an ongoing study of multi-grade, multi-age classrooms in 17 schools throughout the State of Arizona.

After discussions of what we believe restructuring to be, and not to be, attention is focused on the preliminary understandings principals should have before embarking on a restructuring effort. The most important of these understandings is the degree of autonomy granted to the school by school district officials.

Descriptions of principals, teachers, and schools that have been involved in restructuring efforts occur throughout the chapter. The people and settings described are those with which we have worked or are working in the two projects just mentioned.

In the concluding section, we have combined the reflections of the principals with our observations, to provide guidelines for principals contemplating a restructuring effort. The one generalization we make is that no restructuring effort will be successful without the leadership and enthusiastic support of the building principal.

Conceptual Frame

What Is Restructuring?

Restructuring means changing the basic structure of the school. Many have ignored this dictionary definition and applied the word to mean any change in programs, instructional techniques, or teaching arrangements. Serious students of change in schools have shown a lack of consensus regarding the term's definition (Liberman & Miller, 1990; Schlechty, 1991). Widespread confusion and lack of understanding have resulted from the many definitional perspectives.

For clarity, we have adopted the definition of restructuring noted in the preceding paragraph. The roots of the definition can be traced easily to the classical era of organization theory when theories were divided into two camps: the structuralists and the functionalists. Probably the two leading structuralists were Weber (1947), a German economist, and Fayol (1949), a French mining engineer. While neither theorist focused exclusively on the structure of the organization, their primary interest appears to have been on how to structure an organization so it could operate both efficiently and effectively. Other early theorists, such as Gulick (1937) and Taylor (1916/1987), were more interested in "what the executive does," or what was the best way to perform a particular task, and for those reasons were known as functionalists.

Our definition of *restructuring* is not in conflict with the perspectives of Liberman and Miller (1990) and Schlechty (1991) cited above. Indeed, we have welcomed their insights because the entire process of restructuring a school is better illuminated by their efforts. Yet the primary act remains *changing the basic structure of the school*.

To be more specific, most American schools are organized in a manner reminiscent of the assembly line in a factory. Twenty-five or thirty students and a teacher work together for about nine months. Then the group moves along to another teacher and the nine-month cycle is repeated. Should a student fail to keep up with the other members of the group, he or she is recycled through the entire nine-month experience, often with the same teacher.

We believe restructuring means changing this assembly-line production model. In our work in Arizona, restructuring has meant (among other things) the adoption of a more static model where students of various ages work with the same teacher over a multiple-year period. As the student demonstrates the acquisition of the knowledge, skills, and behavior expected of students in the setting, he or she moves individually to the next multi-age, multi-grade setting. Groups are not moved; individuals move as they are ready.

The focus on the progress of the learner in the Arizona Project is not a new concept. Its roots can be traced to The Winnetka Plan of the 1930s and the Continuous Progress programs of the late 1960s and 1970s (Kapfer & Ovard, 1971).

Several critical differences exist between the Winnetka Plan and the Continuous Progress plans of the past and the Arizona program. The essential distinction rests on the fact that the Winnetka and Continuous Progress plans conceptualize the learning programs for individual students as linear. The Arizona Program does the following things:

1. It places great emphasis on the local systems' adaptations of the Arizona Essential Skills required of all students in the state (combining the essential skills with additional outcomes deemed important within the district).
2. It depends on the students learning from one another. The metaphor of the family is used to describe the dynamics of the Arizona classrooms. Young students enter the classroom, and older students leave. Learning takes place in a variety of settings: in small groups where all the students share a common learning need (regardless of age), individually (with and without technology), and in occasional total group settings (usually to take advantage of some current event or issue).
3. It uses a variety of assessments of student progress (portfolios, observational data, writing examples, and so on) are used to document the progress and learning needs of each student. The planning of the subsequent activities for the student then proceeds according to the accumulated performance data.

In addition to the Arizona Educational Restructuring Project, many other plans are under experimentation that change the basic structure of the school. Some middle and high schools have turned away from their graded formats in favor of multi-grade arrangements. In middle schools, one may find the expected interdisciplinary teams serving heterogeneous, multi-grade groups of students. A number of high schools have dropped their traditional department formats in favor of "schools within schools" arrangements focused on the particular needs of subpopulations of students. Still other secondary schools are experimenting with "house plans" designed to offset the negative effects of school size on students and to foster the students' sense of belonging to a subunit of the total school.

Such fundamental changes to a school's structure permit us to declare the school *restructured* according to our definition. After the school has been restructured, however, we see the ideas of writers such as Barth (1990), Lieberman and Miller (1990), and Schlechty (1991) as being very helpful. Further support for this dual approach to restructuring can be found in the organizational development and change literature. Writers such as Schmuck and Runckel (1985) and Miles (1965) have demonstrated in their research the importance of focusing a school's change efforts on the *process* as well as on the objective(s) of the innovation.

What Restructuring Is Not

The definition of *restructuring* we use in this chapter excludes many innovations commonly called "restructuring efforts" because the basic structure of the schools has not been changed. In the schools where these innovations occur, students continue to be divided by age into grades, and traditional departments continue to function as they have since the school was founded. We reject calling such efforts, worthy though they might be, *restructuring projects*. Undoubtedly, they are innovations, and many are extremely beneficial to students, but they should not be popularized as examples of restructuring.

Empowerment, as we have used the term in our research, is a process that results in the shared governance of a school. Teachers and other stakeholders share in making the basic decisions governing the operation of the school. Areas that may be included are the decisions related to the school's programs, instruction, budget, personnel, students, and so on.

The sharing in such vital decisions does not automatically mean the structure of the school is changed. In our recent nine-school study of the empowerment process (Greer & Short, 1993), bona fide empowerment efforts resulted in only one restructured school.

A Vignette: Abraham Lincoln High School

At Abraham Lincoln High School in Denver, the decision makers of the school (the principal, teachers, and community leaders) decided that the existing department organization of the school did not serve the students well, nor did it enable the school to offer programs the students in the school needed. The decision was then made to abandon the departments in favor of a "schools within the school" structure. The result was "schools" for targeted groups of students. Lincoln's Alternative Milestone Program (LAMP), for example, is a largely self-contained "school" designed to serve high-risk students that otherwise would be unlikely to graduate from Abraham Lincoln High School. The School of Global Studies is designed for a heterogeneous group of students and features an interdisciplinary team of teachers and thematic teaching.

Without a lengthy description of Abraham Lincoln High School and all its change efforts, suffice it to say that the school's multiple-year empowerment effort brought about a restructured school, unique in the Denver Public School system. Nevertheless, one could not describe the empowerment process as *restructuring*. In this case, empowerment was the catalytic process that brought about a restructured school.

What Does the Principal Need to Know?

School Autonomy

In our experience with the empowerment project and the present restructuring project in Arizona, we have come to the conclusion that the most important thing the principal needs to know is the degree of autonomy the district officials are willing to give the school. This generalization also applies to principals of site-based management schools. The question is, "How much freedom do we as a school have to make the decisions necessary for the change we are contemplating?"

This is a far more complicated question than it appears. One aspect is that the word *freedom* implies resources. After all, what good does it do for a school to have a bright and shiny new idea about a better system for teaching reading to the youngsters attending the school if no monies are available to purchase the materials and employ the personnel needed to implement the experimental program? It may be easy for district administrators to give lip service to a school's autonomy, but actually making such autonomy possible is a different matter.

A more difficult aspect of the autonomy question is what an autonomous school does to the district's sense of coordination and order. A myriad of questions falls from this dimension. How can we be called a *system* if schools are allowed to establish their own programs? How do we maintain control if we allow schools to go their separate ways? How do our district's administrators supervise schools that are all different? How do the superintendent and the board of education members know what is going on?

We offer no answers to these questions other than to say that autonomous schools shatter the traditional school district's pattern of order, supervision, and control. Many have argued for this eventuality because the students being served in the schools of a district differ dramatically from one school attendance area to another. Some neighborhoods are affluent and stable; others are poor and transient. Yet the traditional district's operation is based on bureaucratic principles with the basic assumption being that every school's students exhibit relatively similar education needs.

The arguments favoring a school's autonomy are essentially based on logic. It makes good sense for each school in a district to make the decisions necessary to best serve the learning needs of its students. But logic alone does not answer the questions related to strong district level coordination and control. There are legal ramifications as well.

Most states expect boards of education to serve as agencies of the state in their local communities. The boards are to ensure that all students receive the type and amount of education other students throughout the state receive and that each student will receive his or her share of the state's education resources. Such objectives are made difficult if not impossible when individual schools are allowed to be too autonomous. Equity for all students cannot be guaranteed or maintained.

Finally, after all the logical and legal arguments are heard and (with any luck) overcome, autonomy is not assured. An uncoordinated district just doesn't look right. It violates all we have been taught as school administration students about school system structure and coordination. It also violates the centralized control assumption that undergirds every board of education policy statement.

The basic question whose answer a principal must know about restructuring is, "How much autonomy will I have should I and my staff decide to initiate a restructuring project?" Closely associated with the first question is one regarding the help or hindrance the school can expect if it embarks on a restructuring effort. It is one thing for district officials to grant autonomy only to have lower-ranking staff members make the effort difficult if not impossible.

During the course of the empowerment and restructuring projects, we have seen several instances of this problem.

- In one school, two teachers representing different grade levels volunteered to serve as a two-teacher team and experiment with the multi-age, multi-grade concept. Their principal's request to the superintendent was denied because the district's outside curriculum consultant felt that not all schools of the district were ready for such experimentation.
- In another school district, the school was withdrawn from the statewide network of experimental schools by the district superintendent who felt the school was departing too widely from the norm established by the other district schools.

These two examples represent what can happen at the beginning of a project. Schools are vulnerable at other times as well.

Two schools in our empowerment project learned to their dismay, after they had been in the project for several years, that their empowerment efforts had not been appreciated by all sectors of the district. In one instance, the principal's recommendation for a vacant assistant principalship of the school was totally ignored by the board of education which then appointed its own candidate. In another district, the superintendent in public presentations went out of his way to praise the accomplishments of the district's second high school at the expense of the project school.

Other examples could be cited by nearly anyone with innovation experience. Whenever an individual school strikes out on its own with an innovation or other creative practice, there is pressure within the district to pull the offending school back into line with the district's other schools. In open systems theory, the phenomenon is known as *maintaining equilibrium*. It is the tendency for multiple-unit organizations to keep the units in some sort of balance. When this balance is upset by the actions of one or another of the units, the system moves to pull the offending unit back to its original position, so the balance of the system is restored.

A Vignette: Gilbert Elementary School

One might ask, "Can anything be done to offset this tendency of a system to pull back an innovative school?" A school in our restructuring project provides some insight to the question. The school is Gilbert Elementary School in Gilbert, Arizona, and the principal is Sheila Rogers. The school is completing its second year with multi-grade, multi-age classrooms. The grades included to date are first, second, and third. In 1992-93, additional classrooms for grades four and five will be added.

Sheila Rogers came to the principalship after 17 years of successful teaching in the Gilbert schools. Her first administrative post was serving as the acting personnel director of the district for one year. She then was appointed principal of Gilbert Elementary School.

One of Sheila's principals during her teaching years was the person who presently serves as the assistant superintendent for instruction. Earlier, the assistant superintendent and Sheila had taught together, so the assistant superintendent knew Sheila very well and trusted her leadership abilities.

Her year in the personnel office at the central office had provided Sheila with the opportunity to work closely with the superintendent, the assistant superintendent for instruction, and members of the board of education. Here again, she was able to demonstrate her competence as an educational leader and to earn the trust of the central office administrators and the board members.

Early in her tenure as principal of Gilbert, Sheila was approached by two primary teachers who wanted to have multi-age, multi-grade classrooms. Their request was welcomed by Sheila who had felt for some time that changes were necessary to serve the school's youngest children more effectively. When Sheila took the request for multi-age, multi-grade primary classrooms to her superiors, both the assistant superintendent and the superintendent readily agreed to the experiment *even though, if successful, the school would depart from the district's standard pattern of instruction*. Here was a request for school autonomy that was not only honored but vigorously supported by the district's leaders.

Analyzing the Gilbert story, we make the following observations:

1. Sheila, through her years as a teacher, established herself as an effective classroom leader, one who was sensitive to the needs of students.
2. Sheila earned the respect and trust of those who one day would be her superiors.

3. The Gilbert experiment followed the dictum, "Think big but start small." Only three classrooms were involved in the initial experiment. The number was allowed to increase only after two years of experimentation.
4. The experiment was initiated by highly respected and effective teachers. These people sincerely believed that multi-age, multi-grade classrooms provide richer learning environments than traditional classrooms.
5. Sheila and her faculty have not advertised the experiment. They have reported their work to the board of education and have joined our project. But they have not lorded the success of their efforts over the other schools of the district. They have not drawn attention to their uniqueness. Thus it seems likely that the Gilbert experiment will succeed. Should others at some future time attempt to draw the school back into line by dismantling the effort, it will be done by those not presently serving as members of the board, the superintendent, or the assistant superintendent.

We have explored the issue of individual school autonomy at great length because we believe it is a facet of school restructuring that has been ignored by other writers. From our perspective, the authority of the school to make those decisions necessary is the prime ingredient in a successful restructuring effort. In the following section, we discuss other ingredients that have enabled the schools in our projects to initiate their restructuring efforts successfully.

Other Initiation Factors

In addition to possessing autonomy, the successful schools in our projects demonstrated a second quality that principals embarking on restructuring projects need to understand. Successful shared governance and restructuring efforts were largely grassroots efforts. At the very least, the projects began with the principal and several teachers discussing the possibility of a new look. In some schools, the idea came from a combination of people that included the principal, teachers, and members of the community (as was the case at Abraham Lincoln High School in Denver). In a few of the schools, the original idea came from members of the faculty. Typically, the originating teachers also volunteered to gather research and other literature about the idea, and agreed to be among the school's first experimenters with the new format (as was the sequence of events at Gilbert Elementary School).

Less successful were those restructuring efforts initiated by principals. In one instance, the teachers simply refused to support their principal's initiative and the effort collapsed. In several other schools, the principal initiated the innovative effort because the principal felt the superintendent or some other person *external* to the school wanted the school to conduct the experiment. Here also, the result was a lackluster effort, without enthusiasm on the part of the principal or the faculty.

In observing these successful and unsuccessful efforts, our conclusion is similar to the conclusion other writers have made. The motivation and commitment of faculty members to an innovation are enhanced when the faculty members are involved in the creation and planning of the innovation.

Community Involvement

Another observation from successful schools regarding the early stages of an innovation is the involvement of the community, particularly the leaders of the business community. The participation of such people can provide all sorts of benefits. Foremost among them is that the resources of the businesses are made available to the school. Nearly always, these resources are in the form of services and expertise rather than financial resources.

In many respects, these supports are more valuable than financial resources, because the business people bring to the table years of experience searching for better ways to organize, challenge, and motivate. Finally, the early involvement of the business community helps overcome the autonomy problems discussed earlier. In our project, schools that reached out early to the business community were the schools that became almost "untouchable"—at least for the period of time the project was being conceptualized, planned, and implemented. Whether the immunity status can be sustained on a permanent basis is a different question.

Our feeling is that long-term survival of an experiment depends more on the widespread adoption of the innovation by other schools of the district than on the political power the school has acquired in the early stages. Nevertheless, early involvement of business leaders has proven invaluable in our project schools because of the businesses' ideas, expertise, and status in the community.

Role of the Principal

An interesting observation we have made during the course of our work is the role of the principal. Principals seem to adopt one of three positions regarding the innovation:

1. They may play the role of the person in charge (usually by saying repeatedly that, after all, they are the ones who will be held responsible if things go wrong).
2. They may consider themselves a member of the team, with a single voice just like any other member. This is not to say that the principal's expertise and wisdom are withheld from the group or that when offered, they are not readily accepted. What it does mean is that the principal is a contributing member to the team but not the sole authority. The principal might very well find her or his suggestions rejected in favor of some other approach.

3. Finally, a principal might adopt a hands-off role. In this case, the principal does not engage in the work of the group. Some principals operating in this mode will accept and support whatever the group wishes to do, so long as it does not contradict mandates of the district. Other principals will say they will support only those plans with which they agree. The rationale for this stance is always the principal's ultimate responsibility for everything that goes on in the school. Plans that depart from the principal's thinking are simply not allowed to go forward.

The Process

Because the empowerment study is completed and the restructuring project in Arizona is still in process, our observations about what happens during the course of a project are taken largely from the empowerment study. We believe that these observations apply to any restructuring project where decisions are made jointly by the principal and faculty.

It should be kept in mind that the shared governance and restructuring changes we are discussing require several years to plan and implement. When successfully implemented, the changes alter the school's culture. The attitudes, values, and behaviors of the school's members are changed to reflect the new reality. Instead of the decisions being made by one person, the school has decisions made by all or many of its members. After such changes are put into place, there is no going back because the new culture is a culture based on shared decision making.

Framing

School faculties view opportunities to change differently. In our empowerment study, we noticed that the faculties of all of the schools wanted to know more about empowerment when they first encountered the concept. After reading articles and obtaining the information they needed, the teachers and administrators approached the task of establishing an empowered school from one of two quite different perspectives. At most of the schools, it was decided that the way to become empowered was to decide on a schoolwide project. The pervading thought was that the participation of the entire staff in making the necessary decisions for the project would provide the experience everyone needed in the techniques of shared decision making.

At several schools, a decision was made to view empowerment as an evolutionary process that required new roles, rules, and relationships. Focusing on the educational needs of their students, these schools concentrated on developing new staff leadership, new communication networks, and new decision patterns to provide for the student needs.

After observing the two groups of schools, we concluded that the schools who viewed empowerment as an evolutionary process progressed more rapidly than those that chose to learn about the process by selecting a project. Part of the reason for the slower progress of the "project" schools was the time it took for the school to decide which project to pursue. A second, less visible, reason was that a project was a relatively "safe" activity. Members of the staff could take risks, trying out new roles on a project being planned. Put off until a later date were the tough, culture-changing procedures that characterize the empowered school.

Culture-Changing

The "process" schools began to work almost immediately on the culture-changing procedures. Though difficult, the strategy focused everyone's attention on new roles and relationships. Feelings, attitudes, and values were discussed openly, and accommodations were made. In the end, this early focus on the basic elements of the empowerment process enabled the schools to evolve more rapidly than the "project" schools.

Trust.   One of the easiest generalizations to make about shared governance is that people must trust each other. Our work in the empowerment project enabled us to factor out the various types of trust that must ideally be present in empowered schools.

The first trust relationship was mentioned earlier: district officials must trust the school to do those things necessary to enhance the learning opportunities of its students. Similarly, the school personnel must trust the district officials not to undo the work they have done or to reverse the decisions the school has made. It is a two-way street absolutely vital to the success of any restructuring effort.

Within the school, a type of trust not generally recognized is teachers and other staff members trusting themselves. Those of us in teacher education institutions believe we have been preparing professional teachers all these years. We also recognize that when the teachers are out on the job, they are often not given the authority to act as professionals. The instructional program is carefully prescribed, teaching strategies are standardized, and the teachers' days are specified by district officers. In short, teachers on the job are not encouraged to act like professionals at all. Their lives resemble those of assembly-line workers more than those of professional educators. Trust in one's ability to make independent and risky decisions is not a quality commonly found in today's teachers. The development of such trust requires time and the support of the entire school.

Closely related to teachers trusting themselves is developing trust in their principal. This is a two-way street, with the equal need for the principal to trust the teachers. Teachers need to trust the principal to allow them to experiment and to sometimes fail. In an empowerment process, this often means that the principal must allow teachers to make decisions that might not be the best decisions. It is only through making less than perfect decisions that people learn to make better choices. At the same time, the principal must learn to trust and support the decisions of the teachers *even when such decisions are not the decisions she or he would make.*

Our experience with schools going through the empowerment process is that teachers typically make decisions the principal would make. Often enough, however, they make decisions that are even more effective in helping students than those the principal would have made.

The final type of trust relationship we found was teachers trusting other teachers. This may seem a bit strange because teachers' lives seem to be forever spent in committee meetings. Actually, however, the life of the typical teacher is a solitary life. The teaching performance takes place in the isolation of the classroom. Rarely do teachers find themselves in positions in which they expose their competencies and deficiencies to colleagues. Overcoming the attitudes that the isolated classroom encourages and establishing an atmosphere of acceptance and trust requires great amounts of time and patience.

Communication.   A characteristic we found in schools undergoing a major restructuring project was a bewildering communication network. Messages and communiques in a traditional school flow in predictable directions: vertically and horizontally. This is not the case in schools evolving as shared governance schools. Communications fly in every conceivable direction and follow every available pathway. In one of the meetings of our empowerment schools, a teacher reported to the group of teachers and principals that on one occasion, she had called a faculty meeting without checking with the principal. The principal sitting next to her acknowledged the truth of the statement and indicated how startled he was by the teacher's action. Nevertheless, he survived the experience, and the evolutionary process was forwarded by the episode.

Risk Taking.   Changes of the magnitude being discussed in this chapter call for a level of risk taking considerably different than that found in the typical school. Risk taking in most schools means trying out a new idea or technique. In the successful schools of our projects, we found teachers and other staff members exposing their basic professional beliefs to the critical scrutiny of their colleagues. It was in such public arenas that the real work regarding shared governance could take place. The hidden values of the school's culture that were known and understood by all the members had to be studied openly and forthrightly. Only after such scrutiny could it be decided whether the value or strongly held belief was suitable for the school's new and emerging culture.

Critical Incident.   In all the schools of the empowerment project, we found some critical incident that affected the process and led to a more empowered school. The critical incident might have been a negative incident, such as the sudden resignation of the principal, or a positive incident, such as the recognition of the school's efforts by the governor of the state. Whichever the case, each of the nine schools of the project could point to a particular incident that helped it realize its success.

Critical Mass.   We found in our project schools a phenomenon similar to that found in the descriptions of other major change efforts. At some point, the number of "true believers" reaches a point where the change effort develops a momentum of its own. No further effort of the school's leadership is required for the project to move forward. We called this point the *critical mass* to reflect the self-sustaining nature of subsequent events.

We also found that the critical mass was attained much more quickly in some schools than in others. The most important variable that determined when the critical mass was attained was the principal's behavior. When the principals could let go easily and encourage wide participation in the decisions and governance of the school, the critical mass was reached early in the experiment. When principals insisted on having the final word, the process bogged down—and in several cases, was never realized.

The other variable that affected when the critical mass was achieved was the decision tradition of the school. Several of the schools had long histories of former principals making the decisions of the school. Moving to a shared decision and governance model in such settings was slower because "it had never been done that way."

Other Process Observations.   Some of the nine schools were more successful in accomplishing their empowerment objectives than others. All of the schools, however, reported that they had made great strides toward becoming empowered. Specifically, all schools believed that they had elevated the levels of trust among their staff members. They also believed that their communication networks were more effective than those they had had before the project. Finally, all schools were able to document how the learning opportunities of their students had been improved because of the project.[1]

Guidelines for Principals

The following guidelines use both question and suggestion formats. The question format seems to be better suited for those items the principal needs to determine or consider. The suggestion format seems to be more useful for highlighting items that have not been as fully developed in earlier sections of the chapter. Both types of statements reflect insights of the principals in the projects and our observations collected in school visits and project conferences. The guidelines are divided into two categories: pre-implementation and implementation. The first group focuses the reader's attention on preexisting conditions and considerations that enhance or inhibit the future success of the innovation. The second

---

1.   Such documentation was a requirement of all schools from the beginning of the project.

group is composed of factors and considerations that appeared during the course of the innovation.

Pre-implementation Phase

1. Autonomy
   - How much freedom does the school have to depart from the district's standards (curriculum, organization, budget, instructional methods, and so on)?
   - How permanent is the district's promise of autonomy?
   - Are waivers from statewide mandates and standards required? If so, have they been obtained?
   - Have arrangements been made with state and regional accrediting associations regarding an experimental designation for the school?
2. Early staff involvement
   - If the innovation is the principal's, how quickly will members of the staff be brought in to improve the idea, debug it, and make plans for implementation?
   - If the innovation originated with the staff, how will the idea be nurtured, expanded, debugged, and implemented?
3. Community involvement
   - When will business leaders and others from the community be invited to join the planning team?
   - What level of participation is expected (planning, advice, resources, and so on)?
4. Parents
   - When will the parents be included in the deliberations? (This needs to be early enough so their ideas can be used in the design of the innovation.)
   - What level of participation will be expected of parents?
5. Project chronicler
   - Who will serve as the gatherer of all the information related to the project? (The person should be available to attend all the meetings. Usually the person is a faculty member or administrator.)
   - What project data (planning documents, meeting minutes, reports, summaries of surveys, and so on) need to be collected?
   - How shall the story of the project be reported (brochures, articles, presentations at meetings, and so on)?

Implementation Phase

1. "Think big, start small"
   - In major change projects, begin with a few volunteer teachers and allow the experiment to evolve. Later, expand project with other volunteer teachers.

- When working with an empowerment project, begin with a small, representative group working on process, strategies for expansion, and so on. Later, encourage other volunteers to join group.

2. Volunteer teachers
   - These must be strong teachers, highly respected by other faculty members, parents, and the community.
   - They must be committed to the experiment and eager to make the experiment a success, *whatever it takes*.

3. Communications
   - Expect an unpredictable communications network to emerge.
   - The principal may not always be included.

4. Trust relationships
   - Trust relationships are improved when an effective communication network exists, all members believe in the worthiness of the project, and all have worked together "in the trenches."

5. Risk taking
   - Risk taking on substantive issues becomes more evident as the communication network becomes more effective and trust relationships are strengthened.

6. Critical incident
   - In all likelihood, some positive or negative event will occur during the course of the project that will coalesce the staff. Expect such an event, and use it to forward the ends of the project.

7. Critical mass
   - Keep track of the number of staff members that truly support the project. At some point, the successful project will have enough support to move ahead on its own. The principal then becomes a facilitator of the group rather than its leader.

8. Fatigue
   - Enthusiasm for the project will wane even among the truest of believers. The principal should anticipate this eventuality and be prepared to expend additional resources to keep the project moving forward.

9. Turnover
   - Expect and prepare for key staff members leaving during the course of the project. It often comes as a surprise that new leaders are able to assume the leadership of a project without disrupting the effort.

10. Celebrations
    - We often fail to celebrate our successes. Principals should constantly be looking for opportunities to organize celebrations of the school's successful efforts.

SUMMARY

This chapter has been a reflection of our work in two, long-term studies of empowerment and restructuring experiments. The first was a three-year, national study of the empowerment process that evolved in each of nine schools scattered across the country. The second study, being conducted in the State of Arizona, is a study of multi-age, multi-grade classrooms at 17 school sites. The studies were funded by the participating school districts, our universities and Northern Arizona University, and the Danforth Foundation.

From the studies, we first described what the word *restructuring* means to us and how we used the term in our studies. We stated that the word *restructuring* meant changing the basic structure of the school. We then focused on what proved to be the most important pre-implementation factor of our studies, *autonomy*. Without a high level of autonomy, the restructuring efforts of a principal and staff are placed in serious jeopardy.

Following discussions of the pre-implementation factors that proved to be important in our project schools, we shared the insights of the project principals and other observers about the implementation process itself. Schools engaged in major empowerment and restructuring projects are vastly different settings than the typical school.

We concluded the chapter with questions and suggestions for schools contemplating major change projects. The list is not exhaustive, but it contains the items found to be important in our project schools.

THEORY INTO PRACTICE: A CASE STUDY FOR REFLECTION

Annette Franklin, the principal of Pinetree Middle School, was attending her district's monthly principals' meeting. Communicating a high level of enthusiasm, the district's superintendent, Dr. Bruce Green, announced that the previous evening, the board had approved his recommendation to give greater authority to the schools of the district. This authority would allow the schools to make their own instructional program decisions. Dr. Green's announcement created a stir among the 30 principals of the district. Everyone seemed to be asking, "What's Bruce talking about?" "Have you heard anything about this before?" The responses to both questions were, "I don't know." and "No."

Dr. Green continued, "I know that this catches some of you by surprise, but I decided we needed to react quickly to the State Department's interest in site-based management. I also want us to respond quickly to our board's action last night."

After a brief pause, he went on, "I hope you will return to your school and set up a meeting with your staff as soon as possible. I would like to report to the board at its work session in two weeks that our schools are hard at work developing their plans for the future. At next month's regular meeting, I would like Jerry [Associate Superintendent for Instruction] to present a summary of our efforts to the board."

Bruce concluded by saying, "Jerry will be available to answer any of your questions as you develop your plans. I know this will be a 'lighthouse' effort for the other districts of the state."

GUIDING QUESTIONS

1. If you were in Annette's position, what would be your first reaction to Dr. Green's announcement?

2. What questions would you want answered by Jerry or Dr. Green before meeting with your staff?

3. As principal, what would you say to your staff? What strategies would you use as you lead the staff in developing Pinetree's plan?

4. What principles would serve as your guides as you begin your change project?

REFERENCES

Allen, P., Greer, J. T., & Slawson, A. (1990). *Arizona education restructuring project: A proposal to the Danforth Foundation*. St. Louis: Danforth Foundation.

Barth, R. S. (1990). *Improving schools from within*. San Francisco: Jossey-Bass.

Fayol, H. (1949). *General and industrial management* (C. Storrs, Trans.). London: Pitman.

Greer, J. T., & Short, P. M. (1993). *The empowered school district*. Newberry Park, CA: Corwin Press.

Gulick, L. (1937). Notes on the theory of organization. In Gulick, L., & Urwick, L. (Eds.), *Papers on the science of administration*, pp. 3–13. New York: Institute of Public Administration.

Kapfer, P., & Ovard, G. (1971). *Preparing and using individualized learning packages for ungraded, continuous progress education*. Englewood Cliffs, NJ: Educational Technology Publications.

Lieberman, A., & Miller, L. (1990). Restructuring schools: What matters, what works. *Phi Delta Kappan, 71*(10), 759–764.

Miles, M. (1965). Planned change and organizational health: Figure and ground. In R. Carlson, A. Gallaher, Jr., M. Miles, R. Pellegrin, & E. Rogers (Eds.), *Change processes in public schools* (pp. 11–34). Eugene, OR: CASEA.

Schlechty, P. C. (1991). *Schools for the 21st century: Leadership imperatives for educational reform*. San Francisco: Jossey-Bass.

Schmuck, R., & Runkel, P. (1985). *The handbook of organizational change* (3rd ed.). Prospect Heights, IL: Waveland Press.

Taylor, F. (1987). The principals of scientific management. In Shafritz, J. & Ott, J. *Classics of organization theory* (2nd ed). Chicago: The Dorrey Press. (Reprinted from *The Bulletin of the Taylor Society*, December 1916)

Weber, M. (1947). *The theory of social and economic organization* (A. M. Henderson & T. Parsons, Trans.). New York: Oxford University Press.

SELECTED READINGS

Barth, R. S. (1990). *Improving schools from within*. San Francisco: Jossey-Bass.

Block, P. (1991). *The empowered manager: Positive political skills*. San Francisco: Jossey-Bass.

Bolman, L. E., & Deal, T. E. (1991). *Reframing organizations: Artistry, choice and leadership*. San Francisco: Jossey-Bass.

Flinders, D. J. (1988). Teacher isolation and the new reform. *Journal of Curriculum and Supervision, 4*(1), 17–29.

Gerth, H. H., & Mills, C. W. (Eds.). (1946). *From Max Weber: Essays in sociology*. New York: Oxford Press.

Greer, J. T., & Short, P. M. (1993). *The empowered school district*.

Lieberman, A., & Miller, L. (1990). Restructuring schools: What matters, what works. *Phi Delta Kappan, 71*(10), 759–764.

Miles, M. (1965). Planned change and organizational health: Figure and ground. In R. Carlson, A. Gallaher, Jr., M. Miles, R. Pellegrin, & E. Rogers (Eds.), *Change processes in public schools* (pp. 11–34). Eugene, OR: CASEA.

Murphy, J. (1991). *Restructuring schools: Capturing and assessing the phenomena*. New York: Teachers College Press.

Sarason, S. (1991). *Predictable failure of educational reform*. San Francisco: Jossey-Bass.

Schmuck, R., & Runkel, P. (1985). *The handbook of organizational change* (3rd ed.). Prospect Heights, IL: Waveland Press.

Schlechty, P. C. (1991). *Schools for the 21st century: Leadership imperatives for educational reform*. San Francisco: Jossey-Bass.

7

The Principal's Role in Curricular Leadership and Program Development

Paula A. Cordeiro
University of Connecticut

"Organizations are to be sailed rather than driven."
  James March

"No matter how favorable the winds, if you don't have a rudder you can't reach port."
  P.A.C.

Overview

A principal intern writing in her journal about the frustration of not being able to find time to reflect commented, "Toilets are leaking, asbestos is flying and parents are calling about typos on the honor roll." The literature on the principalship is replete with such examples of "putting out fires." However, the firefighting metaphor of the principalship is an image from the past. It is time to take a different perspective of what principals should do. Researchers such as Mintzberg (1973), Martin and Willower (1981), and Kmetz and Willower (1982) have described the principalship as local, verbal, choppy, fragmented, brief, controlling, and varied. Perhaps their findings were due to the methodology they employed. If we break up a principal's life moment-by-moment as they did, it is likely that we will see the parts. But do we see the whole? How do the pieces fit together?

These researchers' descriptions and analyses of what principals do barely touch on the principal's role in program development. As Fullan (1991) pointed out when discussing the works of Crowson and Porter-Gehrie (1980) and Morris, Crowson, Hurwitz, and Porter-Gehrie (1981), their ". . . 'natural' description of what principals do rarely mentions attention to program changes" (Fullan, 1991, p. 148). I will argue in this chapter that most research on the principalship has not captured the underlying threads that bind together successful principals with their schools. Those threads are tightly woven through the principal's role in program development, a role requiring the principal to be a generalist who through collaboration distributes and coordinates leadership opportunities.

This chapter is organized into four sections. The first section discusses the administrator's role in program development within two frameworks. The first framework deals with Senge's ideas (1990) on "learning organizations" and how these ideas might be applied to schools. The second framework focuses on the importance of the principal understanding the sources and processes of change in relation to program development. The second section describes principal competencies and how school administrators, through their roles in program development and implementation, can foster learning organizations. This is followed by discussion in section three of a model for program development. A metaphor of a play director is used to illustrate the role of the principal in program development. The fourth section explores the role of program development for two principals—one elementary and one high school—and the role of change in the development of their programs. The chapter ends with a case study for reflection.

Conceptual Frame

Since the effective schools movement began in the United States, we have tended to talk about the "key characteristics" of effective schools, and in teaching we have discussed "effective teaching practices." Although the dialogues created by these models of innovation have been interesting, they have produced more harm than good. Just as a person does not become a leader by copying a leader, a school does not become effective by adopting effective characteristics or an effective model. Let us begin by discussing Senge's ideas (1990) on practicing a discipline which ". . . is different from emulating a 'model'" (p. 11).

In his book *The Fifth Discipline*, Senge (1990) describes the new skills needed by leaders to build what he calls "learning organizations." In a *learning organization*, the leadership continuously provides opportunities for generative learning to occur. As people learn, their abilities expand. An organization that generates learning is able to grow and develop in an infinite number of ways. Most organizations are adaptive but not also generative. Schools have become proficient at adapting models: students begin failing a class, and schools provide afterschool remediation programs; students drop out, and schools begin dropout prevention programs. Thus, the school deals with the symptoms of the problem rather than with the underlying causes. Perhaps the student is failing the class because of lack of motivation for irrelevant, outdated content taught by a weak teacher. Perhaps students drop out for economic reasons—they are too tired to be at school at 7:30 after working the night shift. Many schools adopt programs but do not integrate them into the overall curriculum. Most schools' responses to dropout prevention tend to be adaptations to educational, societal, and/or economic conditions. Schools become reactive institutions rather than proactive or catalytic in their approaches to dropouts. Purposeful opportunities for generative learning to occur are not part of the administration's plan. Instead, a Band-Aid approach, to tutorial programs for example, is yet another metaphor.

The Principles of Learning Organizations

Learning organizations are not models that can be copied and simply transplanted to other organizations. The uniqueness of each organization precludes this; nor is it sufficient to adapt a model to that uniqueness. Many schools today adopt and adapt models, stopping at this point rather than striving to generate learning.

For example, schools using Sizer's Coalition of Essential Schools approach can be found throughout the United States. Schools planning to adopt this approach provide many staff development opportunities for teachers. They might read books as *Horace's Compromise* (Sizer, 1984) and *Horace's School* (Sizer, 1991). Next the staff begin to adapt the model for their school. Thus far, the school has taken on a role of adaptive learning. The staff has adjusted the model for such factors as the size of school, the size of teaching staff, and the grade levels included. However, have opportunities for generative learning been built into the infrastructure? If a model is approached idiosyncratically, rather than as a generalizable one, then there is a far greater likelihood that generative learning will occur.

For Senge (1990), the leader of a learning organization is not the archetypical charismatic great leader. The leader is designer, teacher, and steward, or as Hughes (chapter 1) describes the leader: artist, architect, and commissar. The leader in a learning organization is "responsible for *building organizations* where people are continually expanding their capabilities to shape their future—that is, leaders are responsible for learning" (Senge, p. 9). These organizations generate learning just as a cell grows and multiplies as it is nourished. Senge proposes that this requires new skills, including systems thinking, personal mastery, mental models, building shared visions, and team learning. When these skills converge, ". . . they will not create *the* learning organization but rather a new wave of experimentation and advancement" (Senge, p. 11). An organization will never *be* a learning organization, just as a person will never be Maslow's self-actualized person. Instead the practicing itself, for better or for worse, is the goal. For Senge, these five new skills woven together form learning organizations.

The Skills of Learning Organizations

According to Senge (1990), there are five skill areas requisite for learning organizations. The first skill, *systems thinking* and *systems theory*, comes from the behavioral and social sciences. School administration borrowed much of the early knowledge base from organizational and behavioral theory. The works of Getzels and Guba (1957), Parsons (1960), Etzioni (1961), and Carlson (1964), among others, focused on social systems theory. Systems theorists placed a major emphasis on an analytic approach. They focused on unifying principles that serve to integrate knowledge and understanding from a wide array of fields. They argue that the boundaries of social systems are not easily identifiable and within each system are subsystems. If we look at individual pieces of a mosaic, we do not see the entire pattern. Similarly, in schools there are classrooms in which, although change can take place in them individually, if that change is not somehow woven into the larger system, then its impact is considerably diminished, if not misunderstood. The body of knowledge generated by these scholars helps show the pieces and patterns making up the mosaics. Systems thinking can be used as a conceptual framework for clarifying the mosaic.

While systems thinking is the first component of a learning organization, a second component is personal mastery. *Personal mastery* refers to "dominance over people or things," but it also includes having a "special level of proficiency" (Senge, 1990, p. 7). Senge considers personal mastery to be the cornerstone of the learning organization—its "spiritual foundation." Personal mastery is defined as "the discipline of continually clarifying and deepening our personal vision, of focusing our energies, of developing patience, and of seeing reality objectively" (Senge, p. 7). Bennis (1989), who refers to this as "passion, energy and focus," states, "Real leaders, of course, persist, because they are unwilling to settle for anything less than the best—in themselves, their organization, and their employees" (p. 109). It is the collective commitment of the organization that is the driving force behind the learning organization. The challenge for the leader is to harness and nurture that commitment so it generates future commitment.

The third necessary component for learning organizations are called *mental models*. "Mental models are deeply ingrained assumptions, generalizations, or even pictures or images that influence how we understand the world and how we take action" (Senge, 1990, p. 8). Barker (1987) refers to this as thinking in paradigms. If we hold certain perceptions, theories, or ideas and do not reflect upon these assumptions by challenging and questioning them, then there is a greater likelihood they will not change. By collaborating with others and sharing our ideas, we will be forced to challenge our mental models. In another way, it can be viewed by what Einstein said, "Our theories determine what we measure" (cited in Senge, p. 175). Perhaps it has been as succinctly stated as possible by the bumper sticker "QUESTION ASSUMPTIONS." Often, because of our conflicting mental models, change or innovation is slow or unable to occur. Senge stresses the importance of "turning the mirror inward; learning to unearth our internal pictures of the world, to bring them to the surface and hold them rigorously to scrutiny" (p. 9). How can school leaders provide opportunities for this to take place in schools? Traditionally, this behavior has neither been encouraged nor nurtured. Firefighting administrators do not hold the solutions.

The fourth required skill is the ability to build a shared vision. With the complexity of today's organizations, it is folly to believe one person—a CEO, superintendent, or principal—can alone create and implement a vision. In education, we often talk about the vision of the principal or superintendent. We write school mission statements that include "the vision." One must chuckle at the inherent paradox. How can an organization, a social system as complex as a school, have a vision or mission that is created by one person—the administrator? Personal vision is crucial, but in a school setting it is the building together of the vision— the true dialogue among the parties—that shapes the vision. It is the commitment of all involved, because they want to be, not because they are forced, that helps the collective vision emerge. Nanus (1989) believes that developing a vision is crucial to an organization. "You need not necessarily set out on this journey alone," he comments. "Often it is wise to draw from the organization" (p. 105). We know also that goals, and especially their means of implementation, become clear only as we attempt to achieve them.

The final component of a learning organization is team learning. This concept is reminiscent of the Gestaltists: "the whole is more than the sum of its parts." If the people in our organizations are collectively discussing issues, then Senge states they will "discover insights not attainable individually" (1990, p. 10). Looking historically at education from the one-room schoolhouse to the large, sometimes gigantic, buildings that today house dozens of classrooms, we realize the complexity of today's schools can no longer fit the "I go in my classroom and shut the door" approach to teaching.

For example, while working with a mid-size, public, suburban high school in its third year of having a variety of councils that have been given considerable decision-making latitude, I observed one council responsible for staff development that was developing strong group-processing and decision-making skills. At times, the teachers on this council were unsure of their direction, but through their collective discussions and with occasional administrative guidance, they were beginning to realize the potential power they held. At the council meetings, ideas were being generated. Those ideas were questioned, debated, and further developed. This group contained people who tried to understand classroom life. Great commitment was taking place simply because people who would be directly affected were involved. The complexity of the programs in our schools and the expanding boundaries of the classroom, make team learning the keystone in the learning organization.

Understanding Change

Throughout the 1980s, the plethora of national reports described the changing environment of our schools (for example, *Latino Youths at a Crossroad*, 1990; *New Voices: Immigrant Students in U.S. Public Schools*, 1988). Demographic changes were usually discussed first. This was followed by the waves of reform. Educators are constantly struggling with questions as these: How do we deal with the inequities in school funding? What are the best ways to provide growth opportunities for teachers? What are appropriate ways to measure student achievement and other forms of growth?

Change is a constant in the field of education. Yet, as we look historically at the many issues and concepts of importance particularly in relation to program development, we experience déjà vu. Perhaps through conceptually understanding how change occurs, we can increase our awareness as to why program development issues have succeeded, failed, or experienced only partial success. Having such an understanding would help the school administrator to better predict and explain changes with additional confidence.

Change is an elusive concept. Hughes and Achilles (1971) point out that, "Change is not a thing. Change is a *process*" (p. 841). The research on change (Berman & McLaughlin, 1976; Fullan, 1991; Klausmeier, Rossmiller, & Saily, 1977; Rosenblum & Louis, 1979; Yin, Herald, & Vogel, 1977) describes various stages that all innovations go through as they become institutionalized. One of the principal's many roles in the change process is analyzing where the staff is in that process.

How can we be sure when change has actually occurred? For example, a large high school in which I was working had five levels or tracks for placing students. There were three major divisions: college-bound, business/vocational, and remedial/Special Education. Within the college-bound group (the largest group) were three types of classes: AP English, Honors English, and English. Due to pressure by parents of students enrolled in English, the school made some changes in the scheduling of students. As a result, English classes that originally enrolled only college-bound students included some business/vocational students. The written curriculum was not altered. Several school administrators, counselors, and teachers were pleased with this change. They felt some of the barriers to heterogeneous grouping had been broken. The school newspaper and district newsletter described the changes that had taken place. In actuality, however, little if any change had occurred. Teachers' attitudes and expectations had not been impacted substantially; instructional strategies had not changed. Why was this change made? Did achievement levels increase? The answers are unknown because ongoing evaluation was not a part of the change process.

Approaches to Change

School changes may be a result of political, authoritarian, and/or democratic processes. Political change may be the election of new school board members. For example, a new board member may have campaigned emphasizing a particular issue (say, greater safety in the schools). Thus during the board member's tenure, educators in the district can anticipate a variety of changes (additional security guards, metal detectors, and so on). Authoritarian change might come in the form of a mandate from a principal. A democratic process to change could involve a volunteer group focusing on a particular issue.

Change can occur incrementally, emerging or developing over time, or it can be thrust upon a school. Incremental change often takes place in schools. For example, suppose the teachers at a school would like to adopt a different reading approach. The literature is investigated, contacts are made, and visits to model programs take place. The change is locally controlled and initiated. School systems that encourage these innovations have formal mechanisms allowing for this growth to occur. Not only does the system have a hierarchy with tasks and functional groupings for implementing and anticipating, but it also has a flexible structure for doing what it does not yet know. This flexible structure allows all players within the organization to participate and develop. There are numerous ways to generate opportunities for growth and development in schools. School curriculum councils with representatives on district curriculum councils are one potential way of generating learning within an organization.

A Model for Program Development

Let us explore a model for school program development (see figure 7–1). The model involves four types of approaches to change:

- top-down (mandate)
- adoption model
- change agent
- catalytic events

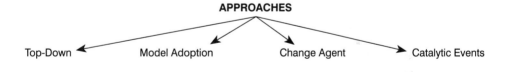

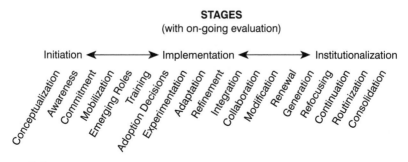

Figure 7–1
A Model for Program Development in Schools

The model also involves stages that occur as change takes place in program development, as shown in figure 7–1. Finally, the players who are involved and the factors affecting program development will be detailed.

Top-Down Approach

Top-down strategies can be thought of as technological. These may be caused by federal and state mandates, accreditation recommendations, central office recommendations, and various other events. Improvement is sought by training teachers in new techniques and then holding them accountable. McNeil (1985) states that, "Top down strategies involve a change in some part of the technology of the school—a testing program, computers, mastery learning—[it is] the most likely element open to immediate influence from outside the school" (p. 196).[1] However, a major concern with top-down strategies involves teacher commitment. Technological changes are often circumvented by uncommitted teachers. Teachers learn to put on "dog-and-pony shows" for evaluators.

A top-down change strategy has become a prevalent mode of change since the 1970s. Federal special education and bilingual education legislation have impacted school districts throughout the United States. Political action groups (PACs) initiated these changes. First, PACs pressed for federal legislation; then laws were passed by Congress. Through pressures exerted at the federal level—grant stipulations and threats to withhold federal funds—states passed matching laws. Next, state departments of education entered the scene by writing regulations requiring school compliance. Some top-down federal legislation resulting from court decisions has only been partially successful, like the ruling in *Brown v. Topeka Board of Education*.

In spite of a plethora of state-level lawsuits, many districts are still reluctant to desegregate, perhaps because compliance involves strong commitment by a variety of people active in desegregation, integration, and equity issues. These change directives have also allowed local districts considerable latitude in implementation, course design, and delivery. For example, in pockets around the country, urban districts and their surrounding suburban districts are forming partnerships using magnet schools as a vehicle for complying to state desegregation laws. Whether this is one of the better solutions remains to be seen. Nevertheless, change is taking place, albeit slowly.

---

1. Madeline Hunter's mastery teaching model, prevalent during the 1980s in school districts throughout the United States, is an example of change in the technology of the school (TTAS, 1984). Training in Hunter's model often included workshops, presentations, videotaping, and so on. In some states, teachers were then evaluated using an instrument based on the principles in the Hunter Model.

Adoption Model Approach

A prevalent strategy for change in education, especially in the 1980s and predictably throughout the 1990s, is the adoption model. With this type of approach to change, a program is disseminated as an innovative package. It may have originated as a project or program at a university or research center. Some models provide little flexibility or opportunity for local adaptation, while others are based on principles rather than being curricular packages. As programs progress, they adapt to the particular school and begin generating on their own. The adoption of a particular model is an example of how program change can take place at the school-site level through a top-down strategy (although the change may also simultaneously be incremental). Examples of this include Comer's School Development Program, Accelerated Schools, Sizer's Essential Schools, Reading Recovery, and the Paideia Model (Comer, 1980; Levin, 1992; Sizer, 1992; Chapman & Turner, 1991; Adler, 1984). These models are being implemented in schools throughout the United States. They may have been brought into the school incrementally, but the decision to be an Accelerated School or a Coalition School came first, in most cases.

Change Agent Approaches

A bottom-up approach to change is individual teachers acting as innovators or change agents. Through their networking both inside and outside the school, these change agents stimulate innovation that usually starts in individual classrooms. For example, after attending a workshop, a teacher may begin using cooperative learning strategies in his or her classroom. Other teachers within the building become aware of this and may be motivated to experiment themselves. Perhaps the teacher does an in-service workshop or an expert is brought in. Incrementally, cooperative learning becomes an integral approach in classes throughout the school.

Another type of change agent approach can result from action research. *Action research* at the site level is another potentially powerful change strategy that can generate learning. A staff looking at its problems and considering alternatives can bring about innovation. Taba (1962) in her seminal work on curriculum development describes how curriculum development should take place and the importance of action research: "It should start with concern and problems identified by teachers and [they should] study these problems scientifically, diagnosing their causes and factors" (p. 483).

Catalytic Events Approach

Change can occur as the direct result of a catalytic event. Outside pressures may exert change, or there could be political actions from within. For example, discontented teachers could petition the board for the removal of the principal or an unhappy middle-school teacher who refused to participate in the afterschool activities program might contact the union to intercede on her behalf. Or, consider such a happening as the schoolyard gun spree that took the lives of five school-age children in Stockton, California, in 1989 (Jennings, 1989). That episode was one of the worst acts of violence that ever occurred on a school campus. As a direct result of this event, school districts throughout the country reviewed their school-safety policies and related curricula. The National School Safety Center, the National Association of Elementary School Principals, and a host of other organizations have produced and/or further developed school safety guidelines and gun safety curricula as a direct result of this event.

Another example of change taking place because of a catalytic event is the impact of the spread of AIDS on school curricula. The majority of school districts in the United States have included AIDS-education in their curriculums. High school student Ryan White, who became a spokesperson for education about AIDS and later died of the disease, played a key role in asserting the rights of children with AIDS to attend classes alongside their peers. His high visibility helped change attitudes toward opening school doors to children with this disease.

A final example of change resulting from a catalytic event is the changing of the school curriculum due to a racial or bias incident in the school and/or community. In recent years, multicultural education has come to the forefront in districts throughout the country, in some cases directly due to local happenings. The event might be a gang fight at a mall, the shooting of one local youth by another, the desecration of the town's synagogue, or the harassment of homosexual students by their classmates. For example, the Fairfax County, Virginia, school board banned the verbal abuse of students on "matters pertaining to sexuality" (Districts, 1992). This ban directly resulted from district reports that intermediate-school students were being sexually harassed by their classmates. These racial, ethnic, and bias acts are catalysts for eventual curriculum change.

Stages of Change

Stages of change occur as a program develops. These stages are along a continuum from initiation through implementation to institutionalization; however, during development, various parts of the program can be at different stages (see figure 7–1). In addition, regardless of the approach to change, overlap may exist in these stages. The first stage is often referred to as *initiation* (Fullan, 1991). At this point, an awareness is developing. Forces are mobilizing, and the players are trying to conceptualize what the results of change will eventually look like. Questions at this stage might include these:

- What is this program about?
- Who will be involved and what role will they play?
- What training and resources do we need?
- Will this be appropriate for "our" students?

Although these questions may be asked throughout the development of a change, they tend to be crucial at the onset of the program. A principal who understands the change process realizes that these questions, and others, will be asked, although they may not be fully answered. Herein lies the ambiguity—what could be called "creative tension" (Senge, 1990). The principal knows where he or she wants to be, but those involved regularly remind everyone of where the school is now. Some might feel they are in a state of chaos, but the principal recognizes that as the program emerges, questions will be answered.

As the group moves toward implementation, other questions surface:

- Is it necessary to buy those materials?
- Could we try it in this class or grade and not in that one?
- Can we change a part that was not successful?
- Don't we need to get "that department" or "those teachers" or "that group" involved?
- How can this be integrated into the other curriculum?

As the school moves toward program institutionalization, many of these questions remain or will be answered only partially, but a host of new questions arise:

- We have been doing this, but it hasn't been appropriate. How can this be refocused?
- The teachers have been working on this for a while now. How can we renew and maintain their high levels of energy and enthusiasm?
- This program has changed over time, and I'm not happy with this part. How can we get back to our original ideas on this?
- We want this to continue because it was successful. How can we assure continuation?

Thus, programs develop in stages with various program parts at different points on the continuum.

Ongoing Evaluation

Evaluation is not something done at the conclusion of a program. Instead, like change, it is a process. As shown in figure 7–1, evaluation is occurring simultaneously with the growth and development of the program.

To evaluate an innovation, the players involved in the development process need to focus on critical questions. These questions vary among programs. However, certain questions are crucial to the ongoing evaluation of any program or innovation:

- Why are we doing what we are doing? (a goals question)
- What are we doing? (a process question)
- Can it be done a better way? (an evaluation question)

For example, if an elementary school has a Reading Recovery program, those three questions should be a part of the ongoing discussions of the parties involved. Then the two or three critical questions unique to this program might be these:

- What outcomes are expected for the Reading Recovery student?
- What instructional strategies work best with Reading Recovery?
- What is the long-term impact of Reading Recovery on the reading skills of students?

After the critical questions have been agreed upon, the next step is to choose techniques for gathering data to answer those questions. At this point, the reader may see a tie to our earlier discussion about change agent approaches to program development through action research. If opportunity is afforded to a staff to continually look at problems and consider the alternatives, then evaluation can be built into the fabric of the program's development. Guba and Lincoln (1985) refer to this type of evaluation as one that is "simultaneously diagnostic, change-oriented, and educative for all the parties involved" (p. 141). Through the players and stakeholders involved in the program changing and refining their ideas, the process becomes an educative and generative one.

Elaborate evaluation techniques and unreasonable data collection methods should not be the evaluation focus. Instead, rich feedback information for refocusing, refining, and modifying the program and curriculum could be collected through a variety of ways including (but not limited to) the following:

- continuous discussion and reflection by those involved
- systematic data collection of students' progress using authentic assessment techniques
- longitudinal follow-up of student progress (possibly through record keeping, surveys, and/or interviews)

The crucial issue is that evaluation can no longer be viewed as something done at the end of a program. In most cases, programs do not suddenly stop one day. Instead, evaluation need not be as complex because the two or three critical questions are being addressed throughout the program's development.

The Principal's Role in Distributed Leadership

To be a principal is to be a generalist. Although many principals have expertise in certain areas, most principalships do not require a principal to be a curriculum specialist, an assessment expert, or a financial wizard. The level of the school, its size, and community expectations have an impact on the principal's role, but on the whole the nature of the job requires a generalist. English (1986) states, "Principals help design curriculum, but not as their major curricular responsibility. Their function is the management of the curriculum" (p. 29). Thus, while principals are leading and managing, they are arranging for things to get done.

Managing program and curriculum changes requires skilled leadership. There are specific competencies needed for this leadership. These competencies fall into four categories:

- technical competencies
- human resource competencies
- political competencies
- architectural competencies

Technical competencies include skills in curriculum development, discipline mastery, understanding of group process, and knowledge of the social and educational values underlying educational decisions. Depending on the school and district's characteristics, the requirements of the principal's competency in these areas differ. In most schools, principals do not write the curriculum; instead, they oversee its development. If they have expertise in a particular content area, their role in writing the curriculum may be greater; however, facilitation of the process and supervising to ensure the curriculum is implemented are more often their roles. To perform well in those roles, the principal needs to understand group dynamics and the community's perspectives about the issues.

The *human resource competencies* are complex and involve many variables. They deal with issues as these: What are the human factors affecting the participants? What degree of change can participants handle at various points in the development? What obstacles need to be overcome? How can people be motivated to get optimum benefit from their ideas and skills? What are the attitudes and perceptions of the participants? How can change be paced so that these attitudes and perceptions are balanced? How can a climate conducive to productive, satisfying work be continued through the development of the program? Thus, human resource competencies place great emphasis on interpersonal issues.

Political competencies involve ways to manage the inevitable competition for resources and power in all organizations. With limited resources, principals will either have to vie for the same resources or develop ways to collaborate and cooperate in sharing those resources. A savvy principal is tuned in to the power structure within the schools in the district and runs a gauntlet as he or she maneuvers through the system. According to Ubben and Hughes (1992), the principal knows "both how to work in the system and how to work the system" (p. 8). (See also Hughes, chapter 1.)

The importance of the principal having political competencies has been recognized by the National Association of Elementary School Principals (NAESP, 1991). Under the rubric of political management, NAESP lists six proficiencies as crucial to principal effectiveness. One key proficiency involves applying "effective strategies for dealing with the political issues and forces that impinge on the school's operation" (p. 18).

Architectural competencies involve a framing of roles and relationships that allow organizations to get things done. Architectural skills include what Hughes refers to as "a decided sense of direction and goal orientation" (chapter 1). They deal with issues as these: Who will be playing a major role in this? At what point will other parties become involved?

The Players—Distributed Leadership

A variety of individuals and groups play important roles in program development. Program leadership and the curriculum development aspects of program development emerge from the ranks of all the stakeholders in the school and the school district including administrators, specialists (curriculum developers, assessment experts, content area specialists, and so on), teachers, outside experts, students, community groups, community leaders and other individuals, and guidance personnel. At different points, players take on different roles, although the primary stakeholders are teachers and administrators. Thus, there is a distributed form of leadership.

Teachers do not buy into an idea simply because the principal tells them they must. This is where the principal uses skills from all four of the competencies. It might be necessary to deal with questions as these:

- In what ways can/should I as principal assist in the curricula needs? (technical)
- What obstacles will teachers need to overcome? (human resources)
- How can we get the resources we need? (political)
- Who would be the best qualified people to serve on the committee and how should the committee be structured? (architectural)

Factors That Have Impact on Program Development

While one school might adopt a model and have considerable success, another might fail with the same model. Why? What are some of the variables affecting program development that might lead to success in one school and little change, if any, in another? We will discuss nine critical factors in program development including the following:

1. *Scale of the program in relation to size of the school.* The principal needs to look at the school itself and the scale of the program. How many classes/grades will be involved with this program? If a model is being adopted, will it be phased in, or will all grades and classes be involved at once?

2.   *Nature of the program.* Is the program and/or curriculum the most appropriate one for that school? The philosophies behind certain programs often tend to match elementary, middle, or high schools, rather than the K-12 spectrum. Most schools adopting Comer's School Development Program are elementary. This is similar for Levin's Accelerated Schools and Gardner's Project Spectrum, while Ted Sizer's Coalition of Essential Schools Approach and Mortimer Adler's Paideia Model are geared toward high schools.

3.   *Players involved.* Who will be involved and what will their roles be? Will this eventually require involvement of all teachers in the school? What if some teachers don't buy in? Is there philosophical agreement amongst the stakeholders about the program?

4.   *Community expectations.* If one class in a grade level is involved and another is not, how will parents view this? Or, if significant changes are being made in the health curriculum in areas as AIDS-education and sex-education, for example, how will the community-at-large react?

5.   *Resources needed.* Program development may involve new resources and certainly will require the reallocation of existing resources. What resources presently exist for this program? How can those resources that are not available, but are needed, be secured? With whom will we need to collaborate to accomplish this?

6.   *Community and school demographics.* The demographics of the school and community, as well as the community's location, are other factors to be considered in program development. Rapidly changing demographics might force the school to take a close look at various areas of the curriculum. Does the school still offer only French even though it is located in an area with a growing Spanish-speaking population? Does the curriculum sufficiently deal with issues of marine science with the district being located in a city with an economic base tied to the sea? Does this program match the community's values and goals?

7.   *Types of incentives.* Does the school want to adopt this model because it will promote its image in the community? As a teacher, why should I support this when it means more work for me? Will this program help the students in my classes? Too often programs are adopted with little advance preparation simply because it "sounds like something we should do."

8.   *Timeline for the program's implementation.* If changes are needed immediately, then the school's leadership team needs to address the issues that will not have a chance to be addressed over time, as they would be with an incremental approach. Commitment often becomes a major issue when awareness, conceptualization, and player's roles are not reflected upon.

9.   *Monitoring of the program's development.* Principals themselves often play a crucial role in this monitoring, although all stakeholders should be included.

Monitoring fuses all four of the competencies discussed earlier. Are those involved really doing what they ought to be doing? Is ongoing evaluation taking place? Did the school get the needed resources? Ways of monitoring might include: attending departmental or grade level meetings, communicating regularly with those who are implementing initiatives, asking teachers to communicate with the community via the school newsletter describing progress towards the program's goals, etc. Too often programs have failed or are diminished in impact because administrators fail to persevere in their monitoring of the program's development. This monitoring is a carrying out of the vision. Through the many ways of monitoring, stakeholders can be reminded of the direction of the vision.

Principal as Play Director

Compare the role of a principal in this learning organization called a school to the role of a play director. A play director works with many constituents: actors, designers, stage managers, producers, composers, choreographer, writers, and so on. Collaboration is a key aspect of the theater. However, the level of involvement of players differs at different points. Plays involve script writing and rewriting, auditioning, casting, costume and prop designing, lighting designing, composing, choreographing, rehearsing, acting, improvising, performing, recasting, managing, and so on. On some days, the director may work with the composer, while another day might be spent dealing with issues of stage management. As director Arvin Brown of the Long Wharf Theatre commented, "I still depend on a good stage manager, and I'm lucky to have worked with the best to help me sidestep certain problems in rehearsal that might accrue later" (Bartow, 1988, p. 27). It is the role of the director to facilitate the collaboration of these disparate players. When the theatergoers sit in the audience watching the performance, the director has accomplished a multitude of tasks but is not the one to receive the accolades.

If a school is to be a learning organization, the principal's role should be that of the play director. The principal needs to anticipate and eliminate potential stumbling blocks and create a climate conducive for students' and teachers' learning, so errors can be tolerated because a safety net is provided. The principal needs to nurture opportunities for staff to learn the skills for collaboration. According to director Zelda Fichandler, "We have to teach ourselves and each other the art of collaboration, 'co-laboring' in order to express a collective consciousness" (Bartow, 1988, p. 114). The principal must find ways to provide the necessary resources be they fiscal, technological, or pedagogical, but this can only be done in collaboration with others. Finally, the principal needs to foster the development of teams collaborating within the school as well as with individuals, groups, and organizations outside the school. However, for the principal—the play director—to direct his or her school, understanding the process of change is crucial.

Vignettes of Program Development

Given the school as a "learning organization" and what is known about change, how can programs in schools be best divulged? What should the school principal's role(s) be in this development? We will discuss these questions by taking a look at two principals: one elementary and one high school. These principals have successfully provided leadership in program development. Change has occurred in their schools. At the same time, they have played a crucial role in creating learning organizations.

A Vignette: Fuller Elementary School

Ron Eckel is the principal of Fuller Elementary School in Gloucester, Massachusetts. After being asked by his superintendent whether any elementary schools in the district were interested in Howard Garner's Project Zero, Eckel decided to investigate Garner's research. In an interview he stated, "I decided if we were heading in this direction as a district I needed to be an educational leader for my teachers. . . . It was a contagious excitement, a spark, a catalyst that began and then other people started buying into it and getting as excited as I was" (Cordeiro, 1991). Eventually he and some of the school's staff decided to further explore multiple intelligences and various assessment techniques.

Teachers went through training at Harvard and began applying Gardner's ideas in their classrooms. In describing what they did, he commented, "Eventually they [the teachers] did what had never been done with Gardner's work. They took the research theory and applied that to a practical model and wrote the curriculum thus creating a program that had at its center multiple intelligence theory" (Cordeiro, 1991).

Ron described his role in the development of this program:

> My job has definitely been to provide pedagogical expertise, but more to provide moral support and almost a checking in once in a while. I go to a lot of their meetings, but I'm not there for all of them. (Cordeiro, 1991)

At a later point in the program development, Ron helped to secure the resources for teachers to get further training, "So three teachers here are now trainers and implementation advisors for the other six kindergarten teachers around the city." Ron also discussed how the nature of the other schools would mean the implementation of the program would differ: "The model that will be used in some of the other schools will be different because if there's only one kindergarten teacher, while Fuller has several, that collaborative nature is not automatically built in." Thus, the adoption and adaptation of the project could result in a very different program at other elementary schools within the district. Ron discussed the importance of the principal working with parents and other community groups. He referred to his role as one of a constant catalyst. Whether it's a new group of parents who have just come to the district or a new teacher, I encourage them. It's a sort of collegial supervision.

Teachers see me as a resource. . . . The biggest thing I hope to see here is a support for innovation. I can come up with a new idea as well as any of the teachers can, but I need to support their new ideas. It's a harder struggle. So I focus on whatever ways I can make their professional lives easier to concentrate on and do what they've been hired to do. I need to be a rusher or the blocker—trying to keep their mission as pure and as safe and as uninterrupted as possible by trying to get through all that morass of paperwork and other things which interrupt their teaching and planning time. I need to leave the actual idea generating to them in its pure form without the outside political pressures. (Cordeiro, 1991)

Ron and his staff are reaching the institutionalization stage for some program aspects. They are addressing questions as these: Should the entire school become involved in the program? When will the other teachers receive their training?

A Vignette: Windham High School

Don Berkowitz is the principal of Windham High School in Willimantic, Connecticut. Due to a perceived need by the administration and staff, Don initiated race/culture seminars that have been in existence at WHS for more than 10 years. The purpose of the seminars is to address those racial and cultural issues perceived by the participants to be of importance to the school and community. There are seminars for two different groups: one group consists of students, and the other is school staff. Seminars are scheduled at camps or similar facilities and usually last two nights and three days. There are group facilitators for every five to seven persons. Group members discuss, role-play, debate, and get to know each other. Each seminar develops an action plan to address various racial and cultural issues in WHS and the community. Participants set specific activities and objectives as well as an evaluation to ensure that the plan is carried out. Berkowitz has attended every student seminar since the inception of the program:

Every seminar has been a learning experience for me. It's similar to what a coach develops. I know I can draw upon this group if there's a problem in the school at a later point. Participants and former participants become a school support group. (Berkowitz, 1992)

Like Ron Eckel, Don sees his role as ensuring that resources are available so seminars can take place every year. During the seminar itself, he said, "I like to be the logistics manager" (Berkowitz, 1992). This provides him with opportunities to work with student groups when it is their turn to cook. It also allows him the opportunity to visit with the various groups—home group, task group, and large group—rather than focusing on one group for an entire seminar. Don also discussed some modifications the program has taken on over the years. "The adult seminars have now been expanded to include all schools in the district," he commented (Berkowitz, 1992).

According to Berkowitz (1992), "This expansion has limited the number of high school teachers who can participate in a seminar at a given time." In addition, approximately five students from one high school in the area are invited to attend each of the WHS student seminars. Although he believes this change has been a positive one, he does not feel comfortable with the adult seminars. "I don't like the idea that the adult seminars are district-wide. There's less impact on WHS." The program has been institutionalized, but Don commented, "I would like to see a refocusing."

These principals recognize the problems generated by change and the inherent uncertainty that accompanies programmatic development. They find comfort with the tension because they realize that through building and developing work teams, marshalling resources, eliminating obstacles, and providing opportunities for reflection in practice, their mutual goals will be accomplished.

SUMMARY

If a school is to be a learning organization, then what role will the principal—the play director—take in the development of programs? We have discussed learning organizations and the five key technologies necessary for their existence: systems thinking, personal mastery, mental models, building shared visions, and team learning. Next, we discussed the importance of principals understanding approaches to change and the stages its development take. Using the metaphor of the principal as play director, we discussed possible stumbling blocks, the art of collaboration (co-laboring), creating a climate tolerant of errors, and providing a safety net so the players are less fearful of taking risks. Babcock (cited in Tanner & Tanner, 1980) tells us that the principal's responsibility "is to marshall all the resources of the curriculum staff to improve the quality of the program in the school" (p. 669). Given the complexity of schools, the principals' role is to create when necessary; to marshall resources when necessary; to facilitate, coach, or protect; to communicate clearly; to build coalitions; and to be persistent. At various times, one or more of these roles will need to take precedence. Recognizing Senge's creative tension is the key. Accurate and complete pictures of the desired situation and the current reality are crucial to success.

In addition, we detailed the four competencies—technical, human resource, political, and architectural—needed by principals to manage program development. The leader of an organization that generates learning—a learning organization—will do what Kanter (1984) called *kaleidoscope thinking*. The dispersed fragments turned within the kaleidoscope reveal a variety of pictures. Principals having this vision of program development provide the direction for the play, so it can be performed with the synergy of co-laboring.

THEORY INTO PRACTICE:
A CASE STUDY FOR REFLECTION

You are the new principal of Coral Middle School. One day after school in early September, a serious racial incident occurs on school grounds between several students from your school and the city's other middle school. Several students are wounded and require medical attention. After a complete investigation that includes community groups, 11 students from the 2 schools were suspended.

During the investigation you discover that numerous racial, ethnic, and religious incidents have occurred over the years. In exploring the curriculum, you see little evidence of issues of cultural diversity being addressed. In addition, although the present population of the district includes only 10 percent African Americans and only 5 percent are Latino, the percentages of these populations, as well as of other racial and ethnic groups, are rapidly increasing.

In response to the information you collect during investigation of the fight as well as through exploring the curriculum, you decide that Coral Middle School cannot continue to be reactive in its approach to dealing with racial, cultural, and religious issues.

The Challenge: What would you do at this point? Develop an action plan.

GUIDING QUESTIONS

1. How should the school address multicultural issues in the curriculum?

2. What types of professional development opportunities for teachers do you recommend?

3. In what ways can all adults in the school be better prepared to deal with issues of cultural diversity?

4. What programs dealing with these issues already exist at the national, regional, state, and/or local levels? Which of them might serve as possible models that could be adopted and adapted idiosyncratically?

REFERENCES

Barker, J. A. (1987). Discovering the future: The business of paradigms [Video]. Lake Elmo, MN: Infinity Limited.

Bartow, A. (1988). *The director's voice*. New York: Theatre Communications Group, Inc.

Bennis, W. (1989). *Why leaders can't lead: The unconscious conspiracy continues*. San Francisco: Jossey-Bass Publishers.

Berkowitz, D. (1992, January). "Race/Culture Seminars." Presentation for the Manchester, CT, school system. Manchester, CT.

Berman, P., & McLaughlin, M. (1976). Implementation of educational innovation. *Education Forum, 40*(3), 345–70.

Brown v. Board of Education 347 U.S. 483 (1954).

Carlson, R. O. (1964). Environmental constraints and organizational consequences: The public school and its clients. In D. E. Griffiths (Ed.), *Behavioral science and educational administration* (pp. 262–276). Chicago: University of Chicago Press.

Chapman, J. W. & Turner, W. F. (1991). Recovering reading recovery. *Australia and New Zealand Journal of Developmental Disabilities, 17*(1), 59–71.

Children's Defense Fund. (1990). *Latino youth at a crossraod.* Washington, DC: Children's Defense Fund Publications.

Comer, J. P. (1980). *School power: Implications of an intervention project.* New York: Free Press.

Cordeiro, P. A. (1991, November). *Interview of Ron Eckel.* Unpublished audio recording.

Districts. (1992, November 18). *Education Week,* p. 2.

English, F. W. (1986). Who is in charge of the curriculum? In H.J. Walberg & J. Keefe (Eds.), *Rethinking reform: The principal's dilemma* (pp. 25–30). Reston, VA: NASSP.

English, F. W., & Hill, J. C. (1990). *Restructuring: The principal and curriculum change.* Reston, VA: NASSP.

Etzioni, A. (1961). *A comparative analysis of complex organizations.* New York: Free Press.

Fullan, M. (1991). *The new meaning of educational change.* New York: Teachers College Press.

Getzels, J. W., & Guba, E. G. (1957). Social behavior and the administrative process. *School Review, 65,* 423–441.

Guba, E. G., & Lincoln, Y. S. (1985). Fourth generation evaluation as an alternative. *Educational Horizons, 63*(4), 139–141.

Hughes, L. W., & Achilles, C. M. (1971, May). The supervisor as change agent. *Educational Leadership, 28*(8), 840–843.

Jennings, L. (1989, January 25). Schoolyard gun spree leaves 6 dead, 30 injured. *Education Week,* p. 5.

Kanter, R. M. (1983). *The change masters: Innovations for productivity in the American corporation.* New York: Simon & Schuster.

Kmetz, J. R. & Willower, D. J. (1982, March). *Elementary school principals' work behavior.* Paper presented at the annual meeting of the American Educational Research Association, New York.

Klausmeier, H. J., Rossmiller, R. A., & Saily, M. (1977). *Individually guided education: Concepts and practices.* New York: Academic Press.

Martin, W. J., & Willower, D. J. (1981). The managerial behavior of high school principals. *Educational Administration Quarterly, 17*(1), 69–90.

Mintzberg, H. (1973). *The nature of managerial work.* New York: Harper Collins Publishers.

McNeil, J. D. (1985). *Curriculum: A comprehensive introduction*. Boston: Little, Brown and Company.

Morris, V. C., Crowson, R. L., Hurwitz, E. & Porter-Gehrie, C. (1981). *The urban principal: Discretionary decision making in a large educational organization*. Washington, DC: National Institute of Education. (ERIC Document Reproduction Service No. ED 207178)

NAESP. (1991). *Proficiencies for principals*. Alexandria, VA: National Association of Elementary School Principals.

Nanus, B. (1989). *The leaders' edge*. Chicago: Contemporary Books.

National Coalition of Advocates for Students. (1988). *New voices: Immigrant students in the U.S. public schools*. Boston: National Coalition of Advocates for Students.

Parsons, T. (1960). *Structure and process in modern societies*. New York: Free Press.

Rosenblum, S., & Louis, K. (1979). *Stability and change: Innovation in an educational context*. Cambridge, MA: ABT Associates.

Senge, P. (1990). *The fifth discipline*. New York: Doubleday.

Taba, H. (1962). *Curriculum development theory and practice*. New York: Harcourt, Brace & World, Inc.

Tanner, D., & Tanner, L. N. (1980). *Curriculum development: Theory into practice* (2nd ed.). New York: Macmillan.

TTAS. (1984). *Texas teachers appraisal system*. Austin, TX: Texas Education Agency.

Ubben, G. C. & Hughes, L. W. (1992). *The principal: Creative leadership for effective schools*. Boston: Allyn & Bacon.

Yin, R., Herald, K., & Vogel, M. (1977). *Tinkering with the system*. Lexington, MA: D.C. Heath.

SELECTED READINGS

Adler, M. (1982). *The Paideia proposal*. New York: Macmillan.

Adler, M. (1984). *The Paideia program*. New York: Macmillan.

Apple, M. W. (1979). *Ideology and curriculum*. Boston: Routledge and Kegan Paul.

Barth, R. S. (1988). School: A community of leaders. In A. Leiberman (Ed.), *Building a professional culture in schools* (pp. 128–147). New York: Teachers College Press.

Bennis, W. (1989). *Why leaders can't lead: The unconscious conspiracy continues*. San Francisco: Jossey-Bass Publishers.

Children's Defense Fund. (1990). *Latino youth at a crossraod*. Washington, DC: Children's Defense Fund Publications.

Comer, J. (1988). *Maggie's American Dream*. New Haven, CT: Yale Child Development Center. (Provides information about School Development Programs.)

English, F. W., & Hill, J. C. (1990). *Restructuring: The principal and curriculum change*. Reston, Virginia: NASSP.

Hughes, L. W., & Ubben, G. C. (1994). *The elementary principal's handbook: A guide to effective action*, 4th ed. Boston: Allyn and Bacon. (See chapters 5, 6, 10, and 11 especially.)

Louis, K. S., & Miles, M. B. (1990). *Improving the urban high school*. New York: Teachers College Press.

McClaren, P. (1989). *Life in schools*. New York: Longman.

Nanus, B. (1992). *Visionary leadership*. San Francisco, CA: Jossey-Bass.

Senge, P. (1990). *The fifth discipline*. New York: Doubleday.

Sizer, T. (1984). *Horace's Compromise*. Boston: Houghton Mifflin. (Provides information about Coalition of Essential schools.)

Sizer, T. (1992). *Horace's School*. Boston: Houghton Mifflin. (Provides information about Coalition of Essential schools.)

Steinberg, Adria. (Ed.) (1991, January/February). Low achievers can catch up: Chapter 1 expects more of schools. *The Harvard Education Letter, 7*(1).

Ubben, G. C., & Hughes, L. W. (1992). *The principal: Creative leadership for effective schools*, 2nd ed. Boston: Allyn and Bacon (See chapters 2, 6, 9, and 10 especially.)

8

The Practical Affairs of Improving Teaching

Laurel N. Tanner
University of Houston

Overview

Principals—like doctors, teachers, and other professionals—are (or should be) continually trying to find and use more effective methods. Drawing on what is known of practice is their responsibility to the public. The word *profession*, after all, means "a public vow." But finding and practicing better methods is also a responsibility to themselves. It is a matter of personal as well as professional development, and it is impossible to separate the two.

When we read the memoirs of famous professionals, this becomes very clear. C. Everett Koop, former Surgeon General of the United States, recounts his experiences as a pediatric surgeon (1991, pp. 107–124). When he first began his career, the mortality rate for some congenital defects, such as esophageal deficits in which the baby's esophagus and its stomach are not connected, was 100 percent. Thirty-five years later, Koop and his colleagues at the Children's Hospital of Philadelphia had performed hundreds of operations for this defect and had not lost a full-term baby for eight years. Even the survival rate for premature infants who often weighed less than 2 pounds was 88 percent. Koop writes that this is "a wonderful testimony to what the advances in pediatric surgery and anesthesia had done for our children" (p. 107).

Koop tells of the personal as well as professional pleasure he got from applying the best that is known when he performed surgery. He continues to receive letters from grateful patients who received the benefit of new techniques and who never knew him because they were only days old when they met him; "Nothing gives me greater satisfaction," he tells us (p. 123). Memoirs such as Koop's provide inspiration for which we are grateful, whatever our professional field.

It is rare to find personal histories of professional achievements by school principals. More's the pity, for a good experiential account can provide counsel and guidance to other building-level administrators. As Robert Stake points out, "a good account invites them to recognize the circumstances never identical to the reader's own, but described in sufficient detail so the reader can decide their similarity and pertinence" (1991, p. 76). The fact is that such accounts *could* be written. The knowledge of how principals should work if they wish to help teachers find the best possible methods to improve teaching is increasing at an accelerating rate. What is more, many principals are already drawing on it as they work with school faculty, individually and collectively, in diagnosing and solving classroom and schoolwide instructional problems. I base this conclusion on what I have found working with prospective and practicing principals, both in university seminars and classes and in visits to schools—my lifeline to reality in education.

Yet much more is known about how to help teachers solve instructional problems than is now being acted on by building-level administrators. These new and not-so-new ideas are the lessons of research and experience combined. They are the approved practices in supervision, and the subject of this chapter. The first section of this chapter discusses the definition and nature of approved practices and their potential for improving teaching. The second section presents three major examples of practices principals can apply in working with teachers on the improvement of instruction. For each practice, the underlying theory and the ways in which the practice can be applied is discussed.

Conceptual Frame

Approved practices in educational leadership are those practices on which recognized authorities agree, and they are found in the professional literature. Approved practices may be based on the best available research evidence or based on demonstrated practical success in the field (Tanner & Tanner, 1987, p. 337). As an illustration, authorities in instructional supervision generally agree that the supervisory modes should be democratic-participative and the communication should be kept flowing between and among the faculty, administration, and supervisory staff (pp. 133–249; 337).

Practices from History

In thinking of approved practices in the professional literature, many people neglect the fact that these practices are not necessarily new ideas. The participatory-group system featuring highly cooperative teamwork in which professional groups feel responsibility for control was a popular way of working with teachers in the late 1940s (Campbell, 1952). The idea fell into disfavor in the years following Sputnik I (1957).

The tone of reform was that teachers were of low quality and site leadership was an inadequate approach to winning the space race. Myron Atkin, former dean of the School of Education at Stanford, noted that the message sent by the public to the schools over the next 30 years was that the "problems and their resolution are universal and that legislators will develop the 'solutions'" (1985, p. 55). In Atkin's view, a dangerous deficiency in efforts to improve public education through legislative prescriptions is that expectations by principals and teachers are lowered for developing creative ways of solving problems (p. 55).

Recently, Atkin's apprehension has been borne out. Some school districts have mandated the formation of teams of teachers who are to work collaboratively toward school improvement. Many principals report resistance from teachers who do not wish to be involved in such efforts to improve the curriculum. A frustrated elementary school principal in my seminar on organization theory put it this way: "These teachers got their training in the teacher-proof curriculum era—when teachers were expected to be technicians, not problem solvers. They have become demoralized with so many changes in direction and priorities, even collaborative programs where they have a chance to be professionals."

Implicit in the idea of teacher-proof curricula—total curriculum packages that preselect learning tasks and specify the amount of time to be spent on each task—is the notion of the teacher as a technician. Patience and support are needed if teachers are to begin to conceive of themselves as more than mere components in the production process of schooling. As Kirk points out, there is much work to be done to "redress this teacher-proofing" (1990, p. 411).

Some teachers and central office supervisors have identified a different problem: site leadership. There are principals who find it hard to work collaboratively with the school faculty in making improvements. They also received their professional training in a different era. But meanwhile, the conception that curriculum improvement is a problem-solving process involving the entire professional staff of the school never left the literature. It is part of the supervision legacy. It is found in the body of research, evaluation, and conception in supervision from which contemporary workers draw. It is an approved practice in instructional leadership.

Practices from Experience

Closely related to history, and in a sense a part of it, is experience. By *experience* is meant the efforts of educational leaders to improve the curriculum over the years. Experience enables us to avoid past mistakes and do better in like circumstances the next time (Tuchman, 1981, p. 249). Educators are often accused of reinventing the wheel. They do, and this is a problem, but they also learn from experience in the field and do better the next time, as shown by the following illustration.

Action Research.   The action research movement of the 1950s was based on the idea that staff development programs should furnish teachers with opportunities to improve the curriculum by investigating their individual classroom problems. The movement was a failure, much of the research was very poor. (Research conducted by teachers should meet the requirements of other scientific research.) Many people were quick to blame the teachers, but it seems reasonably clear that teachers received little or no guidance from consultants and statisticians. It has already been pointed out that there has been a renewal of interest in teachers conducting their own investigations into real classroom and schoolwide problems. The lesson of the action research movement was that along with the commitment to teacher participation in curriculum research must go a commitment to giving teachers the kind of help required to do the job. In its most recent form, action research involves teachers and researchers "who work together to solve school and classroom problems" (Clift, Veal, Johnson, & Holland, 1989, p. 2).

Teachers, individually and collectively, should be encouraged to conduct investigations into their classroom and school problems. The encouragement is, in itself, a professional behavior, and is an approved practice in the literature of supervision. Some teachers are interested in improving the curriculum through systematic experimentation. Ideally, the principal should possess research skills. He or she would then be in a position to help teachers acquire the research skills necessary to solve classroom problems. But this may not be the case at all, and the principal's role then becomes that of resource identifier: to help teachers identify persons with expertise. Universities can be helpful, as well as research personnel in the central office. (Teachers should also have the freedom to seek assistance on their own.)

Teacher Participation: Learning the Lesson the Hard Way.   An approved practice that springs from the experience of educational leaders over the years is this: teachers should participate in making the decisions that they are expected to implement. Some policy makers have had to learn this the hard way. The lesson has also caused hardship for teachers and principals. In the period from 1960 until 1990, arguments favoring centralization of curriculum decision making prevailed. The ultimate result, as two observers noted, was that "resources that might have gone into programs to help teachers become better decision makers were channeled into programs dedicated to the development of schemes for preventing teachers from making decisions" (Tanner & Tanner, 1980, p. 633). The objective was excellence in education. But the attitude of many state legislators, large foundations, and the federal government was that the goal of excellence would be achieved despite the teacher not because of him (or her).

Not surprisingly, some who held this position felt later that they had made a fatal error in judgment. They attributed the failure of some well-funded programs to meet expectations to two major factors: teachers' problems were not permitted to be the starting point for innovation, and teachers were barred from participating in critical decisions influencing their classroom work. An outstanding example of this radical change in viewpoint came from the Ford Foundation, which was a prime mover in shaping the managerial-efficiency policy in education in the 1950s and 1960s. The Foundation's push for the 1960s was the Comprehensive School Improvement Program, which included some 25 school systems. The program's purpose was to "create a climate congenial to innovations already developed" (Ford Foundation, 1972, p. 18), such as programmed instruction, flexible scheduling, and the major discipline-centered curriculum projects like the Physical Science Study Committee (PSSC) physics course and the Biological Sciences Curriculum Study (BSCS) course. Looking back on its efforts, the Ford Foundation reported that while the program had not met expectations, it furnished guidelines for future efforts to improve school programs. "One lesson gleaned," said the report, "was that *the people who are expected to put new programs into operation should participate in defining problems and developing solutions, and to do that often requires retraining*" (Ford Foundation, 1973, p. 3). The Ford Foundation had rediscovered an approved practice that had long been in the professional literature of supervision. It was there in the first place because curriculum specialists had had experiences similar to those of the Ford Foundation in working with teachers over time.

Education Is Not Alone.   Interestingly, the rediscovery of old practices is not confined to education; it happens in other fields as well, including medicine. For example, some surgeons have recently resurrected a 4,000-year-old technique for healing badly infected wounds. The treatment, which originated on the battlefields of ancient Egypt, involves packing the depths of the wounds with sugar. The treatment is used by some doctors today to overcome stubborn bacteria that are resistant to all modern drugs. Experts indicate that the treatment probably works because the sugar absorbs fluid from the wound, promoting tissue growth and dehydrating the infection-causing bacteria (Rosenthal, 1990, p. B7).

Discussing the treatment, one surgeon pointed out that "despite nearly 4,000 years of use, there are no comparative scientific studies of sugar dressings to be found" (Rosenthal, 1990, p. B7). Nevertheless, noted another surgeon, a remedy "sometimes comes more from history and experience. That's good, too" (p. B7). This is also true in the practical affairs of improving teaching. Some approved practices come from experience. They have demonstrated their effectiveness in the field. Others have been validated by research—case studies, historical studies, and other modes of research in addition to comparative studies. Certainly, as McGill (1991) points out, there is a "need for solid, field-based research" (pp. 261–262).

Practices from Research

Research on teaching, psychology, sociology, supervision, organizational behavior, and curriculum development all have made contributions to knowledge on the practical affairs of improving teaching. And one need not stop there. As Dewey counseled in *The Sources of a Science of Education* (1929), "The scientific content of education consists of whatever subject-matter, selected from other fields, enables the educator, whether administrator or teacher, to see and to think more clearly and deeply about whatever he is doing" (p. 75). In one sense, education is an eclectic field. It draws on knowledge from other disciplines to solve its problems.

But the problems are education's own. Dewey goes on to warn that the function of other fields is "not to supply objectives to him [the educator], any more than it is to supply him with ready-made rules" (1929, p. 75). Thus when confronted with the need to make schools more effective, educators drew on the literature on organizational behavior and rediscovered the potential of shared participation for improving organizational effectiveness (Likert, 1977; Tanner & Tanner, 1987).

Looking Outside: Breaking the Bonds of Isolation.   Literature reviews on the strategies used by effective principals for improving teaching are an excellent source of validated approved practices. One such practice is helping the staff obtain access to resources outside the school (Leithwood, 1990; Leithwood & Montgomery, 1982). Breakthroughs in solving problems can be made when the principal or teacher has the assistance and support of experts. Operationally, "outside" can mean one of many things: observing teachers in other schools, bringing in paid educational consultants (school systems spend enormously on this), or calling on central office supervisors for assistance. According to Loucks-Horsley and Hergert, in school districts that are sufficiently large, "a central office person, depending on role and authority, can play an outsider's role in an individual building" (1985, p. 5).

Another older and more fundamental approved practice merits attention: school systems should establish a central department of curriculum with responsibility for helping individual teachers in local schools with instructional problems, and for a continuous and comprehensive program of curriculum development. This is a very old practice—dating back to 1926. A group of well-known professors of curriculum conducted a survey to find out what effective schools do. They found that provision was made for teacher assistance within the school system itself—that outstanding school systems made certain that principals and teachers obtained the assistance of the system's own professionally prepared curriculum specialists (Rugg & Counts, 1926).

This idea runs counter to the recent prevailing educational fascination with site-managed schools that do everything by themselves and for themselves. In some cases, that scenario means scratching and scrambling for human resources that are in very short supply because the central curriculum department has all but closed up shop. Curriculum departments were established for a reason, and it is important for school principals and teachers to know what the reason was. That reason becomes clear when we examine the historical relation between school administration and curriculum development.

A Marriage for Life.   According to Cremin (1961), the curriculum field began as a subfield of educational administration. The story begins in Denver in the 1920s. Superintendent Jess Newlon developed a plan for curriculum revision in urban school systems that involved teachers in preparing courses of study that were tested experimentally. Cremin relates, "Once the Denver pattern caught on, it was obvious that specialists other than the superintendent would be needed to manage the process, and it was for the purpose of training such specialists that the curriculum field was created" (p. 213). Curriculum specialists were needed as consultants in the preparation of new courses of study and to coordinate the process itself.

The status of curriculum as an academic specialization has long since been established. In no way is it still a subfield of educational administration. And yet the relationship between the two is irrevocable, a marriage for life, as it were. The union has produced a sturdy offspring: instructional supervision, which is concerned not only with improving instruction but also with the interrelationships of the various subjects and learning activities that comprise the entire school curriculum. These twin concerns lie at the heart of the local school administrator's educational leadership role.

Developing a coherent curriculum and improving instruction are also concerns of the curriculum staff at the school-district level. In fact, curriculum articulation between levels of the school system is probably impossible without them. In a good deal of the literature, there is recognition that offering educational programs at continually higher levels depends enormously on the leadership of the principal. At the same time, however, the district's role has been downplayed, if not derogated. School and district are often treated as adversaries rather than as professionals cooperating to improve educational programs (Glatthorn, 1987, p. 103). The conception of *individual school* is often interpreted in the literature as *individual school district*. This is actually the case in Chicago under school decentralization legislation (Wong & Rollow, 1989). Each school is expected to look inward for its own curriculum improvement resources, without supervisory help from the district. In the early 1990s, this conception, coupled with an economic recession, led to reductions in central office curriculum staff in some cities. Indeed, the terrible fiscal bind in which many school districts found themselves was probably the unspoken justification for the new school-as-district-unto-itself fashion.

Teachers and principals need to draw upon resource people for ideas. In his study of schooling, Goodlad (1984) found that teachers were already too isolated.

The teachers "appeared, in general, to function quite autonomously. But their autonomy seemed to be exercised in a context more of isolation than of rich professional dialogue about a plethora of challenging educational alternatives," and Goodlad found further that teachers were isolated "from sources of ideas beyond their own background of experiences" (p. 186). The idea of school-as-district can only reinforce such isolation.

Principals and teachers should not be beguiled by the oddly popular notion that isolation from the central office and other schools leads to a more effective school program. Research seems to point to just the opposite: schools that make the most use of consultants in their curriculum improvement efforts are the most effective. One of the most important studies in this regard was the famous experiment in secondary education known as the Eight-Year Study (1933–1941), possibly the largest-scale longitudinal study ever undertaken in education (Tanner & Tanner, 1987, pp. 41, 340). The study was generated from the need to free the high school curriculum from college-dominance in order to establish an experimental basis for curriculum development.

Thirty schools that seemed interested in making creative changes in their curriculum were selected for the study. The curriculum staff of the Eight-Year Study served as consultants for the 30 schools. Staff members visited each school once in order to get mutually acquainted. After that, visits were made by invitation only. Some schools made little use of the staff, either because they were not actually doing much curriculum revision or because they felt that they could bring about even comprehensive change without a great deal of help. Other schools that were trying to totally reconstruct their curriculum asked for all the help that could be given them. The consultants did the following: they informed each school (those that called on them) of developments in other schools, made class visits, taught demonstration lessons, and conducted "curriculum clinics" (workshops). The study found that students from schools that made the most use of consultants were the most successful in college (Aikin, 1942).

One might argue that the teachers who asked for assistance were committed to the improvement of instruction and that this significant teacher factor was not controlled in the experiment. But special assistance for teachers (of which some took little advantage) was part of the experimental variable (Tanner & Tanner, 1980, p. 370). According to Aikin, those schools that took the most advantage of assistance made the most significant changes in their curriculums (1953, p. 14).

As has been indicated, even before the Eight-Year Study, a committee of experts in curriculum, which was then still a subfield of educational administration, pointed to the importance of provision within the school system of consultative help for teachers. Their study of curriculum development practices in school systems found that "instructional work very generally constitutes the major work in administrating the school systems" (Rugg & Counts, 1926, p. 440). This is—or should be—still true.

A Climate of Professional Inquiry.   When all is said and done, the most significant approach to improving teaching is probably not in specific strategies or staff development activities; it is the development of a spirit of inquiry in the staff, modeled of course by a principal who is an effective consumer of research and who works with teachers in applying the best available evidence to improve practice in the school and classroom. As Leithwood points out, the school culture must be based on the norm of professional inquiry (1990, p. 82). Establishing such a climate in a school may sound to the reader like a complicated matter and a very subtle one at that. It is neither complicated nor subtle. The main ingredient, as Dewey wrote early in the twentieth century, is that administrators and teachers are "possessed by the spirit of an abiding student of education" (1904, p. 16).

In 1904, Dewey made this observation:

> The willingness of teachers, especially of those occupying administrative positions, to become submerged in the routine detail of their callings, to expend the bulk of their energy upon forms and rules and regulations, and reports and percentages, is evidence of the absence of intellectual vitality. (p. 16)

Recently, educators have rediscovered the importance of a climate of intellectual vitality for school improvement. As a staff development specialist in a school district in New Jersey notes from his experience, a prerequisite for school improvement is the willingness of principal and teachers to look at their school's strengths and needs, to learn how to solve problems of the entire school collaboratively, and to use the best available knowledge to reach their goals. To be successful, such efforts must take place with a principal whose belief and skills support this kind of process (Squires, 1991, p. 477).

The evidence supports a climate of professional inquiry for schools. Of considerable interest in this regard is a study by researchers at the Rand Corporation of six large urban school systems that managed to reverse the trend toward decline (Hill, Wise, & Shapiro, 1989). The school systems were those of Atlanta, Cincinnati, Memphis, Miami, Pittsburgh, and San Diego. These school districts had shown improvement in such attributes as lower absenteeism, higher achievement scores, and rates of school completion. The report focused on the school system level and the nature of the superintendent's leadership. Nevertheless, both superintendents and principals are administrators with broad concerns and the superintendents' strategies related to improving instruction are generalizable to principals. Four of the superintendents showed their commitment to improving instruction by spending the major portion of their time in the schools. "In part," concluded the researchers, "the superintendents who made the greatest internal changes treated teachers and administrators as professionals and led them by means of general guidance and modeling" (p. 26).

It is the nature of that modeling that so deeply concerns us here. The report describes what one superintendent (Payzant, San Diego) did:

> Payzant used modeling to induce an atmosphere of intellectual excitement and experimentation. According to San Diego administrators, the fact that Payzant always read the latest research and cited the results in everyday meetings encouraged others to keep up with the literature. As a result, they claimed that everyone understood that change and improvement, rather than routine execution of administrative tasks, was the valued activity. (Hill et al., 1989, p. 26)

Although a big-city superintendent, who could deal directly only with a small fraction of the school district's professional staff, Payzant was an instructional leader. Administrative tasks were only a means to an end: improving the quality of instruction. They were not the focus of his activity. It is of interest and importance that the same quality has been identified in research on effective principals. Leithwood and Montgomery (1982) conducted a study to find what is known about the behavior of effective elementary-school principals that would be useful to prospective and practicing principals. Principal effectiveness was defined in terms of effect on pupil achievement. Leithwood and Montgomery came to the following conclusion in their reviews of the literature: "Whereas the effective principal acts as an instructional leader, leadership provided by the typical principal is largely administrative" (p. 322).

This is not to say that "highly effective" principals do not face the same demands as "typical" principals. It is, rather, that

> the glue that holds together the myriad actions and decisions of highly effective principals . . . is the goals that they and their staff have developed for their schools and a sense of what their schools need to look like and to do in order to accomplish those goals." (Leithwood, 1990, p. 85)

Less effective principals are unable to bring this consistency to their decisions and actions. They may base decisions about discipline, staffing, scheduling, and other matters all on different criteria. The effects of the decisions may be in conflict rather than fostering school improvement and teacher development (Leithwood, 1990, p. 85). Effective principals view teacher and school improvement as inextricably related. Effective principals are able to link their actions—even on matters that are seemingly remote from instruction—with the goal of improving instruction. When all is said and done, however, that goal, rather than the actions and decisions, is their driving force.

Ways that a principal can develop a school culture characterized by inquiry and experimentation are considered in the second part of the chapter.

Cooperative Relationships as a Means.   Like typical principals, effective principals are concerned with establishing and preserving cooperative interpersonal relationships among the professional staff. According to Leithwood and Montgomery (1982), this is where the similarities between effective and typical principals end on the matter of interpersonal relationships. "Unlike typical principals," they report, "this strategy is viewed [by effective principals] as an instrument to goal achievement, not an end in its own right" (p. 334). Thus, the effective principal appoints teachers to curriculum committees based on their professional competence, not for political reasons (not for the sake of running a smooth ship and keeping the school's social leaders happy). Unlike typical principals, who perceive building good relationships with the staff and among the staff as a worthy objective in its own right, effective principals are likely to sacrifice such relationships readily for the sake of pupil growth, if forced to do so (p. 334).

What is of particular interest here is that the principle of basing teacher appointments to committees on their competence is an old, established one in the literature. As early as 1926, Rugg and Counts laid down this principle in their study on curriculum development practices in effective school systems:

> Teachers who are released from the classroom (to do the work of preparing new curricula) must be selected in terms of intelligence, technical training in curriculum-making, understanding of child learning and general research attitude. *They should be chosen for professional rather than for political reasons.* [italics added] (p. 441)

This idea seems obvious, something that any intelligent person would conclude. It is, as N. L. Gage points out, a "truism" (1991, p. 13). But Gage goes on to tell us that to "have value for research and practice the research does become necessary" (p. 13). How much better it is to know that our common-sense practices have been confirmed by research. In addition, it is good to bear in mind that we need to confirm (or refute) them, if education is not to remain at the level of folk medicine (Cremin, 1990, p. 124). Finally, research can enhance a general principle with specifics; it can provide necessary details for practitioners on the conditions under which it can be applied most effectively.

Policy and Approved Practices

The best available knowledge provides guidelines for educational policy makers as well as practitioners. Policy makers are as concerned as educational leaders that teachers use methods that will have productive consequences. Nevertheless, as Barbara Tuchman (1984) observes, governments often pursue policies that are contrary to the direction in which available information points. Like individuals, governments can be perverse:

> Woodenheadedness, the source of self-deception, is a factor that plays a remarkably large role in government. It consists in assessing a situation in terms of preconceived fixed notions while ignoring or rejecting any contrary signs. It is acting according to wish while not allowing oneself to be deflected by the facts. (pp. 6–7)

"Folly or perversity," according to Tuchman, is "a specific manifestation" of misgovernment (1984, p. 5). An important criterion for folly is that it was viewed as counterproductive in its own day, not simply by hindsight. In this way, we avoid judging by present-time values.

Control by Authority: A Classic Case of Folly

In 1976, Herbert A. Simon stated the following:

> Administrators have increasingly recognized in recent years that authority, unless buttressed by other forms of influence, is relatively impotent to control decisions in any but a negative way. The elements entering into all but the most routine decisions are so numerous and so complex that it is impossible to control positively more than

a few. Unless the subordinate is himself able to supply most of the premises of decision, and to synthesize them adequately, the task of supervision becomes hopelessly burdensome. (p. 227)

Simon's ideas earned him a Nobel Prize and much acclaim. Although not Nobelists, all principals can attest to how well the ideas in Simon's statement apply to school settings. To control the teachers' numerous instructional decisions behind closed doors is impossible and to attempt to do so is foolish. A wise principal knows that control by sheer authority is nonfunctional and is bound to have unproductive consequences. Teachers are going to make the decisions, so they might as well make them based on their professional knowledge and continually try to improve their decisions. What is true of workers in industry is doubtlessly more so of teachers: It isn't so much a question of whether teachers *should* have autonomy: like it or not, they have it. The question is one of how they can be helped to make decisions well. In Simon's words, "Functional supervision necessarily takes the form of advice rather than authority" (1976, p. 226).

Most teacher educators (pre-service and in-service) also believe—and have for a long time—that attempts at authoritarian control of teachers' decisions have negative consequences. Margaret Lindsey, at a curriculum conference held at Columbia's Teachers College in the early 1960s, put it this way:

> Thus, in the end, the teacher makes the crucial decisions. The quality of the teaching-learning process depends in the last analysis on whether the decisions are made with professional competence by a person shouldering a professional responsibility or whether they are made by an employee following orders, deliberately not becoming involved as an agent responsible for using his own intelligence in the situation. (p. 39)

The conceptions of supervision held by Lindsey and Simon are not divergent ideas in their respective fields. They are basic principles in the literature of administration and education. They are widely available. They are based on certain realities of the work setting. There is no way that sound educational policies regarding supervision can get around such realities.

Yet many states continued to pursue policies that were contrary to available knowledge and their own best interests. These policies were based on the idea that education is an established situation, that teachers' decisions are specifiable and predictable, and therefore can be standardized (Tanner & Tanner, 1987, p. 124). Teaching was viewed as mechanical and supervision as control—prescribing in detail how teachers are to work with students. But education is an emergent situation—variable and complex, particularly when teaching is idea-oriented, rather than limited to facts and skills (p. 126). Teachers must have the freedom to deal effectively with emergent situations, but the intent of the policies was to reduce teachers' freedom. This freedom is the very essence of professionalism. As Margaret Lindsey foresaw, the quality of teaching in many schools declined because teachers were not allowed to use their own intelligence.

Each legislative act that conceived of teaching as a set of routine decisions that can be standardized and prescribed from afar (some state capitol) was folly. And much of the legislative activity concerning issues associated with the improvement of education was based on this view of teaching (Atkin, 1985, p. 48; Darling-Hammond & Sclan, 1992). That was in the 1980s. We have continued to live with the damaging effects of such policies on teachers and children, which have persisted beyond the political lifetimes of many legislators.[1]

Principals as Policymakers.   But all is not lost. Lest we forget, principals and teachers also make policies (Clark, 1988). The principal's policy may be to practice the approaches to supervision that support a professional conception of teaching. This begins with the view of teaching as an emergent situation. It also may be to oppose policies that seek to limit teachers' decision-making autonomy. Principals are professionals. A profession has to have something to say about policy; otherwise it is not a profession. The principal should be helping to solve problems, not leaning whichever way the wind is blowing. Principals, unfortunately, have historically gone *with* the wind—acting as the arm of the administration to implement policies, no matter how unwise. For example, in the early 1980s the National Association of Secondary School Principals issued a publication on "reducing the curriculum," taking the line of least resistance in response to back-to-basics (NASSP, 1982).

Some readers may think that I am unduly hard on principals. I am not trying to blame anyone for the unwise policies of the past, only to suggest that principals and teachers might do better in the future in responding to policies. Collective responses to unwise policies and pressures are more apt to be effective than individual responses (Anderson, 1988).

Recently, the wind has been blowing in a favorable direction where a professional conception of teaching is concerned (Darling-Hammond & Sclan, 1992). Some states continue to mandate what Darling-Hammond and Sclan call "the bureaucratic model" of supervision—"an inspection system featuring supervisors bearing checklists on brief visits to classrooms" (p. 8). But other new laws are clearly legislative responses to reform proposals concerned with the professionalization of teaching. Some, for example, are concerned with providing mentors for beginning teachers; others with creating mechanisms for collaborative decision making in local schools. The fact that some of these proposals were generated by professionals, such as The Holmes Group (1986), is of more than passing interest, for it indicates that education professionals *can* influence politicians. The conventional wisdom is that influence travels only one way: from the politician to the teacher. Perhaps the problem is that policy initiatives affecting supervision seldom originate with teachers and school administrators. As Darling-Hammond and Sclan suggest, "teachers and teacher educators must become

1.   According to Tuchman (1984), "to qualify as folly . . . the policy in question should be that of a group . . . and should persist beyond any one political lifetime" (p. 5).

proactive in developing—and informing—the standards by which they would like teaching to be judged" (p. 25). They did not include administrators. Yet as we have learned, effective principals and superintendents view themselves as instructional leaders, and they also need to be involved in developing the standards.

What Practices Are Conducive to Instructional Improvement?

This section of the chapter is organized around approved practices that are basic ingredients in educational leadership. Although the emphasis of the discussion is on practical applications, the research and experience behind each practice are very important, for they can help the principal do a better job in applying the practices. Consequently, they are included in the discussion.

First Practice: Follow a professional style of supervision.

Theory.   This model places emphasis on cooperative schoolwide decision making. Teachers are engaged collaboratively in working with one another and with the principal in addressing schoolwide problems and in making schoolwide decisions. The contrasts with traditional supervision are striking. In the traditional style of supervision, the administration develops a new way of doing things and tries to get teachers to "buy into" the innovation. Under professional supervision, any approach to change that attempts to "sell" an innovation to teachers is inadequate. The new methods are developed and implemented from shared decision making.

This is the basic idea, and it is not just another faddish theory, for teachers have considerable autonomy. The literature is quite conclusive about this: "teachers have a considerable control over the decision of whether and how to implement a change" (Richardson, 1990, p. 13). They might as well—in fact, might *better*—make the decisions to begin with, in the course of their own professional work. All professionals have to solve problems. Why should teachers be an exception?

Furthermore, teachers are the closest to the problems associated with teaching. This has been obvious since the first teachers and pupils, and it has been in the literature for a long time, too. In 1939, Hollis Caswell, a pioneer in the curriculum field, observed that

> . . . all teachers are curriculum workers and directly associated, by the very nature of their work, with curriculum improvement. It is impossible to isolate a teacher through any administrative organization from curriculum work. Arguments may wax and wane as to whether the expert or the teacher should make the curriculum, but the fact remains that no curriculum can be made without teachers though one may be developed without experts. (p. 456)

Applying the Practice.   In following a professional style of supervision, a principal can profit from the experiences of other principals. This can be done by networking, followed by visits to schools that are engaged in collaborative problem solving. It is unwise to plunge ahead without hearing the experiences of others. The principal may have to expand his or her network to include administrators who have accepted the concept of participatory decision making and are using the collaborative style. Fortunately also, some principals have written about their own experiences in educational journals. Kenneth Tewel (1989), a former principal in New York City, offers these start-up suggestions, based on his own practical experience in launching a program.

1.   Gain the complete support of assistant principals and department heads. "Without such support no effort to alter the school's governance, planning, and management procedures could ever succeed" (Tewel, 1989, p. 74). At a retreat, Tewel introduced the new goals, theoretical background, and ways for involving teachers.

2.   Re-educate and train department heads so they can hold productive problem-identification meetings with their teachers. The actual collaborative process is to be entrusted to chairpersons of departments; therefore, it is absolutely essential that the training address in detail leadership methods appropriate for use in working with groups of teachers, "a skill most supervisors (department heads) lacked when the program began" (Tewel, 1989, p. 75).

3.   Pave the way for the department head. The principal should open the first meeting with a description of the program, explaining "how the school could be enriched by broadening the problem-solving and decision-making processes," and, "that often the real expert at identifying and solving problems connected with teaching is the person closest to the scene—the teacher" (Tewel, 1989, p. 78). Of particular importance is to communicate the commitment of the administration to improving teaching and learning through the involvement of teachers in real decision making. (Many faculty members will be understandably skeptical after so many rapid-fire policy changes in education.) Here is an example of what a principal might say to them:

> Many of you—especially long-term faculty members—have seen school improvement programs come and go over the years. Some of you, no doubt, may be saying to yourselves "Here it comes again" or "What did he say the improvement program will be called this time?" Well, this time, we're really serious about a new approach and we want to see it work. We're going to devote ourselves to it. But you're the ones that have to give it a chance to work. (Tewel, 1989, p. 78)

4.   An effective program requires that there be a continuous cycle of problem-solving meetings involving teachers and their department heads. Tewel found that when groups met on a continuous basis, "the candor and openness of the group members increased" (1989, p. 81), and efforts were more likely to lead to substantial improvements.

5.   The department head should assist the group in identifying problems and, if unable to get volunteers, assign responsibility for problem solution. Tewel suggests that "to enhance trust and promote participation," department chairpersons assume responsibility for solving the problems that require administrative resources.

6.   Between meetings, department heads should hold brief but frequent sessions with teachers to make certain that the teachers do not procrastinate with problem-solving responsibilities and to offer support where needed. This is important, for "without the assistance of the department chairpersons in such areas as fact finding, some groups come to the second meeting to raise additional problems without first clarifying those identified in the first" (Tewel, 1989, p. 79).

7.   In assessing whether goals have been met, groups should select measures over which they have control. For example, a group of art teachers established the goal of reducing the number of students who failed courses due to absence. Six months later the figures had not shown much improvement, and the teachers had become discouraged. They felt that their attempt to improve the percentages of students who passed was a waste of time and energy. The principal and the department head helped the teachers see the difficulty of accomplishing their goal in view of the school's social environment and the reasons for student absences.

Nevertheless, without realizing it, the art teachers had influenced two other variables: "Class cutting decreased and the number of high-risk students attending class on a more regular basis increased" (Tewel, 1989, p. 80). More important for our purposes here is Tewel's observation that: "By initially selecting a measure over which they had little control, the group members felt frustrated and were on the verge of disbanding, even though their efforts had resulted in substantial improvement in a different area. Once they recognized both their success and error, the group moved ahead to successful goal setting" (p. 80).

It is important that department goals be attainable and that department heads assist teachers in developing appropriate criteria for assessing the project's impact.

8.   The principal should expect "occasional resistance" (Tewel, 1989, p. 82) by a department head. After all, some heads with more traditional supervisory views will find the collaborative way of working with groups very difficult and may reject it. Tewel found that this resistance was the most important difficulty he encountered but that it was not enough to ruin the program. Indeed, the program was generally seen by teachers and department heads as effective in solving school problems.

According to Tewel (1989), an important ingredient in successful programs is that department heads communicate to teachers that the administration is really committed to broadening the way decisions are made to include teachers.

Department heads must immediately counter staff opinions that the new supervisory process is just another passing fancy in education. Not to do so is to invite failure. It is imperative also that department heads and, indeed, principals not become discouraged about teachers' reluctance, for whatever reason(s), to participate in what for years have been viewed by all concerned as strictly managerial functions.

Adequate leadership is based on the understanding that changing old patterns is something that must be worked at. The moving spirit behind it is the belief that the process is good. Many years ago, Hollis Caswell, an expert on the teacher's role in curriculum improvement wrote this:

> Teachers will not decide to take on larger responsibilities merely because the administrative organization is changed. Leadership must be ever present, stimulating, guiding, suggesting; leadership which is concerned with procedure and has faith to trust the outcome so long as the procedure is sound. (1939, p. 474)

It also helps to know that in the past, instructional leaders confronted the problem of teacher reluctance and dealt with it in their own time, in their own way. Times have changed, but the problem is a persistent one in democratic school administration. The insights of our forebears into this and other problems are their legacy; we should take the dusty books from the shelf and read them. Tewel recalls an incident in his school that conveys the true effect of collaborative decision making and participatory management:

> Two teachers were overheard talking in the hall. One, a member of a department in which the process was successful, described the great involvement of teachers in the collaborative problem-solving process to a second teacher from one of the departments in which the program was not working. The second teacher responded: "You may not be turning the school into St. Augustine's *City of God* but you're bringing about small improvements and planning even bigger ones. More important, you're excited about your job and you enjoy coming to work again. At the very least in your department, supervisors and teachers are now treating each other like professionals. (1989, p. 83)

Second Practice: Orchestrate time and schedule factors to bring about opportunities for teachers to collaborate on curriculum and instructional problems.

Theory.   We have long known that when teachers are expected to do the work after school, the results are often disappointing. Indeed, this knowledge goes back to the 1920s when Superintendent Jesse Newlon put into operation his famous plan for curriculum revision in Denver. The plan put teachers at the heart of the process. Teacher committees worked out courses of study and tests to assess student progress (Cremin, 1961).

The various phases of the Denver program of curriculum revision are discussed in *The Transformation of the School*, Lawrence A. Cremin's classic history of the progressive education movement (1961). They will not be considered here, except to point out that in the initial phase (in 1922), teachers were asked to study the literature in their field of professional specialization with a view toward reconstructing courses of study. According to Cremin, "no official principles were laid down, and no time limit was set. The teachers were simply asked to read widely and to think as deeply as possible in the pursuit of their enterprise" (p. 300).

Newlon was apparently pleased with the progress that the teachers made, for in 1923 he proposed to his board that the committees meet during school hours and that teachers so engaged be provided with substitutes. He also proposed that university consultants be called in to meet with the teacher groups and integrate their efforts.

The revised courses of study were published as a monograph series. "Not surprisingly," wrote Cremin, "they were snapped up by the thousands for use in other school systems, not only in the United States but abroad" (1961, p. 301). And not surprisingly, other school systems attracted by Newlon's enthusiasm about the program, tried curriculum revision by committees of teachers. Frequently the results were disappointing. Puzzled and dismayed, the other superintendents failed to recognize that there was at least one very significant difference between their programs and the Denver program: they expected teachers to do the work after school.

Newlon treated the teachers as professionals. He knew that the quality of the new syllabi depended on providing teachers with favorable conditions under which to do the work. This principle continues to be valid. A critically important condition for curriculum improvement is time to do the work. As experience has shown, this requires that teachers be released from instructional responsibilities. In the late 1970s, this practice was far from common. Howey and Joyce (1978) reported that less than one in five teachers surveyed across the country indicated that they were given released time from classroom duties to work on curriculum and instructional matters. Lieberman and Miller (1978) identified time as one of three resources that teachers must have for problem solving—the others being expertise (the help of supervisors and outside experts) and materials (books, curriculum materials, and other instructional aids).

But the issue of time still looms large, in fact, larger than ever, for time is now viewed by many teachers as part of the professional equation. A recent survey of Iowa teachers, for example, concluded that many Iowa schools are much as they were in 1983, when educational reform became a major issue (Pipho, 1991). The report stated that "Permanent structural changes in schools have not occurred," and that, "in part, this is because the recommendations of teachers have not been heard clearly" (p. 182). Topping the list of factors with the most potential for transforming the schools was time—"time to plan for comprehensive school change through participatory decision making; time for team planning, team teaching, and cooperative education at the building level; time to participate in state-level professional activities" (p. 182).

Time is a critical factor. Nevertheless, principals can influence the time factor at the local school (and elsewhere) to create opportunities for teachers to participate in the kinds of activities identified by the Iowa teachers.

Applying the Practice.

> There are a number of time and schedule dimensions of school life that principals can orchestrate to bring about the time and space opportunities for the participatory decision making noted above. (Griffin, 1988, p. 252)

So writes Gary Griffin, a former principal who is presently working in teacher education and staff development. Griffin offers the following ideas, based on his own experience:

1. Most teachers have daily professional preparation periods in their schedules. This time may or may not coincide with other teachers' preparation time. Thus the preparation period may not be the time during the school day when the teacher may engage in professional activity with other teachers. "Principals can arrange for these times to coincide for certain groups," suggests Griffin. "For example, teachers in the same subject fields or grade levels, so that opportunities to engage together about curriculum become a reality" (1988, p. 253).

2. Principals can plan large-group events such as school assemblies, thus freeing teachers to work together on curriculum development activities.

3. Principals can serve as advocates with district-level administrators to provide professional days for teachers, days when there can be uninterrupted dialogue.

4. Principals can plan for substitute teachers to enable teachers to observe exemplary programs in their professional field.

This list is by no means complete, but the ideas should help principals see that the principal is in an excellent position to ensure that there is enough time for teachers to talk together. It should also be pointed out that an articulated, coherent curriculum is not really possible unless teachers talk and plan together.

Third Practice: Promote higher-order thinking in school.

Theory.   Thus far we have been concerned in this chapter with the participative group system as a general administrative model. Our focus has been on a supervisory process that is educative rather than coercive. But as has been pointed out elsewhere,

> At the same time, the effective teacher knows that sheer control over students by authority not only is nonfunctional but is miseducative, since education requires the development of productive self-control and self-direction. (Tanner & Tanner, 1987, p. 149)

The research literature on school "climate" or "environment" points to the interdependence of variables (Anderson, 1982).

Of equal importance is that the various aspects of a system of operation must be mutually consistent. Simply grafting elements of the participative-group system onto a basically autocratic system will not produce effective results because "the various behavioral, attitudinal, and structural parts of the organizational whole have a fundamental interdependence, and they must be mutually consistent" (Bowers, 1976, p. 100). If they are inconsistent, the more powerful elements will win out. In the words of Bowers, an expert on organizational systems,

> Where an attempt is made artificially to implant intervening or lower echelon processes of a participative nature in an organization in which causal or upper echelon processes are more autocratic, it is likely that the whole system will shift, or revert, toward autocracy. (p. 144)

Obviously, teachers must be inquirers if pupils are to be inquirers. What is less obvious is that the reverse is also true: pupils must be inquirers if teachers are to be inquirers. Just as teachers should be engaged with principals and supervisors in solving schoolwide problems, so should teachers foster the development of pupils' ability to think critically and independently in examining problems and issues. The nature of teacher-pupil interactions in the classroom is an important variable in the environment of the school. If the school is to move to a participative system, it must do so inside classrooms. It must do so as a whole.

Goodlad's large-scale study of schooling (1984) investigated both dimensions of school climate. He found that teachers "rarely worked together on some school-based issue or problem" (p. 279) and that many principals lacked the major skills required for problem solving to effect schoolwide improvement (p. 306). Since Goodlad's findings (and perhaps in part because of them), many schools have initiated participative decision-making programs. Principals' interest in having the decision-making process extend organically throughout the school is widespread, but it is by no means universal. Increasing numbers of principals are beginning to note that collective intelligence applied to problems by those closest to the scene can yield effective solutions to problems. "More heads are better than one" is something that wise principals are finding out. Others are interested in moving to a collaborative approach but do not know how to operate with teachers in "a strong professional culture" (Rallis, 1990, p. 203). In this regard, some school districts are setting up partnerships between principals to share and get feedback on their individual implementation problems (Roberts, 1991).

Turning to the second dimension of school climate, Goodlad (1984) found that inside their classrooms the teachers initiated nearly everything. Most teachers recognized that this is not an approved practice. They expressed the view that students should be increasingly independent in making decisions concerning their own education:

> On the one hand, many teachers verbalize the importance of students becoming increasingly independent learners; on the other, most view themselves as needing to be in control of the decision-making process. (p. 109)

Telling and explaining, which most teachers do most of the time—followed by asking students to "fill in the blanks"—do not promote higher-order thinking (Goodlad, 1984, pp. 108–109). Goodlad reported his findings in the mid-1980s. It appears from the literature that little has changed since then as far as students' opportunities to solve real problems are concerned. The opportunities are few and far between. "Cooperative learning," it is true, has been widely promoted as a teaching technique, but cooperative learning should not be confused with collaborative problem solving. Goodlad expressed it well: "A great deal of what goes on in the classroom is like painting-by-numbers—filling in colors called for by numbers on the page" (p. 108).

In most cooperative learning programs, the teacher chooses the assignments, and groups of students answer the questions cooperatively—filling in the colors, so to speak. These assignments are typically at the lowest cognitive level. Problem solving, on the other hand, involves the application of information to a situation and the development of a plan for dealing with the problem. Evaluation, the highest cognitive process in the taxonomy developed by Bloom, Hastings, and Madaus (1971), is also essential for problem solving.

The participative-group system of operation in classrooms, in which students use knowledge as a resource for inquiry, encompasses a wider range of cognitive learning than classroom recitation, pupil assignments, and teacher made tests (Tanner & Tanner, 1980, p. 169). More importantly, perhaps, collaborative problem solving is a democratic procedure. As Caswell (1942) pointed out,

> democratic procedures cannot be applied on a mechanical basis but must take into account the ability of various persons to assume responsibility. In the elementary school, children should be guided into participation and decision making as rapidly as they are able to assume responsibility for their decisions. (p. 65)

The implication is that democratic procedures will lead to democratic action. Something will happen as a result of decision. The procedures will not simply be empty exercises.

In recent years, there has been much interest in teaching critical thinking. In this connection, Dewey's work on inquiry (reflective or critical thinking) is of great interest. Dewey believed that critical thinking is motivated by a problem. It must be a real problem—the pupil's own. As I have pointed out elsewhere, simulated problems and practice problems intended to help pupils do well on tests do not meet this qualification (Tanner, 1988). As Dewey said, "they are his *only* as a pupil, not as a human being" (1916/1966, p. 183). Yet critical thinking has gone the ready-made lesson way, rather than the firsthand experience way on which Dewey's complete act of thought is based.

We have departed far from our legacy as far as cooperative, participatory learning methods are concerned. The legacy is this: children learn democratic processes and develop a sense of social responsibility while applying scientific methods to genuine social problems at their level of development, which is often higher than we think it is. And as noted, they also need opportunities to make decisions about their own education—what they will do in the classroom.

Applying the Practice.   Principals can play an important role in raising the thinking level in classrooms. One means is organizational reform. Principals are often prone to criticize teachers for being apathetic (or failing altogether) about engaging students in learning that is classified at the higher cognitive levels. Yet the organizational characteristics of their schools may also have something to do with the kinds of instructional activities designed by teachers. There is no doubt, as McCartney and Schrag (1990) point out, that "the routine features of school organization, viz., class size, scheduling, and the structure of the subject disciplines . . . are significant constraints on higher-order thinking" (p. 535). In their study of the principal's role in promoting higher-order thinking, McCartney and Schrag found that principals "do not emphasize organizational or structural reform as a strategy for achieving higher-order thinking in their schools" (p. 535).

Yet organizational reform—for example, dividing time into larger blocks— removes some constraints on interdisciplinary teaching. Teachers often complain that they must fit their lessons to time blocks instead of the needs of students (Jacobs, 1989, p. 4). Obviously, integration cannot be accomplished by mere organizational reform. Nevertheless, as Jacobs points out, if principals have flexibility in their schedules, they can encourage team planning and teaching or change the sequence of subjects (p. 18). Many principals are able to make these kinds of adjustments.

McCartney and Schrag (1990) studied principals' efforts to promote higher-order thinking in five high schools. Interestingly, although the principals had little exposure to recent research on higher-order thinking, McCartney and Schrag found

> a remarkably shared vision among principals of what a higher-order thinking classroom should look like. This vision involves less teacher domination, teachers posing challenging questions or tasks, and teachers allowing students to tackle questions from diverse perspectives. (p. 534)

The principals viewed their administrative responsibilities, which they felt had been increasing, as the major impediments to their efforts to promote thinking in classrooms. The other demands on them meant that they had only limited time for dealing with instructional issues. Their leadership styles varied, as did the ways that they supported higher-order thinking.

Not all five principals received district support for promoting higher-order thinking. One principal felt that the district had its priorities confused:

> There is no significant contribution or promotion (of higher-order thinking) from the district. District concerns are more mundane, focused on test scores and developing a consistent and district-wide curriculum. (McCartney & Schrag, 1990, p. 540)

Be that as it may, this principal was a strong instructional leader who spent time talking and working with teachers to gain an understanding of what they needed to do the job well. He encouraged—even urged—the eight mentor senior teachers at his school to embark on curriculum improvement projects. Some of the projects involved interdisciplinary collaboration between departments—no easy task in a high school.

McCartney and Schrag (1990) used data gathered from an observational study in the five schools to determine the schools' relative success in promoting higher-order thinking in social studies classes. They administered questionnaires and conducted interviews with the administrators as well as with teachers and students. Based on their data, they offer four guidelines for school-based administrators.

1. A department-based program that is systematically focused on developing higher-order thinking is necessary for classrooms that do well in this area.
2. Department heads must be strong and dynamic leaders who work to help teachers promote higher-level thinking in their classes.
3. The principal must work closely with department heads in supporting their efforts.[2]
4. Success hinges on a collegial atmosphere in the department characterized by sustained and focused discussion of curriculum and teaching.

Summing things up, they offered this conclusion: "Collegial school culture and institutional leadership from department heads and principals help teachers promote higher-order thinking in their classrooms" (McCartney & Schrag, 1990, p. 543). Their study was concerned with higher-order thinking, not with problem solving. It is entirely possible that principals and department heads could have a similar impact on student involvement in making decisions about their classroom work and in cooperative problem solving in the classroom. These must first be valued activities.

SUMMARY

Today, the responsibilities of teachers have expanded vastly, to include involvement in decision making. Principals have been given a new role to play in the conduct of the schools. The practical affairs of improving teaching include working with teachers on school-based issues or problems. The principal should provide educational vision and leadership for people who, like the principal, are professionals. The problems involved challenge principals' skill and ingenuity, yet meeting these problems can be a source of personal as well as professional pleasure.

---

2.   The principal who felt that he received no support from the district in promoting critical thinking played an active role in supporting the department heads. His school was one of three schools where students scored highest in critical thinking (McCartney, & Schrag, 1990, p. 541).

Research and the experiences of educators in the field have produced a body of approved practices from which principals can draw in order to carry out their newly-conceived functions. However, the word *new* does not really apply to these procedures. What has been called a new mode of instructional leadership—the democratic participatory approach—was developed by educators in the first half of the twentieth century and is based on Dewey's concept of problem solving for instructional improvement.

In 1922, the famous Denver curriculum revision program was based on this approach to improving instruction, introduced by Superintendent Jesse Newlon. Teachers, administrators, and supervisors engaged collaboratively in curriculum revision. Newlon had great confidence in teachers as professionals, which distinguished him from other superintendents. His faith was justified, and the Denver curriculum revision program was an instant success and gained national recognition. Other superintendents tried to institute Newlon's theory of curriculum reform in their own schools—with one difference. Teachers were expected to do the work after school. The results were disappointing. In Denver, the curriculum committees met during school hours, and substitutes were provided for teachers so involved.

The principle that emerged from Newlon's work remains valid: teachers must have time for problem solving. Freeing teachers to work on instructional problems is an approved practice in instructional leadership. Principals can adjust schedules and plan large-group activities, for example, to provide time for teachers. Such strategies make team planning and interdisciplinary teaching more possible.

Three basic ideas undergird teacher involvement in solving instructional problems. First, teachers are closest to the scene—the classroom. Their insights are crucial to the problem-solving process. Second, control by sheer authority as a way of supervising teachers cannot work because the elements involved in all but the most minor and routine decisions are too complex and it is impossible to control them all. Teachers will make these decisions anyhow (their autonomy is a fact of life), and they should make them on the best available evidence. Third, many heads are better than just one. Participatory decision making is a way to draw upon the collective knowledge of professionals and use it in the solution of problems.

Participatory decision making in school and classroom are inseparable parts of a whole. Just as teachers must share in schoolwide decisions affecting them, students must become increasingly independent in making decisions about their own education. The total organizational system, including how classrooms work, must be consistent. Principals can promote higher-order thinking and problem solving in classrooms by spending time talking and working with teachers—finding out what teachers need to do the job well. Principals who urge teachers to embark on projects involving interdisciplinary collaboration have been found to be effective in promoting higher-order thinking in the classroom.

Many principals have established successful programs for involving groups of teachers in solving instruction-related problems. Some school systems have instituted peer coaching programs so that principals can share their ideas and experiences. Fortunately also, some principals have seen fit to set their experiences on paper and make valuable suggestions. Emerging from such experiences is this cautionary note: principals must quickly counter teachers' impression that participatory decision making is just one more educational fad that will go away. Teachers are often reluctant when asked to assume decision-making functions they were schooled to believe are centralized in the administration. Principals must be patient and believe in the process. The key is to treat professionals as professionals.

THEORY INTO PRACTICE:
A CASE STUDY FOR REFLECTION

You are the principal of Holmes High School, a school of almost 2000 students. Until last year, management in the school district followed a centralized, top-down model. Schoolwide decisions were made and problems solved by the principal (with occasional input from an assistant principal) and then approved by the superintendent. But last year a pilot program involving collaborative problem solving and shared decision making was set up at another high school in the district, Angell High School. The feelings expressed by the participants were so successful that the area high school superintendent was prompted to recommend that the participative-group system of identifying and resolving teaching-related problems be instituted in all of the district's high schools.

The program at Holmes has been in operation for three months. You receive this memo from your social studies department chairperson.

To: Arthur Rolph
From: John Percy
Subject: Collaborative Supervision

You will remember that I was initially quite impressed with the reports that I heard about the pilot project. But after conducting problem-solving meetings with my teachers, I have come to a different conclusion: teacher involvement in making decisions about policy and instructional problems is just a worthless approach to school management. My teachers are interested only in dealing with the issues within their own classrooms. They resent the extra work that is coming out of the new program.

I ended our last meeting by asking "Are there any more gripes?" There were none, and our group would like your permission to disband.

GUIDING QUESTIONS

1. Which of the ideas presented in this chapter seem particularly relevant to this case? Explain.

2. What kinds of additional information would you want to have before responding to Mr. Percy's memo?

3. Under what conditions would you think it most appropriate for you to respond to Mr. Percy in a person-to-person meeting? Under what conditions would you think it most appropriate for you to respond in writing?

4. Obviously you have implementation problems. What (if any) resources can you call upon?

REFERENCES

Aikin, W. M. (1942). *The story of the eight-year study*. New York: Harper.

Aiken, W. M. (1953). The eight-year study: If we were to do it again. *Progressive Education, 31*(10), 11–14.

Anderson, C. S. (1982). The search for school climate: A review of research. *Review of Educational Research, 52*(1), 368–420.

Atkin, J. M. (1985). Changing our thinking about educational change. In J. H. Bunzel (Ed.), *Challenge to America's schools: The case for standards and values* (pp. 47–60). New York: Oxford.

Bloom, B. S., Hastings, J. T., & Madaus, G. F. (1971). *Handbook on formative and summative evaluation of student learning*. New York: McGraw-Hill.

Bowers, D. G. (1976). *Systems of organization: Management of the human resource*. Ann Arbor, MI: University of Michigan.

Campbell, C. M. (Ed.). (1952). *Practical application of democratic administration*. New York: Harper & Row.

Caswell, H. L. (1939). Administrative considerations in curriculum development. In H. Rugg (Ed.), *Democracy and the curriculum: The third yearbook of the John Dewey Society* (pp. 455–474). New York: D. Appleton-Century.

Caswell, H. L. (1942). *Education in the elementary school*. New York: American Book.

Clark, R. W. (1988). Who decides? the basic policy issue. In L. Tanner (Ed.), *Critical issues in curriculum: The 87th yearbook of the National Society for the Study of Education* (Part 1, pp. 175–204). Chicago: University of Chicago Press.

Clift, R., Veal, M. L., Johnson, M., & Holland, P. (1989, June). *Strengths and limitations of collaborative action research: Implications for teacher learning*. Paper presented at the conference of the Canadian Association of Teacher Education, Laval University, Quebec.

Cremin, L. A. (1961). *The transformation of the school*. New York: Knopf.

Cremin, L. A. (1971). Curriculum-making in the United States. *Teachers College Record, 73*(2), 207–220.

Cremin, L. A. (1990). *Popular education and its discontents*. New York: Harper & Row.

Darling-Hammond, L., & Sclan, E. (1992). Policy and supervision. In C. Glickman (Ed.), *Supervision in transition: The 1992 yearbook of the Association for Supervision and Curriculum Development* (pp. 7–29). Alexandria, VA: ASCD.

Dewey, J. (1904). The relation of theory to practice in education. In C. A. McMurry (Ed.), *The relation of theory to practice in the education of teachers: The third yearbook of the National Society for the Scientific Study of Education* (Part 1, pp. 9–30). Chicago: University of Chicago Press.

Dewey, J. (1929). *The sources of a science of education*. New York: Liveright.

Dewey, J. (1966). *Democracy and education*. New York: Macmillan. (Original work published 1916)

Ford Foundation. (1972). *A foundation goes to school*. New York: Author.

Ford Foundation. (1973). *Annual report*. New York: Author.

Gage, N. L. (1991). The obviousness of social and educational research results. *Educational Researcher, 20* (1), 10–16.

Glatthorn, A. A. (1987). *Curriculum renewal*. Alexandria, VA: Association for Supervision and Curriculum Development.

Goodlad, J. I. (1984). *A place called school*. New York: McGraw-Hill Publishing Company, Inc.

Griffin, G. A. (1988). Leadership for curriculum improvement: The school administrator's role. In L. Tanner (Ed.), *Critical issues in curriculum: The 87th yearbook of the National Society for the Study of Education* (Part 1, pp. 244–266). Chicago: University of Chicago Press.

Hill, P. T., Wise, A. E., & Shapiro, L. (1989). *Educational progress: Cities mobilize to improve their schools*. Santa Monica: The Rand Corporation.

The Holmes Group. (1986). *Tomorrow's teachers*. East Lansing, MI: The Holmes Group.

Howey, K., & Joyce, B. (1978). A data base for future directions in inservice education, *Theory Into Practice 17*(3), 206–211.

Jacobs, H. (1989). *Interdisciplinary curriculum: Design and implementation*. Alexandria, VA: Association for Supervision and Curriculum Development.

Kirk, D. (1990). School knowledge and the curriculum package-as-text. *Journal of Curriculum Studies, 22*(5), 409–425.

Koop, C. E. (1991). *Koop: The memoirs of America's family doctor*. New York: Random House.

Lieberman, A., & Miller, L. (1978). The social realities of teaching. *Teachers College Record, 80*(1), 1–201.

Leithwood, K. A. (1990). The principal's role in teacher development. In B. Joyce (Ed.), *Changing school culture through staff development: The 1990 yearbook of the Association for Supervision and Curriculum Development* (pp. 71–90). Alexandria, VA: ASCD.

Leithwood, K. A., & Montgomery, C. (1982). Role of the elementary school principal in program improvement. *Review of Educational Research, 52*(3), 309–339.

Likert, R. (1977). *Past and future perspectives on system 4.* Ann Arbor, MI: Rensis Likert Associates.

Lindsey, M. (1962). Decision-making and the teacher. In A. H. Passow (Ed.), *Curriculum Crossroads* (pp.27–40). New York: Teachers College.

Loucks-Horsley, S., & Hergert, L. F. (1985). *An action guide to school improvement.* Alexandria, VA: ASCD.

McCartney, D., & Schrag, F. (1990). Departmental and school leadership in promoting higher order thinking. *Journal of Curriculum Studies, 22*(6), 529–543.

McGill, M. V. (1991). The changing face of supervision: A developmental art. *Journal of Curriculum and Supervision, 6*(3), 255–264.

NASSP. (1982). *Reducing the curriculum.* Reston, VA: National Association of Secondary School Principals.

Pipho, C. (1991). Teachers, testing and time. *Phi Delta Kappan, 73*(3), 182–183.

Rallis, S. F. (1990). Professional teachers and restructured schools: Leadership challenges. In B. Mitchell & L. L. Cunningham (Eds.), *Educational leadership and changing contexts of families, communities, and schools: The 89th yearbook of the National Society for the Study of Education* (Part 2, pp. 184–209). Chicago: University of Chicago Press.

Richardson, V. (1990). Significant and worthwhile change in teaching practice. *Educational Researcher, 19*(7), 10–18.

Roberts, J. (1991). Improving principal's instructional leadership through peer coaching. *Journal of Staff Development, 12*(4), 30–33.

Rosenthal, E. (1990, April 4). Four-thousand-year-old treatment revived to heal wounds. *The New York Times*, p. 87.

Rugg, H., & Counts, G. S. (1926). A critical appraisal of current methods of curriculum-making. In G. M. Whipple (Ed.), *Curriculum-making, past and present: The 26th yearbook of the National Society for the Study of Education* (Part 1, pp. 435–447). Bloomington, IL: Public School Publishing Company.

Simon, H. A. (1976). *Administrative behavior* (3rd ed.). New York: Free Press.

Squires, D. A. (1991). [Review of F. H. Klein, *Curriculum reform in the elementary school: Creating your own agenda*]. *Journal of Curriculum Studies, 23*(5), 474–479.

Stake, R. E. (1991). Retrospective on "the countenance of educational evaluation." In M. McLaughlin & D. Phillips (Eds.), *Evaluation and education: The 90th yearbook of the National Society for the Study of Education* (Part 2, pp. 67–88). Chicago: University of Chicago Press.

Tanner, D., & Tanner, L. N. (1980). *Curriculum development: Theory into practice* (2nd ed.). New York: Macmillan.

Tanner, D., & Tanner, L. N. (1987). *Supervision in education: Problems and practices.* New York: Macmillan.

Tanner, L. N. (1988). The path not taken: Dewey's model of inquiry. *Curriculum Inquiry, 18*(4), 471–479.

Tewel, K. J. (1989). Collaborative supervision—theory into practice. *NASSP Bulletin, 73*(516), 74–83.

Tuchman, B. W. (1981). *Practicing history.* New York: Knopf.

Tuchman, B. W. (1984). *The march of folly*. New York: Knopf.

Wong, K., & Rollow, S. (1989). *From mobilization to legislation: A case study of the recent Chicago school reform*. Paper presented at the annual meeting of the Western Political Science Association, Salt Lake City, UT.

SELECTED READINGS

Cremin, L. A. (1971). Curriculum-making in the United States. *Teachers College Record, 73*(2) 207–220.

Goodlad, J. I. (1984). *A place called school*. New York: McGraw-Hill Publishing Company, Inc.

Griffin, G. A. (1988). Leadership for curriculum improvement: The school administrator's role. In L. Tanner (Ed.), *Critical issues in curriculum: The 87th yearbook of the National Society for the Study of Education* (Part 1, pp. 244–266). Chicago: University of Chicago Press.

Leithwood, K. A. (1990). The principal's role in teacher development. In B. Joyce (ed.), *Changing school culture through staff development: The 1990 yearbook of the Association for Supervision and Curriculum Development* (pp. 71–90). Alexandria VA: ASCD.

McCartney, C., & Schrag, F. (1990). Departmental and school leadership in promoting higher order thinking. *Journal of Curriculum Studies 22*(6), 529–543.

Simon, H. A. (1976). *Administrative behavior* (3rd ed.). New York: Free Press.

Tanner, D., & Tanner, L. N. (1987). *Supervision in education: Principles, problems and practices*. New York: Macmillan.

Tewel, K. J. (1989). Collaborative supervision—theory into practice. *NASSP Bulletin, 73*(516), 74–83.

9

The Principal and Novice Teachers

Kay R. Weise
University of Houston
Patricia E. Holland
University of Houston

Overview

You probably will never forget that first year of teaching—the eagerness, anticipation, exhilaration you felt entering the first classroom full of 6-year-olds (or 16-year-olds) waiting to see how you would change their lives. And, yes, the apprehension, anxiety, uncertainty you felt entering a profession long revered as one of civilization's most noble enterprises. Why did the principal of this school choose you? What did the principal expect of you? What could you expect from the principal? Did you know the answers to these questions? We propose in this chapter that if you did, you probably learned a great deal and now enjoy pleasant memories of that first year; if you *didn't*, you should have. Viewing the first-year teacher from the principal's perspective, we hope to stimulate your thinking about the fragility of the novice and about the principal's responsibility to protect and guide a new career in our profession.

For over a decade now, the educational community has been issuing an unequivocal directive that principals assume a proactive stance as "instructional leaders." The changing demographics of the teaching force promise to make this role even more challenging as principals will have to assume responsibility for increasing numbers of new teachers. As instructional leaders, principals will have to pay close attention to the instructional needs and performance of these novice teachers and to make sure they receive direction and assistance in their professional development.

It is easy to recognize how important a principal's leadership can be for a novice teacher, but the topic has not received much attention in the professional literature nor is it often discussed. We intend to address that attention gap and raise several important questions about what principals need to know and do to provide help for novice teachers.

What demands do principals face when they undertake the task of helping new teachers? What are the special needs of these teachers for knowledge, guidance, and support? What can principals do to determine that new teachers get both the kind and the amount of assistance they need for professional growth? These are questions we will address, first by considering what literature on the principalship, instructional supervision, and induction suggests about the principal's role. Next we will offer the views of several principals about their work with novice teachers and examine discrepancies between what they say novice teachers need from them and what they are actually able to do. Finally, we will generate propositions describing an appropriate role for principals in their work with novice teachers.

Conceptual Frame

The principal will naturally be anxious to learn how a first-year teacher performs in the classroom. However, the major tenets of instructional supervision (discussed below) suggest clearly that the principal, by necessity, often delegates much of the direct observation, feedback, and guidance to other instructional specialists. This does not relieve the principal of responsibility for closely observing teacher behavior and growth. It merely shifts active involvement in the process from collecting specific data about classroom strategies to gathering more comprehensive information about the teacher's progress in adapting to school norms, establishing a positive instructional image, and furthering the mission of the school in general.

What might be thought of as a kind of common professional knowledge about the relationship between novice teachers and principals is included in a number of places in the literature on teaching and administration. Literature on effective schools, instructional leadership, learning to teach, mentoring and induction, supervision, and school culture all offer ideas that increase understanding of how principals can better function as a key figure in the new teacher's professional development.

Needs of Beginning Teachers

As noted earlier, professional literature offers sparse data regarding the principal's role with novice teachers; however, considerable research has explored the perceived needs of beginning teachers (Gray & Gray, 1985). Veenman (1984) reviewed 83 separate studies that revealed the key problems facing new teachers as *person-specific* and *situation-specific*. Sacks and Brady's study (1985) of 602 novice teachers in New York City supports that generalization by identifying more specific needs felt by teachers entering the profession for the first time. A substantial number of these teachers (24 percent) expressed a need for moral support, guidance, and feedback from a mentor—i.e., personal attention. Other needs expressed in this study included discipline management (20 percent), curriculum and lesson planning (18 percent), and school routines (15 percent), all of which reflect largely site-specific policies and procedures.

Lortie (1975) contends that the vast majority of beginning teachers (92 percent) wish, above all, to attain professional autonomy and status equality with their colleagues. This supports the notion of person-specific and situation-specific needs. Furthermore, though they do "swap stories" with peers, novice teachers typically avoid seeking direct help from colleagues for fear of revealing their weaknesses. According to Lortie, 93 percent of teacher stress related to professional performance stems from inexperience, unavailability of expertise, and ambiguity regarding goal attainment. Because "story swapping" tends to do little to reduce these sources of stress, Gray and Gray (1985) have suggested that "a sense of community must be established, consisting of interdependency, shared concerns, a sense of common fate, and a sense that others 'stand by' when one is under stress or uncertainty about what to do" (p. 39).

A mentor teacher could provide the most immediate and tangible resource for addressing all these issues, and formal programs of mentor assistance for novices are springing up throughout the country, at both district and state levels. However, common sense tells us that even the most well-conceived mentor program will thrive only within a broader context of mutual trust, support, and collegiality. Enter, the person uniquely positioned to influence that context, the principal.

Instructional Leadership

During the past several years, descriptions and definitions of instructional leadership may have increased more rapidly than any other single topic in reform literature. One could turn to almost any study of school improvement to find a new list, or perhaps more accurately, a new treatment of various *earlier* lists, of principal behaviors and characteristics that promote student achievement. The findings of research on beginning teachers' needs cited previously address a number of elements found in those studies—instructional support, performance feedback, collegiality, goal-setting and attainment, and professional growth. Therefore, we will focus on a few principal traits and behaviors commonly associated with general school effectiveness that might yield fruitful implications for the principal's specific leadership role with novice teachers.

Goal Attainment

The categories of *person*-specific and *situation*-specific needs expressed by first-year teachers echo key issues embedded in two underlying questions of most organizational theory:

1. How does a leader attain organizational goals?
2. How do the personal needs of its members influence the organization's goal attainment?

Though schools differ from other large organizations in very important ways (see Norris, chapter 3), most studies attribute, directly or indirectly, a large measure of school effectiveness to the principal's success in answering the same questions.

People (their perceptions, attitudes, behaviors, etc.) can hardly be separated from the organizations (professional, social, political, etc.) in which they operate. The two phenomena interweave so tightly, and often so imperceptibly, that an observer could defensibly isolate one from the other only for purposes of discussion. With this caution in mind, the following argument pursues two distinct, though inextricably connected, lines of analysis for insight into how principals go about meeting the special needs of novice teachers:

1. the teacher's personal needs as a new professional
2. the teacher's situational needs as a contributing member of the organization

Characteristics of Effective Leadership

From the earliest to the most recent, studies have consistently cited numerous variables commonly associated with effective school leadership (Brookover, Beady, Flood, Schweitzer, & Weisenbaker, 1979; Clark, Lotto, & McCarthy, 1980; Edmonds & Frederiksen, 1978; Norris, Baptiste, Weise, & Macaluso, 1988; Rutherford, 1985; Ubben & Hughes, 1992; and a host of others). With no intent to suggest any rank of importance, we need focus on only the following:

- a visionary principal who communicates a distinct school mission
- clearly articulated goals for its attainment

- continual monitoring of teaching practices, with specific feedback
- collaboration among faculty
- staff development that advances the school's mission while augmenting professional growth of teachers

Investigators of effective schooling carefully avoid assigning *causation* to the principal who leads a high-achieving school; however, research conclusions commonly reflect clear inferences, if not assumptions, about the principal's direct influence on most attributes generating a distinct campus "personality" (Purkey & Smith, 1983).

Vision.   Norris (chapter 3) has provided an extensive analysis of traits, behaviors, and processes inherent to visionary leadership. Without repeating the substance of that discussion, we do feel the need briefly to consider the concept's implications as principals establish relationships with novice teachers.

The notion of *vision* implies substantial reliance of human resources to transform it into practice. A principal who understands the nature and dynamics of that reliance will recognize intuitively the value and power of making a *personal* investment in every staff member. The more precise a principal's vision, the more important that members of the school community be invited to *share* values, attitudes, and beliefs that shape it. We will more fully explore the dynamics of those elements later in this section of the chapter as we view the novice teacher merging with the context of the school culture. We wish to note here, however, that every staff member who *enters* the school setting with a clear set of key values and beliefs will strengthen the overall sense of vision for the school. Therefore, in considering new teacher candidates, the principal focuses keenly on eliciting evidence of philosophies and working styles that reflect a "fit" with an established vision of excellence. If successful, the selection process can prevent issues arising from philosophical differences between principal and teacher or from the teacher's lack of commitment to educational values driving the school's mission. Effective schools research has produced a vivid interpretation of traits and behaviors that characterize exemplary principals. The following excerpt captures the essence of that portrait:

> The principal provides the *voice* and the *vision* which move the school beyond achieving competence to maximizing potential. Such a leader inspires students and staff to embrace the mission/purpose of the school; to awaken their own untapped resources; to reach constantly higher; to trust one another in the pursuit of common goals; and to expect success. . . . In every facet of the leadership process, the exemplary principal models the type of behavior expected of students and staff. The leader's vision must be clearly communicated through behavior, and it must be shared by those who can make it a reality. Therefore, the leader must stand as a developer of human beings, directing much of his or her energy toward building relationships, inspiring trust, and unleashing the power of human resources within the school. (Norris et al., 1988)

Long-term Goals.   Sergiovanni and Starratt (1988) propose three assumptions of instructional leadership particularly important to the novice teacher:

1. Leadership implies relationships with other people that inspire loyalty, commitment, and regard for others.
2. Leadership is enacted over *time*—with no expectation of "quick fixes" or immediate changes.
3. Leadership is always exercised within some *community*, organization, or group—some societal entity that the leader creates or re-creates.

All three of these assumptions lend a particular character to "how things are done" in a school, suggesting that a strong leader executes central responsibilities by aiming directly at the growth and development of followers. The principal with firm resolve to create an environment that nurtures mutual trust, collaboration, respect for others, and learning as the primary goal for everyone, chooses new teachers who share this view of humanity and who are likely to demonstrate loyalty and commitment to that vision for the school. Equally important, perhaps, the principal expects that it will take *time* for the novice to develop both a proactive stance for school improvement and the instructional skills required to accomplish it.

Instructional Supervision

We turn now to ways a principal can best influence instructional skill development and to another of the most consistently observed attributes of effective schools: the direct supervision of the novice's performance in the classroom. Much of the literature on instructional supervision reflects an assumption that supervision is particularly important for beginning teachers. Consider, for example, that clinical supervision, a common form underlying just about all contemporary practice of supervision, originated in the Harvard MAT program to prepare new teachers (Cogan, 1973). The conventional process of student teaching also reflects the importance placed on supervision for beginning teachers, as does the emerging practice of mentoring, a process that provides beginning teachers with on-the-job guidance and feedback from experienced teachers and university personnel. However, these familiar processes imply another underlying assumption: ideally, supervisory intervention occurs before a teacher has developed routines and habits that would interfere with effective teaching and learning. This assumption may have the unfortunate consequence of introducing supervision to a beginning teacher's mind as primarily judgmental and hierarchical; nonetheless, it operates at a tacit level and for beginning teachers helps establish permanent expectations of what supervision entails.

This emphasis on supervision for beginning teachers makes perfect sense; what makes *little* sense, however, is the notable absence of any discussion of the principal's involvement in the process. According to supervision literature, the task falls to other teachers or persons at a district level who hold such titles as *staff development specialist* or *curriculum coordinator* or *supervisor* (Pajak, 1989). Granted, the principal's formal performance evaluations of new teachers are acknowledged, but these evaluations meet summative rather than formative purposes, and they apparently occur too infrequently to influence much growth.

Intensive and Sustained

Regardless of whether principals directly supervise novice teachers, certain assumptions about supervising teachers help articulate an appropriate role for principals in the process. The first of these assumptions is that in order to be effective, supervision must be intensive (Goldhammer, 1969; Acheson & Gall, 1987). Cogan justifies the intensity of clinical supervision this way:

> The teacher needs a sustained, expert program to help him relinquish his existing classroom behavior in favor of new behavior, a program strong enough to help him apply such new competencies to the specific conditions that obtain for each child, for each class and for the teacher himself. (1973, p. 4)

The repeated cycle of clinical supervision assists novice teachers with planning and provides sufficiently frequent feedback on their developing teaching practice to serve as both support and reinforcement. Ideally, the clinical supervision cycle is repeated weekly to accomplish this goal. Such intensive clinical supervision obviously consumes a great deal of time—a minimum commitment of two hours per week per teacher. Small wonder that most principals don't do it!

Intensive supervision also requires a high level of skill and knowledge about the specific subjects and grade levels taught by the novice teacher and about the practice of supervision itself. Noreen Garman describes the "skilled service" of supervisors who "offer a service to teachers in the educational community as a result of prolonged and specialized intellectual training and practice" (Garman, 1982). For this reason, if for no other, it becomes unreasonable to expect a principal to act as primary provider of supervision to new teachers. How could any principal—even at an elementary level, much less at a secondary level—possibly have the content knowledge and the practical experience to effectively help novice teachers in all of a school's different instructional settings?

Tailored to the Individual

Another assumption found in the literature is that supervision is most effective when it is individually tailored to both the teacher and the context of teaching (Cogan, 1973; Blumberg, 1980; Grimmett, Rostad, & Ford, 1992). Again, this is a fundamental assumption of clinical supervision, albeit one that reflects the still-too-common view that a teacher's sphere of influence is bounded by classroom walls. Nonetheless, the clinical approach to supervision does provide a novice teacher with valuable knowledge about progress in developing classroom skills.

By observing specific events of teaching and learning in a teacher's classroom, the clinical supervisor gathers information specific to that teacher and teaching situation. That information is then used by the supervisor and the teacher in analyzing and discussing the teacher's practice and in planning subsequent lessons.

Such individualization of supervision has been more specifically articulated in Glickman's model of developmental supervision (1985). According to this model, a supervisor must diagnose a teacher's particular level of practical and conceptual skill in order to determine whether to work with that teacher in directive, collaborative, or nondirective ways. The model assumes that the supervisor can consciously select from a repertoire of supervisory strategies those that will best promote professional development of an individual teacher.

Tailoring supervision to individual novice teachers requires considerable skill. Even though principals generally have some training in supervision, they don't often have the time or opportunity to develop as wide a repertoire of supervisory skills as they would wish. Realistically, principals recognize that while they might be able to provide novices with help on generic aspects of teaching, such as classroom management, they assume that other professionals will assume responsibility for the level of specific diagnostic and curricular assistance a novice needs to fine-tune teaching.

Colleagueship or Peer Supervision

Yet another assumption about supervision concerns what Cogan (1973) has described as the "colleagueship" that characterizes the optimum relationship between supervisor and teacher (Alfonso & Goldsberry, 1982; Smyth, 1984; Little, 1987). The essential feature of colleagueship (or, as others have called it, "collegiality") is that it is nonhierarchical; it "derives from a conviction that both the teacher and supervisor give and receive support" (Cogan, 1973, p. 69). Although Garman (1982) has urged expansion of the collegiality concept to encompass identification "with the community of teachers and especially with the heritage of the teaching-learning and schooling" (p. 41), the traditional view of supervisory collegiality doesn't include anyone other than the supervisor and the teacher. The supervisor is implicitly assumed to be a primary and even a sole resource for the teacher's professional growth. Interestingly enough, though, the converse is not assumed to be true. The supervisor is tacitly assumed to be involved in collegial relationships with other teachers as well as with administrators and supervisory peers. The supervisor's extended network of relationships raises possibilities of a contrived collegiality that masks an inherently unequal relationship between supervisor and teacher.

Perhaps this assumption of collegiality—contrived or genuine—in supervisory relationships poses the greatest obstacle for a principal who would directly supervise novice teachers. The very nature of the school leadership position accords the principal full responsibility and authority to *evaluate* each faculty member's teaching competence and professional growth. How can a principal then expect a beginning teacher to willingly reveal personal limits in knowledge or skill? It is simply too much of a risk.

Evaluation of Teaching

The question of whether a teacher's supervisor should also evaluate that teacher stimulates continuous discussion. Advocates of combining the roles claim that the supervisor's extensive knowledge of the teacher's skill and growth work in the competent teacher's favor (Hunter, 1984; Tanner & Tanner, 1987; McQuarrie & Wood, 1991). Other, perhaps more realistic, writers hold it unlikely that teachers can ever develop sufficient trust in an evaluator to be completely open about their teaching practice (Blumberg, 1980; Gitlin & Smyth, 1989). Perhaps a more fruitful discussion of the supervisor as evaluator construes evaluation more broadly as a process of interpretation and decision making rather than simply measurement of the teacher's success in meeting certain specified standards (Sergiovanni & Starratt, 1988). Regardless of which argument one accepts, however, the "cold war" (Blumberg, 1980) continues between teachers and evaluators whom they perceive as infiltrating their ranks in the guise of supervision.

Principals who want to help novice teachers improve their practice need to recognize the influence of this war. Given their role as formal evaluators, and the power of this role to affect a teacher's professional life, they can reasonably expect their direct supervision of novices to produce some degree of caution and compliance rather than risk-taking on the teacher's part.

Induction

One might expect the professional literature regarding induction of new teachers to yield helpful information about how principals can best help teachers at the start of their careers. This literature acknowledges the unique needs of beginning teachers with a specificity not found in discussions of either instructional leadership or supervision. Nevertheless, it gives the principal no special role in meeting these needs. Instead, mentor teachers, district level personnel, and possibly university teacher education faculty are identified as the most appropriate professionals to work with beginning teachers (Brooks, 1987; Huling-Austin, 1988).

This omission of an expressly identified role for the principal in the induction process may reflect a general perception of induction as an extension of teacher education. Much of the literature on induction emanates from scholars in that field. The failure to include principals in the induction process may say more about how the balkanized structure of university colleges of education maintains clear separation between programs to prepare teachers and those to prepare administrators than it does about how best to meet novice teachers' needs.

Assignment of Mentor Teachers

Certain assumptions in the induction literature warrant examination in terms of implications for the principal's role in the induction of new teachers. The first of these addresses the assignment of experienced teachers as mentors as a primary vehicle for providing help to new teachers (Galvez-Hjornevik, 1986; Little, 1990). Most often the principal identifies and assigns mentors. The literature suggests that successful mentoring depends largely on a careful match between mentors and novices in terms of their teaching assignments and their proximity to each other. Furthermore, principals must understand that in addition to exceptional teaching skills, a mentor must also possess the willingness and an ability to offer the beginning teacher helpful assistance and feedback on teaching. All too often, mentors do not receive sufficient training to provide these services, in which case principals may need to take a more active role in monitoring mentors' performance and in providing the appropriate training.

Issues of Adult Learning

In all phases of facilitating growth for the novice teacher, a principal will do well to tailor the process to adult needs. A body of research on adult learners points to a very specific mind-set adults bring to most learning experiences (Weise, 1992). Adults generally choose educational activities as a result of experiencing some inadequacy in coping with current life problems, and they want to apply today's learning tomorrow. This time perspective of immediate application creates a problem-centered orientation to learning that is satisfied only by activity organized around concrete problem areas recognized by the learner as authentic to field experience (Knowles, 1980). One widely accepted model for accommodating this orientation outlines a process in which the instructor serves primarily as a facilitator who designs strategies to acquire content and only secondarily as a content resource. The model assumes access to a variety of content resources (peers, experts, media, field experiences) other than the instructor, whose chief responsibility is to know appropriate resources and to direct learners to them at appropriate times (Knowles, 1980).

In addition to appropriate content, the novice's learning experiences should include elements known to nurture self-esteem in the adult learner (Knowles, 1980). The psychological environment should communicate the following:

- mutual respect (acknowledgement of the value of the learners)
- collaborativeness (sharing rather than competition, using peers as a resource for learning)
- mutual trust (as opposed to the power of teacher)
- supportiveness (learners accepted rather than judged)
- openness and authenticity (teacher modeling by expressing honest thought and feelings)

- pleasure (learning experiences that are enjoyable and adventurous)
- humanness (physical comfort and safe, accepting atmosphere)

The process itself should actively engage novices in several key events:

- mutual planning, to gain commitment through a feeling of ownership in decisions
- diagnosing their own learning needs, using school expectations as a standard
- formulating learning objectives
- designing learning plans
- evaluating their learning

Perhaps the principal's key function in the process is to help the novice actually carry out the plan and to monitor progress through completion.

Professional Initiation

A second assumption culled from the literature is that induction efforts, like supervision, focus on individual novice teachers. Common practices place considerable emphasis on developing generic skills of teaching, such as classroom management or lesson planning. Often, such development activities directly address successful performance evaluations required for the novice's permanent certification (Berry & Ginsberg, 1988; Darling-Hammond & Sclan, 1992). Such individually-focused efforts to meet specific competence requirements may help develop basic knowledge and technical skill, but they don't necessarily address what Huling-Austin (1988) has identified as a responsibility to transmit the culture of the system to beginning teachers.

Learning to operate successfully within a specific *culture* adds a new dimension to the concept of induction—making entry into the *profession* of teaching as opposed to entry into the *practice* of teaching currently highlighted in the induction literature. Herein may lie the principal's most critical role with novice teachers, a role that moves beyond the lists of instructional leadership behaviors to a holistic notion of cultural leadership. If we accept the idea, as the literature on supervision and induction suggests, that a principal does not necessarily provide the beginning teacher with the practical training needed for successful classroom performance, we should not infer that the principal has no key function in the induction process. Evaluation studies of induction programs (Swanson, 1968; Brooks, 1986) reveal a principal's interest and involvement as an important ingredient for their success. In programs where the principal maintains a visible and positive presence, beginning teachers feel accepted and approved by the primary authority figure in their school (Hoffman, Griffin, Edwards, Paulissen, O'Neal, Barnes, & Verstegen, 1985).

The Holmes Group (1986) recommends that principals make a rather dramatic distinction between experienced teachers and novices. In fact, this group suggests that first-year teachers not even be inducted as full professionals, but rather as instructors *preparing* for the profession. Addressing the policy implications of such a drastic measure would not serve our purposes here. However, the recommendation includes certain specific strategies principals might consider equally valuable within the traditional framework of induction:

- New teachers would not have formal responsibility for taking part in setting school policy, evaluating programs or personnel, counseling students and parents, or deciding curriculum. This would not preclude novices' *observing* such processes; in fact, observation of such activities could provide key opportunities to learn the situation-specific skills needed by beginning teachers.
- Novices would be expected to do only what their limited background and experience prepares them to do *well*, i.e., interact with others about their subjects. Early communications of this expectation could pave the way for novices to participate freely in collaborative activities by sharing their expertise and successes with colleagues.
- The principal would carefully define responsibilities for the first-year teacher, avoiding assignments that inexperience might cause to end in failure.

Such strategies might serve as useful vehicles for facilitating the novices' transition from learning *about* the school as a student in teacher education programs to learning *within* the school as a new member of the culture.

Cultural Leadership

The concept of school culture, which is receiving increased attention in professional journals, provides a broad, rich context for analyzing principal behaviors intended to communicate the school's mission, in this instance to beginning teachers. Purkey and Smith (1983) cite three process variables evidenced by school cultures that produce notable student achievement:

1. collegiality and collaborative planning
2. a sense of community—a feeling of *belonging* to a supportive organization clearly perceived as such by all members
3. a clear mission, supported by definite goals and high expectations

The latter, which requires continual monitoring, can stimulate and direct both the energy and attention of teachers—*if* the principal has managed to achieve consensus on goals and expectations. Cultural leadership assumes that consensus wields far more power than does control. Helping the new teacher to develop a sense of membership in the community and to take initiative as a participant in the consensus process presents one of the most important (and most *challenging*) tasks the principal undertakes.

Synergy

A principal acts as cultural leader by establishing and reinforcing key values, beliefs, rituals, and social norms associated with the school's mission. The process builds a synergy that sparks both the organization as a whole and each of its members as individuals. Kottkamp (1984) states that "when a culture is strong and cohesive, it provides a sort of multiplier effect for individual work efforts. Individuals are supported, guided, and given identity by a social web which moves them toward common goals" (p. 152). Beginning teachers have named these same elements among their strongest needs as they enter the profession. A principal may be able to offer some measure of support, guidance, and identity through direct interventions. However, for the novice to accomplish and sustain meaningful growth from the efforts, the larger school context must provide continuous reinforcement. Furthermore, learning within this type of environment may exert a more lasting influence on the new teacher than on any other member of the staff.

Risk Taking

We have mentioned the principal's vision of excellence as a key factor in promoting such an environment. However, vision and understanding alone do not make things happen. As Barker (1990) so aptly puts it, "Vision without action is merely a dream. Action without vision is just passing time. Vision with action can change the world" (p. 7). Studies on school improvement abound with strategies devised by principals to foster and maintain a mission-oriented synergism. Principals often approach the task by encouraging, even requiring, teachers to set personal goals for professional growth (Leithwood & Montgomery, 1982). In the process, principals clearly and publicly express support for innovations aligned with school goals. Most first-year teachers have not yet developed confidence in even the most traditional practices. At the same time, recent studies have identified the willingness to take risks as a major predicator of the novice's success (Chandler, Robinson, & Noyes, 1990). Therefore, it is especially important that the novice receive a clear, unequivocal message of support for innovation before risking anything new. And that message must come directly from the principal.

Rallis and Highsmith (1986) associate these actions with the vision of a *developmental* leader, who demonstrates a willingness to experiment and change, a tolerance for messiness, and the ability to invest in long-term outcomes—traits that provide a safety net for novices practicing new skills. The developmental leader understands that failures often yield more valuable insight into the learning process and the craft of teaching than does reliance on proven techniques. Ideally, the principal also serves as a model by sharing personal experiences with risk-taking, self-improvement, and goal-setting. Perhaps most important, the principal treats all teachers, including the novice, as professionals capable of improving instruction, thereby creating a safe environment for change and growth. Burns' related concept of transformational leadership (see Hughes, chapter 1) centers on the inevitability of change and the leader's opportunity— even obligation—to facilitate growth in human resources as a way of influencing its direction. No member of the school community stands to benefit more from the transformational approach than does the novice teacher.

Ubbens and Hughes' (1992) "culture builders" corroborate the value of the risky practices of experimentation and modeling. As one incentive for innovative efforts, they suggest that faculty meetings highlight teachers' sharing of new ideas. Principals can emphasize the importance of reaching out to the knowledge base by expecting teachers to demonstrate active curiosity about the expanding information base in the field. As leaders, they influence most, perhaps, by modeling their own love for learning and desire to improve as they share *their* new learnings with faculty individually and in groups. This spirit of learning among colleagues provides the ideal setting for novices to "try their wings" without fear of failure or threat of violating accepted norms.

A Learning Community

The school culture we have described thus far transcends the use of recipes gleaned from observing effective leaders. The character of each school is unique in so many ways that blanket transfer of strategies from one to another probably creates more problems than it solves. Barth's (1986) perspective on current reform may reflect the sentiments of many visionary principals who "are growing weary of the logic of lists and would prefer that their own common sense be honored" (p. 295). He cites several projects (the Coalition of Essential Schools and the Bay Area Writing Project, for example) that represent, in his words,

> a vision of a school quite unlike a center of production for principals, teachers, and pupils. . . . [They] seem to value and honor learning, participation, and cooperation above prescription, production, and competition, . . . [embracing instead] the concept of the school as a *community of learners*, a place where all participants—teachers, principals, parents, and students—engage in learning and teaching. . . . School is a place where students discover, and adults rediscover, the joys, the difficulties, and the satisfactions of learning. . . . Many conditions appear to foster learning, such as posing one's own problems, risk taking, humor, high standards coupled with low anxiety, collaboration with another learner, and the importance of modeling. . . . *That* a principal is learning something is far more important to the school than any list of *what* a principal should know. (pp. 295–96)

Barth's concept (1986) of a community of learners embodies several assumptions that bode extremely well for novice teachers.

- School improvement depends on the right conditions.
- Adults and students alike learn when conditions are right.
- The greatest need in schools is to improve the culture in terms of interpersonal relationships and learning experiences.
- Schools should provide an environment that promotes and sustains learning among *all* members of the school community.

At the risk of indulging in the very practice Barth criticizes, we would be hard pressed to create guidelines more propitious than this "list" for a principal dedicated to the professional development of beginning teachers. Within these parameters, the principal acts as head *learner*, not teacher, engaging in "the most important enterprise of the school—experiencing, displaying, modeling, and celebrating what it is hoped and expected that teachers and pupils will do" (Barth, 1986, p. 296). We can think of no better way to communicate that learning does *not* indicate deficiency (a perception often feared by novices) but rather provides an avenue to growth and satisfaction.

Principals' Views of Novice Teachers

We turn now from the world of theory analyzed in the literature to the world of practice. In this and following sections of the chapter, we will consider what, at least in principals' opinions, new teachers need to learn and how principals themselves might best promote that learning.

For information about what principals think, we undertook a secondary analysis of interviews conducted earlier with seven principals—two high school, one middle school, and three elementary. The interviews, part of a larger study funded by the Danforth Foundation on collaborative decision-making in the principals' schools (Clift, Veal, Holland, Johnson, & McCarthy, in press), had initially been developed to gather general information about the principals' professional experiences and philosophies of practice and about issues they were currently facing in their schools.

Interview data reflect administrators' growing concern about the increased demands implied in calls for "instructional leadership," as well as uneasiness about how, as principals, they can meet additional demands. These concerns surfaced particularly when principals spoke about new teachers. We therefore decided to look specifically at the principals' comments about new teachers learning to teach and about their leadership responsibility for such learning. Comments were initially divided into two groups: those indicating the principals' view of what novice teachers *need* to learn and those describing the principals' responsibility for *helping* them learn. We then recognized, and summarize below, five themes that cut across the material in each of these categories.

Content of Learning Needs

School Setting.   Principals unanimously identified novice teachers' need to learn, and learn quickly, about their particular school settings. For immediate survival, they need to receive adequate nuts-and-bolts information, such as the campus layout (especially in large secondary schools), certain bureaucratic details (e.g., completing enrollment and attendance records), and the daily bell schedule. Beyond survival, they need a thorough acquaintance with social and cultural norms of the school, including how to line up students, how to keep corridor traffic flowing, how to work with colleagues (in clusters, grade level, or content area teams), and how to communicate with parents. They also need to learn the more subtle dimensions of school structure, such as who the unofficial school leaders are and which colleagues are approachable and willing to share materials and ideas.

Principal's Expectations.   Several principals also mentioned the need for novices to learn about the principal. One principal noted that she expects new teachers to develop an understanding—and hopefully an appreciation—of her strong management skills. Another adamantly insisted that teachers share her commitment to "meet the total needs of the child." To illustrate, she recalled a teacher's sending to her office a child who had missed breakfast, knowing that "there are rules and there are rules," and that a hungry child could not learn much. It is often difficult to determine whether a principal's expectations reflect personal goals or a more general school mission. For example, the principal of a predominantly minority high school expected teachers to work toward the "primary goal of the school," which was "learning what motivates minorities."

Students' Backgrounds.   Principals universally acknowledged the need for teachers—both new and experienced—to learn more about students' various cultural backgrounds. Even in a suburban school with more than 95-percent white, middle-class students, the principal—like urban and near urban counterparts—wants teachers to learn how to interpret behaviors of students from other cultures and to recognize the values various cultures assign to such issues as corporal punishment or placement in a pre-first grade class. In suburban schools, teachers working with only a few students from other cultures can learn rather easily about those cultures through individual cases—usually from the students' parents. However, teachers in urban and near-urban schools serve large numbers of students from cultures other than their own, and even teachers who share students' minority status often represent significantly different social and economic backgrounds. (For a discussion of multi-cultural issues, see Baptiste, chapter 4).

Principals believe that teachers can overcome these differences by learning more about students' home environments, including communities in which they live. More than one principal mentioned the importance of teachers gaining a sense of the community by driving through it. One high school principal told of taking teachers on a narrated bus tour of the community. In addition to awareness of the general community environment, principals believe that if teachers hope to involve family members in helping students succeed in school, they also need to learn about specific circumstances in students' homes. One principal, for instance, noted how teachers had learned that although notes and phone calls to Hispanic parents rarely produced results, those parents did respond to conferences. Novice teachers in this school are now expected to hold conferences with parents.

Interpersonal Skills.   Two of the elementary principals spoke of new teachers needing to learn and refine interpersonal skills. For one principal, this means learning to care about the children so that they can identify and meet social as well as academic needs. In talking about how teachers must care about children, the principal revealed a view of caring that closely resembles the nurturing provided by a good parent. This principal believes that a teacher must have the sensitivity to solve the kinds of nonacademic problems that kids bring with them to school. "If you don't have the time," she says, referring to teachers, "if you don't have the caring necessary to work with the total child, it's like an empty home."

Opportunities for Learning

Experience—The Best Teacher.   Invariably, the principals expressed a belief that novice teachers learn best from experience. Perhaps the most dramatic expression of this general belief came from a principal who described "the clinical approach to teaching," in which prospective teachers actually work in schools and classrooms as a major part of their teacher education program. He compared this training to that of physicians who, as medical students, learn by treating actual patients with a senior physician directing them to "Stick your hand in here, let's feel for this part of the body. . . . Let's get your hands in there and feel it and touch it. Let's get the different layers of skin and pull them back and let you see it and touch it." Teachers, he maintains, need the same kind of experiential learning; they "need to see for themselves." Or, in the words of another principal, "You just don't know until you get in there and experience it and do it."

Principals' comments about the value of experience contain implicit (and occasionally explicit) criticism of current approaches to teacher education. One secondary principal, recalling his own preparation for teaching, admits that the theory he learned in university courses and six weeks of student teaching left him woefully unprepared for the reality facing a novice teacher. Another principal made a more sweeping criticism of teacher education: "What we are doing now is not 'cutting it,' and we are losing a lot of good potential teachers."

Personalized Support.   The principals mentioned a number of opportunities or occasions that help teachers learn and grow professionally. For novice teachers, the principals all supported assignment of a mentor or buddy teacher to help the newcomer. Most of them also saw great benefit in arranging for novice teachers to observe experienced teachers in the classroom and in providing individual help, particularly for dealing with individual students or managing the classroom. In fact, principals mentioned a number of direct ways they see themselves helping teachers to improve their practice. One example was to provide teachers with instruction on criteria for assessing teachers in mandated evaluation processes. Such instruction would include specific illustrations of teaching techniques identified by the evaluation instrument as excellent practice.

Group In-service Training

Invariably principals cited in-service presentations and workshops as opportunities for all teachers, novice as well as experienced, to gain new information, particularly about policies and practices expected by the district. They also mentioned the importance of teamwork, although again new teachers were not singled out as the only ones to benefit from collaborative experiences. Two of the principals (one secondary and one elementary) designed faculty team structures as the primary organizational units within their schools. These principals believed that teachers must be able to discuss and solve their own problems of practice with their team members.

The principals expressed differing notions about the nature and sources of assistance they can provide new teachers. Taken collectively, the principals' comments present polarized views of principals' roles and responsibilities in helping teachers. Some depended largely on sources outside of the teacher, the principals, and even the school, relegating major responsibility for helping novice teachers to the district through in-service programs. This view limits not only the principals' responsibility for identifying teachers' needs and strategies to meet those needs but also the teacher's role in recognizing learning needs and choosing appropriate responses. In fact, reliance on central office clearly implies that helping new teachers learn and grow does not fall within the everyday responsibilities of the principal and workings of the school. It also creates a hierarchy for assistance; the novice teacher as a compliant recipient of help is essentially cast in a student role, subservient to and dependent upon the giver of such help.

Empowerment of Teachers

Evidence suggests that principals believe teachers should become more self-directed. It is interesting, though, that these principals make no distinctions between novice and experienced teachers' needs for autonomy and decision-making power, nor do they acknowledge any process by which teachers can gradually assume such power as their understanding and experience increase. In one secondary school, for instance, the principal organized the faculty into five clusters of five teachers, each of whom represented a content area, and all of whom taught the same 150 students. While the principal described how enthusiastically teachers, students, and parents received the cluster arrangement, he did not distinguish between its impact on novice and seasoned teachers.

Elementary principals conveyed an impression that they too have essentially disregarded the disparate needs of novice and experienced teachers for independent decision-making. Efforts toward empowerment still target the faculty as a homogeneous group. Only one of the seven principals even alluded to helping teachers acquire power by providing them with opportunities to make decisions. Perhaps the failure of principals to think about novices developmentally in terms of their decision-making ability fosters a certain inertia in terms of teachers developing beyond dependence on the principal. One elementary principal poignantly expressed her frustration with such a condition, wishing that teachers would "release their talents" and take on more decision-making responsibility, rather than always looking to her to make decisions.

Instructional Support and Feedback

Not all of the principals referred directly to novice teachers' need to learn specific techniques of teaching, but this need was implied in their references to evaluation criteria—these principals use a state-mandated observation form—and also in the references to district level in-service programs focused on curriculum materials and instructional methods. Comments about specific instructional learning needs included novices' particular need to master classroom management techniques, a need recognized at both elementary and secondary levels. One elementary principal also referred specifically to novices needing to learn the elements of the "lesson cycle" that comprises the nucleus of the adopted teacher appraisal instrument.

Elementary principals offered the most specific comments about techniques needed by the novice. These principals tended to reflect a keener sense of the content area and instructional strategies used by their teachers. Their schools were smaller, with fewer faculty members than those of their secondary counterparts. Accordingly, while a secondary principal talks generally of teachers needing to include critical thinking in their lessons, an elementary principal talks of working directly with teachers as they learn how to pace delivery of a new reading series, or of working with a teacher on how to make up work missed by a student who has been absent for 11 days.

Classroom Observation

The principals recognize observation of instruction as benefiting novice teachers more than any other form of assistance. Given the evaluation observations required of principals, it is not surprising that this strategy would be mentioned frequently. The principals rely on classroom observations to offer the novice "tips" on effective teaching methods developed through their own experience as good teachers. At the same time, principals' opinions of the positive value of classroom observation are quite generalized. They see themselves not only as direct observers offering guidance based on events that occur during the lesson, but also as facilitators of various other observation experiences. Principals talked of their obligation to arrange occasions for novice teachers to visit experienced teachers, for a teacher needing help with a particular teaching area to observe a teacher skilled in that area, and for teachers to observe colleagues using new materials or techniques.

Principals also agreed that various levels of feedback provide the clearest learning opportunity for novice teachers. Most obvious to the principals and cited by almost all of them is the formal process of teacher evaluation. They see the process providing teachers with performance-specific information based on some general standards of good teaching. For some principals, no other occasion arises to observe teachers and comment on their instructional expertise. Surprisingly, however, these principals acknowledged no differences in evaluating novice and experienced teachers. This lack of distinction raises some fundamental questions about levels of expectation and about the developmental use of observation and feedback.

Other Forms of Feedback

Evaluation of teaching does not constitute the only means of feedback for teachers. One principal mentioned several other important sources of feedback that teachers ought to consider, including parents, who usually inform the teacher if some problem arises. A teacher's colleagues provide another source for such feedback. A teacher gains important information from other teachers "if everybody is coming in and wants to know how you do something," says the principal, "or if people are turning their backs on you when they see you coming." Finally, this principal see students' performance in the classroom as feedback to a teacher about quality of teaching and classroom management.

School Culture

Several principals acknowledged a socializing influence the school culture exerts on novice teachers. Novices not only need to learn *about* that culture, but they also learn by *joining* it. They learn from their contacts with other teachers the norms of behavior in that school—whether the principal expects teachers to spend considerable time working in teams or to concentrate more on individual efforts, and so on. The principals recognize that while some contact among teachers centers strictly on school business, a social dimension also allows informal sharing of information and experiences.

School Size.   Principals believe the size of the school directly influences the relative ease with which novice teachers actively join the school culture and learn what they need to know about the school. In large secondary schools, principals admit that they themselves can't be aware of all facets of the school culture. Three of the secondary principals described these schools as difficult and demanding places to work. The fourth principal agreed that his school is demanding, but he also recognized the benefit of larger schools enabling teachers to acquire deeper knowledge about content and instruction in their content areas by allowing them to teach several sections in the same grade and often at the same ability level.

Collaboration

One elementary principal stressed skills that teachers need to acquire for dealing effectively with parents. She wanted teachers to develop the ability to discuss children's problems with parents in an informative as well as a sensitive way. She also focused on novice teachers' gaining confidence in their own professional judgments so that they deal with parents more comfortably. This concern about learning to work with parents came the closest of any principal's comments to addressing the possibility that novice teachers might need to learn *how* to work with other adults. The omission is interesting inasmuch as all of the principals, elementary and secondary, described their *expectation* that teachers work with administrators as well as with other teachers in clusters, grade level, or content area groups.

The expectation suggests an alternative view of help generated within collaborative relationships—of principal and novice, of novice and mentor teacher, or of novice and other teaching colleagues. Situations occurring in actual practice within a particular school stimulate instructional questions and problems for which colleagues seek answers together. While solutions may come from outside sources, responsibility for deciding the *usefulness* of those solutions rests with teachers and administrators who will carry out the decisions. The process places both principals and teachers in the role of learners, all seeking to increase their professional knowledge by addressing incidents of teaching practice. This view assumes a working relationship among adults, each with a unique knowledge and experience base, and each respecting what the others bring to the task. Uncertain about their ability to contribute and somewhat fearful of *risking* contribution, novice teachers may approach such activities rather timidly. Before principals can expect novices to participate, they themselves, as well as experienced teachers, must explicitly acknowledge the value of the novice's opinions and must carefully guard against disdaining questionable suggestions that might naturally accompany inexperience.

Discrepancies Between Principals' Expressed Views and Observed Behaviors

In their discussions of novice teachers' needs, principals also included references to ways of addressing those needs. While such remarks provide useful information for helping to isolate and define specific aspects of the principal's role with new teachers, they do not alone tell the whole story. They offer only the "normative" dimension of principals' own views of what their role should be. To understand the full story, we must hold this normative view up against what principals actually do in interacting with novices and facilitating their professional development. This comparison produces interesting discrepancies between what the principals say and what they do, or to use Argyris and Schon's (1974) terms, between their "espoused theory" and their "theory-in-action."

Using the same framework that we used to classify what the principals said about new teachers' learning needs, we will now examine what principals say and what they actually do to help novice teachers. In particular, we will explore the discrepancies revealed between the two.

Content of Learning Needs

The first discrepancy concerns the principals' expressed belief in their ability to identify and articulate common learning needs of all beginning teachers and also the individual needs of each novice to learn specific policies and practices that will enhance performance in a particular teaching assignment. The anxiety principals feel about insufficient time to work with beginning teachers grows largely from the belief that they could really help these teachers if they just had time.

However, principals' belief in their potential value to novice teachers doesn't necessarily hold up to scrutiny. Most principals, for example, have only rudimentary training in the skills of clinical supervision. Furthermore, their practice of the supervisory skills of classroom observation, analysis, and conferencing consists primarily of mandated summative evaluations of teaching performance using criteria specified by the state or district. The evidence suggests overwhelmingly that such evaluations contribute little if anything to teachers' understanding and improvement of their teaching practice.

It is also questionable whether principals can possibly possess the wide range of knowledge of content and curriculum they need to advise teachers adequately in various subject areas with students across the spectrum of ability and motivation. In other words, principals can't reasonably expect to be all things to all teachers. Only one of the principals we spoke with, and that one the principal of a large high school, acknowledged these limitations.

Another aspect of this discrepancy between principals' belief in their ability to help new teachers and the help they actually give is the principals' strong conviction that teaching skill develops only through experience. This school-of-hard-knocks philosophy clearly contradicts their professed affirmation of basic precepts of supervision and induction—that novice teachers will grow and develop in their teaching skill with intensive time, individual assistance, and specific feedback. Apparently the principals are not only unaware of the discrepancy between what they say and do to help novices, they are also unaware of the inconsistencies in their beliefs about how new teachers learn to be better teachers.

Opportunities for Learning

Principals reveal a second discrepancy between their espoused theory and their theory-in-action in maintaining the importance of providing novice teachers with opportunities to learn but reporting little responsibility for the opportunities that do exist. Formally structured learning opportunities for novice teachers are usually orchestrated at a district level, in the form of either in-service training sessions or requirements that experienced teachers be assigned as mentors to work with novice teachers at the building level. As for more informal learning opportunities—team or department members sharing lesson materials with the novice, conversations occurring between novice and mentor, etc.—these events are by their very nature beyond a principal's direct control.

To more closely align their actions with their commitment to providing appropriate learning opportunities for novice teachers, principals might develop a calendar of activities and meetings to address novice teachers' special needs. These occasions could focus exclusively on communicating what the new principal expects of new teachers and how the teachers can go about meeting those expectations successfully. None of the principals we spoke with did such planning for new teachers.

Empowerment of Teachers

The principals revealed a third discrepancy between their overt commitment to empowering teachers as decision-making professionals and actual practices subverting that commitment. For example, one principal spoke eloquently about recognizing the talent and skill of his teachers and wanting them to feel free to express themselves and to make decisions. That same principal invariably dominated any meeting he attended at the school by talking nearly 95 percent of the time during any given meeting.

The issue of empowerment for beginning teachers is particularly sensitive. The principal must maintain a delicate balance between providing essential information and direction for the novice and at the same time allowing the novice to participate actively in setting a meaningful agenda for professional development. It is a good guess that the principal who was frustrated when a novice teacher failed to use information provided by teammates had not been paying attention to whether teachers in that school were encouraged to be selective about what was useful to them and to interpret the information they received to fit their personal styles.

Classroom Observations

A fourth discrepancy between the principals' espoused theory and their theory-in-action concerns the high value they place on observing instruction as an essential means for helping novice teachers improve their teaching. The principals frequently observed novice teachers during their brief and informal "walk-through" visits to their classrooms, but none of the principals engaged in systematic data collection during those visits. In fact, the only times principals documented their observations were during summative evaluations.

Granted, time constraints may limit the principal's using classroom observation as part of a formal clinical supervision process that also includes analyzing and using the collected data in a conference with the teacher. However, if a principal understands that a teacher benefits from observation only as part of a supervision cycle that includes sharing and interpreting observation data, then that principal should restrict observation to the framework of the complete process. The principals we observed didn't.

Instructional Support and Feedback

Their espoused theory suggests that principals would ensure that novice teachers receive frequent and useful feedback on their performance. Though not necessarily providing that feedback personally, the principal should monitor the process of new teachers receiving and applying feedback. The principals we observed were more reactive than proactive in providing feedback to novice teachers, reflecting an implicit assumption that no news from the principal was good news regarding a novice's performance. Only when a principal perceived the novice to be in trouble would the principal intervene with direct advice and assistance or delegate others to help the teacher with whatever problem had arisen.

Additionally, the principals didn't *appropriately* delegate responsibility for observing the instruction of novice teachers. Each of the principals assigned mentors to novice teachers, but neither the districts nor the principals themselves provided these mentors with sufficient training in conducting observations or using observation data effectively. Moreover, none of the principals engaged in any creative scheduling to provide released time for mentors to conduct observations, to analyze observation data, or to confer with novices.

School Culture

Collaboration.   A final discrepancy occurs between the principals' clear endorsement of teachers working collaboratively with other professionals and the structures the principals create and maintain in schools to make collaboration difficult or impossible. Although the principals have promoted collaborative working arrangements such as interdisciplinary clusters or grade-level teams, they have not taken the next steps to ensure that these groups have sufficient time to work together at anything beyond the most basic operational levels. Nor have the principals arranged comfortable, private, and functional meeting space for teachers. The principals' failure to support collaboration certainly does not appear to be a conscious attempt to subvert teachers' efforts. Rather, it suggests that principals are unaware of the difficulties teachers face when they try to work collaboratively in conventional school settings.

The process they use to evaluate teachers also contradicts the principal's espoused value of collaboration. Granted, the principals we observed had no choice but to conduct classroom observations as part of a state-mandated teacher evaluation system. However, these principals did nothing to help teachers or themselves envision this required evaluation process in ways that would prevent it from threatening teachers' collaborating among themselves or with administrators. Teachers continued to view the evaluation of their teaching as a risky ordeal. They also continued to perceive the evaluation process as inherently competitive, pitting teachers' performances against each other in a contest for financial reward and recognition of distinction among peers.

Secondary School Principals.   We don't question the fact that sheer size of the unit may place demands on secondary school principals that consume far more time than those facing elementary school principals. In fact, a high school principal might not be able to meet the full range of responsibilities inherent to high school operation without assistance. But we recently visited a high school of approximately 2,500 students, a sizable enrollment by any standards, in which the principal places classroom instruction at the top of any list of priorities—immediate or long-term—for faculty, staff, and students. He demonstrates that commitment every day as he visits personally with teachers, either formally or informally, and talks (often at length) about learning and student achievement.

He assigns at least one assistant principal or counselor to attend *every* school activity, and he himself attends as many as possible. This principal occasionally receives criticism for lack of interest in school activities other than classroom instruction (e.g., student organizations). He does not respond to the criticism by compromising his idea of the *real* business of schools—student learning. Devising a schedule that includes daily excursions into the classroom wings requires him to delegate a sizable share of other management responsibilities to assistant principals and other staff members.

We have heard high school principals claim that it's impossible to delegate *enough* administrative responsibility to allow them daily classroom contact. Not so. This principal has somehow managed to accomplish the task, and he says that he can't imagine approaching school leadership any other way.

Test scores in his school set the standard among districts in that area, and though his measure of achievement extends far beyond scores, he studies test data regularly and presents his analysis to the faculty as one piece of the foundation for planning instruction or adjusting curriculum to meet students' needs.

How does he do it? He says it's rather simple: "I merely plan my day to address the *real* priorities and not to be, in the words of the poet, 'tripping on every nutshell or mosquito's wing that falls on the track.'" Schools are littered with nutshells and mosquito's wings. The principal who wants to act on what is most important will anticipate minor obstacles and not be tripped. He will accept the same poet's challenge to "live by dead reckoning" with eyes fixed on the charted destination—a school where students, teachers, staff, and administrators engage in the adventure of learning. The novice fortunate enough to begin teaching in such an atmosphere stands an excellent chance of developing into a master of the profession—*and* of deciding to *remain* in the profession long enough to one day help nurture first-year teachers toward the same achievement.

Implications

In general, our analysis of what principals say about a new teachers' needs and what they as leaders can do to meet them suggests that they understand these needs at only a tacit level. The principals hold strong values and beliefs about learning to teach and about their responsibilities to novice teachers; nevertheless, they have not consciously tested these values and beliefs in terms of either the theory or the realities of administrative practice.

Our observation that principals do not exercise a consistent, clearly articulated role in their work with novices supports the intent of this chapter to bring new awareness to the question of how principals can help beginning teachers improve their professional practice. In the following section, several propositions synthesize what we have learned about principals and novice teachers from an examination of relevant literature and consideration of how working principals describe and execute their role with novices.

We offer the following four propositions to more clearly define the principal's role with novice teachers.

> ***Proposition 1: The principal's role with novice teachers requires the principal to communicate clearly expectations for novices' performance.***

This is perhaps the most important aspect of the principal's role with novice teachers, and one that, unfortunately, receives conspicuously little attention. Too often principals operate on the assumption that a new teacher will learn best from experience or that someone else—a mentor or a district-level supervisor—will explain directly what the novice needs to know. By not taking the initiative in communicating how novices are expected to learn and grow as teachers, principals miss a valuable opportunity to influence the quality of inducting new teachers into the profession.

The position of authority figure in the school creates an ideal opportunity for the principal to act not only as spokesperson for policies particular to the school and district but also as a standardbearer of professional excellence. If, as principals claim, they know what it is new teachers need to learn—at least in general terms—then they should communicate these things directly to the novice in very clear language. They should also establish a two-way flow of communication and should meet with novices, either individually or as a group, to respond to their questions and to process their feedback on experience. The principal who takes a leadership role in communicating expectations to novice teachers is also sending a message to the rest of the faculty that novice teachers are important in that school and deserve everybody's time and attention.

Proposition 2: The principal needs to plan specifically for the learning needs of novice teachers and to schedule time for that learning to occur.

This proposition actually contains three points about the principal's role with novice teachers:

1.   Novices have unique needs that aren't addressed by the regularly scheduled faculty, team, or department meetings. In addition to these meetings, novices need specially scheduled sessions that cater to their special issues and questions. That requires a substantial amount of meeting time for a beginning teacher who is already struggling to find the time needed to keep up with planning classes, locating materials, and keeping track of unfamiliar paperwork.

2.   Principals should actively collaborate with novices to plan how they spend their time. Establishing this two-part process will demand creativity on the part of a principal, a willingness to open the box that is a school schedule and think beyond traditional assignments of faculty and time. The best thing a principal can do for a novice teacher is provide an extra planning period to observe other teachers and meet with a mentor or other colleagues. The next best thing a principal can do is give the novice a schedule that maximizes use of time. Such a schedule may include several sections of the same class for a secondary teacher, or a relatively homogeneous and motivated class for an elementary teacher.

In planning the novice's schedule, the principal also needs to ensure that the mentor's schedule be compatible. If possible, the novice and mentor should have designated time during the school day when both are free from teaching responsibilities and can meet together. Expecting such meetings to occur before or after school makes them appear to the teachers as extra work rather than a rightful or *important* part of the school day. Principals should verbally point out to novice teachers the special efforts to schedule specific learning opportunities for them. Not only does this communicate the principal's personal investment in their success, it also gives them a frame for their learning if they know what they are expected to learn from a particular kind of experience or event.

3.   All learning opportunities especially designed for novice teachers should reflect sound consideration of their needs as adult learners. Therefore, the principal should see that such activities center on real first-year problems and that they occur in an appropriate learning environment for adults.

Proposition 3: The principal should help novice teachers set professional goals for themselves, monitor progress toward those goals, and provide help in achieving them.

This proposition articulates a special mentoring role for the principal. While a teaching mentor is appropriately concerned about working with the novice on immediate needs for instructional strategies, record-keeping, or classroom management questions, the principal ought to guide the novice toward a more global self-study as a maturing professional. Principals who ask novices to consider what they want to know about or be able to do at some future time—next year or three years from now—not only show interest and concern for the teacher's individual professional development, but they also deliver a clear expectation that teachers continue to learn and grow as professionals. In addition, this proposition creates accountability for the principal to see that novices engage with their profession in ways that extend beyond the classroom. Such involvement might mean joining school or district committees, attending in-service training sessions or conferences of special interest to the novice, or engaging in action research along with a mentor, supervisor, or other colleague to investigate the effectiveness of particular curriculum or instructional strategies.

Proposition 4: The principal must set an example of collaborative working behavior for novice teachers.

Implicit in the previous propositions is the principal's collaboration with other professionals—mentors, supervisors, team or department mates—to plan and oversee the novices' professional development. Not only does such collaboration provide the principal with ongoing information about the support the novice is receiving, but it also allows the principal to set reasonable limits on personal commitment of time and direct responsibility for the new teachers.

The principal who sets the example for collaboration is creating an environment conducive to the novice teacher's professional growth. Through collaboration, teachers, novice and experienced alike, gain access to more information and ideas than they could generate on their own. They also are more likely to develop greater willingness to question their own previously taken-for-granted assumptions about teaching and learning, as they explore different approaches. Finally, in a school where collaboration is a valued norm, teachers are apt to feel supported in their efforts and be more comfortable with change and innovation.

SUMMARY

A review of the literature provides little insight into a principal's specific responsibility for leading novice teachers into the profession in a way that augments both personal growth and commitment to educational excellence. However, by extending certain aspects of current thought about visionary leadership in today's schools, we can frame a few recommendations that might hold promise for helping new teachers develop into exemplary professionals.

School culture may influence teacher performance more than any other single factor cited in studies of effective school practices. We found wide agreement on key elements that promote excellence in a school community:

- a clear vision of excellence articulated by the principal and shared by its members
- a strong sense of mission
- common goals with high expectations
- a focus on learning for *all* members of the school community
- collegiality and active collaboration among faculty
- fundamental beliefs, values, and attitudes shared by faculty and staff
- continual, visible efforts to grow personally and professionally

Novice teachers who launch a career in such a stimulating environment will long remember—and benefit from—their early experiences in the classroom. The principal can influence first-year experiences more dramatically than any other single figure in the school community. Positive learning outcomes for the novice will not occur accidentally and should not be left to happenstance. We agree that a fair amount of learning comes only with experience. However, careful planning by the principal can prevent a number of anxieties, uncertainties, inaccurate perceptions, errors in judgment, and miscommunications that might cause difficulty for the new teacher.

First of all, the principal must not overlook or *forget* the novice's absolute unfamiliarity with the school's culture. This new teacher arrives on the scene as a veritable "blank slate." Many expectations, processes, and procedures that seasoned faculty members have *internalized*—do naturally, take for granted—hold little or no meaning for the first-year teacher, who is encountering them for the first time. The principal should assume sole responsibility for ensuring clear communication down to the last detail, explicitly spelling out for the novice how visible events, circumstances, and activities are *connected* to the underlying philosophy, beliefs, and values that are already crystal clear to veteran teachers. This may require principals to spend some time reflecting on their early days of leadership, to recapture strategies they used to communicate vision, promote the school's mission, and invite commitment from teachers.

We do not suggest that principals won't need to delegate portions of this task to reliable colleagues (see Achilles, Keedy, & High, chapter 2). We *are* saying that principals should make no assumptions about the novice's understanding of important issues. They should "check it out"—*personally* confirm that the new teacher has received and understood accurate information. Time so invested early in the year will yield long-term dividends far beyond the measure of investment. Even if that were not a guarantee, we believe novice teachers offer a unique challenge for *principals* to grow as leaders. Thinking about the growth of a new professional and key expectations held for teacher performance in a particular school setting provides an ideal opportunity for the principal to do some serious self-assessment—to re-think, perhaps even *re-vitalize*, goals and priorities, as well as to analyze whether current routines and activities still focus on these goals and priorities.

The exercise could offer surprising enlightenment for the principal who genuinely embraces the vision and mission that purportedly drive school activities. If approached with an open mind, it would undoubtedly raise important questions. Are key goals and expectations still visibly promoted throughout the school culture? Is professional growth and development a non-negotiable expectation for both teachers *and* principal? Does the principal still keep a finger on the pulse of the classroom operation? Introducing a novice to the teaching profession provides an ideal opportunity, *reason*, for the principal to revisit most fundamental purposes of leadership.

THEORY INTO ACTION: A CASE STUDY FOR REFLECTION

The following vignette, though it provides only brief glimpses of a teacher-principal relationship, synthesizes many of the key points we have considered regarding the principal's role in working with novice teachers. It centers on an actual incident and surrounding circumstances during one teacher's first year of experience, described by him as follows:[1]

> I was hired to teach eleventh grade mathematics in [a large inner-city school that was undergoing substantial change]. Someone in the office, not the principal, had told me early on that it was against school rules for students to wear hats. The principal had established the rule because hats had become a symbol of gang affiliation.
>
> This was my first time ever to teach; so I was very concerned about following the rules, and this school also had a reputation for tough kids. I had heard from a lot of other teachers that it was real important to be firm with rules, or [the students] would run right over you. It was very early on, maybe during my first week, when a girl came to class with a hat on. I told her to remove her hat, and she just refused. I mentioned that there was a rule that students shouldn't wear hats, and that we had to follow those school rules. She continued to refuse, and a few of the other students got excited about it, particularly a male student. They were saying that the rule applied to males but not to females. I wasn't sure about that, but I thought they were "pulling the cap over my eyes," so I said, "Well, I'm not sure about that rule, but I want you to

1.   The incident was recounted in an interview with Dr. Phil Carspecken, now a professor in the Department of Educational Leadership, University of Houston. He began his teaching career in an inner-city school of a large urban school district. The school principal had been placed there three years earlier, in hopes that he could eradicate the gang activity and violence occurring in the school. Conflict among students had been so intense that a homicide had occurred shortly after the new principal arrived. The principal had hired Carspecken primarily because of his counseling background.

take the hat off." One guy got so excited that he just ran out the door. I got them quieted down by "asserting my authority." The girl hadn't removed her hat, but I just didn't know what to do. As I recall, I just decided I wasn't going to mess with that issue, that I would find out later what the rule really was, rather than just force it.

Not long afterwards, in fact in a *very* short time, the boy came back into the room, and [the principal] came in with him. [The principal] began by saying some complimentary things to me, about the classroom or something, in front of the students. So I instantly felt his support. Then he said to the class, "Mr. Carspecken is a new teacher, so he doesn't know the rules real well yet. Of course, *you* know that the rule applies only to males, so she can keep the hat on." He said it in a way that didn't undermine my authority at all; I felt really well-supported. The students had become totally quiet and were giving him all their attention. Then he turned around and looked at my blackboard. I had a lesson on the board, and he could tell what the lesson was about—he was a former math teacher himself. He said something like, "Well I see you've been studying such-and-such (I forget what the subject was). Then he gave a little lesson about what was on the board. It was totally appropriate—he went on for about five minutes, and it fit in exactly with what I had been teaching. It was amazing, really. The students gave him all their attention, and then he said, "Now I'll let Mr. Carspecken continue," and he walked out the door. It was great. The students were well-behaved after that, and class went well.

Later, I went to see him in his office, and I was amazed at how accessible he was— I could just walk in. His office had easy chairs and sofas, and he was sitting in one of those. He talked to me as if I were an old buddy of his—it was so *informal*. He said, "Well, how's it going with the new teaching? You seem to have good rapport with the kids." I thought, "My God, that was a potential *blow-up*, and he's telling me I seemed to have good rapport with the kids." About the incident, he mentioned the student's name who ran out of the room—he knew the guy real well, knew his first name, last name, knew his family. And he said, "Yeah, that guy's a little bit 'squirrelly,'"— I remember he used the word *squirrelly*—"but he's a good kid." My overall feeling was that he really accepted the kids, really liked the kids, and that he really accepted me as a teacher and liked me, and that he was totally accessible—not authoritative but supportive, a *guide* rather than an authority figure. . . .

I'll never forget the first assembly in that school. [The principal] sort of prepared me in advance by commenting that I was probably in store for a totally new experience. He asked, "Have you ever been to one of these before?" I said I hadn't, and he sort of smiled as if to say, "It's kind of crazy, but this is what the kids like." It was a musically-based assembly. The kids were standing up, not sitting down, shouting with enthusiasm, and they had these magnificent performers who were kids themselves, from the student body. They could sing and play like you wouldn't believe. And the audience, even though they were standing and keeping time with the music, didn't get out of control. Throughout my year there, music was one of the big unifying forces in that student body. They had a lot of assemblies with music. The kids loved it, and they were so talented.

I also remember one day when I was eating lunch in the faculty lounge and he [the principal] came in and sat down next to me to have lunch. He asked me questions about my personal life, just chit-chatted. That was another way he made us feel that he wasn't just a distant figure but just a regular guy who was very accessible. Another time, I stopped by his office, and he was in there with a couple of parents. They were just chit-chatting away. They seemed on real friendly terms. These were parents who were involved in the whole school; they weren't just in there because of their own kids, but because of the relationship of that school to the community. Once again, I saw this real familiarity—they called him by his first name—so he seemed to have real good community relations.

GUIDING QUESTIONS

1. What did the principal do to communicate expectations for the novice's performance? Was the communication effective? Why or why not? What else might he have done?

2. From this vignette, can you identify some learning needs of this new teacher? What are some other ways the principal could have provided opportunities, formally or informally, to meet these needs?

3. How did the principal demonstrate collaborative working relationships in this school? Was his method effective? Why or why not? What else might he have done?

4. What do you know about the culture of this school from the vignette, and particularly from the principal's actions? How did this principal communicate values, beliefs, etc., of the school culture? Was his method effective? Why or why not? What else might he have done?

REFERENCES

Acheson, K., & Gall, M. (1987). *Techniques in the clinical supervision of teachers*. New York: Longman.

Alfonso, R., & Goldsberry, L. (1982). Colleagueship in supervision. In T. Sergiovanni (Ed.), *Supervision of teaching: 1982 ASCD yearbook* (pp. 108–118). Alexandria, VA: Association for Supervision and Curriculum Development.

Argyris, C., & Schon, D. (1974). *Theory in practice: Increasing professional effectiveness*. San Francisco: Jossey Bass.

Barker, J. A. (Producer). (1990). *The power of vision: Discussion guide*. Burnsville, MN: Charterhouse Learning Corporation.

Barth, R. (1986). On sheep and goats and school reform. *Phi Delta Kappan, 68*, 293–296.

Berry, B., & Ginsberg, R. (1988). Legitimizing subjectivity: Meritorious performance and professionalization of teacher and principal evaluation. *Journal of Personnel Evaluation in Education, 2*, 123–140.

Blumberg, A. (1980). *Supervisors and teachers: A private cold war* (2nd ed.). Berkeley, CA: McCutcheon.

Brookover, W. B., Beady, C., Flood, P., Schweitzer, J., & Weisenbaker, J. (1979). *School social systems and student achievement—schools can make a difference*. Brooklyn: Praeger.

Brooks, D. (1986). *Programmatic teacher induction: A model for new teacher professional development*. Richardson, TX: Richardson Independent School District.

Brooks, D. (1987). *Teacher induction: A new beginning*. Reston, VA: Association of Teacher Educators.

Chandler, P., Robinson, W., & Noyes, P. (1990). Is initial training nurturing proactive teachers? *Educational Research 32*(2), 130–137.

Clark, D. L., Lotto, L. S., & McCarthy, M. M. (1980). Factors associated with success in urban elementary schools. *Phi Delta Kappan, 61*, 467–470.

Clift, R., Veal, M., Holland, P., Johnson, M., & McCarthy, J. (in press). *Cases in collaborative leadership*. New York: Teachers College Press.

Cogan, M. (1973). *Clinical supervision*. Boston: Houghton Mifflin.

Darling-Hammond, L., & Sclan, E. (1992). Policy and supervision. In C. Glickman (Ed.), *Supervision in transition: 1992 ASCD yearbook* (pp. 7–27). Alexandria, VA: Association for Supervision and Curriculum Development.

Edmonds, R., & Frederiksen, N. (1978). *Search for effective schools: The identification and analysis of city schools that are instructionally effective for poor children*. Cambridge: Harvard University, Center for Urban Studies.

Galvez-Hjornevik, C. (1986). Mentoring among teachers: A review of the literature. *Journal of teacher education 37*(1): 6–11.

Garman, N. (1982). The clinical approach to supervision. In T. Sergiovanni (Ed.), *Supervision of teaching: 1982 ASCD yearbook* (pp. 35–52). Alexandria, VA: Association for Supervision and Curriculum Development.

Gitlin, A., & Smyth, J. (1989). *Teacher evaluation: Educative alternatives*. New York: The Falmer Press.

Glickman, C. (1985). *Supervision of instruction: A developmental approach* (2nd ed.). Boston: Allyn and Bacon.

Goldhammer, R. (1969). *Clinical supervision: Special methods for the supervision of teachers*. New York: Holt, Rinehart and Winston.

Gray, W. A., & Gray, M. M. (1985). Synthesis of research on mentoring beginning teachers. *Educational Leadership, 43*(3), 37–43.

Grimmett, P., Rostad, O., & Ford, B. (1992). The transformation of supervision. In C. Glickman (Ed.), *Supervision in transition: 1992 ASCD yearbook* (pp. 185–202). Alexandria, VA: Association for Supervision and Curriculum Development.

Hoffman, J., Griffin, G., Edwards, S., Paulissen, M., O'Neal, S., Barnes, S., & Verstegen, D. (1985). *Teacher induction study: A final report of a descriptive study*. Austin, TX: University of Texas, Research and Development Center for Teacher Education.

The Holmes Group (1986). *Tomorrow's teachers: A report of the Holmes Group*. East Lansing, MI: The Holmes Group.

Huling-Austin, L. (1988, April). *A synthesis of research on teacher induction programs and practices*. Paper presented at the annual meeting of the American Educational Research Association, New Orleans.

Hunter, M. (1984). Knowing, teaching and supervising. In P. Hosford (Ed.), *Using what we know about teaching, 1984 ASCD yearbook* (pp. 169–192). Alexandria, VA: Association for Supervision and Curriculum Development.

Kottkamp, R. B. (1984). The principal as cultural leader. *Planning & Changing, 15*(3), 152–160.

Knowles, M. S. (1980). *The modern practice of adult education: From pedagogy to andragogy* (2nd ed.). New York: Cambridge Books.

Leithwood, K. A., & Montgomery, D. J. (1982). The role of the elementary school principal in program improvement. *Review of Educational Research, 52*, 309–339.

Little, J. (1987). Teachers as colleagues. In V. Richardson-Koehler (Ed.), *Educator's handbook: A research perspective* (pp. 491–518). New York: Longman.

Little, J. (1990). The mentor phenomenon. In C. B. Cazden (Ed.), *Review of Research in Education, 16*, 297–351. Washington, DC: American Education Research Association.

Lortie, D. C. (1975). *School teacher: A sociological study*. Chicago: University of Chicago Press.

McQuarrie, F. and Wood, F. (1991). Supervision, staff development, and evaluation connections. *Theory into Practice, 30*(2), 91–96.

Norris, C. J., Baptiste, P. H., Weise, K. R., & Macaluso, L. (1988, Fall). A practical model to prepare for campus level accreditation. *Texas study of secondary education research journal, 43*, 18–28.

Pajak, E. (1989). *The central office supervisor of curriculum and instruction: Setting the stage for success*. Boston: Allyn and Bacon.

Purkey, S. C., & Smith, M. S. (1983). Effective schools: A review. *The elementary school journal, 83*, 427–452.

Rallis, S. F., & Highsmith, M. C. (1986). The myth of the "great principal": Questions of school management and instructional leadership. *Phi Delta Kappan, 68*, 300–304.

Rutherford, W. L. (1985). Styles and behaviors of elementary school principals: Their relationship to school improvement. *Phi Delta Kappan, 67*, 31–34.

Sacks, S. R., & Brady, P. (1985, April). *Who Teaches the City's Children? A Study of New York City First Year Teachers*. Paper presented at the annual meeting of the American Educational Research Association, Chicago.

Sergiovanni, T., & Starratt, R. (1988). *Supervision: Human perspectives* (4th ed.). New York: McGraw-Hill.

Sergiovanni, T. J. (1982). Ten principles of quality leadership. *Educational Leadership, 39*, 330–336.

Smyth, J. (1984). *Clinical supervision—collaborative learning about supervision: A handbook*. Geelong, Australia: Deakin University Press.

Swanson, P. (1968). A time to teach—and a time to learn. *Bulletin of the National Association of Secondary School Principals, 52*(330), 74–84.

Tanner, D., & Tanner, L. (1987). *Supervision in education: Principles, problems and practices*. New York: Macmillan.

Ubben, G. C., & Hughes, L. W. (1992). *The principal: Creative leadership for effective schools*. Boston: Allyn and Bacon.

Veenman, S. (1984). Perceived problems of beginning teachers. *Review of Educational Research, 54*(2), 143–178.

Weise, K. R. (1992). *A contemporary historical study of the Danforth Principal Preparation Program at the University of Houston.* Unpublished dissertation, University of Houston.

SELECTED READINGS

Acheson, K., & Gall, M. (1987). *Techniques in the clinical supervision of teachers.* New York: Longman.

Barth, R. (1986). On sheep and goats and school reform. *Phi Delta Kappan, 68,* 293–296.

Deal, T., Meyer, J., Scott, W., & Rowan, B. (1983). *Organization environment: Ritual and rationality.* Beverly Hills, CA: Sage.

Garman, N. (1982). The clinical approach to supervision. In T. Sergiovanni (Ed.), *Supervision of teaching: 1982 ASCD yearbook* (pp. 35–52). Alexandria, VA: Association for Supervision and Curriculum Development.

Kottkamp, R. B. (1984). The principal as cultural leader. *Planning and Changing, 15*(3):152–160.

Sarason, A. (1971). *The culture of school and the problems of change.* Boston: Allyn and Bacon.

Shulman, J. H., & Colbert, J. A. (1987). *The mentor teacher casebook.* Los Angeles: Far West Laboratory for Educational Research and Development.

Schulman, J. H., & Colbert, J. A. (1988). *The intern teacher casebook.* Los Angeles: Far West Laboratory for Educational Research and Development.

10

Stimulating the Academic Performance of Pupils

C. M. Achilles

University of North Carolina–Greensboro

P. Smith

University of North Carolina–Greensboro

Overview

Improving poor performances or maintaining excellent ones is the major task of an instruction leader. The yardstick by which policy makers and others measure their investment in schools usually is the performance of the nation's children on some quantitative test. So, to be considered effective, educational administrators must ensure that accountability measures (test scores, graduation rates, basic workforce skills) meet expectations. Results occur where you pay attention and place your emphasis, so how administrators invest time and energy in schooling determines the likelihood of student success in school. Instructional leaders help

The authors thank Raymond Garcia of the Spring Branch, Texas, Independent Schools who developed the initial working outline for this chapter. The present chapter reflects elements of that initial outline in several places, including some of the basic assumptions, topics addressed, and actual text. Garcia's preliminary work helped provide direction and focus for parts of the final text. Other people also provided helpful comments: Larry W. Hughes, George Michel, Paula Short, Vernon Farrington, Susan Hoover, William Purkey, Dale Brubaker, Michael Waggoner, Cindy Bumgarner, and anonymous reviewers.

establish a foundation conducive to effective teaching, monitor closely the instructional process, and accept the moral responsibility for making difficult curricular, personnel, and organizational decisions. Research and evaluation results, anecdotal reports of successful practice, and even common sense provide some guidelines in the quest for academic successes.

The focus of this chapter is the principal's role in stimulating the academic performance of pupils[1] in the schools. Because the public, the media, and policy people have made academic performance—or more accurately, the measurement of academic performance in a narrow vein—a high-stakes, highly visible aspect of schooling, a successful principal necessarily has pupil performance in its broadest sense high on the agenda. Nearly all studies of schools where pupils demonstrate high achievement have shown the importance of strong principal leadership. Practically speaking, these principals have the conceptual, technical, and human-relations skills to coordinate, guide, and improve the instructional process; to build and deploy human resources; to establish achievement as a school-wide goal; and to monitor school progress in meeting pupil achievement goals. These principals "set the tone" of the school and, metaphorically, become the spark-plug in the engine of school success.

The chapter begins with introductory comments, four caveats, a brief discussion of selected issues, and some ways to address effective instructional leadership in three broad categories:

- foundation issues
- instruction issues
- moral/ethical issues

The chapter concludes with a summary and a case study for reflection and application.

Four Caveats

This chapter addresses some ways for improving pupil academic achievement. At the outset, we offer four caveats:

- Things often are not what they seem at first glance.
- Change, ambiguity, and diversity are increasing daily
- The principal is but one member of a team sharing instructional leadership tasks.

---

1.   *Pupil* is from Latin *pupilla* or *pupillus*, an orphan or a ward of the state. Use of this word captures the state-mandated education idea. *Student*, on the other hand, derives from *studeo*—to desire, to be eager—and seems an appropriate designation for those who are in school by their own volition, and especially appropriate for those who stay in schools after mandatory-attendance age.

- The path to improve pupil performance is not an unencumbered straight line.

A little skepticism is probably salutary; things seldom are exactly as they first seem. The authors have reservations that there is a single, agreed-upon mission of public schooling that is clearly and easily defined. For example, the author of *Friday Night Lights* (Bissinger, 1990) found that the money one Texas high school athletic department spent on tape for the ankles of its football players exceeded the budget of the entire English department for the year. Nevertheless, academic performance is the stuff of missions mentioned in the public rhetoric of legislative halls, of state and local school boards, and of the business leaders who routinely criticize education. Academic performance results also provide the data for state report cards, national "wall charts" of education's efficacy, commission reports, editorials, and evaluations of all sorts.

Change, ambiguity, and diversity are rampant in schooling today. Any discussion of issues related to academic achievement must take into account that the target, the ammunition, and the location of the hunter are *all* in motion— even the ways that people judge success in hitting the target are in motion. Consequently, actions an administrator takes to increase success one year may lead to less success another year as the school's student population or the public's expectations change. Change, Ambiguity, and Diversity together constitute the CAD factor, and the only stability today seems to be the exponential growth of change, ambiguity, and diversity. The successful principal's response to the CAD factor includes flexibility and creativity, and a dash of wit and humor.

There is a current debate about the appropriateness of a principal serving as the instructional leader of a school. Deal (1987) argued that a principal must serve as a counselor, an engineer, a pawnbroker, and a poet. Hughes (chap. 1) avers that the leader must be an artist, an architect, and a commissar. Rallis (1988) noted that "if a principal neglects these duties to concentrate on instructional leadership, the grease that keeps the school's wheels rolling may be gone, and people may no longer perceive the school as effective" (p. 645). Instructional leadership belongs to teachers. Lieberman (1988) identified as an "unexamined assumption" the idea that the principal was the sole instructional leader of a school, suggesting that by relieving teachers of responsibilities for curriculum, instruction, and evaluation educators have compromised the likelihood of school success. Greenfield (1987) found that

> despite the passage of time and the numerous calls for "more and better" instructional leadership during the past eighty years or so, the idea itself remains ambiguous, and evidence supporting any sort of direct cause-and-effect relationship between the efforts of school principals and the accomplishments of teachers and pupils remains muddled to a large degree. (p. 57)

Research designs used to measure school effectiveness are insufficient to project a causal relationship between principal behaviors and school outcomes

(Hallinger & Murphy, 1987). However, after a synthesis of research, Ellett (1987) supported the proposition that "principals, through their instructional leadership roles, can and do make a difference in school productivity" (p. 303). The difficulty appears to be in how one casts the role of instructional leader, or in what variables one includes in defining that role. Elements that some might consider outside of that role, such as establishing a clear mission associated with student achievement, actually can be behaviors classified within it. Also, informal, almost casual reinforcement of such a vision through brief contacts with students and staff in hallways or drop-in classroom visits can be considered exercises in instructional leadership (see also Achilles, Keedy, & High, chapter 2).

Finally, in preparing this material the authors have followed the pattern of Isaiah Berlin's (1953) fox and not his hedgehog. Rather than focusing in depth on one or two strategies related to improving pupil performance, the chapter includes a broad view, built on research/theory and successful practice and bolstered by current readings. Either approach has inherent limitations, but chapter length, the audience, the nature of educational administration and the "CAD factor" form an environment more suited to the fox's darting, exploratory ways than to the hedgehog's plodding linear path.

Conceptual Frame

Public schools in the United States are supposed "to educate" all eligible youth, where "to educate" is popularly conceived and overtly explained *primarily* as "academics" or "academic performance" that can somehow be measured, evaluated, or assessed. Educators and others charged with this responsibility work, for the most part, in traditional settings that house pupils from preschool to some state-established, mandatory-attendance age. School buildings look much alike, as do the processes inside them; when Rip Van Winkle woke from his long sleep there were no surprises—at least from education's arena.

Youth spend from fewer than six to more than eight hours a day in schools for about 180 days per year for 13 years if they progress from kindergarten to high school completion at grade 12. For some, this is a productive and stimulating experience with high levels of participation in academic/curricular and extra- or co-curricular events. Many others simply tolerate school, derive some benefits from it, "get by," and hope that their part-time jobs will lead into full-time work after graduation. For still others, school is dull, disappointing, even demeaning and debilitating drudgery, full of rote, repetition, and regurgitation of "the basics," with little or no time for anything else. These will drop out, or simply put in time until they exceed mandatory-attendance age.

In the 1990s, teachers, schools, and even states may be ranked or rated based on, among other things, pupil academic performance that is most commonly determined by pupil "scores" on some standardized or norm-referenced tests

(NRT). The successful principal attends to and stimulates the academic performance of all pupils in the school, especially as education becomes a "front-burner" political agenda item and school report card results increase in use as a public indicator of school "quality." A major challenge is to stimulate the academic performance of those who are low or slow achievers, or who learn differently.

Any schoolwide concentration on pupil academic performance is driven by an unflagging belief that all children not only can learn what schools offer, but that they can learn well when provided a safe, nurturing, and stimulating environment. Given that pupil academic performance is one expected and legitimate school outcome—and the logical corollary that improving or increasing this legitimate outcome is desirable and good—the successful principal devotes time, energy, funds, knowledge, and skills to meet this expectation. In targeting available resources on improving pupil performance, the principal fulfills the role of instructional leader.

One major premise of this chapter is as clear as 1-2-3-4: The academic performance of pupils can be stimulated when:

1. Those pupils are in schools.
2. Those schools provide a safe, inviting, learning-oriented environment.
3. A large portion of in-school, high-quality time is spent with dedicated, skilled, and concerned *people*.
4. Those people are committed to helping pupils learn the outcomes or knowledge/skill/attitude base that will be measured.

Surrounding this central role are important supporting casts, such as home and community, appropriate curricula aligned to the assessment criteria, fine faculty, strong leadership, a clearly focused school mission, and nurturing school-site climate. Although this quite simply tells *what* needs to be done, *how* each principal orchestrates the variables to get the job done will vary based upon the context, the audience and the individual.

Foundation Issues

On the surface, some key issues may not seem *directly* related to instruction, yet unless an administrator assures that these dimensions are thoroughly addressed, instruction and student outcomes will suffer. Among the foundation issues are these:

- attendance
- climate or culture
- community involvement
- clear and well communicated mission (no secrets)
- a primary reliance on people not programs, with a recognition that programs, too, are important

Attendance

Part—perhaps the major part—of the principal's task in stimulating academic achievement at the school has to do with pupil attendance. After reviewing issues and studies of education quality in the 1970s and 1980s, Orlich (1989) commented "if students did not attend school regularly or did not take basic academic courses in science, English, and mathematics, they scored poorly on standardized tests" (p. 515).

In analyzing data on the state of Tennessee's 1989–90 report card for each school district, researchers found that the key variables on the report card that could be expected to influence pupil outcomes as defined by test results collectively accounted for about one fourth (26.5 percent) of the variance in pupil outcomes, and almost half of that influence (10.9 of the 26.5 percent) was related to the rate of pupil school attendance. *The single strongest predictor of pupil outcomes as measured by tests given in schools was whether or not pupils attended school regularly* (Bobbett, French, Achilles, McNamara, & Trusty, 1992).

Should it surprise anyone that those who attend school most do best on tests of school-type information? On the surface, it makes sense; below the surface, educators know that those who do best in school, who are rewarded by school participation, and who like school are also those who are most often not absent and not drop-outs. Thus, some aspects of stimulating pupil performance are found in the research and literature on truancy, pupils "at risk," and student participation and involvement in school activities. After an extensive study of data from 50 states and the District of Columbia on student outcomes, fiscal issues, and student persistence in schooling (not dropping out), Hashway (1989–90) concluded: "The most influential factor upon school persistence is school achievement. Students who view themselves as successful will stay in school" (p. 69). The reciprocal relationship between attendance and achievement as usually measured in schools seems clear.

Because pupil attendance at school is a primary, direct way to increase pupil academic achievement, administrators seeking to make that achievement more likely take actions to keep youngsters in school. Lindsay has shown the positive benefits of participation in school activities on satisfaction and attendance (1982) and on future citizenship activities of young adults (1984). In reviewing the research on dropouts, Finn (1989) posited two approaches to drop-out reduction—the self-concept model and the participation-identification model. Finn showed that if pupils participated in school-related activities they identified with, they were less likely to withdraw from school. While the changing of self concepts is difficult and time-consuming, changing the school environment to provide expanded opportunities for pupil participation is administratively mutable—the principal can make decisions to offer participation events for all pupils.

Participation includes such things as clubs, activities, governance, and even active involvement in school academic efforts (Finn & Cox, 1992). Research supports the importance of teachers actively involving all pupils in classroom participation because doing so has not only direct academic benefits but also indirect benefits on academics by decreasing a student's likelihood of withdrawing from school. Why, for instance, must there be "cuts" in cheerleading squads or in band (Ryan, 1992)? Changing the participation rules at the school level can get more students "hooked on school" by providing events that hold their interest and participation.

A person cannot be actively involved in something at school and also be absent. Structuring participation opportunities schoolwide (through clubs, athletics, class offices, and community service opportunities) and working with teachers to structure classroom participation (through peer tutoring, cooperative learning, and small and interactive classes) are ways that principals can exercise leadership in the quest for improved pupil outcomes.

Climate/Culture

If they had free choice, most people would not willingly stay where they felt unwanted, unwelcomed, and unappreciated; they would not go daily to a job that was harassing and impossible to do well. They would avoid a site where they felt threatened or unsafe, or where they worked with people who didn't like them. Children quickly learn the espoused and sometimes conflicting norms of the school workplace, and whether or not people at school seem to like them or want to teach them.

One of Edmond's (1979) "effective schools" correlates is a safe and orderly school environment that is conducive to learning. In this setting, pupils and teachers feel secure, and the overall culture (language, stories, myths, heroes, rewards, icons, and so on) exudes the idea that learning is the school's major "business"—learning is important, exciting, fun, and rewarded. Such a climate does not happen by chance (see Norris, chapter 3). The principal *must* emphasize this goal and reward students and staff as knowledge workers engaged in high-quality work (Glasser, 1990) through behaviors, priorities, staff development, and involvement.

An Invitation to Learn.   A global approach to making school a welcome place is to apply strategies of "invitational theory." In offering a clear and cogent synopsis of invitational theory, Purkey and Novak (1984; Purkey, 1992) defined its major components: the assumptions, dimensions, levels, and areas of concern that underlie Invitational Education. People in the invitational setting consciously summon others cordially to share and to enjoy the events in the setting. Purkey noted that "inviting is an ethical process involving continuous interactions among and between human beings" (1992, p. 5). The assumptions of invitational theory are "trust, respect, optimism, and intentionality" where an *invitation* is "an intentional act designed to offer something beneficial for consideration"

(p. 9). Although invitational theory applies to any arena of human interactions, consider the five areas of the theory (people, places, policies, programs, and processes) relative to the school work setting. At what *level of functioning* are the five areas operating in the school setting (see figure 10–1)?

Does the school look inviting? Are the policies and rules fair, encouraging, helpful, and supportive? Do the principal and others at the school act like they enjoy themselves, each other, their work, those with whom they work (pupils, parents, patrons)? Do people have fun at the school? Are high-quality programs for all pupils and effective processes for achieving school goals firmly in place? Does the school's particular blend of the 5 P's (people, places, policies, programs, and processes) reflect an inviting philosophy? If so, people will want to

	WORST ← → BEST			
	Disinviting		Inviting	
	Intentional	Unintentional	Unintentional	Intentional
Sample Descriptions	Purposely insulting. Items that on purpose demean, debase, defeat.	Lack of care: condescending, sexist, racist, dictatorial. Do not intend to hurt/harm, but do!	Unconsciously do right. Explain what to do, but not why. Succeed without trying but don't know *why*. No philosophy or intent.	Work from a philosophy of trust, optimism, and respect and do it on purpose– intentionally.
Personal	Disinviting		Inviting	
With Self and Others	Negative internal dialogue (self-talk); apart from others; isolated, manipulative.		"Know Thyself" and *then* be able to consider the feelings/wishes of others.	
Professional	Cautious and Fearful		Confident and Correct	
With Self and Others	Suspicion, reliance on coercive power; take "doing to" stance, rather than "doing with."		Ethical awareness. Staying current with your field; to contribute. Application of beneficence to persons. Above all, do no harm.	

Figure 10–1
The Four Levels of Functioning of Invitational Theory—Disinviting (Intentional and Unintentional) and Inviting (Intentional and Unintentional)—With Examples
Adapted from Purkey, 1992, pp. 10–13. Thanks to W. Purkey for reviewing the materials.

be there and succeed. Each principal sets the tone—"as is the principal, so is the school"[2]—and research shows consistently that two major elements in pupil achievement are pupil attendance at school and work at good academic programs. Invitational theory provides the 5-P framework to guide efforts to make the school environment invite increased academic success. As a check on a school's invitingness, the principal can set up work groups or committees to analyze, review, and make recommendations to be sure the school's people, place, policies, programs and processes (5 P's) are inviting. Interviews and judicious use of "climate" questionnaires can support the process of improving a school's learning environment.

Safe and Orderly.   Discipline and safety are linked to pupil achievement in several ways. An expression often heard in Project SHAL, an "effective schools" effort in inner-city St. Louis in the early 1980s, was that the school should be the safest and best place the youngster would experience during the day. The principal *must* ensure a safe environment that encourages learning. Pupils need to feel safe so they can attend to the school's learning goals; pupils who are trying to learn must be free from harassment, violence, and external diversions that distract them from the tasks of learning. Teachers should be free to work at teaching rather than at order and control. A statement by Dr. Karon Crow-Rilling, an educational administrator in Humble, Texas (quoted in Ubben & Hughes, 1992), sums up succinctly the issues of school safety and the need for a supporting, nurturing environment for today's youth:

> We have to insure that while these children are with us they will be safe and they will be treated well. For some that may be all we can do but we must do that. We may not be able to control what goes on in any child's life before or after school. But here they will not be abused and they will be treated fairly. And they will be protected and they will be respected. And we're going to help them learn how life can be. (p. 95)

Teachers may complain about the time they must spend attending to discipline, but they may not see the full extent of the effect of lack of discipline and safety as disruptions to pupil performances. The public constantly ranks poor discipline and specific discipline issues (such as drugs, truancy, fighting/gangs, drinking) as the biggest problem facing public schools (Elam, Rose, & Gallup, 1991). While people perceive that public school pupils lack discipline and that improved discipline is the answer to many education problems, teachers believe that discipline problems are less serious "than parents' lack of interest and support . . . and pupils' lack of interest and truancy as major problems" (Elam, et al., p. 56). These two seemingly different perceptions are not unrelated;

---

2.   This quotation has been attributed to Ellwood P. Cubberly; variations of it appear in discussions of education administration, but we have been unable to find and therefore cannot cite its exact source.

discipline at school is tied to parental interest in and support for the work of those in the schools.

Involvement

Education is but one primary institution of society, and formal schooling is only a part of education. In a balanced, healthy society each institution contributes to the progress and well-being of the society. The major institutions (family, religion, government, health, economics, protection, etc.) should complement and help the goal achievement of all, but no one institution can be responsible for assuming the core purposes of other institutions. Elements of sharing between social institutions are included in such concepts as cooperation/co-optation, parental or home and community involvement, and school/community relations.

Not all individuals enter schooling with the same abilities or propensity to do "school" work, and not all have the same support from other institutions (health, family). Representatives of education and other social institutions need to cooperate in the broadly-defined teaching function and in working with increasingly diverse—and often troubled—entrants into schooling. More and more youngsters come to school with health and emotional problems, from dysfunctional families and from poverty (Hamburg, 1992). Hodgkinson (1991) bares the tip of the iceberg:

> This is the nature of education's leaky roof: about one-third of pre-school children are destined for school failure because of poverty, neglect, sickness, handicapping conditions, and lack of adult protection and nurturance. There is no point in trying to teach hungry or sick children . . . *educators can't fix the roof all by themselves.* (p. 10. Emphasis in original.)

Preparation for successful pupil performance begins even before the pupils enter school; it includes nutrition, health, mental health, and a supporting home environment.

Although there is some movement toward year-around schooling and extended-day or extended-year programs, the agrarian calendar still thrives in the information age; youngsters continue to spend more time each day out of school than they spend in school, and more days each year out of school than in school. To help in the time problem, two very important adjuncts to school learning are the home and the school community, and work with these two groups is often blended into the category "community involvement."

Nettles (1991) defined *community involvement*, especially as it influenced disadvantaged pupils, as "actions that organizations and individuals (e.g., parents, businesses . . . social service agencies . . .) take to promote student development" (p. 380). Among the categories of involvement were these:

- mobilization—actions to increase citizen and organization participation
- allocation—actual provision of resource to pupils
- instruction—efforts to assist pupil intellectual development and the understanding of rules and values of the community

Mobilization is necessary to focus attention and to build a critical mass of interest, but these activities (e.g., citizen advisory committees or the 1990s Local School Councils in Chicago) have only indirect influence on pupils. Some mobilization efforts (e.g., school/business partnerships or "adopt-a-school") may support pupil academic achievement directly. The principal's role here is seeking support, taking the lead in calling meetings, developing role expectations, publishing and distributing progress reports, and serving in liaison and support roles.

Successful principals garner and distribute resources to support the school's mission, and allocation of resources is a demonstrable level of community involvement. Involvement as allocation can be simple, such as the principal encouraging parents to help the pupil set aside a time and place for study, or it can be complex and involved. Nettles (1991, pp. 382–383) pointed out several large-scale examples of allocation, such as The Boston Compact, where public high school graduates were given priority in job applications, and the I Have a Dream Foundation, where students who graduated were assured of support to attend college. Small-scale allocations might include rewards for pupil attendance and/or achievement through "adopt-a-school" efforts, school-business partnerships or small grants from local businesses or agencies.

A direct link to improved academic performance is community involvement as instruction. This can be as uncomplicated as the principal working with parents to show them how to read to pupils, to help with homework, or to review work. Involvement as instruction can also be more complex, such as setting up homework telephone hotlines, establishing tutoring links with higher education/ teacher preparation programs, business tutors, or big brother/sister tutoring plans. There are some formal church-related instructional assistance programs. The effective principal seeks and coordinates these programs so they complement the school's mission and goals.

Law-enforcement groups have begun to move closer to and work directly with groups and agencies that can use their help. A school example is the DARE (Drug Abuse Resistance Education) program in which police officers work in schools with youngsters. In some communities, the police are establishing contact points and offices in trouble spots, such as housing projects. Similarly, in some communities, educators are working closely with community agencies. For example, in Kansas City, educators have worked with housing project managers to provide study rooms for students and to deliver parent education directly to the parents in the project. As educators tackle opportunities raised by the increasing diversity in schools and by the growing poverty and deficits in children's school readiness, intense community involvement and cooperation with other agencies will be required. The school is becoming a social service hub and a place for coordinating integrated social services not just for humanitarian value but also as support for the learning goals of schooling. This powerful trend will continue.

Community involvement has been successful in improving school efforts. Nettles (1991) noted that "evidence suggests that parental participation in children's efforts to learn in schools as well as in the broader community can have positive effects on students' school achievement" (p. 384). As Hodgkinson (1991) said, educators can't do this job alone—especially as more and more children come to the school without the requisite knowledge and skills that educators had come to expect. Although important at all levels, community involvement to address pupil academic achievement seems especially crucial at early stages of schooling.

A Clear Mission: No Secrets

A major source of support for school goals can come from each pupil's home environment *if people there know about and are encouraged to be part of the school's goals for pupil learning*. While teachers work with children in classrooms, the principal helps educate parents, guardians, and extended family about the school's mission and goals; as part of this process, the principal interprets the community expectations and translates these into schooling processes. The principal may use various involvement strategies such as parent/teacher organizations, advisory or review teams, planning groups, volunteer programs, and informal meetings, to assure that the school's goals and mission are constantly emphasized.

What the school is doing—or trying to do—should not be a secret. If all appropriate and involved people (the stakeholders) know what is important and if they are kept informed of progress and needs, they are likely to become supporting partners in achieving the goals. One concrete example is a statement of desired exit skills developed by teacher committees for each subject area for each grade. These clear and brief explanations (one page per subject) are sent home each year with the pupils, and the grade-level statements carry an important inclusionary message on the cover. The following example is from the First Grade Learner Objectives (1989), Clovis Unified School District, Clovis, CA:

> The Grade Level Objectives are statements of desired learning outcomes. . . . They should provide *teachers and parents* specific direction for learning activities *at school and at home*. . . . Decisions about learning materials, methods and sequencing of the objectives will be made at the school site. Objectives are listed where *mastery is desired of all students* [Italics added].

There is a strong positive relationship between the clarity of a leader's vision and a person's likelihood of actualizing it. Knowing where one is going makes planning and directing the journey possible. Instructional leaders have a clear sense of what the result of instruction should resemble. They focus on what students will know or be able to do at the end of the academic journey. They are able to communicate those ideals to staff members, to students, and to parents, and in so doing, to create a school culture that is imbued with a belief that all students will learn.

Keedy (1982) and Doll (1989) found that effective principals established the educational norms and did whatever was necessary to promote pupil achievement. Rutherford (1985) noted that effective principals who served as curriculum leaders had specific visions for their schools, translated those visions into goals and expectations, and established school climates conducive to achieving them. In comparing principals to potters, Blumberg (1987) argued that administrators needed to know what their final products would resemble and to understand the nature and eccentricities of the materials with which they must work. Greenfield (1987) suggested that there were two major ideas that served

> as the cornerstones of effective instructional leadership. The ability to exercise "moral imagination" underlies one's capacity to develop a compelling vision regarding what is possible and desirable to achieve in a given school situation . . . [and] "interpersonal competence," the ability to elicit desired task responses from another, . . . [which] refers to the knowledge and skills needed to influence teachers and others in desired directions. (p. 64)

In high-achieving high schools, Boyer (1983) found "a clear sense of community" and that the principal made the difference in establishing that perception (p. 219). Leadership extends beyond the efficient technical management of a school: "It rests upon meanings as well as actions. Leaders make meanings" (Hoy & Miskel, 1991, pp. 296–297). Instructional leaders possess what Sheive and Schoenheit (1987) have labeled *professional missions*.

Specifically how principals translate their school missions and expectations will vary according to the pupils and teachers with whom they work. For instance, Hallinger and Murphy (1987) discovered that the leadership role an individual principal took in defining missions and goals varied with the populations served in particular schools. Principals judged to be effective who worked with lower-socioeconomic-status students were more likely to be assertive in formulating specific goals than were their peers working in more affluent institutions. Tillman (1991) found that context, situation, and purpose influenced how principals translated their school visions into action.

People, Not Programs

Although it is tempting to point to programs that may be successful with one group or another, the keys to pupil achievement are the people involved: excellence depends on people more than on programs. In his welcoming speech to new teachers when he was superintendent of the Clovis, California, schools, Floyd Buchanan, the 1990 California Superintendent of the Year said, "We've learned an interesting thing—if you really want to develop winners you've got to surround children with winners" (Strother, 1991, p. 34). Buchanan's "People not Programs" philosophy puts a burden on the principal's recruitment, selection, staff development, and human relations skills. The principal is responsible for developing educational "winners" and then distributing support and resources to those teachers who help pupils achieve academic goals.

Even if the principal and faculty introduce new or improved *programs* to stimulate pupil learning, *people* must make the programs work. Usually those people are teachers, and to apply their skills most beneficially, they must be free and empowered to make appropriate decisions (see Greer & Short, chapter 6). As teachers work directly with pupils, the principal supports and encourages teachers, coordinates teacher and pupil work toward common goals, and builds the tone or the culture of the school; what the teacher is for the classroom, the principal is for the school—and more.

Although people are key to pupil academic achievement, thus requiring that the principal be adept at matching of staff development processes to ways that people can help pupils achieve, sometimes people *and* programs must be orchestrated to stimulate pupil achievement. A seemingly limitless array of programs is available to address almost every conceivable issue of pupil learning. Educators learn about programs in many ways: conferences, word-of-mouth, professional publications, mandates, and advertising. The principal should help the teacher determine the need for the program, the priority and costs associated with the program, the goals and objectives to be met by the use of the program, and how the program will be evaluated—what will be considered "success."

In informing people of proven programs, the principal would do well to *start* with recommending that the teacher check programs that have been carefully evaluated and shown effective. One place to start is the many programs available since 1974 through the U.S. Department of Education's National Diffusion Network (NDN). Using a rigorous evaluation process, NDN programs are "validated" as successful and promoted for use with *specific groups* (grade levels, demographic groups such as rural, urban, or ethnic) for *specific purposes* (reading improvement, geography, arts) for students with certain characteristics (general, gifted, at risk). Outstanding projects from Chapter 1, Head Start, Bilingual Education, etc., are also listed. Programs are reviewed and annually a list of *Educational Programs that Work* is available through the NDN State Facilitator in each state. Many of these programs were developed at great cost, and the NDN can make them available at little or no cost through its process of needs analysis, matching needs and audience with programs, awareness materials, training, adoption/use assistance, and follow-up and evaluation. Starting with the NDN provides an extensive base of programs that have a sort of "Good Housekeeping Seal of Approval."

Other federal help for stimulating pupil achievement is available through services of regional educational laboratories, research and developmental centers, and the Education Resources Information Clearinghouse (ERIC) database networks, readily available on CD-ROM and other media. By intelligently using the vast resources available through the U.S. Department of Education and State Education Agencies, a principal can often efficiently help faculty identify and use proven programs to aid in improving pupil achievement.

Programs will be most successful in the hands of those who have selected them; the content to be taught and the methods of instruction are most appropriately decided by the teachers after they have understood the needs of the clients they will serve (see Achilles et al., chapter 2). The principal's five-fold task is to do the following:

1. *Inform* people about sources of proven programs.
2. *Help* people select the *most* appropriate program(s).
3. *Provide* resources (for training, for materials, etc.) so people can learn to use the programs effectively.
4. *Guide* people through the change process so they adapt/adopt the program as part of regular instruction.
5. *Coordinate* the adoption of any new program carefully with the school's primary mission so that programs don't seem like add-ons or afterthoughts.
6. *Evaluate* results as a basis for decisions.

Developed in this way, programs are tightly coupled to the school's mission while the teacher's methods of instruction are determined by "teaching moments" that arise (loosely-coupled events).

Instructional Issues

Traditionally, the domain of instructional leadership includes a consideration of who will be taught, what they will be taught and with what resources, under what conditions, by whom and in what ways, and how we will know if what was taught was actually learned. Although many of the decisions about aspects of these areas have been determined by agencies outside the school (the state legislature, the state or local board of education, various committees or commissions, a central office administrator), a principal is still presented with choices. What choices that principal makes can influence pupil academic performance.

Who Will Be Taught?

Students in schools today are unlike those a mere decade ago. A significant number come from homes with incomes below the poverty line. Reed and Sautter (1990) found that during the 1980s, at a time when the number of American billionaires quintupled, 23 percent more children were classified as poor. According to the National Commission to Prevent Infant Mortality, the United States ranks 20th among world nations in infant death. One-fourth of pregnant mothers receive no prenatal care during the first three months of pregnancy. According to Hodgkinson (1991), two million school children are unsupervised in the afternoons; another two million are being reared by someone other than a parent.

Simons, Finlay, and Yang (1991), reporting for The Children's Defense Fund, found that the birth rates for unmarried adolescents have never been higher. Homicide is the second leading cause of death for young people and, in some cities, it is the leading cause of death for young black males. Alcohol abuse is widespread and not confined to a particular socioeconomic class; generally adolescents begin drinking around the age of 13. The number of reported cases of child abuse had tripled between 1976 and 1987. The most likely victim of sexual abuse is an adolescent female. As Kotlowitz documented in *There Are No Children Here* (1991), the lives of many of the nation's youngest citizens resemble a Hobbesian state: "continual fear and danger of violent death . . . solitary, poor, nasty, brutish, and short" (Hobbes, 1651/1991, p. 89). As Hodgkinson concludes:

> The fact is that more than one-third of American children have the deck stacked against them before they enter school. Although America's best students are on a par with the world's best, ours is undoubtedly the worst "bottom third" of any of the industrialized democracies. (1991, p. 10)

Students come to schools with profound health and social problems (Hamburg, 1992). The number of children diagnosed with learning disabilities has increased dramatically, rising 140 percent during the past decade (Reed & Sautter, 1990). In the 1990s, the nation's schools will receive an unprecedented number of children whose intellectual potentials have been compromised by their mothers' addiction to crack cocaine and to alcohol and tobacco use during pregnancy. The current debate about fetal child abuse reflects a growing concern for the medical, social, and educational implications of fetal alcohol syndrome and drug-addicted infants. Our "worst third" has not benefitted from the economic boom times of the 1980s and will likely not benefit from the economic recession of the early 1990s. Yet they will come to school.

Charged with teaching all children well, how can public school educators address simultaneously the needs of those youngsters and the requirements of the twenty-first-century workplace? Certainly it's tempting to declare that the problem belongs at someone else's door—the White House, Congress, Wall Street, excessive violence expressed in the media. The public schools did not create the conditions of the street that compete for a child's attention. They did not encourage the proliferation of poverty, the declining access to health care, or the increasing divorce rate.

As some observers have noted, the children entering schools are the best ones we have. No one has stockpiled the good kids somewhere else. The fact that educators are unable, in isolation, to repair the damage caused by economic stress does not excuse the obligation to provide all young people with the best possible educational opportunities. "But you should see our children" cannot be a rationale for inaction; it can and must, however, be an imperative for alternative actions and a call for creative problem solving.

A school administrator might be unable to select the pupils for the school but he or she can select actions to enhance the likelihood of their success at school. Specifically, the principal can articulate and perpetuate a belief system that sets high expectations for all children: "Everyone can learn in this school, and everyone can learn the good stuff."

The schoolhouse door stands open for every youngster eligible to attend classes in that building. The principal cannot serve as a gatekeeper, accepting those who are more likely to succeed and rejecting those who might have a lower potential for academic success. However, the leader's role in setting forth a clear set of expectations about why schools exist and how the business of schooling will be enacted within a particular building influences the achievement of the youngsters who enter that building.

What Will Be Taught and with What Will It Be Taught?

The nature of curriculum in a school depends on various constituencies outside that school. Board policy sets the broad parameters, sometimes informed by state recommendations, and sometimes determined by state-adopted standard courses of study. State curriculum guides, competency goals and indicators, and curriculum frameworks proliferated in the 1980s, often reinforced with state testing programs keyed to the curriculum. Simultaneously, the textbook selection process used in several key states resulted in the adoption of materials that were considered educationally suspect. The list of textbook sins is a long one. Texts do the following negative things:

> take on too many topics and treat them superficially; there are too many unexplained facts, and there is not enough context; new knowledge is more often piled on than assimilated; the prose is dumbed down to accommodate . . . poorer reading skills . . . ; faddist and special-interest-group messages, however meritorious, appear as bulges or snippets of content; flashy graphics and white space further compress the already compressed text; instructors are becoming seduced by, and addicted to, teaching manuals and ancillary products that promise to take the work (and the judgment) out of teaching (Tyson-Bernstein, 1988, p. 194).

In some states, educators can use money only for officially sanctioned materials. They are required to make a choice between an inadequate textbook or none at all, a decision often difficult to explain to parents who see the possession of a text by every child for every subject as one of the givens of public schooling. When given a choice among books, administrators generally find that their teachers are the subjects of intense lobbying campaigns by vendors, each of whom tout the virtues of a particular product with a vast array of supplementary materials. As a result, decisions are sometimes made not on the compatibility of a textbook with a particular curriculum, but on the range and potential user-friendliness of the audio-visual, workbook, and testing program extras that accompany the text.

In a world where many teachers will start on page 1 in August and conclude on page 300 in May, and will teach the textbook rather than using it as a resource for teaching a curriculum, book selection is not a trivial issue. The principal is responsible for assuring that the text and other resources are aligned with the curriculum and that they serve to strengthen the curriculum rather than serving as a *replacement* for it.

Hallinger and Murphy (1987) observed that the technology for an organization is the ways it chooses to meet its goals. For schools, "the technology designed to produce student learning is the curriculum and instruction to which students are exposed" (p. 182). They claim that there are two aspects to that technology: clarity and complexity.

Technical clarity is the extent that what is to be taught and how it is to be taught are understood. To increase the likelihood of technical clarity, the administrator must help staff to understand the parts of the school's curriculum and to adopt a coordinated approach to teaching that curriculum to all students. For example, Ms. Jones's class and Mr. Smith's class, assuming those students are responsible for mastering the same curriculum, should be taught the same topics, but probably not in precisely the same way or in the same sequence.

Technical complexity refers to how the curriculum is interdependent—how skills are reinforced by various disciplines and depend upon previous instruction. An administrator can influence achievement by addressing technical clarity issues through curricular articulation. Although sixth-grade teachers must ensure that all sixth graders are introduced to the same competencies, the administrator is responsible for ensuring that those competencies make sense based on prior education, that they will not unnecessarily be repeated in succeeding years, and that they provide an adequate foundation for future learning.

A principal can choose several actions to help ensure that the curriculum will contribute to student achievement. For example, the administrator can make sure that the following things are true:

1. The staff knows the curriculum that will form the basis for judging pupil achievement; they know what they are expected to teach.
2. The staff clearly understands the curriculum.
3. Staff members act on that knowledge.
4. The resources selected with which to teach the curriculum are applicable and appropriately used.

The principal becomes a steward for the school curriculum. Smith and Andrews (1989) found that administrators judged to be effective instructional leaders were more likely to engage in certain behaviors than their peers who were deemed either average or weak instructional leaders:

- They communicated clearly to the staff about instructional matters.
- They were likely to pay attention to student test results and to discuss with staff members those data as they applied to curriculum and instruction.
- They communicated both to students and to parents the extent to which learning objectives had been mastered.
- They were a visible presence in and around the school, to students, to the staff, and to school patrons and parents.

Visibility has been related to student achievement and the implementation of new programs in a number of studies (see, for example, Andrews & Soder, 1987; High & Achilles, 1986). Blase and Kirby (1992) found that teachers perceived effective principals as being visible. MBWA (management by walking around) has been a staple of the business excellence literature popularized in the 1980s. In schools, purposeful MBWA provides a way for principals to observe how and how well goals are being attained.

Under What Conditions?

Schools continue to be the way they have always been. Individual classrooms open off long corridors. There is a cafeteria and, perhaps, a gymnasium. The library, renamed now the media center, houses print and other supplementary materials for student and staff use. The year is divided into semesters of approximately 90 days. Classrooms contain a teacher and approximately 25–30 youngsters. The curriculum remains remarkably constant.

Yet none of these or other organizational realities is necessarily cast in stone; many offer opportunities where administrators can be creative, although certain forms of creativity, such as reducing class size, require a reallocation of resources. Isn't it possible to reduce the student–teacher ratio in some classes some of the time? Mental barriers to thinking creatively about class size have restricted educators to thinking of same-sized groups for all things throughout the day. Lortie (1975) noted the "cellular" notion of education, whereby when there are more pupils, administrators add another teacher and classroom—with the efficient ratio common to the district, and without thinking about creative alternatives. Perhaps educators can reconsider how to assemble student groups within a building (see Greer & Short, chapter 6). Taking a cue from Adler's *The Paideia Proposal*, perhaps some instruction might work best in small groups (seminars), in large groups (didactic presentations), and in very small groups (coaching), and perhaps principals can find ways to schedule programs of study that include the possibilities of such variations (Adler, 1982).

Another way to improve pupil achievement, at least in early primary grades, is a direct class-size reduction. Few elements of schooling have stirred as much debate or been the focus of as much research as the issue of class size. "Special" youth, such as handicapped or gifted, usually are taught in small classes while "regular" youngsters are taught in classes of 25, 30, or even more. Early debates about reducing class size as a way to improve pupil achievement spurred some 1980s large-scale efforts, such as Indiana's Project Primetime. In reviewing the research on class size to that time, Robinson (1990) noted that "the most positive effects of small classes on pupil learning occur in grades K-3 . . . [and] smaller classes can positively affect the academic achievement of economically disadvantaged and ethnic minority students" (p. 82).

A large-scale (over 7000 pupils) longitudinal (1985–89 for grades K–3) experiment in Tennessee (The Student–Teacher Achievement Ratio project, or STAR) has shown positively that small classes (average of 1:15 teacher–pupil ratio) increase pupil achievement, especially in reading and mathematics when compared with the control classes (1:24 ratio) and with 1:24 classes also having a full-time teacher aide. The Lasting Benefits Study (LBS), a continuation of STAR, showed that two years after STAR ended and all pupils returned to "regular" classes, those who were originally in the STAR small classes were still outperforming those who were in regular STAR classes (Achilles, Nye, Zaharias, Fulton, & Wallenhorst, 1992; Nye, Achilles, Zaharias, Fulton, & Hooper, 1992). Of Project STAR, Finn and Achilles (1990) said, "This research leaves no doubt that small classes have an advantage over larger classes in reading and mathematics in the early primary grades" (p. 573).

Researchers rank-ordered STAR classes by reading achievement scores each year and then categorized the top 10 percent into their class types. In kindergarten, 55 percent of the top-scoring 10 percent were small classes, but small classes were 78 percent of the top-scoring 10 percent by third grade. Being in small classes has a cumulative effect on pupil achievement (Bain, Achilles, Zaharias, & McKannea, 1992). By 1993, preliminary analyses were showing substantial positive achievement gains in 17 counties in Tennessee where elementary (K–3) class sizes had been reduced to an average teacher–pupil ratio of 1:15 by using Federal Chapter 1 and state funding (Achilles et al., 1992; Nye, Achilles, Zaharias, Fulton, & Wallenhorst, 1993).

Researchers (such as Bloom, 1984, and others) have noted that one-to-one tutoring can provide very positive pupil gains but that the cost is not feasible for educating large numbers of youngsters in the public school system. Continuing study of class size is not so much a question of class-size reduction as it is a way to determine reasonable-sized groups so the pupils and teachers can achieve positive learning outcomes.

Organization and the mechanics of instruction (grades arranged by chronological groups and evaluations based on a bell-shaped curve, for example) can make student achievement more or less likely. A teacher who sees 50 students a day, rather than 150, will be more able to know them as individuals, to understand their particular learning problems, and to design instruction to address those needs. The teacher will also be more likely to make assignments that require additional evaluation time, simply because his or her class load has been reduced. Yet principals continue to assign high school English teachers five classes of students a day, rather than to consider how to change class structures to reduce the number of contacts a staff member might encounter in, say, a given semester.

Research shows that retention in grade rarely has a positive impact on the pupil retained and that retention is quite likely to contribute to school ineffectiveness as measured by such statistics as drop-out rates (Shepard & Smith, 1990). Yet few educators have implemented a comprehensive evaluation system to eliminate the concept of failure, so the idea of retention thrives in the face of contrary evidence (Doyle, 1989). A pupil in need of remediation is generally required to wait 180 days, or until the doors of summer school open, to receive that help.

The school calendar could be designed so that a pupil is no more than nine weeks away from necessary remediation, thereby reducing the likelihood that he or she will fall further behind. Educators can also work to eliminate a long summer hiatus of formal educational opportunities, an educational lull that adversely affects students. Year-around schooling offers teachers more time to teach new skills because it eliminates the need to review or renew skills that had been mastered three months ago but were extinguished after a significant period of non-use.

Some forms of nongraded or continuous-progress programs also offer alternatives to retention in grade. Instructional variations such as peer tutoring, cross-age grouping, cooperative learning, and other adjustments can reduce retention in grade.

What stops a school administrator from implementing such possible redesigns? Often it is the limitations of educators' collective imaginations. Educators have become so acculturated to schools as they have always been that it is very difficult for them to think beyond the long-held stereotypes. The stages on which students perform—middle schools or junior highs, essential schools or Horace's high school, a traditionally calendared school or a year-round school, a graded or a non-graded school—actually influence those performances.

No blueprint yet exists for the creation of schools that overcome all barriers to student success. However, almost monthly researchers publish reports of fledgling efforts to design new organizations, more flexible or student-friendly schedules, and more valid ways to assess student learning. For that reason alone, principals must survey the literature on schools and on schooling to become what Barth (1990) has termed the "head learner" in a school community.

By Whom

The teacher directs the student performances in the classroom. The teacher is the educational leader for that group of youngsters. Criticism of public school educators was prevalent in the reform documents of the early 1980s. There was a sense that the individuals who became teachers were ineffective because they were lazy or inept. A declining number of the best and brightest college graduates appeared to elect education as a career, and of those individuals who did become teachers, the best and brightest seemed more likely than the others to leave the profession early (Schlechty & Vance, 1981, 1983). Teacher preparation programs came under attack. The National Council for the Accreditation of Teacher Education (NCATE) revised its standards, making accreditation more rigorous. Some colleges moved to five-year teacher preparation programs; some colleges adopted five-year credentialing plans. A National Board of Professional Teaching Standards has been developed to help teaching as a profession.

There remained problems within the teaching pool. The percentage of minority candidates continued to drop as other employment opportunities opened for women and minority college graduates. The number of men interested in classroom positions in primary grades remained low. Good teachers found that the avenue to higher compensation and more autonomy led outside the classroom toward administration.

Teachers who remained in those classrooms found themselves facing a challenging student population. Competition for the time and attention of the nation's children has increased during the past decade, while the number of children adversely affected by fluctuations in the nation's economy has increased. Students are more likely to hold jobs after school, to be responsible for the care of their younger brothers and sisters, to be latchkey children, to engage in behaviors that can seriously compromise their health, and to be poorer than they were 20 or 30 years ago. They are also more likely to watch television than to read a book. Their heroes include Bart Simpson, who has elevated pride in academic underachievement to a T-shirt slogan. Students seem no longer able to learn from lectures, to sit quietly and work independently, to complete homework, or to care about the quality of their work products. It has become uncool to do school.

Although the workplace conditions of teaching might not have deteriorated—teachers today rarely have to fill the coal bucket and start the furnace—the tension between workers who perceive themselves as professionals laboring within a bureaucracy and those outsiders who view them as ineffective and incompetent has increased. That tension has been exacerbated by a tendency of some reform efforts to make the bureaucracy more rigid and to deny teachers freedom to practice their profession. Teachers are often told what to teach (a state curriculum), how to teach it (a state-approved instructional method required by a standardized evaluation system), and with what to teach it (state-adopted teaching materials). Their performances are judged by state-designed evaluation instruments and often considered independent of whom they teach or of the available resources. Given recent economic reverses, all too often needed educational resources have been curtailed, salaries held static, and equipment purchases postponed while expectations and criticisms have risen.

An instructional leader recognizes the tensions that undergird professional practice in public schools. In addition to ameliorating working conditions that most directly interfere with the capacity to teach and that are within the principal's power to address (e.g., turning off the intercom during class hours, making supplies available for instruction), effective principals take advantage of teacher strengths in designing schedules, in determining faculty loads, and in pairing students with teachers.

Peterson (1987) identified six behaviors linked to effective instructional leadership in working with teachers.

- providing regular observation and feedback
- monitoring of student performances frequently
- constructing a coordinated instructional program
- promoting of staff development
- insisting that teachers are responsible for student learning
- serving as an information resource about instructional issues

Blase and Kirby (1992) found that three attitudes and two behaviors characterized principals deemed effective by teachers. The attitudes included optimism (a hard task, but we can do it), honesty, and consideration. The actions were modeling and visibility. Effective instructional leaders "walked the talk" and they did it constantly.

Smith and Andrews (1989) found that effective instructional leaders communicated with teachers, supported participation in staff development, displayed knowledge of the curriculum and instructional methods, visited classrooms frequently, and provided clear and helpful feedback during evaluations. They clustered behaviors that facilitated student achievement into four areas of interaction among teachers and administrator: the principal as resource provider, instructional resource, communicator, and visible presence.

Effective principals were more likely than their less effective colleagues to encourage the use of different instructional strategies, to provide during the evaluation process information that improved teaching, to be sought out by staff members for help in solving problems related to instruction, and to engage in "creative insubordination" to see that school goals were addressed. (This idea is captured in the expression, "It is easier to ask forgiveness than to get permission"; see Hughes, chapter 1.) Barth (1990) contended that principals who failed to take advantage of the possibilities for adult learning available in public schools were missing opportunities to improve the effectiveness of schools. This makes the case for the principal in the role of staff developer to emphasize what research has shown about ways to improve student performance. Examples are research on homework, on retention and tracking, and on using other good education processes. The principal can also guide the school into adapting "new" change efforts, such as empowerment and restructuring.

Homework.   Many teachers assign homework because it's the thing to do. Yet there is considerable research on homework effectiveness. A standard for improving pupil academics has long been homework. Cooper (1989) found that over the years homework has been praised and cursed by educators and others. There have been various definitions of *homework*, so Cooper established a working definition as "tasks assigned to students by school teachers that are meant to be carried out during non-school hours" (p. 86). This excludes, for example, guided in-school study.

Cooper's research provides some surprising and some not-so-surprising answers about the impact of homework on pupil achievement. Homework may have other purposes than pupil achievement, such as encouraging responsibility, perseverance, and parent involvement, but if it is for those purposes, the goals should be clear, well-recognized, and followed. Cooper arrives at three major conclusions about homework and achievement (p. 88):

1. Homework influences achievement positively, *but* the effect varies by grade level: there is strong benefit for high school pupils' achievement, about half as much benefit for junior high pupils, and negligible benefit for elementary pupils.

2. "The optimum amount of homework varies with grade level" (p. 88). No specific amount of homework increases achievement for elementary pupils, and junior high pupil achievement continues to improve until total assignments "last between one and two hours a night" (p. 88). Within reason, high school pupil achievement increases with increased homework.
3. No clear pattern of homework effectiveness in particular subjects has been established. "Homework probably works best when material is not too complex or completely unfamiliar" (p. 88).

Cooper provides model guidelines and a recommended homework policy for districts, schools, and teachers. Generally, a need exists for coordinated policies, especially at the teacher and building level. Principals and teachers should understand the rationales, strengths, and weaknesses of homework as an important tool in instructional improvement. Homework provides an arena for teacher professional decision-making based on current research and principal initiation and coordination of such an initiative is part of instructional leadership, perhaps in staff development. Without knowing this body of information, how could a principal help teachers and parents establish policy and guidelines for constructive use of homework?

Retention and Tracking.   Years of research have not shown benefits on pupil performance from retention in grade (Doyle, 1989; Shepard & Smith, 1990). Educators need to apply both the strong research results against grade retention and persuasive human-relations skills to combat the folk-wisdom-driven emotional issue of grade retention. The practice of "tracking," declared illegal (*Hobson v. Hansen*, 1967), has also been seriously questioned by a continuing strand of research results (Oakes, 1985, 1992; Braddock & McPartland, 1990), although some grouping seems to help gifted pupils (Rogers, 1991). What would be the outcome if principals and teachers applied the test of *cui bono* (who benefits) to retention and to tracking?

Using Research-Established Processes

To increase pupil achievement, the principal needs to keep current research results in front of teachers, to guide the teachers to use the results, and to avoid what Glickman (1991) calls "pretending not to know what we know." The principal's role in staff development must be focused on improving pupil performance, because what the principal pays attention to is what will improve.

Empowering.   As administrator, the principal is responsible for solid management and for sound leadership of the enterprise (see Achilles et al., chapter 2). In the early 1990s, several concepts dominated the literature and themes for school improvement, where improvement often meant increased pupil achievement on norm-referenced tests (NRTs). Some of the emphases providing targets for leadership are restructuring, reinventing, site-based management, shared decision making, new teacher-preparation ideas, teacher improvement through strategies such as mentoring or lead-teaching initiatives, and teacher empowerment.

Successful leaders use power to increase it. They empowered their followers. Heck, Larsen, and Marcoulides (1990) found that teachers were more involved in determining aspects of the instructional program in high-achieving schools than were their counterparts in low-achieving schools. Principals in low-achieving schools were more likely than peers in high-achieving schools to rationalize non-participation by teachers in decision making as a way to preserve their valuable time for teaching. Glickman found improved student performances in Georgia schools where administrators provided more opportunities for teachers to become involved in governance issues. Teachers respond favorably to increased teacher involvement in decision making (Blase & Kirby, 1992), but there are limits to involvement—when it interferes with teaching responsibilities or when it seems token and is clustered about things of little interest to teachers (High & Achilles, 1986; High, Achilles, & High, 1989). Areas of high interest include curriculum and instruction issues, while management details such as scheduling are not usually productive areas for involvement.[3]

Examples of strategies to improve teacher empowerment or to strengthen shared decision making are communication skills, goal setting, expanded decision-making steps such as consensus, and cooperative learning. These skills can become the agenda for faculty meetings, workshops, and retreats.

Restructuring.   School restructuring, or changing the basic structure of a school (see Greer and Short, chapter 6; Achilles et al., chapter 2) includes such things as nongraded primaries, school-within-a-school organizations and individual governance boards. Restructuring may provide alternatives to the usual grade/age organization in schools, or to the rigid departmental organization found in some secondary schools. Restructuring might also include creative use of time, such as extended-day or extended-year programs or year-around schools. One key is that efforts at restructuring should have as their goal the improvement of pupil learning and the achievement of the school's mission.

In an attempt to build upon and use effectively the expertise of all faculty, some principals experiment with expanded concepts of school governance and ways to empower teachers to use their skills to improve student learning. Teachers and administrators may cooperate in strategic planning and in sharpening the vision of the results of schooling. Developing and working with visions

---

3.   A considerable strand of research on teacher involvement in school decision making suggests that involvement can be a powerful tool for school improvement. However, involvement can be a two-edged sword. If it is overused or seen as perfunctory, involvement will be seen as a waste of time or a ploy to get endorsement for already-made decisions. Teachers are interested in being involved in substantive issues of curriculum and instruction but prefer not to be bothered with details of scheduling or maintaining the status quo; they do not actively seek extensive involvement in personnel issues. For more details see, e.g., Alutto & Belasco, 1972; High & Achilles, 1986; High et al., 1989; Imber & Duke, 1984; Mohrman, Jr., Cooke, & Mohrman, 1978.

of pupil achievement provide a basis for people to exercise leadership. As faculty refine the vision with goals/objectives and a mission statement, they consider the strategies, tactics, and activities that will need careful management—such things as planning, coordinating, oversight, and evaluation.

As leader, the building principal is the "keeper of the vision." The principal constantly, clearly, and cogently keeps the vision in front of everyone in the school and articulates it at every opportunity to those in the school and to other publics. Expressed visions such as "All students here learn daily" and a goal of "80 percent of pupils here will equal or exceed the national norms on tests each year" guide efforts to improve pupil academic achievement. In increasing pupil achievement, there may be few goals but there are many methods.

Measuring Pupil Achievement

The principal and the faculty should use results of measurements of pupil learning to set goals and to plan programs of improvement rather than to sort, label, track, fail, or otherwise demean the individual. This complex concern is incorporated in such concepts as the purpose and use of testing and test results, curriculum and test alignment, media and public understanding of testing and test results, and other touchy subjects.

It is beyond the scope of this chapter to debate the role of standardized testing in determining the curricula of schools, the time spent on particular subjects, the way teachers teach, or the "quality" of schools relative to pupil performance. Events on the education landscape have shown that policymakers, parents, patrons, pupils, and others perceive that pupil performance, as measured by tests, is a major indicator of education quality. Tests most often cited as indicators of education quality are standardized or norm-referenced tests (NRTs), and comparisons of group scores (e.g., "school average") are used in national wall charts and state report cards for schools (e.g., Bobbett et al., 1992).

A standardized test is "normed" so that half of those who take it are below average. If the test is not normed regularly (an expensive act), then in a few years more than half of the test-takers are "above average" and educators get criticized for pupil success (Cannell, 1987). Test makers then re-norm tests so half of the test takers are again below average. Some critics have singled out subject areas and tried to determine whether today's or yesterday's youth have known more.[4] Ravitch and Finn (1987) argued that 17-year-olds in the United States performed "shockingly" poorly on a national assessment of American history and literature and (by inference) knew less about these subjects than did yesterday's youth. Whittington (1991) undertook to determine what 17-year-olds knew in the past and concluded that:

---

4.   If pupils today are doing less well than their predecessors, then we must determine when and by how much today's tests have been normed *downward*.

the perception of a decline in the "results" of American education is open to question. Indeed, given the reduced dropout rate and less elitist composition of the 17-year-old student body today, [and, we might add, the knowledge added over the years] one could argue that students today know more American history than did their age peers of the past. (p. 778)

As long as NRTs, or tests that are treated as NRTs, are the accepted and usual ways to assess pupil academic performance, the principal will work within "the system" while trying to make sense of it. Contemporaneously, the principal has a professional and moral responsibility to lead the movement to find alternative, authentic ways to assess pupils, and to advocate productive, appropriate uses for results of NRTs. For example, NRT results can profitably survey academic strengths and weaknesses of pupils so that teachers can define and work to remediate deficits. To do this usefully, the NRTs could be given early in a school session, and when results become available, the principal can help teachers understand and plan to use them. Just as a person's blood pressure, pulse rate, EKG, and other vital statistics help doctors determine that person's general health and help doctor and patient to plan for improvement, so NRT results can help educators and parents build appropriate education experiences for children.

Perhaps the issue isn't how well a pupil does on a test, but how people *use* knowledge; inert knowledge isn't of much value in a pragmatic sense. Whitehead (1929) has noted that "Education is the acquisition of the art of the utilization of knowledge" (p. 16), and that "Knowledge does not keep any better than fish" (p. 102). How can we measure how people *use* knowledge? One point is clear: If we change how we assess student performance, changes in curriculum and instruction will follow.

Moral Issues

Research results that strongly contradict practice or conventional wisdom emphasize the magnitude of moral issues facing principals. In other fields, such as medicine, a practitioner would be subject to malpractice for failing to know about and to use the most current research in the field. As Glickman (1991) points out in "Pretending Not to Know What We Know," educators constantly neglect employing the results of substantial research on such practices as retention in grade, tracking, and class size, for example. In other cases, not everyone agrees—for example, on the purposes and goals of schooling (knowledge and/or socialization)—so there is considerable room for debate. Nevertheless, a principal desiring to see improvement in pupil achievement needs to know research results that offer promise of direct and indirect influences on pupil outcomes.

Although pupil academic achievement is a major school outcome often used as an indicator of education "quality," the nature of schooling in the United States dictates that other outcomes may be classified under the rubrics of equality, equity, and quality. The *intersections* of these legitimate outcomes provide areas where the principal must make decisions based on sound *research* on one hand and on *ethical/moral and community values* positions on the other hand (see Craig, chapter 5). In these instances, the principal may need to employ research on various positions to advance two or more legitimate outcomes (e.g., quality and equality) simultaneously. The issues of tracking and of pupil retention in grade are examples of these types of leadership opportunities.

Tracking as an education strategy has supporters and detractors. Some people argue that teachers can teach better with more homogeneous groups of students and that good students do not get a fair opportunity when they are taught in classes with less able students. Others argue that tracking harms students by sorting them early into winners and losers, that once so placed students seldom catch up or move to higher groups, that low tracks are inequitably filled with males and with minority students or pupils of color, and that the content of low tracks is uninteresting and trite. Tracking has been used for a long time; since it gained widespread use, methods, content, and technologies of teaching have changed—but not the strategy of grouping/tracking. Researchers (e.g., Braddock & McPartland, 1990) have shown successful alternative strategies to traditional grouping and tracking. How might cooperative learning, peer tutoring, self-paced learning, or outcome-based instruction provide teachers with tools that will improve instruction for all pupils—and increase achievement—while eliminating old strategies that research suggests are harmful for pupils?

As educators try "untracking," some are having success—but not without making important concomitant changes in the content and methods of instruction. Just untracking without applying professional knowledge and other research results won't get the job done (Cone, 1992).

Some research results challenge spoken and unspoken norms in education. One such norm has been that teachers in "regular" classes should all have about the same number of pupils as a measure of fairness. In using results of class-size research, the principal's leadership ability will be sorely tested. In the past, principals typically have arranged nearly equal pupil assignments for all teachers. Present research, however, suggests that in at least K–3 the teacher–pupil ratio should be about 1:15. This is increasingly important as pupils come to school less well prepared for schooling than they were in the past (Hamburg, 1992; Hodgkinson, 1991). Pupils who start their school experiences in small classes arrive at later grades better prepared for schooling than do their peers who start in larger classes.

The issue of reducing class size to improve pupil performance offers an interesting challenge for principal leadership. How might a principal use results of the class-size research, equalize the teaching load, and embrace another stimulus to pupil academic performance—parent or home involvement? One way is to encourage teachers of small classes to make *home visits* as a means of parent interest and involvement in the school. Hamburg (1992) noted that a program of home visitation, while useful for all pupils, was particularly useful with poor and neglected children (p. 84) and those with developmental and educational problems (p. 66).

Research on retention in grade shows that the practice does not benefit pupils and, to the contrary, often is harmful (Doyle, 1989; Shepard & Smith, 1990). In addition to some public opinion against grouping and tracking, courts have ruled against tracking (*Hobson v. Hansen*, 1967) and research has shown some of its detrimental effects (e.g., Achilles, Campbell, Faires, Jackson, & Martin, 1982; Braddock & McPartland, 1990; Oakes, 1992, 1985). On the other side, research (Rogers, 1991) has also shown that gifted youngsters learn well when homogeneously grouped.

There are a few examples where legitimate schooling outcomes (e.g., quality, equity, and equality) seem to intersect. The principal must navigate carefully while

- improving pupil outcomes by using research
- addressing community concerns
- exercising responsible, ethical leadership (Giroux, 1992)

Decisions have a moral/ethical dimension. It is not enough for a principal to address the "whats and hows" of schooling—attention to the "why" questions will help the principal steer a moral and ethical course in helping pupils achieve the goals of inquiry and scholarship.

SUMMARY

This chapter includes some perspectives and strategies relating to one key school outcome that many people equate with school quality—pupil academic achievement. A major portion of the principal's leadership job relates to monitoring, understanding, and stimulating pupil achievement, and this complex task interacts with other important aspects of administering an effective school. Analyses of test results and other factors of schooling have shown that a major influence on pupil performance on standard achievement measures is attendance: pupils who attend school and study a curriculum that is aligned with what is tested do better on the tests than pupils who do not attend school. A considerable part of pupil achievement relates to pupil attendance in a school that is safe, orderly, and inviting and that projects a culture of learning, caring, motivation, and success. The task of engendering such an experience is complicated by the challenge of doing the right thing and doing it right.

In reporting the work of the National Center for Educational Leadership (NCEL) at Harvard and the National Center for School Leadership (NCSL) at the University of Illinois, Krug (1992) highlighted the concept of instructional leadership. The five dimensions he noted, essentially a synthesis of major tasks for the principal concerned with helping increase pupil academic achievement through "instructional leadership," are summarized here (pp. 432–433):

1. *Defining mission.* Effective schools have clearly stated purposes, goals, and missions that principals clearly and frequently communicate to all stakeholders.
2. *Managing curriculum and instruction.* Because a school's primary and expected mission is to offer instruction on some agreed-upon curriculum, the principal needs to manage and coordinate these tasks and use these concepts as criteria for the distribution of resources.
3. *Supervising teaching.* In this area, the principal's role is emerging *from* the narrow, evaluative role of performance assessment to the use of supportive and proactive staff-development modes.
4. *Monitoring student progress.* The effective principal will use assessment results to "help teachers and students improve" and to "help parents understand where and why improvement is needed" (p. 433). To do this, the principal must understand the uses and misuses of testing and test results.
5. *Promoting instructional climate.* The principal's task here is "to motivate people by creating the conditions under which people want to do what needs to be done" (p. 433). Although the emphasis is on motivation, a positive instructional climate clearly must include a safe, orderly, and inviting environment.

The stimulation of pupil academic performance is a continuing challenge for the principal as instructional leader. Improvement will not occur without the principal's time and attention, for "as is the principal, so is the school." The principal is the coordinator of the learning environment and must demonstrate a commitment to pupil performance: the principal, the teachers, and the pupils *are a learning team.*

THEORY INTO PRACTICE: A CASE STUDY FOR REFLECTION

This state's Department of Public Instruction, like agencies in many other states, has developed an extensive testing program in response to the demands of various constituencies for public school accountability measures. Various test scores and related indices, such as attendance and drop-out rates, are combined and used to determine annual district-level report cards. One element of the testing program that is considered in generating report-card assessments is a holistically scored essay exam given each February to all sixth and eighth graders.

Because school districts are rated partially on the basis of such test scores, because the report cards are announced with considerable media hype and publicity, and because the scores of individual schools are subject to scrutiny in central offices and influential in setting goals for principals, school-level administrators must pay attention to such things. They do so, as one educator said, "so we can do well enough to be free to do some of the things that we need to do for our students but which are not measured by standardized tests."

Consider the case of one inner-city middle school in a traditional Southern industrial (textiles and furniture) town. The socio-demographics of the school are the stuff of administrative cop-outs and for "it can't work here" rationalizations. Yet student performances on the writing exams, a measure somewhat less susceptible to claims of class and racial bias than certain standardized tests and directly linked to curriculum, suggest the power of administrative activism in the areas of curriculum and instruction.

GUIDING QUESTIONS

Consider the following questions relative to the state testing data presented in table 10–1.

1. The current principal came to the school after the essay testing sequence had been begun. "When I first came to the school, I didn't pay attention to the writing tests, because they had not been part of my experience as an elementary school principal."
   - In what year did the new administrator arrive?
   - What indicates a shift in focus?
   - In what ways might that administrator communicate that shift in focus so it would stimulate pupil achievement?

2. "The school lost two key teachers and the system was involved in an unpopular, comprehensive study of merging three middle schools—a study I was asked to chair. At the same time, we were focused on the new set of legislatively required goals. Our scores reflected our preoccupation with other matters."
   - In which year did administrative attention shift from writing?
   - What other factors might compromise the attention of either administrators or staff, shifting it to other issues?
   - How can administrators limit the negative consequences of such attention shifts?

Table 10–1
State writing assessment, 1983–92. Scores reflect percentage (rounded) of students scoring 2.5 or better on a 4-point holistic scoring scale.

End of School Year	'84	'85	'86	'87	'88	'89	'90	'91	'92
Percentage of 6th Graders	20	26	50	16	57	42	43	24	41
Percentage of 8th Graders	N/A	N/A	36	26	64	55	67	30	74

REFERENCES

Achilles, C. M., Campbell, E., Faires, C., Jackson, C., & Martin, O. (1982, March). A study of issues related to discipline, grouping and tracking, and special education in New Castle County, Delaware, desegregation area. Vol. I, Discipline; Vol. II, Grouping and Tracking. Dover, DE: Delaware State Department of Public Instruction. (ERIC: ED 220967; ED 220968)

Achilles, C. M., Nye, B., Zaharias, J., Fulton, D., & Wallenhorst, M. (1992, August). *Class size is a reasonable policy alternative for educational excellence—or is it?* Paper presented at the meeting of the National Conference of Professors of Educational Administration, Indiana State University, Terre Haute, IN.

Adler, M. (1982). *The Paideia proposal: An educational manifesto.* New York: Macmillan.

Alutto, J., & Belasco, J. (1972). A typology for participation in organizational decision-making. *Administrative Science Quarterly, 17,* 117–125.

Andrews, R. L., & Soder, R. (1987). Principal instructional leadership and school achievement. *Instructional Leadership, 44,* 9–11.

Bain, H. P., Achilles, C. M., Zaharias, J. B., & McKenna, B. (1992, November). Class size does make a difference. *Phi Delta Kappan, 74*(3), 253–256.

Barth, R. (1990). *Improving schools from within.* San Francisco: Jossey-Bass.

Berlin, I. (1953). *The hedgehog and the fox: An essay on Tolstoy's view of history.* New York: Simon and Schuster.

Bissinger, H. G. (1990). *Friday night lights: A town, a team, and a dream.* Reading, MA: Addison-Wesley.

Blase, J., & Kirby, P. (1992). *Bringing out the best in teachers: What effective principals do.* Newberry Park, CA: Corwin Press.

Bloom, B. (1984, May). The search for methods of group instruction as effective as one-to-one tutoring. *Educational Leadership,* 4–17.

Blumberg, A. (1987). The work of principals. In W. Greenfield (Ed.), *Instructional leadership: Concepts, issues, and controversies* (pp. 38–55). Boston: Allyn and Bacon.

Bobbett, G. C., French, R., Achilles, C. M., McNamara, J., & Trusty, F. (1992, April). *What Policymakers Can Learn from School Report Cards: Analysis of Tennessee's Report Card on Schools.* Paper presented at the meeting of the American Educational Research Association (AERA), San Francisco, CA.

Boyer, E. (1983). *High school: A report on secondary education in America.* New York: Harper and Row.

Braddock, J. H., II, & McPartland, J. M. (1990, April). Alternatives to tracking. *Educational Leadership, 47*(7), 76–79.

Cannell, J. J. (1987). *Nationally normed achievement testing in America's public schools: How all fifty states are above the national average.* Daniels, WV: Friends for Education.

Clovis Unified School District. (1989). *Grade level objectives, grades K–6.* Clovis, CA: Author.

Cone, J. K. (1992, May). Untracking advanced placement English: Creating opportunity is not enough. *Phi Delta Kappan, 73*(9), 712–717.

Cooper, H. (1989, November). Synthesis of research on homework. *Educational Leadership, 47*(2), 85–91.

Deal, T. (1987). Effective school principals: Counselors, engineers, pawnbrokers, poets . . . or instructional leaders. In W. Greenfield (Ed.), *Instructional leadership: Concepts, issues and controversies* (pp. 230–245). Boston: Allyn and Bacon.

Doll, R. C. (1989). *Curriculum improvement: Decision making and process* (7th ed.). Boston: Allyn and Bacon.

Doyle, R. P. (1989, November). The resistance of conventional wisdom to research evidence: The case of retention in grade. *Phi Delta Kappan, 71*(3), 215–220.

Elam, S., Rose, L., & Gallup, A. (1991, September). The 23rd annual Gallup poll of the public's attitudes toward the public schools. *Phi Delta Kappan, 73*(1), 41–56.

Edmonds, R. (1979, October). Effective schools for the urban poor. *Educational Leadership, 37*(1), 15–24.

Ellett, C. D. (1987). Emerging teacher performance assessing practices: Implications for the instructional supervision role of school principals. In W. Greenfield (Ed.), *Instructional leadership: Concepts, issues, and controversies* (pp. 302–327). Boston: Allyn and Bacon.

Finn, J. D. (1989, Summer). Withdrawing from school. *Review of Educational Research, 59*(2), 117–142.

Finn, J. D., & Achilles, C. M. (1990, Fall). Answers and questions about class size: A statewide experiment. *American Educational and Research Journal, 27*(3), 537–577.

Finn, J. D., & Cox, D. (1992, Spring). Participation and withdrawal among fourth-grade pupils. *American Educational Research Journal, 29*(1), 141–162.

Giroux, H. A. (1992, May). Educational leadership and the crisis of democratic government. *Educational Researchers, 21*(4), 4–11.

Glasser, W. (1990, February). The quality school. *Phi Delta Kappan, 71*(6), 424–435.

Glickman, C. D. (1990, September). Pushing school reform to a new edge: The seven ironies of school empowerment. *Phi Delta Kappan, 72*(1), 68–75.

Glickman, C. D. (1991, May). Pretending not to know what we know. *Educational Leadership, 48*(8), 4–10.

Greenfield, W. (1987). Moral imagination and interpersonal competence: Antecedents to instructional leadership. In W. Greenfield (Ed.), *Instructional leadership: Concepts, issues and controversies* (pp. 56–74). Boston: Allyn and Bacon.

Hallinger, P., & Murphy, J. (1987). Instructional leadership in the school context. In W. Greenfield (Ed.), *Instructional leadership: Concepts, issues and controversies* (pp. 179–203). Boston: Allyn and Bacon.

Hamburg, D. A. (1992). *Today's children.* New York: Time Books, Random House.

Hashway, R. A. (1989–90). Does money make a difference? An econometric analysis of school outcomes. *National Forum of Applied Educational Research Journal, 2*(2), 59–71.

Heck, R. H., Larsen, T. J., & Marcoulides, G. A. (1990). Instructional leadership and school achievement: Validation of a causal model. *Educational Administration Quarterly, 26*(2), 94–125.

High, R. M., & Achilles, C. M. (1986, Winter). An analysis of influence-gaining behaviors of principals in schools of varying levels of instructional effectiveness. *Educational Administration Quarterly, 22*(1), 111–119.

High, R. M., Achilles, C. M., & High, K. (1989, March). *Involvement in What? Teacher Actual and Preferred Involvement in Selected School Activities.* Paper presented at the meeting of the American Educational Research Association, San Francisco. (ERIC ED 336856)

Hobbes, T. (1991). *The leviathan.* R. Tucker (Ed.). Cambridge: Cambridge University Press. (Original work published 1651)

Hobson v. Hansen, 269 F. Supp. 401 (D.D.C. 1967).

Hodgkinson, H. (1991, September). Reform versus reality. *Phi Delta Kappan, 73*(1), 8–16.

Hoy, W. K., & Miskel, C. G. (1991). *Educational administration: Theory, research, practice* (4th ed.). New York: McGraw-Hill.

Imber, M., & Duke, D. (1984, Winter). Teacher participation in school decision making: A framework for research. *Journal of Educational Administration, 22*(1), 24–34.

Keedy, J. L. (1982). A factor in principal effectiveness: Norm setting. *The Catalyst for Change, 11*(3), 26–29.

Kotlowitz, A. (1991). *There are no children here.* New York: Anchor Books.

Krug, S. E. (1992, August). Instructional leadership: A constructivist perspective. *Educational Administration Quarterly, 28*(3), 430–443.

Lieberman, A. (1988). Teachers and principals: Turf, tension and new tasks. *Phi Delta Kappan, 69*(9), 648–653.

Lindsay, P. (1982, Spring). The effect of high school size on student participation, satisfaction and attendance. *Educational Evaluation and Policy Analysis, 4*(1), 57–65.

Lindsay, P. (1984, Spring). High school size, participation in activities and young adult social participation: Some enduring effects of schooling. *Educational Evaluation and Policy Analysis, 6*(1), 73–83.

Lortie, D. (1975). *Schoolteacher.* Chicago: University of Chicago Press.

Mohrman, A. M., Jr., Cooke, R. A., & Mohrman, S. A. (1978). Participation in decision-making: A multidimensional perspective. *Educational Administration Quarterly, 14*(1), 13–29.

Nettles, S. M. (1991, Fall). Community involvement and disadvantaged students: A review. *Review of Educational Research, 61*(3), 379–406.

Nye, B., Achilles, C. M., Zaharias, J., Fulton, D., & Hooper, R. (1991 and 1992). *The lasting benefits study: Technical reports (grades 4 and 5).* Nashville, TN: Tennessee State University Center of Excellence for Research in the Basic Skills.

Nye, B., Achilles, C. M., Zaharias, J., Fulton, D., & Wallenhorst, M. P. (1993, Winter). *Tennessee's bold experiment: Using research to inform policy and practice, 22*(3), 10–17.

Oakes, J. (1985). *Keeping track: How schools structure inequality.* New Haven, CT: Yale University Press.

Oakes, J. (1992, May). Can tracking research inform practice? Technical, normative and political considerations. *Educational Researcher, 21*(4), 12–21.

Orlich, D. (1989, March). Education reforms: Mistakes, misconceptions, miscues. *Phi Delta Kappan, 70*(7), 512–517.

Peterson, K. (1987). Administrative control and instructional leadership. In W. Greenfield (Ed.). *Instructional leadership: Concepts, issues and controversies* (pp. 139–152). Boston: Allyn and Bacon.

Purkey, W. W. (1992, Winter). An introduction to invitational theory. *Journal of Invitational Theory and Practice, 1*(1), 5–16.

Purkey, W. W., & Novak, J. (1984). *Inviting school success: A self-concept approach to teaching and learning* (2nd ed.). Belmont, CA: Wadsworth Publishing Co.

Rallis, S. (1988, May). Room at the top: Conditions for effective school leadership. *Phi Delta Kappan, 69*(9), 643–647.

Ravitch, D., & Finn, C. (1987). *What do our 17-year-olds know?* New York: Harper and Row.

Reed, S., & Sautter, R. C. (1990, June). Children of poverty: The status of 12 million young Americans. *Phi Delta Kappan, 71*(10), K1–K12.

Robinson, G. E. (1990, April). Synthesis of research on the effects of class size. *Educational Leadership, 47*(7), 80–90.

Rogers, K. B. (1991, October). *The relationship of grouping practices to the education of the gifted and talented learner.* St. Paul, MN: University of St. Thomas. (Produced by National Research Center on the Gifted and Talented, Storrs, CT: The University of Connecticut.)

Rutherford, W. L. (1985, September). School principals as effective leaders. *Phi Delta Kappan, 67*(1), 31–34.

Ryan, M. (1992, March 15). Here, everybody gets to play. *Parade Magazine*, p. 10.

Schlechty, P. C., & Vance, V. S. (1981). Do academically able teachers leave education? The North Carolina case *Phi Delta Kappan, 63*(2), 106–112.

Schlechty, P. C., & Vance, V. S. (1983). Institutional responses to the quality/quantity issue in teacher training. *Phi Delta Kappan, 65*(2), 94–101.

Shepard, L. A., & Smith, M. L. (1990, May). Synthesis of research on grade retention. *Educational Leadership, 47*(8), 84–88.

Sheive, L. T., & Schoenheit, M. B. (1987). *Leadership: Examining the elusive (1987 ASCD yearbook).* Alexandria, VA: Association for Supervision and Curriculum Development.

Simons, J. M., Finlay, B., & Yang, A. (1991). *The adolescent and young adult fact book.* Washington, DC: Children's Defense Fund.

Smith, W. F., & Andrews, R. L. (1989). *Instructional leadership: How principals make a difference.* Alexandria, VA: Association for Supervision and Curriculum Development.

Strother, D. B. (1991). *Clovis, California schools: A measure of excellence.* Bloomington, IN: Phi Delta Kappa Center for Evaluation, Development and Research.

Tillman, J. B. (1991, March). *Implementing the Vision of the High School Principal.* Unpublished doctoral dissertation, University of North Carolina at Greensboro.

Tyson-Bernstein, H. (1988, November). The academy's contribution to the impoverishment of America's textbook. *Phi Delta Kappan, 70*(3), 192–198.

Ubben, G. C. and Hughes, L. W. (1992). *The principal: Creative leadership for effective schools.* Boston: Allyn and Bacon.

Whitehead, A. N. (1929). *The aims of education and other essays.* New York: A Mentor Paperback.

Whittington, D. (1991, Winter). What have 17-year-olds known in the past? *American Educational Research Journal, 28*(4), 759–780.

SELECTED READINGS

Fiske, E. (1991). *Smart schools, smart kids: Why do some schools work?* New York: Touchstone.

Foster, W. (1986). *Paradigms and promises: New approaches to educational administration.* Buffalo, NY: Prometheus Books.

Heller, R. (1992). *The super chiefs: Today's most successful chief executives and their winning strategies for the 1990s.* New York: Dutton.

Johnson, S. (1990). *Teachers at work: Achieving success in our schools.* New York: Basic Books.

Smith, F. (1986). *Insult to intelligence: The bureaucratic invasion of our classrooms.* Portsmouth, NH: Heinemann.

3

The Legal Framework

THERE IS only one chapter in this concluding part of the book, but it is a very important one. The legal framework that guides administrative action is the subject. Strahan identifies seven critical legal areas about which the principal must be knowledgeable if the school environment is to be at once lawful, orderly, and humane. Students and teachers may not always be right, but they always have rights. So do principals. And so do principals, students, and teachers have responsibilities. Chapter 11 concludes with specific guidelines for the practitioner, to establish and maintain an orderly school environment.

11

Building Leadership and Legal Strategies

Richard D. Strahan

University of Houston

Overview

Shifting the locus of authority to the individual campus unit has a concomitant extension of legal responsibility. Administrative decision making at the building level involves relationships with fundamental issues that include parents, students, and faculty and other employees. The administrator functioning at the building level must be prepared to effectively lead the instructional program while administering a plethora of policies, regulations, state statutes, and federal law that control various facets of behaviors exhibited by various student and professional personnel.

The literature concerning legal issues in schools is expanding quite rapidly, and its growth is expected to continue. The building principal is not likely to maintain mastery of such voluminous material. An informational base must be developed that supplies the principal with sufficient knowledge and intuitive insight to successfully administer existing policy and contribute to the shaping of future administrative practices. Although many administrators possess insights or sensitivities that help them solve human-relations problems, it is unlikely that skills to avoid legal problems will exist without appropriate knowledge and training. It is essential for the leadership to recognize when issues arise that require the guidance of the attorney, who is part of the administrative team of the district or under retainer to the district. Fundamental mistakes in threshold decision-making situations often initiate the emotions that energize litigious efforts.

This chapter is designed to provide the building administrator insights into legal parameters in the organization and delivery of the educational program in a site-based organizational setting. Conceptual frameworks will be emphasized rather than specific case law. Substantive issues in the management of legal concerns appear to stabilize and provide a framework for practice. State or federal legislation often generates new controversies that directly impact schools. These problems are the subject of litigation and are reflected in policy formulation. Issues that arise in these cases of first impression must become a part of the administrator's repertoire for professional growth. Fundamental legal concepts will be discussed in this chapter in relation to the following practice areas:

- Human resources management
- Curriculum design and implementation
- Teaching
- Special populations
- Supervision of co-curricular activity
- The campus and criminal behavior
- Growth of malpractice pressures
- Exercises in preventive law

The overall guiding principle will be leadership practiced substantively with fundamental fairness. The chapter will conclude with a case study for reflection.

Human Resources Management

One of the principal characteristics of the educational reform movement is a significant strengthening of the role of the building administrator. The human resources management function has been one of the areas in which the authority and responsibility of the building administrator has been enhanced. This organizational concept has been embodied in statute in several states such as the following statutes in Texas:

> (d) Each principal shall:
> (1) approve all teacher and staff appointments for that principal's campus from a pool of applicants who meet the hiring requirements established by the district, based on criteria developed by the principal after informal consultation with the faculty; . . . (Vernon's Revised Texas Statutes Education Code, Section 13.352 Principals (d) (1))

Statutes of this character place an increasing responsibility on the campus administrator for developing and managing a human resources plan. School boards will be responsible for mission statements, but the site-based administrator is being charged with strategic campus planning to accomplish organizational goals and objectives. Such planning must accommodate all phases of campus management of both classified and professional personnel. The personnel problems that generate litigation have their situs in the operational function of the delivery system. Many federal laws and regulations have an effect on the various aspects of personnel decisions. Current projections indicate that a significant number of legal assaults on school practices will arise from various personnel problems where administrative practice diverts from federal law, rules and regulations of administrative agencies, and state legislation.

Federal Legal Constraints

Educational organizations share the responsibility of eliminating employment decisions that deny equal opportunity for employment. The Equal Employment Opportunity Commission (EEOC) is charged with enforcement of Title VII of the Civil Rights Act of 1964 as amended (which applies to race, color, religion, sex, and national origin); the Age Discrimination in Employment Act of 1967 as amended (ADEA); the Equal Pay Act of 1963 (EPA) and Section 501, Rehabilitation Act of 1973 as amended; and the Americans with Disabilities Act of 1990 (ADA). The EEOC actively prosecutes these complaints to obtain full compensation and benefits for employees who have been victimized by employment decisions based on forbidden discriminations. The increased role that principals will exercise under a decentralized or site-based philosophy in personnel decisions will extend more extensive risk to them. The principal must consciously refrain from any act that could be interpreted as retaliation against any employee who files a charge or complaint or who participates in an EEOC investigation. Each administrator should remember that it is unlawful for the school as an employer to discriminate with regard to:

- job advertisement
- recruitment
- testing
- hiring and firing
- compensation, assignment, or classification of employee
- transfer, promotion, layoff, or recall
- use of company facilities
- training and apprenticeship programs
- fringe benefits such as life and health insurance
- pay, retirement plans, and disability leave
- causing or attempting to cause a union to discriminate
- other terms and conditions of employment

Litigation to Remain High

As a local administrator, the principal must keep abreast of various developments under state and federal law. The increase of litigation that has occurred during the latter half of the twentieth century has been personally noted by the author, a school attorney. School attorneys report a high incidence of cases and complaints involving employment contracts, special education concerns, and discrimination in employment. Significant changes in programs often occur because of a fear of litigation. A 1990 study from the National School Boards Association (NSBA) (Underwood & Naffle, 1990) estimated attorneys' fees paid by school districts at more than 200 million dollars a year. This does not account for costs related to preparation for suit and remediation of problems the litigation highlights.

Litigation is likely to remain high in those areas that arise from employee concerns. National media coverage has highlighted cases of sexual harassment and creation of a "hostile working environment." Such publicity tends to foster additional legal complaints. The principal who wants to exercise effective leadership must maintain an awareness of decision making where the risk of litigation is high or increasing. Particular attention should be given to new federal or state legislation and to new legal theory and its application to practice arising from appellate court decisions. Human resources management must be approached with high priority for effective control of law suits or administrative complaints. The possibility of successful litigation creates anxiety that tends to impede the decisions needed for innovation or experimentation. Competent administrators must develop a sensitivity to problem areas and be prepared to act decisively and appropriately. Deferred decisions seriously impede progress.

Curriculum Design and Implementation

It has long been determined that the state has plenary power to prescribe curriculum elements for the public schools of the state. Such authority is restricted or directed only by federal and state constitutional parameters. Such power includes the authority that good citizenship be taught and that public policy may prohibit that which is considered to be detrimental to public welfare.

Problems Related to Academic Freedom

Issues that arise in local schools are often generated under the guise of academic freedom. Various pronouncements of professional groups encourage the recognition of the teacher's role in stimulating a spirit of inquiry, the acquisition of knowledge and understanding, and thoughtful formulation of worthy goals. A knowledgeable administrator in a site-based school organization when participating with his or her advisory groups should guide them into goal formulation that avoids known areas of legal contention. In spite of the fact that there have been numerous cases where the U.S. Supreme Court has recognized the academic freedom concept, there have been many cases involving related issues at the elementary and secondary levels. Few cases have restricted legislative authority to control curriculum content (*Meyer v. Nebraska*, 1923) or the method of communicating ideas. Other constitutional parameters have curbed legislative attempts to foster religion, such as *Ambach v. Norwick* (1979).

Teaching Methods and Materials

Other courts have protected the role of the faculty in subject-matter approach in the classroom. Various methods that have evoked parental intervention have included a number of controversial practices. A simulation technique that involved role-playing by students in recreating a period of history was upheld in *Kingsville Independent School District v. Cooper* (1980) although it evoked strong student feeling on racial issues. Similar pronouncements have occurred in *Minarcini v. Strongville City School District* (1969) and *Sterzing v. Ft. Bend Independent School District* (1972). In *Sterzing*, the court suggested that "a teacher must not be manacled with rigid regulations which preclude a full adaptation of a course to the times in which we live."

The courts have placed some limitations on various teaching techniques where the school district has by policy restricted the selection of teaching materials and methodology. It seems clear that substantive concepts designed and maintained in the curriculum by the district may be sustained, although some protection has been given to the sensitivity of parents and students in the community. The use of profanity, material inappropriate for the subject, improper selections for grade level, and subject matter not reasonably related to the course are not likely to be upheld. In a recent Fifth Circuit case, *Kirkland v. Northside Independent School District* (1989), the court created some concern among teachers by upholding a teacher's termination on the basis of the teacher's utilization of a supplemental reading list that was not approved by the district's administrative process. Building administrators should approach various adverse actions where academic freedom is espoused with documentation of abuse rather than negative evaluation of concepts or ideas being presented. The media are seemingly eager to attack claimed abuses of academic freedom, so such attempts as discipline of staff without careful analysis may have political or other ramifications that would be detrimental to the educational climate. Numerous groups are now organized that seek to impose private agendas on the school program. Organizations such as Parents Opposed to Paddling Students (POPS) are prepared to oppose and publicize issues about which they are organized.

Authority to Determine Curriculum Content

In all states, it has been consistently held that the local school must offer a curriculum that the state prescribes. Where some discretion lies with the local board of trustees, state law often requires curriculum selections to be within state guidelines. Courts liberally construe statutory authority for the local district to add various disciplines that exceed the state's minimum requirements. When analyzing practices concerning curriculum requirements for individual students, the local school boards are empowered to make rules and regulations by delegation of board authority to it by the state. In Massachusetts, parents were empowered by statute to compel the local school committee to offer courses not regularly included in the curriculum. In *Johnson v. School Committee* (1977), the court upheld parental demands for driver education. Unless especially granted power by state statute or under a constitutional provision, district residents cannot force a local board to add or delete a course from the curriculum.

Delegated Duties Must Operate within Statutory Schemes

A site-based philosophy normally delegates much programmatic decision-making to community councils or professional committees. These delegated duties must operate within the statutory scheme laid down by the state legislatures. Generally, state minimum requirements will not be altered by such philosophical change. Courts are reluctant to attempt to restrict actions taken in expanding curriculum content or elective course offerings. Courts will not make an independent judgment of administrative decisions unless there is an abuse of discretion or violation of Constitutional limitations. Even though courts recognize and follow the rule of limited review, errors of law are always reversible even if innocently or reasonably made. As an Ohio case stated:

> In the absence of fraud, abuse of discretion, arbitrariness, or unreasonableness the court will not interfere with that authority nor substitute its judgment for that of an independent school board upon matters delegated to it in conducting the affairs of its schools. (*Dworken v. Cleveland Board of Education*, 1951)

Numerous cases are of record where courts have invalidated employment termination where statutorily mandated procedures have not been followed (see *Hill v. Dayton School District*, 1974; *McKelvey v. Colonial School District*, 1975). As a site-based manager, the first responsibility that must concern a principal is acquisition of a thorough knowledge of local school board policy along with state and federal law. Recent trends have held principals and other decision makers to comply with the specifics outlined in the sources.

The Constitution and the Curriculum

In developing curriculum innovations, a recent reminder by a court should be kept in consideration: "no court has found that teachers have a first amendment right to choose their own curriculum or class management techniques in contravention of school policy or dictates" (*Bradley v. Pittsburgh Board of Education*, 1991). That statement arose from a case in which Learnball, a classroom management technique, had been prohibited. The teacher complained that she was subjected to harassment and that the school administrators were interfering with her academic freedom protected by the First Amendment. Administration or board policy in connection with instructional method, classroom management technique, or curriculum content should be clearly spelled out to eliminate conflict of this kind. Where policy is vague or nonexistent, the courts will uphold as an aspect of academic freedom the teacher's right to exercise professional judgment to choose curriculum content or materials for classroom use.

In *Parducci v. Rutland* (1970), the court indicated that teachers must be provided some notice of standards or regulations concerning what behaviors or practices are not acceptable. Vague and ambiguous oral warnings have been held to be ineffective notice of unacceptable practices. Cases that illustrate the principle are *Pickering v. Board of Education* (1968) and *Dean v. Timpson I.S.D.* (1979). Attention should be given to Constitutional standards for dismissal in this area because teachers are still filing suit and prevailing in cases involving impermissible reasons.

Responsibility for Instructional Leadership

The site-based leadership philosophy will increase the responsibility assumed by the principal for instructional leadership. Issues to be approached in this area began to be highlighted in the 1980s. William D. H. Georgiades, Dean of the College of Education at the University of Houston, in an article in 1985, emphasized the necessity for change in the traditional role exhibited by the principal in regard to instructional leadership (Georgiades, 1985). When choosing and developing a leadership style in the school setting, several kinds of legal issues often arise. School administrators at the campus level may not have been kept well informed of the legal risks assumed in this area.

For over a decade, the courts have recognized the principal's responsibility as an instructional supervisor. In a Minnesota case styled *Larson v. Independent School District No. 314* (1979), a principal was held to be negligent for failing to closely supervise the planning and administering of the physical education curriculum. When the principal failed to make decisions about teaching and developing the physical education curriculum, his failure to do so was considered to be evidence of his negligence. The principal was functioning under a school district policy that required the administrator of the school to develop, organize, and implement the school curriculum. Further, that policy made the principal responsible for assigning duties to teachers, supervising classroom instruction, providing orientation for new teachers, and administering requirements of the board of education.

This ruling arose from a student performing what is known as a "headspring over a rolled mat," which was a required activity for an eighth grade physical education class. The injury resulted in quadriplegic paralysis. The class was being taught by a first-year teacher properly certified to teach physical education. The principal was held to have a duty to exercise reasonable care in supervising the development, planning, and administration of the curriculum; in supervising and evaluating the work of the teachers within the school; and in maintaining conditions conducive to the safety and welfare of students in the school. When the teacher took over a class in mid-semester, the principal had given him a copy of the curriculum bulletin and no other assistance. The teacher and principal had a verdict returned against them for more than $1,000,000 in damages.

The duties of the principal as stated by a Minnesota court would be typical of many schools:

> The duties prescribed for a principal by manuals of the department of education and the school district included: (1) administering the rules and regulations of the board of education; (2) making recommendations to the superintendent regarding courses of study and changes in the curriculum; (3) developing, organizing, administering and implementing the curricular activity program; (4) observing the work of teachers in classrooms and serving as a consultant for improving and revising the curriculum; (5) providing for the orientation of new teachers on school policies and classroom procedures; (6) holding staff meetings; (7) organizing the program of studies and preparing individual class schedules; and (8) maintaining conditions that would ensure the safety and welfare of pupils during the school day. (*Larson v. Independent School District No. 314*, 1979, note 6)

The court cited another Minnesota case (*Spanel v. Mounds View School District No. 21*, 1962), stating, "School children have a special status in the eyes of the law and deserve more than ordinary protection." As the statute and responsibility of the site-based administrator emerges, greater scrutiny is likely to be given to the instructional supervision responsibility.

Responsibility for Subordinate Personnel

Other recent court decisions suggest that courts may hold supervisory or administrative personnel liable for acts of subordinate personnel where Constitutional rights are violated. As an illustration, in *Stoneking v. Bradford Area School District* (1987), a principal, assistant principal, and superintendent of schools became defendants because of a series of sexual assaults that occurred between a band director and his student. The student's complaint alleged that these defendant supervisors violated his Constitutional rights by failing to remedy the situation at the high school with which they were familiar. Where supervisory personnel exhibit behaviors that evidence "callous disregard or reckless behavior" and that invade Constitutionally protected areas, they ignore such behaviors at their own risk. The courts have no difficulty in finding the necessary "special relationship" between supervisors and students to provide the threshold duty to support litigation.

Principals may continue to expect community pressures for the recruiting and contracting with teachers of demonstrated competence. It should be recognized that competency is no longer likely to be based on college credentials, grade-point averages, or professional certificates. Student progress has become a public obsession. Many states now require regular or periodic testing of students, including competence tests for high school graduation. The assumption that accompanies such programs is that student progress or the lack of it would assist in the identification of incompetent or inefficient teachers. It would appear that the goal of quality instruction is at the heart of public concern and legislative intent. Principals striving to improve the quality of instruction should develop a comprehensive evaluation technique that will withstand various legal attacks such as those associated with disparate impact or other civil rights litigation.

Academic Freedom and Site-Based Management

Although a search of court decisions regarding academic freedom for public school teachers leaves unclear dimensions, it is likely that the quest for teacher autonomy in the classroom will continue. The U.S. Supreme Court in its decision in *Meyer v. Nebraska* (1923) addressed this issue stemming from two concerns, "the freedom of teachers to teach and of students to learn." The *Meyer* case overturned a legislative act concerning the grade levels or ages at which the German language could be taught or used as a medium of instruction. In other cases, such as *Ambach v. Norwick* (1979), the court noted "in shaping the student's experience to achieve educational goals, teachers of necessity have wide discretion in the way the course material is communicated to students." It is a generally accepted principle that a public school teacher should have the right to teach the subject matter in his or her specialty field without undue interference from school officials or parents and to create an educationally appropriate atmosphere.

Primary problems in the area of academic freedoms are generated by two areas of professional behavior:

- the manner in which controversial topics are approached
- speech activities in the classroom that are, or have the potential to be, disruptive

The first area would involve cases such as *Sterzing v. Ft. Bend I.S.D.* (1972) and *Kingsville Independent School District v. Cooper* (1980). Sterzing had been terminated because of the methods he had used in approaching issues that were controversial in the community. The court ultimately sided with Sterzing when no evidence could be produced on material disruption, insubordination, or abuse of professional standards. While granting monetary damage, the court denied reinstatement. On review, the appellate court remanded it strictly on the basis of the remedy. The trial court opined "a teacher should not be manacled with rigid regulations which preclude the full adaptation of a course to the times in which we live." Later in the opinion, the judge noted that classroom academic freedom places a heavy responsibility on the teacher to maintain objectivity and sensitivity. In attempting to balance various interests, the court added

> it must . . . be the teacher's duty to be exceptionally fair and objective in presenting his personally held opinions, to actively and persuasively present different views, in addition to open discussion. It is the duty of the teacher to be cognizant of and sensitive to the feelings of his students, their parents and their community. (Sterzing, 1972)

In the *Cooper* case, the same court announced its standard for determining disruptive impact as "whether such disruption overbalances the teacher's usefulness as a teacher." The court held that the simulation utilized in the instructional process was a protected activity.

A strong presumption arises that teachers are capable of judging and selecting the best methods, materials, and reading lists in teaching their recognized specialties. In reality, other interests limit complete freedom from restraint. Public schools are a state function, and the state has a strong interest in the education and welfare of its children. Such interest is recognized as an aspect of the state's plenary powers over its schools. The state therefore has an inherent power to provide some control or power to regulate teacher conduct and minimal curriculum content. Teachers and administrators should use those standards and related judicial guidance in evaluating teacher performance as impacted by controversial issues. The generally accepted overall standard is that of "material and substantial disruption" in regard to freedom of speech in the classroom, as promulgated in *Tinker v. Des Moines Independent Community School District* (1969).

Limitations on Classroom Speech

Several types of classroom speech are not within the protections of academic freedom or of the first amendment. These include

- the repeated use of profanity in the classroom (*Martin v. Parrish*, 1986)
- using the classroom as a forum to criticize school administrators and policies (*Robbins v. Board of Education of Argo Community High School District No. 217*, 1970)
- espousing political points of view in academic classes (*Goldwasser v. Brown*, 1969)
- discussion of various personal experiences unrelated to curriculum assignment, i.e., concerning prostitutes, homosexuals, and masturbation (*Moore v. School Board of Gulf County, Florida*, 1973)

The use of derogatory epithets, obscene, pornographic, or illegal materials will not be protected under the umbrella of academic freedom. One of the more recent cases concerning academic freedom from the Tenth Circuit Court of Appeals, styled as *Miles v. Denver Public Schools* (1991), involved a teacher's comments in a ninth-grade government class. He remarked that it was rumored that students had been having sex on the tennis court during lunch. This court stated that a classroom is a closed forum and that it was improper to use that forum to repeat a rumor. The teacher was suspended for four days, and the administrative leave was upheld. Teachers and administrators should understand these limitations and guide their professional conduct by them.

Teaching

The teaching profession has since its beginning in this country been confronted by various stereotypes that many educators would prefer to relegate to a past era. Increasingly, the parameters on teaching behavior are being tested in the courts in an attempt to overturn those with which teacher organizations disagree. Principals are the most accessible members of the administrative staff and are in daily contact with members of the teaching cadre. The building administrator must become sensitive to a climate that emphasizes collegiality and joint decision making.

Critical Components of Teacher Evaluation

Several aspects of teaching performance are critical components for evaluation. One of the most common problems relates to classroom management or control. Although various teaching models involve different patterns of student activity and noise level, one primary characteristic is maintaining such classroom control as to permit the teacher and class to accomplish various learning objectives. This has been a common charge in teacher discipline and termination but should not be used indiscriminately. In *Stoddard v. School District No. 1* (1979), a teacher received a letter from her principal stating that her contract would not be renewed because of her failure to maintain order in the classroom and lack of dynamics in motivating students. In the hearing, the teacher alleged successfully that the principal had informed her that the "real" reasons were rumors about an affair, her propensity for playing cards and not attending church regularly, and her obesity. Her nonrenewal was reversed. Reasons included in notices of various negative professional actions should reflect actual conditions that would justify such disciplinary actions.

A recent case on professional growth reached the U.S. Supreme Court. In *Harrah Independent School District v. Martin* (1979), the district had a growth policy that stipulated that a teacher holding a bachelor's degree must earn at least five semester hours of college credit every three years. The defendant teacher, though tenured, was dismissed for failure to meet the policy requirement. The courts have consistently upheld such growth policies, and this discussion strengthens this area for administrative decision making.

It should not be necessary to remind administrators that equitable and fair administration of policy is important. The failure to uniformly apply policy may render it unenforceable. Such was the case in *Gosney v. Sonora Independent School District* (1979) when a district attempted to nonrenew a teacher's contract for violation of a policy against outside employment when others had been permitted without penalty to engage in such employment.

Legal Concerns about Teacher Speech

Principals are often distressed by public or private communications from subordinates. Although the courts have expressed reluctance to establish a standard by which all statements may be judged, the case law gives sufficient guidance to prevent the administrator from making employment or disciplinary decisions based on inappropriate speech behaviors. Speech that is entitled to First Amendment protection may not be the sole basis for decisions regarding termination.

The speech or communications elements that are most troublesome are those which are made publicly. In *Connick v. Myers* (U.S., 1983), the court generally established that statements related to a public interest would be protected by First Amendment standards. Those generated by personal interests would not be protected. Although this was not a case generating disciplinary acts in an education setting, it has been widely cited in cases in which teachers' comments have been generated in problems related to the complainant's employment. *Connick* made such comments to be unprotected by constitutional standards. In an educational setting, *Pickering v. Board of Education of Township High School District 205* (1968), the U.S. Supreme Court established the principle that public school teachers may enjoy a protected right of expression in certain circumstances. Pickering had written a letter critical of school board and administrative practices concerning budget allocation and communication with the local citizen clientele. The court upheld Pickering's right to speak up as a citizen on such public interests. The local board had responded by terminating his employment. The board charged that his statements were false and that they impinged on the integrity of the board and administration and would foster controversy, conflict, and dissension among teachers, administrators, the school board, and the community. In that case, the court ruled that in absence of proof of false statements knowingly or recklessly made by him, a teacher's exercise of his rights to speak out on issues of public importance may not be the basis for his dismissal.

In subsequent decisions, a two-step analytical process has evolved in determining whether an employee's public speech enjoys First Amendment protection. First, the speech must be directed toward a matter of public concern. Second, the Constitutional interests of the employee must be balanced against the interest of the state as an employer in delivering an efficient public service through its employees. The second determination, known as the "Pickering balance" examines a number of factors related to the employer–employee relationship. These factors include an analysis based on the following:

- the need for harmony in the school or workplace
- the need for a close working relationship between the speaker and coworkers and whether the speech in question undermines that relationship
- the time, place, and manner of speech
- the context in which the disputed speech arose
- the degree of public interest in the speech

- whether the speech impedes the employee's ability to perform his or her duties

When making a decision in regard to subordinates' communication activity, it would be wise to analyze the facts in light of the probability of judicial balancing of the interests. An analysis of the circumstances from which the speech communication arose becomes very important. In *Mt. Healthy City School District Board of Education v. Doyle* (1977), Doyle was a representative of the teacher's organization and on a number of occasions was associated with various incidents. He involved himself in an argument with another teacher who slapped him. Doyle refused an apology and demanded punishment for the teacher. His persistence resulted in a one-day suspension for each of them. A number of teachers staged a walkout and achieved a lifting of the suspension. As supervisor of the cafeteria, he complained about the employees giving him small portions of food. On another occasion, he cursed students and made obscene gestures. Finally, he related an internal memorandum to a local radio station that made a news item out of it. The memo was one that involved teacher appearance. A short time later, the superintendent in his annual recommendations recommended that Doyle, who was untenured, not be reemployed for the following year. Although his communication to the radio station was said to have First and Fourteenth Amendment protection, the U.S. Supreme Court vacated the decision and remanded it for further proceedings. Although this case appeared to grant First and Fourteenth Amendment protection to public speech to an untenured faculty member, termination without granting a continuing contract could still occur when the school district meets its burden of showing that its decision was substantially based upon reasons other than protected expression. Where there exists a long history of inadequate performance, one exercise of a protected speech activity will not prevail over such record. If the teacher's appraisals document deficiencies and the failure of efforts at remediation, the exercise of protected rights of expression is not likely to prevail. Where dismissal of a cafeteria worker (*Brantley v. Surles*, 1985) was based on the parent's choice to transfer her child to a private school and a Chapter I coordinator being retaliated against by the administration for unfavorable testimony in a court proceeding (*Reeves v. Claiborne County Board of Education*, 1987), the court ruled both were protected acts because no other reason for the acts of retaliation could be produced. Under *Mt. Healthy*, the acts could not be supported.

Other Factors in Classifying Speech as Personnel Matter

The manner and place where the speech occurs may support the right of expression in a school situation or leave it unprotected. In some of the circumstances, which involve various commonly utilized practices, judicial decisions become quite confusing. Supervisory intervention must be influenced by various rulings. A court has denied the district the authority to terminate a teacher for refusing to participate in a flag salute ceremony in the classroom (*Russo v.*

Central School District No. 1, 1972). In a second case (*Palmer v. Board of Education of the City of Chicago*, 1979), a court upheld the discharge of a teacher who, based upon her religious faith, refused to lead her kindergarten students in patriotic exercises and failed to carry out certain curriculum requirements. In the first case, the teacher stood silently at attention while her children recited the pledge of allegiance, while in the second case, the teacher refused to follow curriculum guides.

Other guidelines can be established from *Givhan v. Western Line Consolidated School District* (1979) in regard to private personal communication between teacher and school principal. Here the court decided that teachers do not forfeit their protection against governmental abridgement of speech under certain circumstances. The court pointed out that superior–subordinate relations are particularly sensitive and that content of what is said, as well as time, place, and manner can be taken into consideration in deciding what is protected by the Constitution. Standards for judging protected speech are altered when employees choose to communicate privately rather than to spread their views before the public. Private speech that negatively affects relationships within a school operation will be carefully evaluated before First Amendment protection is granted.

In the following cases, speech that produced hostile working relationships was not protected:

- In *Barbre v. Garland I.S.D.* (1979), an aide's remarks and subsequent strained relationship were not protected, although some were made before the school board. Her remarks were openly critical of her immediate supervisor and generally expressed hostile attitudes toward the school administration.
- In *McDaniel v. Vidor I.S.D., Texas Education Agency* (1982), a teacher's comments in the cafeteria and in front of the children ("I don't give a damn what the principal said, I'm going to do as I please") and further her references to the principal as "asinine and paranoid" resulted in her dismissal, which was upheld by the Commissioner of Education in Texas. Her refusal to follow the principal's instructions and her comments "disrupted harmony among her co-workers."

In judging private or public speech activity, the speaker's method of expression cannot be disruptive or materially interfere with legitimate educational endeavors.

Classroom instruction that includes profanity is not a protected speech activity. In *Martin v. Parriah* (1986), a college case, the professor alleged that he used profanity to motivate students. He stated that his exhortations such as "hell, damn, and bullshit" provided "motivation." When he continued the speech after a warning, he was terminated. Whenever disciplinary action is contemplated based on speech activity, whether in or out of school, a careful audit of its impact should be made. Hostile and disruptive speech activity by a professional is seldom upheld in the special environment of school.

Special Populations

The public schools have been subject to an expanded responsibility for education of students with disabilities since Congress passed the Education of all Handicapped Children Act (EHA) (1975) and the Rehabilitation Act of 1973. The site-based emphasis will not alter this responsibility. For almost two decades, school professionals have wrestled with the implications of these statutes and regulations. Philosophically, the school structure was not prepared to extend egalitarian rights to children with disabilities. It is now well established that access to a free appropriate public education for people with disabilities is a Constitutional interest protected by the equal protection concept of the Fourteenth Amendment to the United States Constitution.

Constitutional Rights of Handicapped Students

The courts have continued to expand the rights first extended in *Mills v. Board of Education of District of Columbia* (1972) and *PARC v. Commonwealth* (1971). Similar cases have further extended such rights as have acts of Congress and legislative decisions. People who have disabilities that are unalterable continue to have effective public support for educational programs "appropriate" for their capacities and related support for their needs.

Turnbull and Turnbull (1978) outlined six major principles by which early law and judicial activity could be analyzed:

- zero reject
- testing, classification, and placement
- individualized and appropriate education
- least restrictive appropriate placement
- procedural due process
- parent participation and shared decision making

Such basic concepts are familiar to many administrators, but the concepts have not been static. In an era of educational change, mandated concepts are dynamic, and expansion often occurs.

In 1990, the EHA was amended by Congress and became the Individuals with Disabilities Education Act (IDEA). The amendment primarily addressed excess costs of educating special education students, which are scheduled to be funded with a gradual increase to 40 percent of costs expended for special education students above those in regular education. The types of entitlements under EHA have been substantively continued under IDEA.

Special Concerns of Statutory Interpretation

Expanded definitions of certain concepts such as "zero reject" model and "education" intensify the attention of the site-based administrator's responsibility. In *Timothy W. v. Rochester, New Hampshire School District* (1989), the First Circuit

Court of Appeals heightened awareness of school districts that services will be required regardless of the type and severity of the child's disabilities. Although the immediate impact is limited to the jurisdiction of the court, the case garnered national attention. This child suffered from severe spasticity, brain damage, joint contractures, seizure disorder, and other profound disabilities. He was unable to communicate verbally, was nonambulatory, quadriplegic, and cortically blind. The court ruled that the "ability to benefit" concept was not a prerequisite for the obligation of the school to provide service. Legal theorists now opine that eligible children must be provided with educational services without regard to the severity of the disabling condition. The "zero reject" concept will test the ingenuity of the professional staff to devise appropriate programs at each campus level.

Other cases have expanded traditional definitions of *education*. Self-sufficiency, self-care, toilet training, and feeding oneself have been identified as appropriate educational goals in individualized plans. Cases such as *Battle v. Commonwealth of Pennsylvania* (1980) have concluded that Congress intended that the school district was obligated to provide programs that address the child's needs.

Expansion of Rights Under Other Statutes

Recent treatment of cases under Section 504 of the Rehabilitation Act of 1973 requires an increased awareness of the problems of both disabled students and employees in regard to decisions that have a discriminatory effect in programs receiving federal financial assistance. The significant language reads as follows:

> No otherwise qualified handicapped individual in the United States . . . shall, solely by reason of his handicap, be excluded from participation in, be denied the benefits of, or be subjected to discrimination under any program or activity receiving federal financial assistance . . . (Rehabilitation Act of 1973, 1977)

The questions then naturally arise of "Who is a handicapped person?" and "What meanings are attached to physical or mental impairment or major life activities?" The Code of Federal Regulations gives a definition of these terms that is more expansive than those under EHA (see 34 C.F.R. §104.3(j)). Handicapped person includes any person who (i) "has a physical or mental impairment which substantially limits one or more major life activities, (ii) has a record of such impairment, or (iii) is regarded as having such impairment." This brings into the scope of eligibility those individuals who have a history of such impairment or may have been previously misclassified as having such impairment. Any physical or mental impairment that is so severe that it results in a substantial limitation of a major life activity will qualify the individual for relief under the Rehabilitation Act of 1973 as amended in 1977. Such criteria are directed toward "major life activities," which includes functions such as "caring for one's self, performing manual tasks, walking, seeing, speaking, breathing, working, and learning." At 34 C.F.R. §104.3(k)(2)—(4), these statutory terms are further defined. It seems likely that people who do not qualify under Section 612 of the Education of the Handicapped Act may be eligible for services. Many of the terms that have become well known to principals under EHA are extended to those who qualify under Sect. 504. Free appropriate public education that is accessible and effective is required for those who qualify under either federal law.

Renewed Emphasis on Least Restrictive Environment

The administrative staff must assume responsibility for parental pressures that will be directed toward them as the decentralization of decision making occurs. The increasing pressures for students with disabilities to be maintained in regular classes is one such illustration. *All Children Can Learn Together*, a recent publication of the Texas Education Agency, addresses that issue. It suggests a critical examination of organizational and administrative support for successful programs in the least restrictive environment. Emphasis is placed on evaluation of the educational program by parents, educators, and community members to examine to what degree the least restrictive environment has been integrated into programs to the maximum extent which is appropriate. Shared decision making will, in all probability, increase the scrutiny of various groups, with attendant attempts to litigate areas of disagreement. The lack of substantive standards by which the various programs can be judged as adequate results in a problematic situation that often can be settled only by a hearing officer or a court.

Attempts to discipline children with disabling conditions has been an active area for court cases. Disruptive behaviors that arise from disabling conditions must be evaluated by people who have sufficient expertise to properly advise the professional staff, and various regulations require a rewriting of the student's individual educational plan before a change in placement may occur. As significant cases are heard and judicial decisions are handed down, policies must be modified to satisfy those legal guidelines. As an example, the "stay-put" provision of the Education of the Handicapped Act (EHA) prohibited school authorities from unilaterally excluding disabled children from the classroom for dangerous or disruptive conduct. This concept was examined in *Honig v. Doe* (1988). The court in examining an attempt to exclude students for more than the 10 days provided in the statute was beyond congressional intent. To accomplish such suspension requires injunctive relief, which school authorities must seek from the court where the disabled child is dangerous or continually disruptive. When such a decision is handed down, it must modify administrative policy and practice. The Handicapped Children's Protection Act of 1986 makes provision for the recovery of attorney's fees by parents who prevail in litigation, even for representation at the administrative level. *Moore v. District of Columbia* (1990) portends a continued increase in such litigation because the court awarded fees for both representation at the administrative hearings and in the court. When attorneys can look only to parents for payment, they are more cautious in recommending further proceedings. The Ninth Circuit Court of Appeals recognized that in addition to equitable remedies, a cause of action lies for damages under §504 against federal agencies. This decision has brought about more intensive litigation and concern as to who was the prevailing party. Significant decisions in this regard include: *McSambodies (No. 2) v. San Mateo City School District* (1990), *E.P. v. Union County Regional High School District* (1989), and *Angela L. v. Pasadena I.S.D.* (1990).

In one especially significant case, *E.P. v. Union County Regional High School District* (1989), the court defined the plaintiffs as prevailing party because they obtained "most" of the relief they were seeking. It also held that fees may be appropriate if a settlement is negotiated prior to an administrative hearing. This decision was recently followed in *Reid v. Board of Education of Lincolnshire Prairie View School District 103* (1991).

In a recent case styled *Aronov v. District of Columbia* (1992), the court authorized an award of the costs of experts to parents who prevail in cases brought under the Individuals with Disabilities Act (IDEA) because such awards were compatible with congressional intent.

Public school administrators need to be especially sensitive to laws whose purpose is to promote openness and accountability in education. The extent of recent litigation indicates that the public intends to assure that schools comply. The site-based principal will bear much of the scrutiny because the programmatic aspects of evaluation and assignment will occur at the building level.

Supervision of Student Activities

Student activities that are sponsored by schools have a prominent part in the activity of many communities. The Friday night spectacle of marching bands, female students' drill and dance teams, spirit groups, and athletic teams are deeply embedded in community life in many areas. Rules and regulations that govern many of those activities are promulgated by state- or legislatively-established bodies. Administrators and coaches are sensitive to penalties that forfeit winning records or championship performances.

An often overlooked area in policy and practice concerns the process of excluding or disciplining students who want to participate in such activity. The increasing value of scholarships available at various colleges increases the likelihood of an increasing number of cases in which parents file suit because they believe that their child has not been equitably treated.

Due Process and Exclusion from Co-Curricular Activity

When issues of due process arise over exclusion, the courts frequently rule that there is no property interest or right to participate in various interscholastic sports. Students have no Constitutional right to participate and no Constitutional right to any process whatsoever (see *Herbert v. Ventetuals*, 1981). Even though this may be the case, good judgment may demand minimal due process. An administrative review committee might solve many of the problems. Problems often arise from personality conflicts, and inequitable results often occur that would be avoided by committee review.

Although public concern has focused on academic performance of students, co-curricular activities are often the source of special concern and generate a considerable amount of litigation. Principals are often the object of community and parental censure when various problems arise. Problems of this nature frequently arise from activities that are curriculum-related, while others occur in settings that arise from athletic teams or interscholastic competition.

Actions Directed Toward Student Press Activity

Student newspapers have been considered by the courts from two points of view. One involved publications produced by students off campus who wanted to distribute them on campus. The second judicial examination was directed toward newspapers produced as a curriculum-related project for journalism classes. Both types of cases attempt to defend their practices under First Amendment protection. In early cases during the student activism era, challenges tended to grant Constitutional protection without regard to authorship, financial sponsor, or place of distribution. Cases such as *Shanley v. Northeast School District* (1972) and *Nitzberg v. Parks* (1975) are illustrative of these opinions. In the latter case, the district had attempted to rewrite its policy three times; and the court in striking its policy the third time noted "we have both compassion and understanding of the difficulties facing school administrators, but we cannot permit these conditions to suppress first amendments rights of students" (525 F.2d at 384).

Other courts have upheld various policies that have restricted communication rights: related to partisan political literature soliciting contributions to antiwar activities (*Katy v. McAuley*, 1971); where student solicitation interfered with schoolwork and discipline (*Peterson v. Board of Education*, 1973); and where, while agreeing that school could control sale of publications by outside parties, the school must show that sale of student newspapers caused material disruption (*Jacobs v. Board of Commissioners*, 1973). When reviewing cases concerning noncurricular publication activity, one should carefully review the large amount of case law in this area because several circuit courts of appeal have not supported attempts to suppress the student press. In *Scoville v. Board of Education* (1970), material felt to be unsuitable for distribution by administrators was dismissed as "adolescent attempts to shock their elders."

Where student newspapers are produced as a class project, the courts are more likely to support efforts of school principals to control content of student newspapers. In a series of cases, various federal courts, led by *Kuhlmeier v. Hazlewood School District* (1986), have held prior restraint policies were not per se unconstitutional. Other cases demonstrate the lack of mature judgment on behalf of students who published newspapers caricaturing faculty members in an unfavorable fashion (*Buch v. Barber*, 1987) or criticizing Martin Luther King's birthday as a federal holiday (*Romano v. Harrington*, 1987).

Speech as It Impacts Dress Codes

Messages recorded or displayed on T-shirts have caused considerable problems. Many schools prohibit shirts bearing advertisements for alcohol and tobacco products in school. These rules have seldom been challenged. In *Gano v. School District No. 411 of Twin Falls* (1987), students had produced the shirts that satirically portrayed administrators in a state of intoxication holding up several kinds of alcoholic beverages. The court refused to grant injunctive relief from administrative enforcement of the school's disciplinary action. The court upheld disciplinary action because the message conveyed would interfere with administrative role models. Courts have also upheld bans on use of symbols or insignia that threaten substantial disorder in the school (see *Hill v. Lewis*, 1971; *Mectan v. Young*, 1972). Where authorities have insufficient proof of threatened disruption, the courts may reverse school disciplinary actions, as in cases such as *Tinker v. Des Moines Independent Community School District* (1989) and *Bretts v. School District* (1961). When there is student gang activity in which distinctive dress identifies group members, such distinctive garments or jewelry can be suppressed. Where regulations are designed to protect student health, safety, or school discipline they will usually be upheld. Where school boards are given broad rules making authority, rules which bear a rational relationship to a legitimate state interest will be upheld in most courts (see *Ferrell v. Dallas Independent School District*, 1968; but see also *Dostero v. Barthold Public School District No. 54*, 1975).

Conflict Generated by Dress Codes.   Dress codes often cause greater conflict than would have been anticipated prior to the 1970s. Parents commonly rely on a judicial analysis in *Pierce v. Society of Sisters* (1925) to support their assertion of parental rights over various aspects of their child's education. They often allege that they, not school administrators or boards of education, are responsible for the appearance of their children. School administrators typically contend that school boards possess the delegated authority to establish policies that enhance the educational environment. The U.S. Supreme Court has avoided these types of cases, perhaps to avoid the trivializing of the Constitution. Even though courts from state to state have not been consistent in decisions in regard to cases involving either dress or grooming, as a general rule, courts have usually upheld policy that prohibited immodest or suggestive clothing, clothing that would be a disturbing or distractive factor, and clothing that would be unsafe or create a health hazard. Few cases have sought to protect dress considered to be immodest, such as the no-bra look or skirts that represent scantily designed clothing, because of the probable distraction.

   It is interesting, however, that courts do not agree that wearing of blue jeans or dungarees to school is appropriate. In *Bannister v. Paradis* (1970), the court invalidated a rule banning boys wearing dungarees to school, as long as they were clean and neat. School bans on girls wearing jeans were upheld in Idaho (*Murphy v. Pocatello School District*, 1971) and New Hampshire (*Bannister v. Paradis*, 1970). In Kentucky (*Dunderson v. Russell*, 1973), they were overturned. Although many would suggest that a Constitutional question is not raised by such policy, *Richards v. Thurston* (1970) stated in its opinion:

> No right is held more sacred, or is more carefully guarded, by the common law than the right of every individual to possession and control of his own person, free from all restraint or interference from others, unless by clear and unquestionable authority of law.

When the school attempts to set standards for appropriate dress, it would do well to remember a warning in *Westley v. Rossi* (1969):

> The standards of appearance and dress of last year are not those of today nor will they be those of tomorrow. Regulations of conduct by school authorities must bear a reasonable basis to the ordinary conduct of the school curriculum or to carrying out the responsibility of the schools.

Proposed policies for dress or appearance should be carefully developed with input from parent and student groups. Basic conflict often develops from policy that has become anachronistic because of a change in social mores.

Discipline as It Relates to Co-Curricular Activities

Various theorists take different positions on the fundamental issue of whether a student has a property interest in participation in co-curricular functions. On suspension from one of these activities the question immediately arises, "What process is due on such discipline which forbids participation?" The courts have divided opinions on the issue in recent cases. In *Pegacem v. Nelson* (1979), the court opined that there is no property interest in each separate component of the educational process. It conditioned its decisions on the concept that total exclusion for a lengthy period of time might require a due-process-type hearing. Similarly, *Albach v. Olde* (1976) viewed education as a broad and comprehensive concept but refused to find a Constitutionally-protected property interest in each of its many components. In three states, the "no pass, no play rule" does not violate the federal equal protection rule, so academic requirements for participation have been upheld.

Policies that bar married students from participation in various activities have been reversed for some time. One of the earlier cases favoring married student participation was styled *Roman v. Crenshaw* (1972) and involved refusal to permit a student to participate in a drama activity.

A number of courts have broadly interpreted *Goss v. Lopez* (1975) to encompass a right to an informal hearing before exclusions from co-curricular activity similar to that of a short-term academic suspension. In *Braesch v. De Pasquale* (1973), suspension of student athletes who violated a well-known rule on student use of alcohol was upheld. The court found that the process involved had met the requirement of due process. It related the following concepts:

- specific advance notice of the rule of conduct
- notice of date, time, and place of the violations
- a prompt hearing before appropriate school officials
- a final order from the school
- failure to exhaust administrative remedies before resorting to court action

Tests of various rules for participation often are judicially tested on allegations that they are

- arbitrary
- unreasonably harsh
- beyond the authority of the school board (ultra vires acts)
- lacking a rational relationship to policy and serving no legitimate end

Where hearings are held promptly, the courts have shown some reluctance to interfere with orderly procedures by the district. The possible availability of various kinds of scholarships and the economic benefits that they offer will motivate increased activity in this area. At least one court, *Brands v. Sheldon Community School* (1987), has indicated that no property interest exists in the prospective award of an athletic scholarship. If such a concept is widely embraced, the status of the individual in terms of performance skills would not require unusual procedural attention beyond the informal process. Each principal needs to have audited the regulations involving co-curricular activities, properly publicized them, and provided immediate appropriate process for hearing appeals from nonparticipation decisions, if litigation is to be kept to a minimum.

The Campus and Criminal Behavior

In many ways, the culture within a school organization mirrors contemporary society. Because this is true, various behaviors that may be prosecuted as criminal acts are likely to occur. A study of causes for termination of professional contracts for faculty and administrators will bring this into focus as to the professional staff. Similarly, a study of student suspension and expulsion cases provides an insight into student behaviors.

Educational Professionals as Role Models

Our society still clings to the position that school boards have the right to expect teachers and administrators to be role models for students. Various cases have tested the personal conduct of teachers. Rumors of various acts of misconduct are not likely to form the basis for termination of a contract (see *Stoddard v. School District No. 1 Lincoln County, Wyoming*, 1979).

Sexual Misconduct

Where nonmarital cohabitation was once widely accepted as immoral behavior and resulted in an automatic dismissal, the courts now are likely to require a showing that such conduct adversely effects the teacher's classroom performance (see *Thompson v. Southwest School District*, 1980).

Sexual misconduct by a professional employee involving a student is a fact situation that often results in both a contract termination and a criminal complaint. Such cases of teacher involvement with students, permitting one student to sexually harass another, and a faculty member dating a student have been resolved against the professional staff member (see cases such as *Board of Education of Sante Fe Public Schools v. Sullivan*, 1987; *Katz v. Amback*, 1984).

Numerous cases involving both gay and lesbian behaviors between consenting adults have occurred and often resulted in termination once such relationship becomes public knowledge. In these cases, the courts have moved toward requiring nexus between the teacher's behavior and adverse effect on classroom performance. One such case is *Morrison v. State Board of Education* (1969). Although a trend exists for establishment of teacher privacy, a teacher risks professional effectiveness in the community if his or her conduct is contrary to community standards.

Substance Abuse by Faculty

Illegal drug use has increased among teachers just as it has in society at large. Although considerable tolerance of the use of beverage alcohol now exists, it has not extended to circumstances in which the teacher has role-model responsibility with students. Dismissals have been upheld where students were permitted to become intoxicated at the teacher's home and where teachers are supervising students on road trips. Incidents involving illegal drug use, possession, sale, or advocacy often result in termination of teaching contracts. Dismissal statutes often do not list drug offenses as specific grounds for termination, so that dismissal charges must often be brought under "fitness to teach the youth of the state" or for other "just cause."

The extent to which some teachers become involved is illustrated by *Adams v. State Professional Practices Council* (1981) where the teachers gave sworn testimony advocating marijuana use and admitted daily use for a period of more than 15 years. The growth of local concern over drug abuse has fostered harsher penalties.

Actions When Criminal Charges May Be Pending

Even though a professional may be arrested and subject to criminal sanctions, the school district may institute proceedings to remove the individual, because administrative hearings and criminal trials are separate and independent proceedings. Although care should be used in taking such actions, removal of a principal before a termination hearing was upheld in *Summers v. Vermilion Parish*

School Board (1986). Summers had been arrested and charged with possession of marijuana with intent to distribute. The court stated "public policy and common sense dictate that a school board have [sic] the power to remove a teacher found guilty of acts constituting a serious felony, especially one involving a serious problem such as drug abuse."

As a general practice, most school districts suspend the professional on arrest and indictment, but delay termination proceedings until after the criminal trial has occurred. Often, the school authority has the burden of establishing the nexus between the act involved and diminished professional effectiveness. Numerous acts such as dishonesty, testing violations, shoplifting, welfare fraud, violation of firearms statutes, and other behaviors have supported termination under a charge of "immorality." "Unprofessional conduct" is another generic type of charge where ethical or policy violations occur. The principal administering a school where authority for decision making has been decentralized should give careful attention to requesting professional legal guidance in preparing various communications related to suspension or termination of employees.

Substance Abuse by Students

Substance abuse among students is an issue with which school administrators are often confronted. The problem first appeared in secondary schools but now also occurs in elementary and middle schools. It appears that no age group is immune to such problems. No school can realistically claim to be free of drug or alcohol problems.

Suppression of possession often involves search issues with attendant lawsuits over Fourth Amendment or privacy violations. Two recent cases have invalidated policies that required urinalysis tests of secondary school students. In a 1985 case, *Odenheim v. Carlstadt-East Rutherford School District*, a policy requiring all students to submit to drug testing was invalidated as interfering with student privacy and failing to meet reasonable search requirements. A similar result developed from a Texas case, *Brooks v. East Chambers I.S.D.* (1989), in which a policy required students to be randomly subjected to urinalysis if they participated in co-curricular activity. The court determined that search standards established in *New Jersey v. T.L.O.* (1985) could not be satisfied. Successful challenges of policies where it was only suspected that a student was smoking marijuana indicated that mere suspicions may not trigger drug testing (see *Anaber v. Ford*, 1985).

After *Horton v. Goose Creek I.S.D.* (1982), school attorneys feared that the court expressing an administrative responsibility for a drug-free environment would generate suits charging that school districts should be held liable for peer pressures experienced at school that initiated student drug problems. Such suits have not materialized, but no administrator may relax strict surveillance over these problems.

The Growth of Malpractice Pressures

For more than three decades, plaintiffs and their attorneys have sought to establish some precedent in the courts that would give them a legal threshold that would enable a recovery for educational malpractice. Often, a course of action that is initially denied on first impression may be successful on subsequent cases. This is especially likely in cases where the losses are so grievous as to shock the conscience of the court or to generate public concern with wide media coverage.

Cases Charging Educational Malpractice

One of the first cases in the malpractice area in education occurred in 1976. In *Peter W. v. San Francisco Unified School District* (1976), a high school graduate brought action against a city school district in which he sought damages for an educational program that deprived him of basic academic skills. The plaintiff alleged seven causes of action that were the substance of his appeal. The basic concept through the court's opinion was determined to be that the plaintiff failed to establish a duty of care that was breached. The court further opined "we have already seen that failure of educational achievement may not be characterized as an 'injury' within the meaning of tort law."

The failure of plaintiffs in *Peter W.* did not discourage others from filing similar suits. In *Donohue v. Copiague Union Free School District* (1978), the plaintiff sought $5,000,000 in damages for breach of a statutory duty to educate. Although he received failing grades in several subjects and minimal ones in others, he was permitted to graduate. He alleged that the Constitutional duty to educate had been breached. Section 1 of article XI of the New York State Constitution reads as follows:

> The legislature shall provide for the maintenance and support of a system of free common schools, wherein all the children of this state shall be educated. (p. 877)

The court went on record as stating, "the courts are an inappropriate forum to test the efficacy of educational programs and pedagogical methods." One statement from which teachers take heart was this: "The failure to learn does not bespeak a failure to teach." The court went further to state that "we hold that the public policy of this state recognizes no cause of action for educational malpractice."

Later that same year, the court heard *Hoffman v. Board of Education of the City of New York* (1978), which reversed a damage awarded in the superior court, appellate division. Damages had been awarded where the school had failed to properly evaluate a child's intellectual capacity and had assigned him to a program for the mentally retarded. The court again held that public policy precluded recovery for such misfeasance. One comment of the court is again of consequence to teachers when it stated that teachers are called upon many times a day to make sensitive judgment calls in working with children: "a teacher must not be made aware of the precariousness of his position, as was Damocles, beneath some economic falchion suspended by the hair of hindsight" (*Hoffman v. Board of Education of the City of New York*, 1978). In *Hunter v. Board of Education of Montgomery County* (1981), a Maryland appellate court announced "we hold that the 'public policy' of this state bars an action for educational malpractice." Similarly, a Florida court, in *Tubell v. Dade County Public Schools* (1982), ruled that mistesting and misclassification of a special education student resulting in an improper educational program for a number of years to his detriment failed to state a cause of action.

Plaintiff's attorneys often are quite creative in drafting their pleadings. In *Myers v. Medford Lakes Board of Education* (1985), the failure to provide remedial education to assist Myers to overcome academic deficiencies was filed as an educational malpractice case. The court ruled that he had failed to state a cause of action under a state tort claims act. Attorneys often attempt to frame the facts of a case involving their client in the most self-serving way possible. Where policy or statutory language is ambiguous, the legal advocate will devise pleadings that seek to exploit that ambiguity. Therefore, drafting of both statutes and policy should be carefully accomplished.

Recent practices such as a policy directive recently issued by the Los Angeles School District may erode currently utilized theories for defending malpractice claims. The district, with some 600,000 students, announced a policy effective in 1994 that "guarantees" that its graduates will possess certain definable skills and knowledge. The district has promised that it will retrain, at no cost to the employer, any graduate who skills are found to be deficient. Such assurances may establish a duty of care standard and objections to public policy defenses that have been common in defending educational malpractice could disappear.

The consistent rulings of appellate courts that no cause of action exists for educational malpractice has not kept such suits from being filed. At both the public school and collegiate levels, such cases continue to be filed. The best defense in all tort claims cases in which students allege educational malpractice is for the professional staff to dedicate themselves to effective teaching practices and appropriate levels of professional supervision.

SUMMARY

Adequate professional knowledge and sensitivity to areas of potential litigation is vital to successful leadership on any level of administrative assignment. It cannot be emphasized enough that appropriate, well-conceived rules and regulations, consistently and equitably enforced often preclude effective litigation. The building administrator must develop sufficient awareness of problem areas to know where the professional services of the school attorney should be secured. Administrative decision making must take into consideration both the academic and legal considerations that are inherent in this expansive leadership concept. Because of increased responsibility, the principal in a district where a site-based management philosophy is implemented will be drawn more frequently into circumstances in which parents are likely to "throw the book at you where you do not follow the book." A consistent performance of professional duties is the best defense in many cases.

Individuals who plan or have current appointments as building principals should carefully evaluate their professional knowledge in relation to hazards that occur from an environment beset with increased legal responsibilities. The public generally views the principal as the person ultimately responsible for the function of the individual school. The "captain of the ship" doctrine has an impact on the legal liabilities of the principal. Career planning and professional growth of each principal should include the following basic legal knowledge:

- a basic course in educational law
- up-to-date reading of the professional literature in the area of legal decisions affecting schools
- mastery of state and local policy guidelines for regular and special academic or vocational programs
- mastery of local school board policy (with decisions relating to student academic and social/behavioral discipline following it)
- awareness of the areas of school operation that generate legal problems
- recognition of problem areas in which the professional judgment of the school attorney should be utilized
- recognition that both academic and legal problems are involved in most of the decisions that relate to both subordinate employees and to students

This chapter has sought to create a professional awareness of a number of areas in which legal problems are likely to occur in the decade ahead. It does not encompass all areas of concern but those of immediate need.

THEORY INTO PRACTICE:
A CASE STUDY FOR REFLECTION

A respected teacher on your faculty comes to you in the privacy of your office and challenges several decisions which you have made in regard to various faculty assignments for duty outside the classroom. The teacher's behavior is respectful, with no evidence of anger, shouting, or profanity. The basic concern of the teacher was that assignment of various unpleasant duties at evening school functions gave evidence of racism. After the conversation, the teacher closed your office door and left without you having an opportunity to respond. The implication seemed to be that several faculty members would file a complaint or grievance if the practice continued or that litigation was possible. The conversation irritated you. What action should you take?

GUIDING QUESTIONS

1. Should you charge the teacher with unprofessional conduct, write up the incident, and place the memorandum in the teacher's file?

2. Should you make a mental note of the incident and have it become an item in the teacher's annual evaluation?

3. Is this protected speech under the First Amendment and should a note of commendation be placed in the teacher's mailbox indicating that you will give attention to such assignments so that all share equitably in such assignments?

4. Should you assign the complaining teacher to assist in supervising the most undesirable activities, to demonstrate your authority over such matters?

   After making your decision you might read the U.S. Supreme Court decisions in *Givhan v. Western Line Consolidated School District* (1979) and *Connick v. Myers* (S.Ct., 1983) to check your judgment.

The student handbook in the high school addresses specifically that all students who participate in athletic programs must follow basic rules of personal conduct in order to be eligible to participate in the sports program. Each student handbook had a page that was detachable and required parental and student signatures of acknowledgement of receiving the handbook and having read it. The policy read: "any student who uses drugs, smokes, or drinks alcoholic beverages should not plan to participate in athletics." Several parents hosted a party for seniors that was referred to as a champagne brunch and that was attended by a number of athletes, both boys and girls. At least one student appeared at school inebriated afterward, and the principal on inquiry discovered the names of the others. The students were promptly called before the principal for a conference that was attended by the parents. After admissions were made by the students concerning the use of alcoholic drinks, they were suspended from spring sports participation. Each student and parent received a letter a few days after the informal conference explaining the action. It included the information necessary for the parents to appeal to the board of trustees. Was the action taken appropriate?

GUIDING QUESTIONS

1. In this circumstance, was the process extended all that was due?

2. Was the action taken of such consequence as to require a full due-process hearing at the initial level of consideration?

3. Were there other considerations that, if taken, would have decreased the likelihood of litigation?

Reviewing cases such as *Dallas v. Cumberland Valley School District* (1975), *Hardy v. Interscholastic League* (1985), and *Braesch v. DePasquale* (1978) might provide adequate information for you to evaluate your responses to this exercise.

REFERENCES

Adams v. State Professional Practices Council, 406 So. 2d 1170, Fla. App. (1981).

Albach v. Olde, 531 F.2d 983, 10th Cir. (1976).

Ambach v. Norwick, 441 U.S. 68, 78 (1979).

Anaber v. Ford, 653 F. Supp. 22, W.D. Ark. (1985).

Angela L. v. Pasadena I.S.D., 918 F.2d 1188, 5th Cir. (1990).

Aroncv v. District of Columbia, 780 F.Supp. 46, D.D.C. (1992).

Bannister v. Paradis, 316 F. Supp. 185, D.C. N. Hampshire (1970).

Barbre v. Garland I.S.D., 474 F.Supp. 687, N.D. Tex. (1979).

Battle v. Commonwealth of Pennsylvania, 629 F.2d 269, 3rd Cir. (1980); cert. denied 452 U.S. 968 (1981).

Board of Education of Sante Fe Public Schools v. Sullivan, 740 F.2d 119, N.M. (1987).

Bradley v. Pittsburgh Board of Education, 910 F.2d 1172, 3rd Cir. (1991).

Braesch v. DePasquale, 265 N.W.2d 842, Supt. Ct. Neb. (1978); cert. denied 439 U.S. 1068 (1979).

Brands v. Sheldon Community School, 671 F. Supp. 627, Iowa (1987).

Brantley v. Surles, 718 F.2d 1354, supplemented 765 F.2d 478, 5th Cir. (1985).

Bretts v. School District, 436 F.2d 728, 5th Cir. (1961).

Brooks v. East Chambers I.S.D., 730 F.Supp. 759 (1989).

Buch v. Barber, 647 F. Supp. 1149, W.D. Wash. (1987).

Code of Federal Regulations. 34 C.F.R. §104.3(j)

Connick v. Myers, 461 U.S., 138 (1983).

Dallas v. Cumberland Valley School District, 391 F. Supp. 358, Pa. (1975).

Dean v. Timpson I.S.D., 486 F.Supp. 302, E.D. Tex. (1979).

Donohue v. Copiague Union Free School District, 407 N.Y.S.2d 874 (1978).

Dostero v. Barthold Public School District No. 54, 391 F. Supp. 376, D. N.D. (1975).

Dunderson v. Russell, 502 S.W.2d 64 Ky. (1973).

Dworken v. Cleveland Board of Education, 108 N.E.2d 103, Ohio (1951).

Education of all Handicapped Children Act (EHA), 20 U.S.C. Sect. 1401 et seq. (1975).

E.P. v. Union County Regional High School District, 741 F. Supp. 1144 D.N.J. (1989).

Ferrell v. Dallas Independent School District, 392 F.2d 697, 5th Cir. (1968).

Gano v. School District No. 411 of Tivin Falls, 674 F. Supp. 796, D. Idaho (1987).

Georgiades, W. D. H. (1985, Fall). The principal as instructional leader: Myth or reality? *Educational Considerations, 12*(3).

Givhan v. Western Line Consolidated School District, 439 U.S. 410 (1979).

Goldwasser v. Brown, 417 F.2d 1169 D.C. Cir. (1969).

Gosney v. Sonora Independent School District, 603 F.2d 522, 5th Cir. (1979).

Goss v. Lopez, 419 U.S. 585 (1975).

Handicapped Children's Protection Act of 1986. 20 U.S.C. Sec. 1415(e) (1986).

Hardy v. Interscholastic League, 759 F.2d 1233, 5th Cir. (1985).

Harrah Independent School District v. Martin, 440 U.S. 194 (1979).

Herbert v. Ventetuals, 638 F.2d 5 (1981).

Hill v. Dayton School District, 517 P.2d 223 Wash. (1974).

Hill v. Lewis, 323 F. Supp. 55, E.D. N.C. (1971).

Hoffman v. Board of Education of the City of New York, 410 N.Y.S.2d 99 (1978).

Honig v. Doe, 108 S.Ct. 592 (1988).

Horton v. Goose Creek I.S.D., 677 F.2d 471, 5th Cir. (1982).

Hunter v. Board of Education of Montgomery County, 425 A.2d 681, Md. App. (1981).

Individuals with Disabilities Education Act (IDEA). 20 U.S.C. Sec. 1401 et seq. (1990).

Jacobs v. Board of Commissioners, 490 F.2d 601, 7th Cir. (1973).

Johnson v. School Committee, 356 N.E.2d 820, Mass. (1977).

Katy v. McAuley, 438 F.2d 1058, 2d Cir., (1971); cert. denied 405 U.S. 993 (1972).

Katz v. Amback, 472 N.Y.S. 2d 492, N.Y. AD 3 Dept. (1984).

Kingsville Independent School District v. Cooper, 611 F.2d 1109 5th Cir. (1980).

Kirkland v. Northside Independent School District (890 F.2d 794, 5th Cir. (1989).

Kuhlmeier v. Hazlewood School District, 795 F.2d 1368, 8th Cir. (1986); cert. granted 107 S.Ct. 926 (1987).

Larson v. Independent School District No. 314, 289 N.W. 2d 112, Minn. (1979).

Martin v. Parrish, 805 F.2d 583, 5th Cir. (1986).

McDaniel v. Vidor I.S.D., Texas Education Agency, Docket No. 78-R-60 (April 1982).

McKelvey v. Colonial School District, 348 A.2d 445, Pa. Comwth. (1975).

McSambodies (No. 2) v. San Mateo City School District, 897 F.2d 975, 9th Cir. (1990).

Mectan v. Young, 465 F.2d 1332, 6th Cir. (1972).

Meyer v. Nebraska, 262 U.S. 390, 401 (1923).

Mills v. Board of Education of District of Columbia, 348 F. Supp. 866, D.D.C. (1972).

Miles v. Denver Public Schools, 944 F.2d 771, 10th Cir. (1991).

Minarcini v. Strongville City School District, 541 F.2d 359, 1st Cir. (1969).

Moore v. District of Columbia, 907 F.2d 335, D.C. Cir. (1990).

Moore v. School Board of Gulf County, Florida, 364 F.Supp. 355 N.D. Fla. (1973).

Morrison v. State Board of Education, 82 Cal.Rptr. 175 (1969).

Murphy v. Pocatello School District, 480 P.2d 878, Idaho (1971).

Mt. Healthy City School District Board of Education v. Doyle, 429 U.S. 274 (1977).

Myers v. Medford Lakes Board of Education, 489 A.2d 1240, N.J. Sup. A.D. (1985).

New Jersey v. T.L.O., 105 S.Ct. 733 (1985).

New York State Constitution, Section 1 of article XI

Nitzberg v. Parks, 525 F.2d 378. 4th Cir. (1975).

Odenheim v. Carlstadt-East Rutherford School District, 510 A.2d 709, N.J. Supreme Ct. (1985).

Palmer v. Board of Education of the City of Chicago, 603 F.2d 1271, 7th Cir. (1979); cert. denied 444 U.S. 1026 (1980).

PARC v. Commonwealth, 334 F. Supp. 1257, E.D. Pa. (1971).

Parducci v. Rutland, 316 F.Supp. 352, N.D. Ala. (1970).

Pegacem v. Nelson, 469 F. Supp. 1134, N.C. (1979).

Peter W. v. San Francisco Unified School District, 131 Cal. Rptr. 854. (1976).

Peterson v. Board of Education, 370 F. Supp. 1208, D.C. Neb. (1973).

Pickering v. Board of Education of Township High School District 205, 391 U.S. 563 (1968).

Pierce v. Society of Sisters, 268 U.S. 570 (1925).

Richards v. Thurston, 424 F. Supp. 1281, 1st Cir. (1970).

Reeves v. Claiborne County Board of Education, 828 F.2d 1096 (1987).

Rehabilitation Act of 1973, Sect. 504, 29 U.S.C. Sect. 794 Implementing Regs. (1977).

Reid v. Board of Education of Lincolnshire Prairie View School District 103, 765 F. Supp. 965 (1991).

Robbins v. Board of Education of Argo Community High School District No. 217, 313 F.Supp. 642 N.D. Ill. (1970).

Roman v. Crenshaw, 354 F. Supp. 868, Tex. (1972).

Romano v. Harrington, 664 F. Supp. 675, E.D. N.Y. (1987).

Russo v. Central School District No. 1, 469 F.2d 623, 2nd Cir. (1972); cert. denied 411 U.S. 932 (1973).

Scoville v. Board of Education, 425 F.2d 10, 7th Cir. (1970).

Shanley v. Northeast School District, 462 F.2d 960, 5th Cir. (1972).

Spanel v. Mounds View School District No. 21, 118 N.W.2d 795, 802, Minn. (1962).

Sterzing v. Ft. Bend I.S.D., 373 F. Supp. 657, 661 S.D. Tex. (1972); vacated as to remedy and remanded 496 F.2d 92 5th Cir. per curiam.

Stoddard v. School District No. 1 Lincoln County, Wyoming, 590 F.2d 829, 10th Cir. (1979).

Stoneking v. Bradford Area School District, 667 F.Supp. 1088, W.D.Pa. (1987).

Summers v. Vermilion Parish School Board, 493 So.2d 1258, La. App. 3rd Cir. (1986).

Texas Education Agency. (1988). *All Children Can Learn Together*. Austin, TX: Texas Education Agency.

Thompson v. Southwest School District, 483 F. Supp. 1170, W.D. Mo. (1980).

Timothy W. v. Rochester, New Hampshire School District, 875 F.2d 954, 1st Cir. (1989); cert. denied, 110 S.Ct. 519 (1989).

Tinker v. Des Moines Independent Community School District, 393 U.S. 503 (1969).

Tubell v. Dade County Public Schools, 419 So.2d 388, Fla. App. 3 Dist. (1982).

Turnbull, H. R., & Turnbull, A. (1978). *Free appropriate public education law and interpretation*. Denver, CO: Lam.

Underwood, J., & Naffle, J. (1990). Good news: The litigation scales are tilting in your favor. *Executive Education, 12*(3), 16–20.

Westley v. Rossi, 305 F. Supp. 714 (1969).

Vernon's Revised Texas Statutes, Education Code, Section 13.352 Principals (d) (1) (Effective September 1, 1990).

SELECTED READINGS

Barr, M. J. (1988). *Student services and the law*. San Francisco: Jossey-Bass. See especially chapter 16.

Hudgins, H. C., Jr., & Vacca, R. S. (1991). *Law and education: Contemporary issues and court decisions*. Charlottesville, VA: Michie.

Imber, M., & Thompson, G. (1991). Developing a typology of litigation in education and determining the frequency of each category. *Educational Administration Quarterly, 27*(2).

LaMorte, M. W. (1990). *School law: Cases and concepts* (3rd ed.). Englewood Cliffs, NJ: Prentice Hall.

McCarthy, M. M. (1991). Severely disabled children: Who pays? *Phi Delta Kappan, 73,* 66–71.

McCarthy, M. M., & Cambron, N. H. (1981). *Public school law: Teachers and students rights.* Boston: Allyn and Bacon. See especially chapter 9.

Rossow, L. F., & Parkinson, J. (1992). *The law of teacher evaluation.* Topeka, KS: National Organization on Legal Problems of Education.

Strahan, R. D., & Turner, L. C. (1987). *The courts and the schools.* New York: Longman. See especially chapter 6.

Thomas, G. J., Sperry, D. J., & Wasden, F. D. (1991). *The law and teacher employment.* St. Paul, MN: West. See especially chapter 1.

Thomas, S. B. (1988). *The yearbook of school law, 1988.* Topeka, KS: National Organization on Legal Problems of Education. See especially chapter 3.

Ubben, G. C., & Hughes, L. W. (1992). *The principal: Effective leadership for effective schools.* Boston: Allyn and Bacon. See especially chapter 5.

Underwood, J., & Naffle, J. (1990). Good news: The litigation scales are tilting in your favor. *Executive Education, 12*(3), 16–20.

Yudof, M. G., Kirp, D. L., & Levin, B. (1992). *Educational policy and the law* (3rd ed.). St. Paul, MN: West.

Index

About the Authors

Larry W. Hughes, Ph.D. The Ohio State University (editor and chapter 1)
Larry Hughes is Professor of Educational Leadership and Cultural Studies at the University of Houston. He is author or co-author of six other books, including three on principalship. Hughes is the author of more than sixty articles in leading educational journals and has written many chapters in edited works and numerous monographs as well. He also writes and produces training films and assessment center stimulation materials. He has held teaching and administrative positions in Texas, Tennessee, Ohio, and Michigan. His research and development efforts focus on organizational management, time management, and assessment center technology. He is a frequent consultant to such federal agencies as the Department of Defense, Department of Justice, and General Accounting Office and to private sector organizations, as well as school systems here and abroad.

Charles M. Achilles, Ed.D. University of Rochester (chapters 2 and 10)
Chuck Achilles is Professor and Chair of the Department of Educational Leadership at the University of North Carolina–Greensboro. He has a long-standing and well-established research and theory-building interest in leadership, change processes, communication and school outcomes. Achilles has directed

many studies of school improvement in both urban and rural environments and is the recipient of many grants from private and public sectors. He has numerous chapters, monographs, and entries in the periodical literature to his credit.

H. Prentice Baptiste, Jr., Ed.D. Indiana University (chapter 4)

Prentice Baptiste is Professor and Chair of the Department of Educational Leadership and Cultural Studies at the University of Houston. His research includes studies of multicultural educational environments, effective schools, and science education. He served for five years as co-editor of the *Journal of Educational Equity and Leadership* and most recently was lead editor of *Leadership, Equity and School Effectiveness*, published in 1990. He conducts numerous workshops and seminars in multicultural education for university and school district faculties and administrators and such professional organizations as ASCD, ATE, and Phi Delta Kappa.

Robert Craig, Ph.D. Loyola University, Ed.D. Wayne State University (chapter 3)

Bob Craig is Assistant Professor of Educational Leadership and Cultural Studies at the University of Houston. He has a rich background of experiences in both private and public sectors and most recently in the health care industry as director of the Office of Values, Ethics and Ministry for the Sisters of Charity of the Incarnate Word Health Care Corporate Office. His primary responsibilities there were to develop programs in ethics and values for eighteen health care facilities and to train administrators in ethical decision making. At the university he continues this work with school administrators and prospective school administrators. Current research interests include value and ethical frameworks for administrative decision making. He is a frequent contributor to the periodical literature.

Paula A. Cordeiro, Ed.D. University of Houston (chapter 7)

Paula Cordeiro is Assistant Professor of Educational Administration at the University of Connecticut and directs the Danforth Principals Project there. Her instructional assignments include courses on the principalship, instructional supervision, and the administration of schools in multi-cultural settings and these assignments reflect her research interests. She has recently co-authored a chapter entitled "Political and School Administration," and has published several articles on at-risk students.

John T. Greer, Ph.D. University of Chicago (chapter 6)

Jack Greer is Professor of Educational Administration at Georgia State University. Currently, he is principal investigator of the "Empowered School District Project," a three-year investigation of the empowerment processes used in nine schools across the United States. The project is sponsored by the Danforth Foundation. Greer is also one of the directors of the "Arizona Restructuring Project." Twenty-four schools are participating in this project which is designed to test the concept of multi-age and multi-grade instruction in grades K through 12. It too is funded by a Danforth Grant. Greer is the author of many journal articles and monographs.

Reginald M. High, Ed.D. University of Tennessee (chapter 2)
Reg High directs two federally funded exemplary education projects for the Bureau of Education Research at the University of Tennessee, Knoxville and is Director of the Tennessee project for the National Diffusion Network. High has served as a principal of schools K-12. His current research interests include school-based management, leadership practices, and curriculum development in public schools. He is a frequent contributor to the periodical literature.

Patricia Holland, Ph.D. University of Pittsburgh (chapter 9)
Pat Holland is an assistant professor in the Department of Educational Leadership and Cultural Studies at the University of Houston and coordinates the certification program for instructional supervisors. She has actively participated as a researcher and consultant to the Danforth Foundation Program to Promote Collaborative Leadership in Schools. She is well published on this topic as well as on the interpretive aspects of clinical supervision and staff development. Holland has recently completed a study of how principals work with novice teachers and is currently co-authoring a book entitled *Cases in Collaborative Leadership in School Settings*.

John L. Keedy, Ed.D. University of Tennessee (chapter 2)
John Keedy is assistant professor of educational administration at North Carolina State University. He has been studying teacher collegial groups (TCG) and effective principals as part of an ongoing funded research agenda. He has been an elementary school principal and an assistant superintendent for instruction in Virginia. As part of his research in how principals set norms in schools, Keedy has identified 14 norm-setting categories. He contributes frequently to the professional literature in school administration.

Cynthia J. Norris, Ed.D. University of Tennessee (chapter 3)
Cynthia Norris is Associate Professor of Educational Leadership and Cultural Studies at the University of Houston and Executive Director of the Metro-Houston Administrator Assessment and Development Center. She was facilitator of the recently completed Danforth Foundation Program for the Preparation of Principals. Norris has been a teacher, a director of special and gifted education, and an elementary school principal. Her research interests focus on leadership and the thought patterns that facilitate creativity. She advocates administrator preparation programs designed to foster holistic thinking. Co-editor of *The Moral Imperatives of Leadership: A Focus on Human Decency* to be published in the spring of 1991 by the Danforth Foundation, Norris has also written articles and research pieces appearing in such journals as *Educational Leadership, Theory Into Practice, NASSP Bulletin*, and *Planning and Changing*.

Paula M. Short, Ph.D. University of North Carolina at Chapel Hill (chapter 6)
Paula Short is Associate Professor of Educational Administration at Pennsylvania State University. She has been a school and district administrator as well as a program consultant with the North Carolina Department of Public Instruction. She has published widely in professional journals including *Educational Research*

Quarterly, NASSP Bulletin, and *Planning and Changing*, and regularly presents scholarly papers at AERA, AASA, NASSP, SRCEA, and NCPEA. She serves as editor of the *Journal of School Leadership* and is on the editorial board of *Educational Administration Quarterly*. Short is co-director of the Danforth-funded Empowered School District Project and is consultant to the Arizona Restructuring Project, which involves 24 school districts.

Penelope S. Smith, Ph.D. Rice; Ed.D. University of North Carolina–Greensboro (chapter 10)

Penny Smith is Assistant Professor of Educational Administration at the University of North Carolina at Greensboro. She has had a distinguished career as a teacher—including being named "Teacher of the Year" in North Carolina—and as a middle school principal, assistant superintendent and associate superintendent. She has been the author or director of numerous grants, the focus of which were innovations in school programming and instructional delivery.

Richard D. Strahan, Ed.D. and J.D. University of Houston (chapter 11)

Dick Strahan is Professor of Educational Leadership and Cultural Studies at the University of Houston. He is a member of the Texas Bar and the Federal Bar, including the United States Supreme Court, and specializes in school law. He lectures extensively before professional law and education groups and associations, at conventions, and at both public school and university levels. He has numerous articles to his credit and has written three books, including *The Courts and the Schools*.

Laurel N. Tanner, Ed.D. Columbia University (chapter 8)

Laurel Tanner is Professor of Educational Leadership and Cultural Studies at the University of Houston. In 1988–89 she was visiting scholar in the Benton Center for Curriculum and Instruction at the University of Chicago. A distinguished scholar with wide-ranging research interests, she is the author or co-author of several books, including *Supervision in Education: Problems and Practices* (Macmillan, 1987). She edited the 1988 National Society for the Study of Education yearbook, *Critical Issues in Curriculum*. She also publishes widely in the periodical literature and is a frequent presenter at AERA and ASCD meetings.

Kay Weise, Ed.D. University of Houston (chapter 9)

Kay Weise is Clinical Assistant Professor of Educational Leadership and Cultural Studies at the University of Houston. A former teacher, building administrator and central office administrator in Texas public schools, she brings an extensive background of experiences to her professional writing. Long interested and practically involved in the solution of problems facing novice teachers, her perspective and insights are fresh. She is sought after as a workshop presenter on teaching and learning styles, developmental writing, and instructional strategies for both gifted and talented studies and learning disabled students.

ISBN 0-02-358441-6